Born   trials
1854   1895
   OW- 41 40
      1980

OSCAR WILDE AT THE TIME OF THE TRIALS

By Count Henri de Toulouse-Lautrec

(From the portrait in the collection of Mr. Conrad Lester in
Los Angeles, California, U.S.A.)

THE TRIALS
OF OSCAR WILDE

H. MONTGOMERY HYDE

DOVER PUBLICATIONS, INC.
NEW YORK

To the Memory of
SIR EDWARD CLARKE

This Dover edition, first published in 1973, is an unabridged republication of the new and enlarged second edition entitled *Famous Trials, Seventh Series: Oscar Wilde,* originally published by Penguin Books Ltd. in 1962. The five appendices and several illustrations have been added from the first edition, published by William Hodge and Company, Limited, in 1948.

International Standard Book Number: 0-486-20216-X
Library of Congress Catalog Card Number: 73-77378

Manufactured in the United States of America
Dover Publications, Inc.
180 Varick Street
New York, N.Y. 10014

CONTENTS

ILLUSTRATIONS

FOREWORD

By the Rt Hon. SIR TRAVERS HUMPHREYS, P.C.

I HAVE been asked to contribute a Foreword to this volume of the excellent series of Notable British Trials published by Messrs Hodge & Co., Ltd.[1] The reason apparently for my being selected is that I had a complimentary brief in the case, as junior to Sir Edward Clarke, Q.C. and C. W. Mathews, delivered by my father, who was acting as solicitor to Oscar Wilde. Everyone else connected with the trials, which took place fifty-three years ago, appears to be dead.

I have accepted the invitation, although I doubt whether I can add any new fact or otherwise improve upon the story of the three trials so admirably told by my friend Mr Montgomery Hyde. That gentleman relies for his facts upon a transcript of shorthand notes, and for his comments upon letters and other writings extending over many years. If I do not always see eye to eye with him in regard to those comments, we differ only in matters of opinion and we shall agree that *de opinionibus*, just as *de gustibus*, *non est disputandum*.

What perhaps I can do is to supply something for the background of the picture which Mr Montgomery Hyde has painted, and at least I hope to dispel once and for all some of the ridiculous suggestions put forward from time to time to account for the course pursued by Oscar Wilde's legal advisers.

From the point of view of the man in the street, the first of these trials undoubtedly exhibited all the features of a *cause célèbre*. It is not every day that a Marquess can be seen in the

1. Sir Travers Humphreys, who died in 1956, wrote this Foreword in 1948 for the original edition of *The Trials of Oscar Wilde*, which I edited for the Notable British Trials series. It is reprinted here on account of its valuable comments by the last surviving lawyer who took part in the three trials.

dock at the Old Bailey charged with libel, and the Marquess of Queensberry was a well-known figure in sporting circles. The prosecutor, Mr Oscar Wilde, moreover, was a man whose name at least was well known as the author of successful plays, one of which was running at the Haymarket Theatre and another at the St James's. It was understood that the libel involved an attack upon the decency and fitness for publication of some of the books or writings of Oscar Wilde. Small wonder then that all classes of society clamoured for admission to the Court, which afforded much greater accommodation for the public both on and off the bench than is to be found in the present Court, completed and opened in 1907.

Those who obtained admission certainly had their fill of sensation and had the opportunity of listening to as brilliant and damaging a cross-examination by Edward Carson as was ever administered to a prosecutor in a criminal case. The witness was in every respect the equal in ability of the counsel; and, so long as the cross-examination was confined to the subject of his writings, many thought that Wilde had scored as many points as Carson. But then came a change. Leaving literature, Carson came to the private life and habits of the witness; and the admissions which Wilde was forced to make as to his association with boys and young men of a class far beneath him left no doubt, I think, in the minds of those present, that he was a homosexual. As name after name was put to him, the names of blackmailers, of boys of the humblest class, and as the story was unfolded of such youths being invited to champagne dinners or suppers in Wilde's own rooms or in a private room at expensive restaurants, the explanation that Wilde's interest in such persons was no more than an expression of his innocent love for youth in all its aspects began to ring terribly hollow, and we at least who were representing him realized that the case was lost.

He had saved his reputation as a writer of books and plays, but as a man he had almost confessed to having at least 'posed', as the libel alleged. Carson had made it clear that he had statements from the two Parkers, from Wood, from Shelley, and others, and was intending to call them as witnesses. Wilde had afforded in advance such deadly corroboration of the stories they would tell that we could not hope that they would be altogether disbelieved, and Clarke was convinced that the only course to take in the interest of Wilde was to bring the case to an end before any evidence could be given in support of the plea of justification.

Wilde was given every opportunity to leave the country if he so desired. He elected to stay; or more accurately, he could not make up his mind to go, though he drew money from his bank and had his bag half packed when arrested late in the afternoon. The authorities would, I believe, have been quite willing that he should go abroad; but, since he did not avail himself of the delay in issuing the warrant, his prosecution was inevitable. Before making some observations upon the two trials that followed, let us see how it was that the unfortunate proceedings against Lord Queensberry came to be taken.

The eighth Marquess of Queensberry no doubt deserved all the unpleasant things which were said about him; but the very fact that he was a coarse-minded and violent-tempered individual, filled with envy, hatred, malice, and all uncharitableness towards the members of his family, made it all the more certain that he would not desist from his persecution of Wilde unless compelled to do so, or unless the cause of his enmity was removed by the parting of his son, Alfred Douglas, and the 'poseur', as he regarded Oscar Wilde. When, therefore, Wilde instructed his solicitor to apply for criminal process against Lord Queensberry, that very experienced criminal lawyer had three possible courses open to him. He could advise Wilde to ignore this particular insult, which would mean waiting for the next attack which would surely follow; he could refuse to accept Wilde's instructions, and invite him to consult some other solicitor; or he could take the step which he, in fact, did. It may be taken for granted that he had not the faintest idea that Wilde had laid himself open to charges such as those upon which he was ultimately convicted.

It is always easy to be wise after the event, but at the time, and with the knowledge of the parties which he then possessed, I venture to think that the action of the solicitor was the natural and proper one. That at least was the view of Mr Justice Wills, who presided over the last trial, and who in the course of his summing up observed that 'the action of Lord Queensberry was one which no gentleman would have taken and left Wilde no alternative but to prosecute or to be branded publicly as a man who could not deny a foul charge'.

In giving to his solicitor, as he afterwards admitted, his solemn assurance of his innocence, Wilde lied, as did Lord Alfred Douglas, who accompanied him. None of Wilde's friends came forward to give to the solicitor even a hint of the life Wilde had been leading, though they were ready enough at a later stage to offer information upon it. Three of them came to my chambers just after Wilde had been committed for trial with the suggestion that the defence should be that 'dear Oscar could not help himself, he had always had these tendencies'. The truth is that the two persons responsible for the débâcle were Oscar Wilde himself and his friend Lord Alfred Douglas.

Alfred Douglas was very annoyed that he was not allowed to give evidence against his father. Suggestions were made then and since that his evidence would have helped Wilde by 'showing up' Lord Queensberry. Such criticisms merely serve to expose the ignorance of the critics. There was no admissible evidence which Douglas could have given, since the issue was not concerned with the treatment of his family by the Marquess, but simply – was it true that Wilde had posed as alleged?

As to the reason why Clarke decided to end the trial before the defence had called their witnesses, I have already explained that in his opinion there was just a chance that the Treasury Solicitor, who then acted as the Director of Public Prosecutions, might be satisfied to leave things as they were. So matters might indeed have turned out if Lord Queensberry had been less vindictive than he in fact was, or if Wilde had decided to leave the country for a time. As it was, the Treasury Solicitor's hand was forced, and he had no choice but to prosecute.

Wilde showed considerable courage in remaining to face his accusers, both then and later when, after the disagreement of the jury at the first trial, he was admitted to bail. The £5,000 bail was in fact put up in cash, and Wilde was told, so I was afterwards informed, that his sureties would not suffer if he absconded; but he elected to remain. What he thought then of his chances we cannot tell. He had a pathetic belief in his own power to influence others; he may have considered, not altogether without justification, that a disagreement is half-way to an acquittal, though that astute advocate Montague Williams used to say 'the second barrel is nearly always fatal'. However that may be, he took his chance – and failed.

On the whole, Wilde had little to complain of in the conduct of either of his trials. Both Mr Justice Charles and Mr Justice Wills were scrupulously fair to him, and he obtained from both of those learned judges rulings on the question of the corroboration of accomplices much more favourable than would be given in similar circumstances today. Indeed, Mr Justice Wills, in refusing to leave the case of the youth Shelley to the jury, was not expressing the law as it existed then or now; but, in the absence of any Court of Criminal Appeal, the learned judge was making sure that no injustice should be suffered by the accused in a case where he himself thought it would be dangerous to convict.

Sir Edward Clarke considered that the Solicitor-General in the second trial had pressed the case unduly against his client, and said so in his speech to the jury, but too much attention need not be paid to these forensic recriminations. The genial Frank Lockwood was a hard hitter and a vigorous advocate, belonging to the school of those who held that the 'duty of a prosecutor is to prosecute', as Richard Muir once put it, but it was not in his nature to be intentionally unfair to anyone.

The newspapers, or some of them, certainly behaved disgracefully, and if there is any truth in the statement to be found in the book, *Oscar Wilde: Three Times Tried*, published in 1912, that a morning paper purported to publish the voting of the jury upon the various charges upon which they failed to agree, the editor of that paper was indeed fortunate in not being sent to prison for a gross contempt of Court.

It may be of interest to refer to one other matter which, however, was not, so far as I remember, mentioned during either of the trials. In every sensational trial by jury, one of the factors to be reckoned with is the atmosphere in which the case is tried, by which I mean the attitude of the public, from which are drawn the jurors, to the particular subject debated, and the likelihood of prejudice for or against one of the parties. Now, Oscar Wilde was accused of offences against section 11 of the Criminal Law Amendment Act, 1885. Until that Act came into force, on 1 January 1886, the criminal law was not concerned with alleged indecencies between grown-up men committed in private. Everyone knew that such things took place, but the law only punished acts against public decency or conduct tending to the corruption of youth. The Bill in question, entitled 'A Bill to make further provision for the protection of women and girls, the suppression of brothels, and other purposes', was introduced and passed in the House of Lords without any reference to indecency between males. In the Commons, after a second reading without comment, it was referred to a committee of the whole House. In committee Mr Labouchere moved to insert in the Bill the clause which ultimately became section 11 of the Act, creating the new offence of indecency between male persons in public *or private*. Such conduct in public was, and always had been, punishable at common law. There was no discussion, except that one member asked the Speaker whether it was in order to introduce at that stage a clause dealing with a totally different class of offence to that against which the Bill was directed. The Speaker having ruled that anything could be introduced by leave of the House, the clause was agreed to without further discussion, the only amendment moved being one by Sir Henry James with the object of increasing the maximum punishment from twelve to twenty-four months, which was also agreed to without discussion.

It is doubtful whether the House fully appreciated that the words 'in public or private' in the new clause had completely altered the law; but, as soon as the Royal Assent had been given and the Act was published, there began a spate of correspondence in the newspapers, both legal and lay, and references to the subject on various public platforms, which were duly reported. A learned Recorder dubbed it 'the Blackmailer's Charter' and an eminent Q.C. prophesied that juries would refuse to convict where the alleged acts were in private and not visible to any member of the public. On the other hand, those interested in the welfare of girls welcomed the Act as a whole so warmly (and indeed it was an excellent Act apart from section 11), and it was so clearly impossible to do anything except to let the law take its course, that after a few weeks the clamour died down and the public interest became centred upon some more savoury topic. The criticisms proved to be not without foundation. The reluctance of juries to convict in such cases is notorious, while no one having experience in such matters would deny that the words 'in private' have materially assisted the blackmailer in his loathsome trade.

I have referred to the history of section 11, not for the purpose of reviving the old controversy as to whether the satisfaction of sending to prison some of those who offend against it 'in private' outweighs the harm done in other directions, but because there was a belief in some minds at the time that its unpopularity would assist Wilde. As it was put by a legal friend of mine: 'We shall see which the jury dislike most – section 11 or Oscar Wilde.' Something caused a disagreement among the jury at the first trial; what occasioned it, we do not know. It is not inconceivable that some one or more of the jurors held views upon the matters I have been referring to. Certain it is that no one has had the hardihood to propose the extension of the law upon the subject to women, though Lesbianism is not unknown in this country.

On the other hand, Oscar Wilde was no popular favourite. The cult of 'Art for Art's sake', in the form in which it was rife at the time when Wilde was an undergraduate at Oxford, and later in London, when he may be said to have been its High Priest, had long been out of favour with the virile youth of the day. Aestheticism had been ridiculed out of existence by W. S. Gilbert in *Patience* during the early eighties. *Patience* had a long and successful career, and though it had been succeeded at the Savoy Theatre by *Iolanthe* and other operas long before 1895, it was still frequently played, while its tunes and its songs could be heard in every drawing-room. Wilde in the witness-box showed himself to be a 'poseur', and 'poseurs' were at a discount with those who had laughed at Gilbert's invitation to cultivate a

'sentimental passion of a vegetable fashion ... an attachment
à la Plato for a bashful young potato or a not-too-French French
bean!'

It is, I think, doubtful whether the average juryman knew
much if anything of Oscar Wilde. As a poet he had never acquired
a reputation, at least with the general public; his name was no
doubt familiar to playgoers as the author of some brilliant and
successful comedies, but after all what does the public know and
what interest does the public take in the private lives of authors?
I think we are bound to assume that the jury convicted Wilde
as another jury had convicted Taylor – upon the evidence in the
case.

Wilde's plays still live, and after fifty years continue to draw
audiences. Some of his books, including *The Picture of Dorian
Gray*, are still being published. For my own part I hope that such
exquisite fantasies as *The Happy Prince* and *The Nightingale and
the Rose* will live as long as the similar stories for children by
Hans Christian Andersen. It was, however, as a talker that Wilde
shone most brightly among his contemporaries. As a conversationalist he was supreme. Occasionally flippant, he was never
dull, and his wittiest sayings were for the most part completely
impromptu. I shall always remember one of them during a conference we had together shortly before the first trial came on. It
was on this occasion that he learned that Lord Queensberry's
solicitor had briefed as his leading counsel Edward Carson, who,
as it happened, had once been a student with Wilde at Trinity
College, Dublin. When I told him that he would be cross-
examined by Carson at the trial, Wilde immediately replied: 'No
doubt he will perform his task with all the added bitterness of an
old friend.'

Oscar Wilde's talents raised him almost to the level of a
genius; his mode of life dragged him down to the depths of a
pathological case.

R.I.P.

PREFACE

THE three trials in which Oscar Wilde formed the principal figure at the Central Criminal Court in London in 1895 have every right to the fame that they have achieved. A well-known dramatic author prosecuted an eccentric and pugnacious peer for criminally libelling him, the libel having been uttered by the Marquess of Queensberry in an alleged attempt to save his son, Lord Alfred Douglas, from the author's evil communications. This proceeding in turn led to the author's own prosecution and ultimate conviction on a serious charge under a recent criminal statute.

The legal drama, which unfolded itself at the Old Bailey between 3 April and 31 May 1895, engaged the best professional brains of the day – on the Bench, Mr Justice Henn Collins, Mr Justice Charles, and Mr Justice Wills; and at the Bar, Sir Edward Clarke, Sir Frank Lockwood, and Messrs Edward Carson, Charles Gill, Willie Mathews, Horace Avory, and Travers Humphreys. At the conclusion of the first trial Mr Justice Henn Collins described Carson's defence of Lord Queensberry, in the course of which he cross-examined Wilde with deadly effect, as the most powerful speech and searching cross-examination to which he had ever listened. In the second trial the accused's description of Platonic love between an elder and a younger man produced an extraordinary outburst of applause in Court, which undoubtedly contributed to the jury's failure to agree upon a verdict. Wilde's remarks were described by some who heard them as the finest speech of an accused man since that of Paul before King Herod Agrippa. In the third and last trial Sir Edward Clarke, who was Wilde's leading counsel throughout, attacked Sir Frank Lockwood, the Solicitor-General in charge of the prosecution, for having gone beyond the bounds of fairness in his presentation of the Crown's case. The action of a former law officer – Clarke had himself previously been Solicitor-General –

15

in thus openly impugning the professional conduct of his successor in office is probably unique, at any rate in modern times. Such are the more prominent features which have combined to make these trials notable in British criminal annals, and which, it is submitted, justify the publication of this very full reconstruction. All those who actively participated in the grim Old Bailey drama, more than sixty years ago, have passed away. First to depart was Sir Frank Lockwood, the Solicitor-General, who was carried off in 1897, seemingly in the prime of his life and approaching the zenith of his career. Two years later, Queensberry followed Lockwood to the grave, a pathetic victim of persecution mania, convinced to the last that he was being harried to the tomb by the 'Oscar Wilders', as he used to describe his imaginary tormentors. Barely twelve months afterwards Wilde himself breathed his last in a small Paris hotel, deserted by all save a few faithful disciples. The others followed at varying intervals, among them, Lord Alfred Douglas in 1945. Although his place had only been, as it were, in the wings of the Old Bailey stage, Douglas had been haunted through a long and stormy life by recurrent echoes of the disaster which had overtaken his friend. The last to die was Sir Travers Humphreys, in 1956.

The accident of my having as an undergraduate occupied Wilde's old rooms in college at Oxford brought me into touch with Alfred Douglas; and, in introducing the trials in the following pages, I have drawn on the information which he gave me in the course of conversations and correspondence.[1] I have naturally not neglected other sources which have been open to me, but

1. I am also indebted to Lord Alfred Douglas's published writings, notably: *Oscar Wilde and Myself* (1914), *Autobiography* (1929), *Without Apology* (1938), and *Oscar Wilde: A Summing Up* (1940), as well as to an interesting series of MS. letters from Wilde to Douglas at present preserved in the William Andrews Clark collection in the University of California. A privately printed edition of the latter, with facsimile reproductions, was published in San Francisco in 1924. The text of the letters has been reprinted by Mr Rupert Hart-Davis in *The Letters of Oscar Wilde* (1962). I should mention too a long and very interesting letter written by Douglas from France to W. T. Stead shortly after the last trial, of which the original is now in my possession.

since I was unborn at the time of the trials, my authority can only be at best second-hand. It is, therefore, particularly fortunate that Sir Travers Humphreys survived to recount his own first-hand recollections of the great *cause célèbre* of the nineties, in the Foreword to the original edition of the trials which is reprinted here.

For those who, like myself, were not alive at the time or were too young to remember, it is difficult to visualize the strong public feelings and prejudices provoked by the Queensberry and Wilde trials. Queensberry's acquittal was received with round after round of cheering in Court.

The judge [so wrote the *Daily Telegraph* on the morning of 6 April 1895] did not attempt to silence or reprove the irrepressible cheering in Court which greeted the acquittal of this sorely provoked and cruelly injured father. As for the prosecutor, whose notoriety has become so infamous . . . we have had enough of Mr Oscar Wilde, who has been the means of inflicting on the public during this recent episode as much moral damage of the most hideous and repulsive kind as no single individual could well cause.

More disgraceful scenes marked Wilde's conviction a few weeks later. In the street outside the Old Bailey prostitutes danced at the downfall of one whom they regarded as a dangerous competitor in trade. Newspaper editorials no doubt reflected their readers' sentiments at the time in their professed vindication of outraged public virtue, but it is impossible to disguise the note of personal spite which characterized the homilies of the press.

No sterner rebuke [to quote the *Daily Telegraph*] could well have been inflicted on some of the artistic tendencies of the time than the condemnation of Oscar Wilde at the Central Criminal Court. We have not the slightest intention of reviewing once more all the sordid incidents of a case which has done enough, and more than enough, to shock the conscience and outrage the moral instincts of the community. The man has now suffered the penalties of his career, and may well be allowed to pass from that platform of publicity which he loved into that limbo of disrepute and forgetfulness which is his due. The grave of contemptuous oblivion may rest on his foolish ostentation, his empty paradoxes, his insufferable posturing, his incurable vanity.

Nevertheless, when we remember that he enjoyed a certain popularity among some sections of society and, above all, when we reflect that what was smiled at as insolent braggadocio was the cover, for, or at all events ended in, flagrant immorality, it is well, perhaps that the lesson of his life should not be passed over without some insistence on the terrible warning of his fate. Young men at the universities, silly women who lend an ear to any chatter which is petulant and vivacious, novelists who have sought to imitate the style of paradox and unreality, poets who have lisped the language of nerveless and effeminate libertinage – these are the persons who should ponder with themselves the doctrines and the career of the man who has now to undergo the righteous sentence of the law.

One more example of contemporary journalism on the subject is, perhaps, worth repeating. This is what the editor of the London *Evening News* wrote on the day of Wilde's conviction:

... Never has the lesson of a wasted life come home to us more dramatically and opportunely. England has tolerated the man Wilde and others of his kind too long. Before he broke the law of his country and outraged human decency he was a social pest, a centre of intellectual corruption. He was one of the high priests of a school which attacks all the wholesome, manly, simple ideals of English life, and sets up false gods of decadent culture and intellectual debauchery. The man himself was a perfect type of his class, a gross sensualist veneered with the affectation of artistic feeling too delicate for the appreciation of common clay. To him and such as him we owe the spread of moral degeneration amongst young men with abilities sufficient to make them a credit to their country. At the feet of Wilde they have learned to gain notoriety by blatant conceit, by despising the emotions of healthy humanity and the achievements of wholesome talent.

Such people find their fitting environment in the artificial light and the incense-laden air of secret chambers curtained from the light of day. Their pretences fall from them in fresh air and honest sunshine. Light has been let in upon them now in a very decisive fashion, and we venture to hope that the conviction of Wilde for these abominable vices, which were the natural outcome of his diseased intellectual condition, will be a salutary warning to the unhealthy boys who posed as sharers of his culture. Wilde's fate will teach them that brilliant talent does not justify disdain of all moral restraints ... a delusion common to them, and by no means unknown amongst more honest folk. It has been the fashion to concede a certain amount of immoral licence to men of genius, and it is time that public opinion should correct it . . . all the more when we find a counsel so distinguished as Sir Edward Clarke gravely submitting to a jury that his client should not be judged as an ordinary man in the matter of decent language and manly feeling because forsooth he had intellectual powers above the average.

While the traditional British sense of fair play was scarcely very pronounced during these trials, on the other hand there can be little if any doubt that Wilde was justly convicted – indeed he admitted as much himself to friends with whom he was in touch both during and after his imprisonment. The best that can be said for him is that, so far as is known, he never debauched any innocent young men. All his accomplices, on the strength of whose evidence he was condemned, were already steeped in vice before Wilde met them, and two at least were notorious and self-confessed blackmailers. Furthermore, the offence of which Wilde was accused had been declared criminal by Parliament less than ten years before,[1] and, according to most if not all continental codes of law, was not a crime at all. But these factors, though they may extenuate, do not really excuse Wilde.

It may also be pointed out that Wilde was not charged with being a sodomite, although, as will be seen, Lord Queensberry, in the defamatory words for which he [Queensberry] was prosecuted in the first trial, accused him of 'posing' as such. Had it been otherwise, Wilde would have been liable to a maximum sentence of penal servitude for life. As it was, the offence of which he was indicted – the commission of acts of indecency *in private* with members of his own sex – carried with it in his case the maximum sentence of two years' imprisonment with hard labour, a sentence which the judge who passed it described as being 'totally inadequate for such a case as this'. Not everyone today would agree with the fairness of this judicial stricture. Indeed, had there existed any facilities for a condemned man to appeal against conviction and sentence half a century ago, it is

1. For the notorious Labouchere Amendment, see Sir Travers Humphreys's Foreword p. 12.

19

possible that the sentence in Wilde's case would have been reduced. My personal belief, however, is that the conviction would have been upheld.

There are still, after such a long lapse of time some people who seem incapable of discussing the Wilde trials either rationally or accurately. Their misstatements may, of course, be due to ignorance of the facts of the trials. It must be admitted that there is good reason for this ignorance. Contemporary newspaper accounts are garbled and one-sided. References to the trials in biographies of Wilde, though numerous, are frequently misleading. The official Court shorthand-writers and compilers of the *Central Criminal Court Sessions Papers*, who might have been expected to present the facts objectively, declined to print the proceedings of any of the trials on the ground that the details disclosed by them were 'unfit for publication'.[1] It was not until 1912 that Wilde's industrious bibliographer, Christopher Millard (otherwise known as Stuart Mason), assisted by the publisher Cecil Palmer, ventured to produce, with an anonymity which public feeling on the subject of Wilde still rendered necessary, the first full length and impartial account of the proceedings. This work has long been out of print.[2] But, though it was by far the fullest record of the three trials which had hitherto appeared, it did not purport to give the proceedings verbatim and with the necessary introductory background such as would enable the evidence to be correctly appreciated.

It is with the intention of dispelling prevalent misconceptions, and at the same time of making the proceedings of the trials substantially available in their proper perspective, that I have attempted not only to set down in the following pages exactly what happened during those dramatic days at the Old Bailey in the spring of 1895, but also to sketch in Wilde's family background, the conflict of personalities which led to the disastrous first trial and the painful exile which followed Wilde's release

1. *Sessions Papers*, cxxi, 531–2.
2. *Oscar Wilde: Three Times Tried*, London, 1912. When it first appeared The Times Book Club refused to circulate this publication among its subscribers.

Preface

from prison and lasted until his death in Paris in 1900.[1]
It is unlikely that any spectator of the trials is alive today.
Fortunately I was able, during their lifetime, to have conversations with five persons who were present for part or all of the
proceedings. They were Sir Travers Humphreys, Lord Alfred
Douglas, Sir Max Beerbohm, Sir Seymour Hicks, and Sir Albion
Richardson; and I gratefully place on record my appreciation of
the help which I received from their impressions of the trials.
Others, who knew Wilde personally and similarly communicated
their recollections to me, were Sir Arthur Quiller-Couch and the
poets, W. B. Yeats and Richard Le Gallienne. I likewise salute
their memory.

Through the incorporation of fresh material, the present new
and enlarged edition differs in several respects from the original
edition, which was published in 1948. In the first place, sustained
by the recent Obscene Publications Act, I have been enabled to
reproduce some portions of the evidence verbatim which discretion obliged me to paraphrase in the earlier edition. In this connexion, I must acknowledge my indebtedness to *The Trial of Oscar
Wilde*, edited by Charles Grolleau and privately printed for
Charles Carrington in Paris in 1906.

Secondly, thanks to the Home Secretary in 1954, Major G.
Lloyd George (now Lord Tenby), the official Home Office and

1. Biographies of Oscar Wilde have been written in English by R. H.
Sherard (1906), Frank Harris (1916), G. J. Renier (1933), Boris Brasol
(1938), Frances Winwar (1940), Hesketh Pearson (1946), Lewis Broad
(1954), and Vyvyan Holland (1960); and studies in literary criticism by L. C.
Ingleby (1907), Arthur Ransome (1912), R. Thurston Hopkins (1913),
Édouard Roditi (1947), George Woodcock (1949), St John Ervine (1951),
and James Laver (1954). The first collected edition of Wilde's works was
edited by Robert Ross (1908). His letters have been edited by Rupert Hart-
Davis (1962). A detailed bibliography down to 1914, with the addition of
much interesting extraneous matter, was compiled by Stuart Mason, who
also translated André Gide's recollections of Wilde (1905). See also R. H.
Sherard, *Oscar Wilde: The Story of an Unhappy Friendship* (1902) and *The
Real Oscar Wilde* (1915); Anna Comtesse De Brémont, *Oscar Wilde and his
Mother* (1911); and Vincent O'Sullivan, *Aspects of Wilde* (1936), an account
of his last days in Paris which Bernard Shaw described as 'the first sane
and credible description of him' in the final tragic period.

Preface

Prison Commission Papers relating to Wilde's conviction and imprisonment were made available to me without restriction. At the same time, the late Sir Lionel Fox, Chairman of the Prison Commissioners, kindly arranged for me to visit the three prisons in which Wilde served his two-year sentence.

Thirdly, the MS. of the work composed by Wilde in prison and generally known as *De Profundis*, which has considerable relevance to the trials, and which had never been published in its entirety, has become available, after having been sealed up for fifty years in the British Museum, where it was deposited by Wilde's literary executor subject to this condition in 1909. It was officially opened on 1 January 1960, and I was the first member of the general public to be allowed to examine it.

Finally, the scholarly and definitive edition of Wilde's *Letters* by Mr Rupert Hart-Davis, which appeared earlier this year, throws some further light on the trials and their background. I wish to thank Mr Hart-Davis for permission to quote from several letters which are still in copyright. A few other additional sources which I have used are indicated in footnotes.

Besides those to whom acknowledgements were made in the original edition, I also wish to thank Constable & Co., Ltd, publishers of *W. E. Henley* by John Connell, for permission to quote from Henley's letters about Wilde.

Nutley, Sussex   H. MONTGOMERY HYDE
September 1962

CHAPTER 1

THE BACKGROUND

1

OSCAR WILDE's parents were remarkable and unusual people, and both of them possessed strong literary tastes in addition to other qualities. On his father's side, the family was Dutch by origin and claimed descent from a certain Colonel de Vilde, who came over to Ireland with King William of Orange at the time of the 'Glorious Revolution' and was granted lands in Connaught, where he married an Irishwoman and changed his name to Wilde. Sir William Wilde was a successful eye and ear surgeon in Dublin, and he founded a hospital there in 1853, a year before Oscar was born; his work gained for him the honorary appointment of Surgeon Oculist in Ordinary to the Queen, a post which was specially created for him. Eleven years later he was knighted, largely in recognition of his work on the medical statistics of the Irish census. Sir William Wilde was also interested in natural history and ethnology – his three-volume catalogue of the contents of the Royal Irish Academy has been described as a monumental work of archaeological erudition and insight – and he published in all twenty books including two excellent works of Irish antiquarian topography, *The Beauties of the Boyne and the Blackwater* (1849) and *Lough Corrib and Lough Mask* (1867), which can still be read with advantage by visitors to the west of Ireland. He also attempted to prove, in a short but most readable narrative, that Dean Swift was not mad in his last days.

Besides these achievements, Oscar's father exercised a powerful fascination upon women, whom he used to pursue with vigour. In addition to the legitimate offspring of his marriage, he had several natural children, including one named Henry Wilson: Henry became a popular Dublin oculist like his father, whom he helped with his professional practice. Sir William Wilde was good company, and, surprising as it may appear in view of his personal habits, he was generally liked by his female patients, although he was alleged to have criminally assaulted one of them, having first given her a whiff of chloroform to make her submit more easily to his will. (This episode involved Sir William in a lawsuit and was the most sensational scandal of the sixties in Dublin.) He was slovenly in his dress and dirty in his physical appearance. 'Why are Sir William Wilde's nails black?' was a popular conundrum of the day in Dublin. The answer was: 'Because he scratches himself.' No wonder the Viceroy's wife refused the soup one evening when dining at the Wilde's house in Merrion Square, after she had seen her host put his thumb in the tureen.

Yet, in spite of his peculiarities, Sir William Wilde was on the whole well liked, particularly by his many poor patients, to whom he willingly gave his professional services free. He earned an unusually large income, which he spent lavishly on himself and his family and in the cause of science and archaeology. His wife, who was reputed to turn a blind eye to her husband's amorous exploits, had a great admiration for him as a scholar. 'There was probably no man of his generation more versed in our national literature, in all that concerned the land and the people, the arts, architecture, topography, statistics, and even the legends of the country,' she wrote after his death, 'but above all in his favourite department, the descriptive illustration of Ireland, past and present, in historic and prehistoric times, he has justly gained a wide reputation as one of the most popular writers of the age on Irish subjects'.[1]

Some years younger than her husband, Jane Francesca Agnes Lady Wilde, known as 'Speranza', had become celebrated in Ireland for her passionate nationalist outpourings in verse and prose. Like her husband, she was also an enthusiastic collector of Irish folklore and was active in the women's rights movement of

1. Sir William Wilde (1815–76) is the subject of an interesting biography by Dr T. G. Wilson, *Victorian Doctor* (1942). See also Patrick Byrne, *The Wildes of Merrion Square* (1953), and Vyvyan Holland, *Son of Oscar Wilde* (1954).

the time. Her father, Charles Elgee, was a country solicitor from Wexford, while her grandfather, Archdeacon John Elgee, also of Wexford, was a scholarly and benevolent Church of Ireland clergyman, who was so popular in his parish that the local rebels spared his life during the rising of 1798. According to one account, which 'Speranza' herself accepted, the family originally came from Florence, the name Elgee being an Hibernian version of Algiati, which in turn was a corruption of Alighieri; and she liked to think that she had some remote kinship with the great Dante and indeed to boast of it. Her immediate ancestry is easier to establish. Her mother, Sarah Kingsbury, was the daughter of Dr Thomas Kingsbury, a Commissioner of Bankruptcy in Ireland and the owner of Lisle House, one of the finest Dublin mansions of the period. She was also a grandniece of the Rev Charles Maturin, the romantic novelist who flourished in the early years of the nineteenth century and whose *Melmoth the Wanderer* was later to prompt her son Oscar to use the pseudonym, 'Sebastian Melmoth', under which he lived out his last years as an exile on the Continent. As a young girl Jane Elgee became an ardent Irish nationalist, contributing both verse and prose to the revolutionary patriot weekly *The Nation* under the pen-name 'Speranza'. It was an inflammatory article in which she appealed to the young men of Ireland to take up arms in defence of their country's liberties, in the revolutionary year 1848, that led to the suppression of *The Nation* and the prosecution of its editor, Charles Gavan Duffy, for sedition. For her part in the affair she became a national figure in Ireland overnight. In fact, at the time of her marriage to William Wilde three years later, she was much better known throughout the country than her husband. Thirty years afterwards, her son Oscar was to write: 'I don't think that age has dimmed the fire and enthusiasm of that pen which set the Young Irelanders in a blaze'.[1]

Oscar Fingal O'Flahertie Wills Wilde was born at 21 Westland

1. A biography of Lady Wilde (1824–98) has been written by Horace Wyndham, entitled *Speranza* (1951). See also her *Poems* (1864) and *Ancient Legends of Ireland* (1887), and Anna Comtesse de Brémont, *Oscar Wilde and his Mother* (1911).

Row, Dublin, on 16 October 1854.[1] He was the second son, an elder brother William Charles Kingsbury Wills ('Willie') having been born two years previously. Victorian children were often given long strings of names, which they would mostly discard in later life; Oscar dropped all of his except the first soon after leaving Oxford. The choice of Oscar as the first of his Christian names was long believed in Dublin to have been dictated by the fact that Sir William Wilde had professionally attended King Oscar I of Sweden, on whom he performed a successful operation for cataract and who became his second son's godfather. But the name is more likely to have been chosen by 'Speranza' on account of its association, like that of Fingal, with legendary Celtic history. At that period there was a great vogue for the poems, popularized by Macpherson's translation, of Ossian or Oisin, the ancient Irish warrior-bard, whose father Fingal had delivered Erin from her enemies and whose chivalrous son Oscar was slain in battle at an early age. 'He is to be called Oscar Fingal Wilde,' she told a friend when the baby was a month old. 'Is not that grand, misty and Ossianic?' As for O'Flahertie, this addition may be traced to some real or supposed family connexion with 'the ferocious O'Flaherties of Galway', in whose country Sir William Wilde had a holiday house and also a fishing lodge. Wills was a somewhat later addition and was adopted by both brothers in their youth out of respect for their Wills cousins, who were landowners in County Roscommon and included James Wills the poet and W. G. Wills the dramatist. Sir William

1. Several biographies and encyclopedia articles, including the *Dictionary of National Biography*, wrongly state that Oscar Wilde was born at 1 Merrion Square, Dublin, on 16 October 1856. The error as to his birthday seems to have arisen from his vanity in habitually understating his age, a foible which was to cause him some embarrassment at the first of his trials (see below, p. 105). Although the registration of births in Ireland did not become legally compulsory until 1867, the date of Oscar Wilde's birth has been placed beyond doubt by his baptismal record, which is still in existence. For a facsimile of the baptismal entry, see article by Dr T. G. Wilson ('Oscar Wilde at Trinity College, Dublin') in *The Practitioner*, Vol. CLXXIII, 473–80 (October 1954). There is no doubt, too, that his parents were living at 21 Westland Row at this time and did not move to the better known house in Merrion Square until about a year later.

The Background

Wilde, who likewise adopted the name Wills, was proud of his 'county' relatives, at whose hands his father Dr Thomas Wilde, who practised medicine in the town of Castlerea, had received many kindnesses.[1]

It has been said that Lady Wilde had longed for a girl and, when her second child turned out to be a boy, she insisted on dressing him in girl's clothes. This incident will be examined in considering the problem of Oscar Wilde's sexual inversion. All that need be noticed here is that Lady Wilde's third and last child was a daughter, who was born in 1858 and was named Isola Francesca. Unfortunately this daughter died young, in her ninth year, and Oscar, who was then a dreamy-eyed schoolboy of twelve and appears to have been devoted to his sister, is said to have vented his 'lonely and inconsolable grief' in long and frequent visits to her grave.[2] Some years later he was to perpetuate her memory in the poem which he called 'Requiescat', and which has been included in numerous anthologies of verse; it has even been set to music and sung at concerts. It is perhaps the most often quoted of all Wilde's poems with the exception of *The Ballad of Reading Gaol*, although its author never regarded it, as he told his fellow countryman and poet W. B. Yeats, as being 'very typical of my work'. Written while Wilde was an undergraduate at Oxford, it owes something at least in metre to Hood. The first two of its five stanzas run as follows:

> Tread lightly, she is near
> Under the snow,
> Speak lightly, she can hear
> The daisies grow.
>
> All her bright golden hair
> Tarnished with rust,

1. Oscar Wilde was not baptized until more than two months after his birth. The ceremony took place in St Mark's Church, Dublin, on 26 April 1855, and was performed by his uncle, the Rev. Ralph Wilde, Vicar of Kilsallaghan.

2. Isola Francesca Wilde died on 23 February 1867, at The Glebe, Edgworthstown, Co. Longford, when staying with her aunt (her father's only sister), who was married to the Rector, the Rev. William Noble.

27

Oscar Wilde

See that was young and fair,
Fallen to dust.[1]

When the time came for him to go to boarding school, Oscar was sent to an establishment in the north of Ireland, Portora Royal School, overlooking the waters of Lough Erne and the ancient town of Enniskillen. His career at Portora was not noticeably distinguished, except in his final year. Willie Wilde was already there when he arrived and seems to have considerably outshone his younger brother at lessons. It was only in his last year that Oscar began to show signs of promise, when he won the school prize for Greek Testament, a Gold Medal in Classics and an entrance scholarship to Trinity College, Dublin. But even then, Dr Steele, the headmaster, in calling him into his study to tell him the news of the scholarship, clearly showed which of the two brothers was his favourite. 'The doctor wound up, I remember,' Oscar recalled long afterwards, 'by assuring me that if I went on studying as I had been studying during the last year I might yet do as well as my brother Willie, and be as great an honour to the school and everybody connected with it as he had been.' While the elder boy carefully studied the prescribed textbooks and excelled both at work and games, Oscar was inclined to confine his reading to what pleased him. Nor did he care for either cricket or football – 'I never liked to kick or be kicked' – although he was certainly no milksop.

A schoolboy contemporary who remembered Oscar at Portora has recorded that he was an excellent talker, his descriptive powers being far above the average: his exaggerations of school occurrences were always highly amusing. A favourite place for the boys to sit and gossip in the late afternoon in winter time was a

1. Although included in the anthology of Dublin University under-graduate verse, *Echoes of Kottabos* (1906), 'Requiescat' was not originally published in the undergraduate journal *Kottabos*, and it is not known whether it ever appeared before its publication in the first edition of Wilde's *Poems* in 1881. George Augustus Sala pointed out at the time of the latter publication that golden hair does not tarnish in the tomb, citing Émile Zola's *Nana* in support of his statement: see Stuart Mason, *Bibliography of Oscar Wilde* (1914), pp. 295-6.

stove which stood in the 'Stone Hall'. Here Oscar was at his best. His friend, whose name was Edward Sullivan and was a son of the Lord Chancellor of Ireland, has recalled that at one of these gatherings a discussion took place about an ecclesiastical prosecution which was making a considerable stir at the time. Oscar seemed to know all about the Court of Arches and showed great interest in the case. Indeed he made a remark of curious prophetic insight. 'He told us there was nothing he would like better in after life than to be the hero of such a *cause célèbre* and to go down to posterity as the defendant in such a case as *Regina* versus *Wilde.*'[1]

2

Oscar Wilde entered Trinity College, Dublin, as a Junior Freshman in 1871, a few days before his seventeenth birthday. For his first year he lived with his parents in the large house in Merrion Square where his father had his surgery and his mother kept a weekly *salon*, which was a popular centre of the city's intellectual life. ('Come home with me,' Oscar is alleged to have said to a friend. 'My mother and I have formed a society for the suppression of virtue.') For his second and third years he moved into college, where he and Willie had rooms in the block known as Botany Bay. Both brothers were members of the Philosophical Society, which held regular debates; but oratory appealed less to Oscar than to his elder brother, who had decided to go to the Bar. No doubt, however, Oscar was present on the occasion on which his father presided as guest chairman and the question of social evils was debated. On this particular evening Willie delivered an impassioned speech in defence of prostitutes, a topic

1. Frank Harris, *Life and Confessions of Oscar Wilde* (1916), I, p. 25. Sir Edward Sullivan, 2nd Bart, published a number of books, including a fine edition of *The Book of Kells* (1918), a descriptive account of the greatest treasure in the library of Trinity College, Dublin, where he was also Wilde's contemporary. He also edited (with Professor R. Y. Tyrell) *Echoes from Kottabos* (1906), mentioned above.

on which both the father and his elder son were reputed to possess first-hand knowledge. On another occasion, Sir William accidentally opened a letter intended for Willie, in which his elder son was accused of having made a girl pregnant. 'Here is a most disgraceful letter,' fulminated Sir William. 'Yes, sir,' replied Willie with a serious air when he had read it, promptly assuming that it was intended for his father. 'What are you going to do about it?'

Unlike his father and brother, what he called 'coarse *amours* among barmaids and women of the streets' had no attractions for Oscar. He preferred the society of intellectual companions and teachers, particularly the University Professor of Latin, Dr R. Y. Tyrell, and his tutor, the versatile Dr John Pentland Mahaffy, who was Professor of Ancient History and also Junior Dean.[1] With teachers and students alike he seems to have been generally popular. 'He was a very good natured man and most amusing,' one of the latter recalled in later life. 'Everyone liked him.' But this statement was not quite true. There was at least one exception to it, in the person of a certain plodding student whom the more brilliant Oscar left far behind in the university examinations. His name was Edward Carson, and his path was destined to cross Oscar Wilde's with tragic effect at the most dramatic moment in the latter's career. But at Trinity, although they knew each other and were on speaking terms, Edward Carson and Oscar Wilde were never intimate friends, as has sometimes been supposed. Indeed, Carson disliked the long-haired student genius and distrusted what he considered to be his flippant approach to life. Yet, even at this early period, Wilde did not fail to recognize the latent ability of this particular classmate. 'There goes a man destined to reach the very top of affairs,' he remarked to a young lady, as they were walking across the Front Square in college and

1. The Rev. Sir John Pentland Mahaffy (1839–1919) eventually became Provost of Trinity College, Dublin. His scholastic reputation rests chiefly on his works dealing with the life, literature, and history of the ancient Greeks, although his general knowledge was literally encyclopedic in range and quantity. He was a great talker and lover of good wine, and wrote a book on *The Principles of the Art of Conversation*, which appeared in 1887.

chanced to pass Carson. 'Yes,' agreed Wilde's companion, adding with a touch of feminine malice: 'And one who will not hesitate to trample on his friends in getting there.'

Under Mahaffy's stimulus, Wilde developed an enthusiastic interest in the classics, particularly those of ancient Greece. His academic career at Trinity was a series of unbroken successes in this subject, as it was later also to be at Oxford. He was twice placed in the First Class in the University Examinations, he won a prize for Greek verse, he was elected to a Foundation Scholarship in Classics, and in his final year he carried off the coveted Berkeley Gold Medal for Greek. (He used regularly to pawn the medal when he needed money, and when he died a pawnbroker's ticket for it was found among his few personal belongings.) Finally, he crowned his brilliant record by winning an Open Classical Demyship to Magdalen College, Oxford, whither he departed in a blaze of academic glory in October 1874. 'My dear Oscar, you are not clever enough for us in Dublin,' Mahaffy is said to have remarked to his most outstanding pupil. 'You had better run over to Oxford.'

After the tragedy of his downfall, most of Oscar's college friends and acquaintances in Dublin, with the commendable exception of Professor Tyrell, refused to have anything more to do with him. Their attitude was typified by Mahaffy, who, if anyone chanced to ask about him, would fix the inquirer with a stony stare and observe ponderously: 'We no longer speak of Mr Oscar Wilde.'

3

'The two great turning points in my life were when my father sent me to Oxford, and when society sent me to prison.' Thus Oscar Wilde was to write more than thirty years later in the solitude of a cell in Reading Gaol. 'I will not say that prison is the best thing that could have happened to me, for that phrase would savour of too great bitterness towards myself. I would sooner say, or hear it said of me, that I was so typical a child of my age, that in my perversity, and for that perversity's sake, I turned the good things of my life to evil, and the evil things of my life to good.'

At Oxford, where he was to repeat on an extended scale his earlier scholastic successes, Wilde confined his perversity largely if not entirely to the intellectual field. Thus the trait found expression in his inclination to oppose by his behaviour the accepted conventional standards of the day. However, the poses which he originally affected to draw attention to himself gradually became a habit, and as will be seen, were to lead to perverse behaviour of a more dangerous kind. For the time being, however, he contented himself with concealing his industry with his books while secretly reading hard, by a *blasé* veneer of assumed idleness, by trying to 'live up' to the blue china with which he filled his fine rooms overlooking Magdalen Bridge and the River Cherwell, and by attending Ruskin's crowded lectures on *The Aesthetic and Mathematical Schools of Florence*, which the celebrated Slade Professor of Fine Art would sometimes suddenly interrupt to exhort his listeners male and female to fall in love with each other.

While no doubt he had a few enemies in college, on the whole he was liked in a society which set more store by social ability than athletic or intellectual prowess – and as in Dublin he was always the best of company. 'How brilliant and radiant he could be! How playful and charming!' one of his college friends, William Ward, later recalled. 'How his moods varied and how he revelled in inconsistency! The whim of the moment he openly acknowledged as his dictator. One can see now, reading his character by the light of his later life, the beginnings of the tendencies which grew to his destruction. There was the love of pose, the desire for self-realization, the egotism, but they seemed foibles rather than faults, and his frank regret and laugh at his own expense robbed them of blame and took away offence.'[1]

1. William Welsford Ward (1854–1932) was one of Wilde's closest friends at Oxford. He had the best set of rooms in the college, on the first floor of Kitchen Staircase, which Wilde took over from him when Ward went down in 1876 to become a solicitor in his family firm in Bristol. His nickname was 'Bouncer'. When I occupied the rooms in 1929–30, a drawing of 'Little

The Background

A characteristic example of Wilde's perverse delight in shocking his elders occurred at the college ceremony known as 'Collections', at which the President and Fellows used (as they still do) to meet the undergraduate members of the college and hear the end-of-term tutorial progress reports.

'How do you find Mr Wilde's work, Mr So-and-So?' the President Dr Bulley asked Wilde's history tutor.

'Mr Wilde absents himself without apologies from my lectures,' replied the tutor with an aggrieved air. 'His work is most unsatisfactory.'

'That is hardly the way to treat a gentleman, Mr Wilde,' the President remarked, turning to the delinquent.

'But, Mr President,' Wilde replied, 'Mr So-and-So is *not* a gentleman!'

Amazement followed this sally, and Wilde was told to leave the hall. No doubt he later apologized with his customary charm, but the incident was hardly calculated to endear him to the college authorities, particularly as he failed to reappear in college at the beginning of the next term, having gone off on a tour of Greece with his old Trinity tutor Mahaffy.

Towards the end of Wilde's first year at Oxford, his mother wrote to a friend: 'My eldest son Willie has been called to the Bar and so has planted his foot on the ladder of fame. His hope is to enter Parliament and I wish it also. Oscar is now a scholar at Oxford and resides there in the very focus of intellect. Ruskin had him to breakfast and Max Muller loves him.' Ruskin's breakfast invitation was the reward for those undergraduates, Wilde among

---

Mr 'Bouncer', which Wilde had scratched on one of the window panes, was still visible. (The pane has since been removed.) The MS. of Ward's short 'Oscar Wilde: An Oxford Reminiscence', together with Wilde's letters to him at this period, was presented by his daughter Miss Cecil Ward to Magdalen College Library and has since been published by Mr Vyvyan Holland as an appendix to his *Son of Oscar Wilde* (1954). For other accounts of Wilde at Oxford, see Mason, op. cit. pp. 100–1; Sir David Hunter Blair *In Victorian Days* (1939), pp. 115–43; and articles by C. T. Atkinson ('Oscar Wilde at Oxford') in the *Cornhill Magazine* (May 1929), pp. 559–64, and A. J. A. Symons ('Wilde at Oxford') in *Horizon*, Vol. iii (1944) pp. 252–64 and 336–48.

them, who had helped the 'Master' to maintain the dignity of manual labour with his celebrated road-making experiment at Hinksey. Friederich Max Muller was the Professor of Comparative Philology and a leading authority on Sanskrit, to whose lectures, like those of John Ruskin and Walter Pater, Wilde was strongly drawn at this time.

Oscar Wilde was in his second year at Magdalen when his father, who had been in failing health for some months, died following a heart attack. Sir William Wilde had been a lavish spender, and, although his professional income had been enormous in the days of his prime, his practice had been declining in recent years. Consequently when his affairs came to be settled up, it was revealed that his estate amounted to only £7,000, in addition to some house property, barely enough to keep his widow in a state of genteel poverty. Oscar was left the fishing lodge in Connemara jointly with his half-brother Henry Wilson, besides a small legacy. The legacy he spent on his trip to Greece with Mahaffy in the spring of 1877.

He set out for Greece with the real intention of going to Rome, as he had become strongly attracted by the Catholic faith and wished to see 'the golden dome of St Peter's' and the Vatican. 'This is an era in my life, a crisis,' he wrote on the eve of his departure. 'I wish I could look into the seeds of time and see what is coming.' (It was just as well that he could not.) In the event, he changed his mind when he reached Genoa. Thence Mahaffy 'carried me off to Greece to see Mycenae and Athens', stopping on their way at Corfu and Zante, landing on the mainland near Olympia, and then riding through Arcadia to Mycenae. In the letter which he sent the Junior Dean at Magdalen explaining that he would be unable to be back for the beginning of term, Wilde wrote:

Seeing Greece is really a great education for anyone and will, I think, benefit me greatly, and Mr Mahaffy is such a clever man that it is quite as good as going to lectures to be in his society.

This excuse did not satisfy the college authorities, and on his return to Oxford he was fined the sum of £47 10s., being half the amount of his demyship, and in addition was 'sent down' for the remainder of the term.

My mother was of course, awfully astonished to hear my news and very much disgusted with the wretched stupidity of our college dons, while Mahaffy is *raging* I never saw him so indignantly angry; he looks on it almost as an insult to himself.

A further depressing piece of news reached him soon after arriving home in Dublin. This was the sudden death from pneumonia of one whom Wilde described to his English friends as 'a cousin of ours to whom we were all very much attached' – in reality, his half-brother Henry Wilson. Fearing his conversion to Rome, Wilson had practically disinherited him.

My brother and I were always supposed to be his heirs, but his will was a most unpleasant surprise, like most wills. He leaves my father's hospital about £8,000, my brother £2,000, and me £100 on condition of my being a Protestant. He was, poor fellow, bigotedly intolerant of the Catholics and seeing me 'on the brink' struck me out of his will. It is a terrible disappointment to me; you see I suffer a good deal from my Romish leanings in body and mind. My father had given him a share in my fishing lodge in Connemara, which, of course, ought to have reverted to me at his death; well, even this I lose 'if I become a Roman Catholic for five years', which is very infamous.

In fact, the testator need have had no fears. The pagan influences which he absorbed during his tour of Greece with Mahaffy postponed Oscar Wilde's conversion until he was on his deathbed.

Wilde had already got a 'First' in Classical Moderations, and in 1878 he carried off the double event by securing a 'First' in 'Greats'. In the same year he won the Newdigate prize for English verse. Fortunately for him the subject for that year's poem was 'Ravenna', and Wilde had visited the city on his way to Greece. Consequently the Magdalen dons relented and not only gave him back the amount which they had fined him, but also extended his demyship for a fifth year. But they did not invite him to become a Fellow of the College, which would have given him an assured income for several years. On the other hand, if they had offered him a Fellowship, he might well have refused it, judging by his reply to his friend 'Bouncer' Ward, who asked him what was his real ambition in life.

God knows, I won't be a dried up Oxford don [he replied]. Anyhow I'll be a poet, a writer, a dramatist Somehow or other I'll be famous, and if not famous I'll be notorious. . . . These things are on the knees of the gods. What will be, will be.

It was a remarkable prophecy.

On migrating from Oxford to London, Wilde established himself in rooms off the Strand, overlooking the Thames, which he shared with a gifted Oxford friend and artist, Frank Miles. Meanwhile he had developed a passion for the theatre and the leading actresses of the day on the London stage – Lily Langtry, Ellen Terry, Genevieve Ward, and Helen Modjeska – on whom he danced attendance, composing sonnets in praise of their beauty, while Frank Miles would sketch them for the magazines. When the 'divine' Sarah Bernhardt arrived for a season from Paris, he met her as she stepped off the boat at Folkestone and flung an armful of lilies at her feet; soon he was working as her unpaid secretary. He went the rounds of the theatres and the picture galleries, met James McNeill Whistler, wrote critical articles on art and kept up a continuous outpouring of poetry, some of which he contrived to get published in various journals. Self-styled 'Professor of Aesthetics', he cultivated a passion for the lily and the sunflower, and he would sometimes be seen in public dressed in a velvet jacket, knee breeches, silk stockings, buckled shoes, and a soft loose silk shirt with a wide turn-down collar and a flowing green tie. But, contrary to the legend in the Gilbert and Sullivan opera *Patience*, which was popularly supposed to burlesque him and his 'aesthetic craze', he never 'walked down Piccadilly with a poppy or a lily in his medieval hand'. ('Anyone could have done that,' he used to say. 'The difficult thing to achieve was to make people believe that I had done it.') He soon became a regular diner-out, much in demand by hostesses for his amusing conversation. Soon too he was on the way to becoming something of a social celebrity, and in a year or so he was caricatured in the pages of *Punch*. But these activities brought in very little money, and he was obliged to mortgage his small paternal inheritance in Ireland to keep going.

He was without malice [wrote Ellen Terry's son Gordon Craig], had a great fund of affection, and his flattery was born of this affection. To be kind was why he flattered – but woe to any fool who *accepted* the flattery. It was the ancient Irish power to charm: the desire to give pleasure. A great-hearted being.[1]

Meanwhile his mother and elder brother had also come to live in London. Willie had given up the Bar and was now trying his luck in Fleet Street, where his journalistic gifts got him a job first with *The World*, a brilliant weekly edited by Edmund Yates, and later on the *Daily Telegraph*, where he became a leader writer. At this time, and for some years to come, the two brothers were the closest of friends. Willie never lost an opportunity, whenever he could, of praising Oscar and his poetry and giving him the utmost publicity in the gossip columns to which he contributed.

Lady Wilde first took a house in Ovington Square, South Kensington, which Willie shared with her. Later she moved to a more commodious mansion in Park Street, Mayfair, as Willie and Oscar began to prosper. Here she succeeded in establishing a literary *salon* on much the same lines as she had in Dublin. 'She is always glad to see my friends,' Oscar wrote soon after her arrival in London, 'and usually some good literary and artistic people take tea with her.' It has been said that of her two sons 'Speranza' always preferred the elder and that it was upon Willie that she lavished most of her attention. The shock of Oscar's downfall, which greatly affected her and possibly shortened her life, may have been responsible for this impression: but it would not appear to be supported by the known facts. On the contrary, she regarded Oscar's genius as the superior from an early age; in her eyes Willie was clever enough, but Oscar was going to be 'something wonderful'. Nor can she have been oblivious of the fact that it was Oscar, when he got on in his career, who regularly came to

1. Edward Gordon Craig, *Index to the Story of My Days* (1957), p. 148.

her rescue with his cheque book and paid her household bills, and that it was largely through Oscar's efforts that she was eventually granted a Civil List pension. That Oscar adored her to the end is clear from his letters. As he wrote to another poet, W. E. Henley, when the latter's mother was dying: 'All poets love their mothers, and as I worship mine I can understand how you feel.'

In 1880, Oscar Wilde wrote his first play which he called *Vera*. The Nihilists in Russia, the conspiratorial heralds of the Bolsheviks, were much in the news at this period, and the author made their activities the background to this immature melodrama. But the play showed signs of promise and contained some characteristic epigrams destined to reappear in his later and more successful dramatic productions. ('Experience, the name men give to their mistakes,' is a typical example.) Public interest in the subject of Nihilism was quickened by the assassination of the Tsar Alexander II by Nihilist revolutionaries in March 1881. Shortly afterwards Wilde arranged for the play to be produced at the Adelphi Theatre with Mrs Bernard Beere in the name part. However, about a fortnight before the performance was due, it was announced in the press that in view of 'the present state of political feeling in England' the author had decided to postpone the production. ('*Vera* is about Nihilism,' *Punch* remarked facetiously; 'this looks as if there were nothing in it.') The new Russian Empress was a sister of the Princess of Wales, and it was probably to avoid giving offence to her as well as to her husband, whom Wilde had already met and who was amused by him, that the author agreed to the cancellation of the production.[1] It was later to be given in New York with some additions and alterations to the original text, but it was a complete failure there and had to

1. Of the few copies of this play which Wilde had privately printed for the caste and for presentation to friends, only three are known to exist in perfect condition. One, which he gave to Ellen Terry, is in the Ellen Terry Memorial Museum at Smallhythe, Kent; the second is in the William Andrews Clark Library in the University of California, Los Angeles; and the third, inscribed to Genevieve Ward and formerly in the possession of Sir Bruce Ingram, is now in my collection. The latter was the copy used by Mason on which to base the description given by him in his bibliography of Wilde.

be withdrawn after a week's run. It then went on tour and met with little better success.[1] A cartoon, which appeared in a theatrical journal of the period, shows the author dressed in the inevitable knee breeches and buckle shoes being consoled by his brother Willie, while that aesthetic emblem the sunflower flutters between them: 'Never mind, Oscar; other great men have had their dramatic failures.'

Shortly before the ill-fated *Vera* went into premature rehearsal in London, its author launched another literary venture in the shape of his collected poems. The *Poems*, which were published at his own expense, made an attractive volume and sold for half a guinea, running into three editions in a short time. But, as each edition consisted only of 250 copies, Wilde can barely have recovered the expenses of publication. Also, the work met with a somewhat mixed reception from the reviewers, in spite of his brother Willie's efforts to promote the sales. As usual *Punch* was in the vanguard of the hostile critics. ('Mr Wilde may be aesthetic, but he is not original. This is a volume of echoes, it is Swinburne and water . . .')

Among those to whom Wilde sent presentation copies was the Oxford Union, the celebrated university debating society, to which he had belonged in his undergraduate days. When the Librarian announced the gift to a crowded house one evening, an undergraduate named Oliver Elton rose to object.[2] 'It is not that these poems are thin, and they are thin,' he said; 'it is not that they are immoral, and they are immoral; it is not that they are this or that, and they are this or that; it is that they are for the most part not by their putative father at all, but by a number of better-known and more deservedly reputed authors. They are in fact by William Shakespeare, by Philip Sidney, by John Donne, by Lord Byron, by William Morris, by Algernon Swinburne, and

1. Mason, p. 272. A second acting edition, also extremely rare, was printed in America during Wilde's tour in 1882. My copy, which formerly belonged to Wilde's son Mr Vyvyan Holland, was bequeathed to him by Robert Ross, his father's literary executor.
2. Oliver Elton (1861–1945) was later Professor of English at Liverpool University.

by sixty more, whose works have furnished the list of passages which I hold in my hand at this moment.' Here Mr Elton displayed the offending volume, and continued: 'The Union Library already contains better and fuller editions of all these poets. The volume which we are offered is theirs, not Mr Wilde's: and I move that it be not accepted.'

The Librarian and his supporters naturally opposed this motion, which they conceived to have been brought forward in a spirit of undergraduate banter. But Mr Elton was serious, and he insisted that his motion should be put to the vote. It was so put – and it was carried. Thus, for the first and only time in the history of the Oxford Union, an author's presentation copy of his work was returned to the author.[1]

No doubt Mr Elton was unduly severe. Wilde was certainly not a conscious plagiarist, although he had steeped himself in the works of some at least of the poets to whom Mr Elton alluded, and he may have owed them more than he realized at the time. Others, including Robert Browning and Mathew Arnold, to whom the author sent copies of the *Poems*, received them courteously.

One feature on which in several of the poems which Wilde's interest in ancient Greek art led him to dwell, with what some may think to be undue emphasis, passed unnoticed at the time. This was the physical attractions of the male human form. At this period – and indeed for some years to come – Wilde's sexual feelings, as will be seen when we come to examine them more closely, ran in normal channels.

4

Although he described himself as a 'professor of Aesthetics and critic of Art', Oscar Wilde was not the founder of the aesthetic

1. This story was first published by Sir Henry Newbolt, who was present, in his memoirs, *My World as in my Time* (1932), pp. 96–7. The rejected copy, which was inscribed in Wilde's hand 'To the Library of the Oxford Union my first volume of Poems, Oscar Wilde, Oct. 27, '81', is now in my collection.

movement, or as some people preferred to call it, the aesthetic craze, in England at this time. The cult of the beautiful, the gospel of art for art's sake, had already gained some support through the teachings of Ruskin and Morris and Pater, long before Wilde descended upon London to take a hand in the movement. What he did, however, was to constitute himself a convenient vehicle for its advertisement, which was considerably promoted by *Punch*'s somewhat ponderous brand of humour. Of this humour Wilde was largely the butt, but he took it in good part, and indeed seemed to relish it, as it undoubtedly kept him in the public eye. Typical of *Punch* was the verse with which the London Charivari greeted the appearance of Wilde's *Poems*; it was printed beneath a drawing of the poet peering out of the heart of a sunflower, accompanied by a vase of lilies, an open cigarette case, and a waste-paper basket:

> Aesthete of aesthetes
> What's in a name?
> The poet is Wilde
> But his poetry's tame.

According to Wilde's friend and biographer Frank Harris, Oscar got his brother Willie to insert a paragraph in *The World* to the effect that owing to the 'astonishing success' of his *Poems* he had been invited to lecture in America. Harris is not always to be trusted, and in this instance there is no knowing whether the story is true. However that may be, Wilde had certainly received no such invitation at this date. But the paragraph may have prompted an offer which reached him shortly afterwards from Mr Rupert D'Oyly Carte, or rather from Mr D'Oyly Carte's New York agent, Colonel W. F. Morse. The offer was for a lecture in New York, to be followed by a tour if the initial lecture proved successful; the lecturer was to get paid his expenses and one-third of the receipts. D'Oyly Carte, who managed the Savoy theatre in London for Gilbert and Sullivan, had recently arranged for the latest London success *Patience* to be produced in America, and it now seems to have struck his American agent that the New York production might be boosted if Wilde, on whom the character of Bunthorne, the 'fleshly poet' in the comic opera, was widely believed to have been based, could come over and lecture on the aesthetic cult. For his part, Wilde was quite attracted by the prospect of meeting American audiences: he also hoped that he might be able to arrange for the production of *Vera* in New York. Accordingly, he accepted Colonel Morse's offer, and sailed from Liverpool on Christmas Eve, arriving in New York on 2 January 1882.

Wilde's American lecture tour was a great personal triumph, from the time he stepped ashore and informed the New York customs that he had nothing to declare 'except my genius', to the time he sailed back to England twelve months later.[1] Everywhere he went he was fêted, and in the intervals of lecturing he was able to meet America's leading poets and writers, including Emerson, Longfellow and Walt Whitman. The two principal lectures in his repertory, later published in his collected works, were on 'The English Renaissance of Art' and 'Art and the Handicraftsman'. Not so generally known is the lecture to a San Francisco audience on the Irish patriot poets of the nineteenth century, in which he gave his mother pride of place. Indeed his references to 'Speranza' and his reading of two of her poems drew great applause in the hall and caused a young lady to rush up to the platform with a fragrant bouquet of violets, 'whereat', so we are told in a contemporary newspaper account, 'the audience again applauded and Oscar bowed his thanks'.[2]

As regards the men of '48, I look on their work with peculiar rever-

1. The best and fullest account of the tour has been given by Lloyd Lewis and Henry Justin Smith in their *Oscar Wilde Discovers America* (New York, 1936).
2. *The Call*, 6 April 1882. 'The Irish Poets of '48' was delivered in Platt's Hall, San Francisco. The original MS. of this lecture, written by Wilde in two exercise books and consisting of thirty-four folios, is now in my collection. It is not mentioned by Mason in his bibliography, although at one time Mason seemed to have considered publishing it, since he sent the MS. which formerly belonged to Robert Ross, to W. B. Yeats for editorial advice. *See University Review*, Vol. I, No. 4 (Dublin, 1955), where it has been partly published, with an editorial note by Michael J. O'Neill, from a copy in the Holloway Collection in the National Library of Ireland.

ence and love, for I was indeed trained by my mother to love and reverence them as a Catholic Child is the saints of the calendar, and I have seen many of them also. The earliest hero of my childhood was Smith O'Brien, whom I remember so well, tall and stately, with the dignity of one who has failed – such failures are at least often grander than a hundred victories.[1] John Mitchel too I saw on his return to Ireland at my father's table, with his eagle eye and impassioned manner;[2] John Savage I met in New York;[3] Charles Gavan Duffy is one of my friends in London. . . .[4]

Of the quality of Speranza's poems perhaps I should not speak – for criticism is disarmed before love – but I am content to abide by the verdict of the nation which has so welcomed her genius and understood the song, notable for its strength and simplicity that ballad of my mother's on the trial of the Brothers Sheares in '98, and that passionate and lofty lyric written in the year of revolution called 'Courage'.[5] I would like to linger on her work longer, I acknowledge, but I think you all know it, and it is enough for me to have had once the privilege of speaking about my mother to the race she loves so well. . . .

1. William Smith O'Brien (1803–64), one of the leaders of the abortive rising of 1848, was convicted of high treason and sentenced to be hanged, drawn, and quartered. The sentence was commuted to transportation, which he served in Tasmania. He was eventually pardoned and returned to Ireland in 1864, where he spent most of the remaining ten years of his life but took no further part in politics.

2. John Mitchel (1815–75) was sentenced to fourteen years' transportation for treason-felony in 1848, but after five years in Tasmania he succeeded in escaping to America. He returned to Ireland in 1872 and was elected Nationalist M.P. for Tipperary but was held ineligible to take his seat. His finely-written *Jail Journal*, first published in New York in 1854, is a classic work of penology.

3. John Savage (1828–88) was an Irish poet who was active in the 1848 rising. He escaped to America, where he spent the rest of his life in New York as a journalist and an organizer of the Fenian movement there.

4. Sir Charles Gavan Duffy (1816–1903) was editor of *The Nation* at the time of its suppression in 1848 on account of an allegedly seditious article by 'Speranza' entitled 'Jacta Alea Est'. Between July 1846 and April 1849 he was tried five times and eventually discharged, as no jury would convict him. In 1855 he emigrated to Australia, where he rose to be Prime Minister of Victoria, and was knighted in 1873. He returned to Europe in 1880 and devoted the remainder of his life to literary work.

5. The poem *Courage*, beginning 'Lift up your pale faces, ye children of sorrow', is entitled *The Year of Revolutions* in the English edition of Lady Wilde's poems.

Oscar Wilde

Indeed the poetic genius of the Celtic race never flags or wearies. It is as sweet by the groves of California as by the groves of Ireland, as strong in foreign lands as in the land which gave it birth. And indeed I do not know anything more wonderful, or more characteristic of the Celtic genius, than the quick artistic spirit in which we adapted ourselves to the English tongue. The Saxon took our lands from us and left them desolate – we took their language and added new beauties to it.

Wilde cleared about £1,200 from the lecture tour. What was left of this sum on his return to England, he used up on a visit to Paris, where he spent the first three months of the year 1883. Here he met the leaders of the French literary and artistic world, Victor Hugo, Verlaine, Stephane Mallarmé, Henri de Régnier, Zola, Alphonse Daudet, Degas, Pissaro, and Coquelin. In Paris he also made the acquaintance of a journalist named Robert Sherard, with whom he was to form a close friendship and who was to become his first and most faithful biographer.[1] He now had his hair curled in imitation of a bust of Nero which he saw in the Louvre, discarding his aesthete's knee breeches and dressing in the height of fashion. 'The Oscar of the first period is dead,' he said. During this visit he completed a blank verse tragedy, *The Duchess of Padua*, which he wrote for the American actress Mary Anderson, who, greatly to his disappointment, turned it

1. Robert Harborough Sherard (1861–1943), journalist and author, was the son of the Rev. Bennet Sherard Kennedy of Stapleford Park, Melton Mowbray, and great-grandson of the poet Wordsworth. He became probably Wilde's most chivalrous defender in print: see his *Oscar Wilde: The Story of an Unhappy Friendship* (1902), *Life of Oscar Wilde* (1906), *The Real Oscar Wilde* (1915), *Oscar Wilde Twice Defended* (1934), and *Bernard Shaw, Frank Harris and Oscar Wilde* (1937). Sherard's later writings on the subject of Wilde verge on the hysterical. The MS. of his last unpublished book, *Ultima Verba*, which he wrote in reply to Bernard Shaw's Preface to the English edition of Frank Harris's biography of Wilde in 1938, is now in my collection. I also have copies of his letters to A. J. A. Symons, written between 1935 and 1938, when Symons was collecting material for his projected biography of Wilde but which he never completed except for two chapters which appeared in *Horizon*. These letters contain important details of Wilde's private life, which Sherard did not feel at liberty to include in his published writings, but which I have used in the following pages.

down.[1] Later in the same year he revisited America for a few weeks to assist in the New York production of *Vera*.

Back in London, he went on another lecture tour, this time in the provinces. Perhaps the most entertaining lecture he gave on this occasion was on his impressions of America, which was first delivered to an audience in Wandsworth Town Hall.

I was disappointed with Niagara – most people must be disappointed with Niagara. Every American bride is taken there, and the sight of the stupendous waterfall must be one of the earliest, if not the keenest disappointments in American married life.[2]

During the tour he announced his engagement to Miss Constance Lloyd, to whom he had proposed in Dublin in November 1883. He described her at this time to Lily Langtry as 'a grave, slight, violet-eyed little Artemis, with great coils of heavy brown hair which make her flower-like head droop like a blossom, and wonderful ivory hands which draw music from the piano so sweet that the birds stop singing to listen to her'. Besides these admirable qualities, Constance Lloyd had a little money of her own, amounting to some £800 a year.

Miss Lloyd's father, who was a Queen's Counsel of the English Bar, had died fairly young, and her mother, who was Irish, had married again. When she was not visiting her mother's people in Dublin, Constance usually lived in London with her paternal grandfather, John Horatio Lloyd, a former M.P. and successful railway lawyer. Her marriage to Oscar Wilde took place in St James's Church, Paddington, on 29 May 1884.

After an ecstatic honeymoon in Paris, the couple returned to London, and with the help of Constance's modest fortune they took a house in Chelsea – No. 16 (now 33) Tite Street – which was to be their matrimonial home until the husband was arrested and sent to prison eleven years later. According to Wilde's idea, the necessary alterations and interior decoration were entrusted

1. It was eventually produced in New York in 1891 under the title of *Guido Ferranti*.
2. *Impressions of America* was published by Mason in 1906 from a contemporary newspaper account of the lecture. It does not appear in the collected edition of Wilde's works, edited by Robert Ross.

to E. W. Godwin, a brilliant but now largely forgotten architect and theatrical designer, who also designed most of the furniture, with some help from Whistler.[1] ('Each chair is a sonnet in ivory,' Wilde wrote at the time, 'and the table is a masterpiece in pearl.') Here the two children of the marriage were born – Cyril in 1885 and Vyvyan in 1886.

It may be noted here that it was in 1886 that Wilde first made the acquaintance of a young man of seventeen named Robert Ross.[2] He was the first of a series of young men with whom Wilde had homosexual relations. (We shall return later to this aspect of Wilde's career.) Ross was destined in the end to become Wilde's literary executor.

About the same time as Oscar and Constance Wilde began their married life in Tite Street, Lady Wilde also moved to Chelsea taking a house in nearby Oakley Street, which she found more congenial for her *salon* than Mayfair, if no less respectable. ('Never use that word here,' she once remarked to a caller who had used it in her presence. 'It is only tradespeople who are respectable. We are above respectability.') Her elder son continued

1. For an account of Edward Godwin, and Wilde's letters to him while the house was being redecorated, see my *Cases that Changed the Law* (1951), pp. 148–63.

2. Robert Baldwin Ross (1869–1918) was the grandson of the Hon. Robert Baldwin, c.b., first Prime Minister of Upper Canada under responsible government, whose daughter had married the Hon. John Ross, q.c., Attorney-General for Upper Canada. He became a journalist and later director of the Carfax Galleries, a firm of picture dealers in London; he was also a Trustee of the National Gallery and Adviser to the Board of Inland Revenue on the valuation of pictures for estate duty. Besides two volumes of essays – *Masques and Phases* (1909) and *Really and Truly* (1915) – he wrote biographies of Wilde's ancestor Charles Maturin (1892) and of Aubrey Beardsley (1908). As Wilde's literary executor, he also edited the first authorized collected editions of *The Works of Oscar Wilde*. After his death his character was bitterly attacked by Lord Alfred Douglas in his *Collected Satires* (1926) and *Autobiography* (1928), and by W. Sorley Brown in *The Life and Genius of T. W. H. Crosland* (1928). More favourable estimates of Ross's character have been given by Sir William Rothenstein in *Men and Memories*, Vol. I (1931), by Siegfried Sassoon in *Siegfried's Journey* (1945), and by his niece Margery Ross in her edition of his correspondence, *Robert Ross: Friend of Friends* (1952).

to live with her, except for two or three years when he crossed the Atlantic to marry Mrs Frank Leslie, a wealthy American widow, whom he had met through his mother. From her husband Mrs Leslie had inherited a popular New York periodical, which incidentally had given Oscar some helpful publicity in his lecture tour of the United States. But the marriage was not a success. The owner of *Frank Leslie's Illustrated Newspaper* expected her new husband to go early to the office each morning and work hard at the valuable property which her late husband had built up. However, Willie Wilde saw no reason why he should do any work at all, seeing that his wife was a millionairess. He preferred drinking in the city bars and taking jaunts with girl-friends to the Catskill Mountains to domestic bliss with the somewhat overpowering Mrs Leslie. A divorce inevitably followed, and Willie returned to London more or less a nervous wreck. What his younger brother used indulgently to describe as 'an occasional alcoholiday' had now become a habit. Coupled with Willie's behaviour over money – 'He sponges on everyone except himself,' said Oscar – this led to a rift between the two brothers, which was never really healed. However, Oscar kept up his visits to Oakley Street, even at the height of his literary and social success, although he ceased to attend his mother's Bohemian gatherings. ('Oscar does not come when I have people here,' said Lady Wilde at this time. 'He is so much in demand everywhere, and he prefers to come when I am alone, as he has so little time now for me that he wishes to have me all to himself.') As Lady Wilde never went to Tite Street and Constance never visited her in Oakley Street, it may be concluded that the mother and daughter-in-law were not particularly drawn towards each other.

Apart from Constance's dowry and marriage settlement, not much money seems to have come into the Tite Street household for the first three years. In 1885, Wilde got some reviewing for the *Pall Mall Gazette* and he also did the dramatic criticism for the *Dramatic Review*; but this can have brought in very little. Urged, no doubt, by his wife to get some regular source of income, Wilde's thoughts again turned to becoming a schools' inspector, for which he enlisted the support of the future Lord Curzon, whom he had known at Oxford, and also of his old Trinity College tutor Dr Mahaffy – but with no success. Eventually, in June 1887, he was appointed editor of *The Lady's World*, a women's monthly journal published by Cassell, which he reorganized and renamed *The Women's World*. He seems to have been an excellent editor. As well as writing the literary notes himself, he collected an impressive band of contributors, who included Princess Christian, the Queen of Romania ('Carmen Sylva'), Oscar Browning, 'Ouida', Walter Pater, W. E. Henley, Richard Le Gallienne, George Saintsbury, Walt Whitman, Mahaffy, Swinburne, and Yeats. But after a while the routine of office hours began to prove irksome, and at the end of two years he resigned.

During this middle period of Wilde's career, which falls between the aesthetic period of his youth and his maturity as a fashionable playwright in the first half of the eighteen-nineties, he showed considerable industry. In addition to his reviewing and editorial work, he wrote the short stories subsequently published in book form under the titles, *Lord Arthur Savile's Crime and other Stories* (1891) and *A House of Pomegranates* (1891), as well as the brilliant critical essays which subsequently appeared as *Intentions* (1891). He also produced a delightful volume of fairy-tales, primarily for his two children, *The Happy Prince and Other Tales* (1888); a curious piece of Shakespearian research, *The Portrait of Mr W. H.* (1889); and a remarkable essay in political theory, *The Soul of Man under Socialism* (1891), said to have been inspired by hearing Bernard Shaw lecture on socialist doctrine. Finally, in 1891, his only novel was published as a book, *The Picture of Dorian Gray*; it had appeared in the previous year in a slightly different and somewhat shorter form in *Lippincott's Monthly Magazine*. This work was to play an important part in the first of the three trials at the Old Bailey.

If the year 1891 marked the height of Wilde's literary output, it also contained the seeds of his subsequent misfortune. For it was in that year that he first met Lord Alfred Douglas, whose father was the eighth Marquess of Queensberry.

The Background

After 1891 there followed the brief period of Wilde's greatest triumphs which need only be touched on here. They began with the production in London in February 1892 of his first successful play, *Lady Windermere's Fan*, by the enterprising actor-manager George Alexander. While *Lady Windermere's Fan* was playing to crowded houses in the St James's Theatre, Wilde's next play, *Salomé*, which he had originally written in French went into rehearsal with Sarah Bernhardt in the name part. Unfortunately the Lord Chamberlain stepped in and refused to license the production for public performance on the ground that it portrayed Biblical characters. This official ban so incensed the author that he threatened to cross the Channel and become a French citizen, a threat which, needless to add, he did not carry out, although he was twitted on it by *Punch*. The censor could not, of course, prevent Wilde from publishing *Salomé*, and this he proceeded to do, both in the original French and in an English translation, the latter being daringly illustrated by Aubrey Beardsley. Meanwhile, Wilde had written another play, *A Woman of No Importance*; this was produced by Beerbohm Tree at the Theatre Royal, Haymarket, in April 1893, and proved just as successful as *Lady Windermere's Fan*. Next came *An Ideal Husband*, first produced at the Haymarket Theatre by Lewis Morrell and H. H. Waller in January 1895; it proved an even bigger draw than its two predecessors, being helped no doubt by the presence of the Prince of Wales in the theatre on the opening night. A few weeks later Wilde's crowning dramatic triumph took place with the staging of *The Importance of Being Earnest* by George Alexander at the St James's Theatre, which must rank as one of the best light comedies in the English language.

At this time Wilde was making close on £3,000 a year. This may not seem a great sum when judged by the present purchasing-power of money. However, it represented a very comfortable income in the England of those days, when it is remembered that the cost of living was relatively low and income tax was eightpence in the pound.[1]

1. Wilde's account book with a Chelsea firm of grocers for the period 1892-5 is now in my possession. It reveals that he paid 3d. for a loaf, 1s. 3d.

Oscar Wilde

An Ideal Husband and *The Importance of Being Earnest* were still running when their author was arrested on a charge of having committed a number of homosexual offences contrary to the Criminal Law Amendment Act, 1885.

5

Wilde must now be considered as a pathological case study. First, there is the question of heredity and early environment. As has already been seen, he was the child of parents of marked eccentricity as well as of exceptional ability. Both qualities became concentrated in himself to a striking degree. They help to explain his congenital antipathy for the ordinary and commonplace, his natural love of paradox and his aestheticism, all of which he sought to express in his conversation and writings. Sir William Wilde, moreover, was a man of abnormal sexual drive; as we have seen, he was a notorious runner after women, by whom he had sundry illegitimate offspring, and he figured in a sensational trial in Dublin in which he was accused of having violated a woman patient in his surgery, having first put her under the influence of chloroform. Lady Wilde, the poetess 'Speranza', on the other hand, exhibited certain peculiar physical characteristics, due to the excessive development of the pituitary gland, which were reproduced in her second son. This excess appeared in a general physical overgrowth. Bernard Shaw has recalled that her hands, for instance, were enormous, 'and the gigantic splaying of her palm was reproduced in her lumbar region'. To Shaw, Oscar Wilde also appeared as an overgrown individual with something not quite normal about his bigness. To people like Lady Colin Campbell, who were repelled by his physical appearance, he was 'that great white caterpillar'. Undoubtedly there was some truth in his fellow Irishman's diagnosis. 'I have always maintained that

---

for a dozen eggs, 2s. per lb. for tea, 3s. 6d. for a bottle of whisky, 3s. 8d. for a jar of caviare, 5s. 6d. for a quart of champagne, and 18s. for a dozen claret. Judging by the quantities ordered, his favourite drink seems to have been hock (at 39s. a dozen) and seltzer water.

The Background

Oscar was a giant in the pathological sense,' wrote Shaw in his *Memories of Oscar Wilde,* 'and that this explains a good deal of his weakness.'[1]

It has been said that 'Speranza' was disappointed that her son Oscar was not a girl, and a good deal has been made of the fact that she dressed him in girl's clothes during his childhood days, decking him out with jewels which made him look like 'a little Hindu idol'. But this treatment has probably little, if any pathological significance in Wilde's case. Victorian mothers were accustomed to dress their children of either sex in petticoats and skirts until they were six or seven years old. And to this day, as the biographer of Wilde's father has pointed out, little boys are dressed as girls in parts of rural Ireland, lest the fairies should steal them, 'for, of course, the fairies are only interested in little boys'.[2] Furthermore, any disappointment Lady Wilde may have endured by reason of Oscar's sex did not last long, for she succeeded in having the daughter she longed for four years after Oscar was born.

Havelock Ellis has expressed the opinion that homosexual germs were latent in Wilde's constitution from the beginning, although they did not become active until he was in his early thirties.[3] Certain it is that Wilde betrayed no signs of abnormality in adolescence and early manhood. On the contrary, his inclinations seem to have been decidedly heterosexual. While an undergraduate at Oxford, or shortly after coming down, he contracted syphilis as the result of a casual connexion, probably with a prostitute. In those days the recognized treatment for this venereal disease was mercury. In Wilde's case this treatment undoubtedly produced the discoloration and decay in his teeth, which remained a permanent feature of his appearance for the rest of his life and added to the general impression of physical overgrowth and ugliness which his person presented on acquaintance. Nor, it may be added, was there the slightest suggestion of effeminacy about

1. These *Memories* will be found at the end of Vol. II of Harris, op. cit.
2. T. G. Wilson, *Victorian Doctor*, p. 324.
3. *Studies in the Psychology of Sex*, Vol. II, pt 2 (New York, 1936), pp 48–9.

him, either at Oxford or at any subsequent period. If somewhat ungainly in movement, he was endowed with an abundant measure of manly strength, as a number of his college contemporaries discovered to their cost when they attempted to subject him to an undergraduate 'ragging'.

While at Oxford he seems to have fallen in love, or at least seriously flirted, with several 'respectable' girls, if we may judge from an indignant outburst from the mother of one of them, when he had followed up a vacation visit to her home by inviting the daughter to meet him in Dublin. ('I was very much pained the last time I was at your house when I went into the drawing-room and saw Fidelia sitting on your knee. Young as she is, she ought to have had – and so I told her – the instinctive delicacy that would have shrunk from it. But, oh! Oscar, the thing was neither right, nor manly, nor gentlemanlike in you! You have disappointed me – nay, so low and vulgar was it that I could not have believed anyone of refined mind capable of such a thing.') The mother was particularly upset by Oscar leaving her to open the front door for herself, while he stayed behind in the hall to steal a surreptitious kiss from the apparently by no means unwilling Fidelia. This conduct incurred a further reproach. ('Do you think for a moment that I was so supremely stupid as not to know that you always kissed Fidelia when you met her, if you had an opportunity?')

His first serious love affair during this early period was with a girl four years younger than himself named Florence Balcombe; she was the daughter of a retired army officer and lived at Clontarf, just outside Dublin. Oscar's passion for Florrie lasted two years – 'the sweetest of all the years of my youth', so he told her afterwards – and no doubt he wished to marry her. But she turned him down in favour of another young man with literary tastes called Bram Stoker, who is chiefly remembered today as the author of the horrific novel, *Dracula*. It took some years for the wound to heal. In 1881, when Florrie got her first stage part, a walking-on one, in Henry Irving's production of Tennyson's verse play, *The Cup*, Wilde wrote to Ellen Terry, who had a leading part, and sent her a crown of flowers which he asked the great actress to give the beginner without revealing its origin. ('I shall like to think she was wearing something of mine the first night she comes on the stage, that anything of mine should touch her . . . She thinks I never loved her, thinks I forget. My God, how could I!') Certainly Wilde never forgot his first true love. A dozen years later we find him sending her a copy of *Salomé* – 'my strange venture in a tongue that is not my own, but that I love as one loves an instrument on which one has not played before' – and subscribing himself 'Always your sincere friend Oscar Wilde'.

Wilde's emerging interest in male physical beauty, as exemplified in some of his early poems, has already been noticed. He may well have been unaware of its significance at the same time as his inclinations gradually became bi-sexual. Before his marriage he certainly had recourse to prostitutes. Besides the professional prostitute at Oxford, known among the undergraduate community as 'Old Jess', from whom he may have quite possibly received his first dose of venereal disease, we know on the authority of his friend Robert Sherard that he had connexions of this kind in Paris and New York, as well as in London. He once told Sherard how surprised he was during his first American visit, when he had just finished a rhapsodical discourse on the beauties of English art, by the matter-of-fact way in which some of the young men in the lecture hall approached him with some such words as: 'And now, Oscar, after all that soulthrob, of course you feel like a bit of skirt' – and took him straight off to a brothel. Sherard also records how Wilde, while staying in Paris in 1883, confessed to him one evening that 'Priapus was calling' and thereupon departed by himself for The Eden, a music hall, which was the place in which to pick up the better-class whores in the town. There, according to Sherard, he picked up and spent the night with Marie Aguétant, a well known *demi-mondaine*. (She was afterwards murdered by one of her lovers named Prado, the illegitimate son of the President of Peru, and a notorious *maquereau* and *homme-à-femmes*, who in a fit of jealous rage 'cut her throat from ear to ear while the lady was astride the *bidet*'.) Next morning, Wilde was 'in great form' when he met Sherard. The first thing he said to him was: 'What animals we are, Robert!'

Sherard's chief care was to make sure that his friend had not been robbed, to which Wilde replied: 'One gives them all in one's pockets.' Although he played up to women and flattered their vanity, which no doubt explains why he was generally liked by them and why he was able to edit *The Women's World* with conspicuous success for two years, Oscar Wilde had no illusions whatever about female virtue. He considered women as being prompted mainly, if not solely, by the sexual urge, and he regarded them as really devoid of what is commonly called 'morality'. On one occasion, he happened to meet Sherard in a London hotel. Sherard was accompanied by a lady, with whom he had eloped from Paris and for whom he had taken a separate room in the hotel, pending arrangements for marrying her. 'Act dishonourably, Robert,' Wilde said to his friend. 'Act dishonourably. It is what sooner or later she'll certainly do to you!' Whether Sherard took this advice is not known; but we do know for certain that he did marry his companion, and also that in the process of time Wilde's prediction came true. So did a similar prophecy with regard to Wilde's elder brother Willie. At the time of Willie's marriage to the wealthy American, Mrs Frank Leslie, Oscar blamed his brother for not having got a good financial settlement from her beforehand. 'When she has glutted her lust on him and used him up,' he told Sherard, 'she'll pitch him his hat and coat and by means of an American divorce get rid of him legally and let him starve to death for all she'll care.' Which is precisely what did happen, the lady in question telling the newspaper reporters after they had parted that 'he was of no use to me either by day or by night'.

Wilde thought that there were barely five per cent of English husbands who had not been deceived by their wives. Sherard relates that he once asked Wilde how a husband should act when he discovered that his wife had a lover. 'Pretend to ignore the liaison and delight in watching them,' was the reply. 'It will get so interesting as the time gets near for his departure, when you three have been spending the evening together. You show yourself more and more marital and you close the *séance* by giving him his *congé* with some such remark as: "Well, so long! We young married folks, you know!" And to the adulterous wife: "*Au lit, darling, au lit!*" The touching scene ends with the husband later going in his pyjamas to the window, while the disconsolate lover stands on the other side of the road gazing up towards "the place where Cressid lay" and sighing. There you attract his attention and wave your hand towards him to imply that he must be on his way, while you hasten to the matrimonial delights that are awaiting you.'

On the other hand, we know that at the outset of their married life Wilde was deeply in love with his wife and that they experienced normal sexual intercourse, which resulted in the birth of their two sons. Indeed, he seems to have been an enthusiastic lover. To a friend whom he chanced to meet during the honeymoon in Paris he spontaneously expatiated upon the physical joys of wedlock. And on the occasion of his first separation from his wife, some months later, when he was lecturing in Edinburgh, he wrote to her:

Here am I; and you at the Antipodes: O execrable fates that keep our lips from kissing, though our souls are one ... The messages of the gods to each other travel not by pen and ink, and indeed your bodily presence here would not make you more real: for I feel your fingers in my hair and your cheek brushing mine. The air is full of the music of your voice, my soul and body seem no longer mine, but mingled in some exquisite ecstasy with yours. I feel incomplete without you.[1]

Before proposing to his wife, Wilde had been to consult a doctor in London, who had assured him that he was completely cured of his youthful malady. On the strength of this assurance he got married. About two years later he discovered to his dismay that all traces of syphilis had not been eradicated from his system; on the contrary, the spirochetes were quite active. It was this unpleasant discovery which obliged him to discontinue physical relations with his wife. In the result, *inter alia*, he turned towards homosexuality.[2]

1. Apart from a few brief notes, this letter (now in the Pierpont Morgan Library, New York) is the only one from Wilde to his wife that is known to have survived.
2. Brasol, pp. 358–9. Brasol got the story from Sherard, who has confirmed it in his unpublished (and unpublishable) letters to A. J. A. Symons.

6

At first Wilde developed what was merely an inquisitive interest in sexual inversion. Such an inquisitive interest, as Havelock Ellis has observed, is sometimes the sign of an emerging homosexual impulse. According to his contemporary, André Raffalovich, he liked to discuss the subject with his friends.[1] 'I do not think,' he used to tell them, 'that the people who do these things derive as much pleasure as I do from talking about them.' Prominent homosexual characters in history began to attract him. He was fascinated by the story of King James I's favourite, Robert Carr, Earl of Somerset, who, on the eve of his trial for the murder of Sir Thomas Overbury, threatened to reveal publicly that 'the King had slept with him' – with the result that two men in long robes were posted on either side of the accused in court with instructions literally to stifle any attempted incrimination of His Majesty. In this context Wilde studied the lives of Plato and Michelangelo, and he conducted a piece of ingenious research into the origins of Shakespeare's sonnets to 'W. H.', whom he claimed to be a boy actor named Willie Hewes whom the dramatist admired.[2] Wilde is also stated by Raffalovich to have shown an increased interest in the subject as the result of reading *Monsieur Vénus*, the extraordinary novel by 'Rachilde' on the theme of male homosexuality,

1. Marc-André Raffalovich (1865–1934), psychologist and writer, became an authority on this aspect of Wilde's life. He belonged to a wealthy family of Russian Jewish bankers in Paris; his sister married William O'Brien, the Irish Nationalist leader. At this time he was living in London and was a friend among others of Aubrey Beardsley, becoming the anonymous recipient of *The Last Letters of Aubrey Beardsley* (1904). His study of male homosexuality, *Uranisme et unisexualité*, which was published in France in the year after Wilde's conviction, contained the first full, though not noticeably sympathetic, account of the Wilde trials and their background to appear in any language, besides a great deal of curious material on the history and prevalence of male inversion in England.

2. *The Portrait of Mr W. H.* In its original form this essay appeared in *Blackwood's 'Edinburgh Magazine'* for July 1889.

which created such a sensation on its first appearance.[1]
Indeed, sin in all its aspects became a preoccupation with
Wilde, which amounted almost to an obsession. This is evident in
such of his writings as *Intentions, Lord Arthur Savile's Crime*, and
Salomé. In *The Picture of Dorian Gray*, too, there is a strong
atmosphere of homosexuality in the background. Charles Hirsch,
a French bookseller in London, who dealt in erotica, has recalled
Wilde's interest in homosexuality and how he supplied Wilde
with various books on the subject. According to Hirsch, Wilde
used to leave the MS. of a pornographic homosexual novel
entitled *Teleny* in the shop, where various young men would call
and borrow it. The bookseller, who also read it, believed that
Wilde had a hand in its composition.[2]

Wilde's attitude towards 'beautiful sins', as exemplified in
Dorian Gray, was generally considered as part of his characteristic
pose at this time. 'It's only Oscar,' people argued. 'He likes to
talk about it, but he doesn't do anything.' For instance, he would
tell any young male acquaintance who happened to catch his
fancy at that moment that he was the only one who could provide
him with a new thrill and knew how to mix romance and cynicism.
Then, his habit of wearing in his buttonhole a carnation artificially coloured green, a distinctive emblem which he knew to be
worn by homosexuals in Paris, was speedily taken up by his
youthful admirers on this side of the channel and did not pass
without adverse comment. Indeed the cult of the green carnation
produced one of the most amusing and successful literary skits of
the times, *The Green Carnation*.[3]

1. 'Rachilde' was the pseudonym employed by the French novelist
Marguerite Eymery, who married Alfred Vallette, founder of the publishing
firm, *Mercure de France*. Her novel *Monsieur Vénus* appeared in 1889.

2. *Teleny*, or *The Reverse of the Medal* was published clandestinely in
London by Leonard Smithers in 1893. A privately printed French transla-
tion, with an interesting Introduction by Hirsch, appeared in Paris in 1934.
The original English version has recently been republished in Paris by the
Olympia Press, which definitely ascribes the authorship to Wilde. On
Smithers, see below, p. 309.

3. First published anonymously in London in September 1894. The real
author was Robert Hichens, who has related the story of its composition
and publication in his *Autobiography* (1947).

However, there were some who pretended to discern in Wilde's behaviour something more than mere posing, and they may have been near the mark. There are strong grounds for believing that Wilde was initiated into homosexual practices in 1886 by Robert Ross.[1] This was the year following the passing of the Criminal Law Amendment Act, of which Section 11 made indecencies between males an offence *even if practised in private*. This legislation thus added a spice of danger to conduct which, however repugnant to the majority of human beings, had not hitherto been regarded as criminal in England. 'It was like feasting with panthers,' as Wilde was to write in *De Profundis*; 'the danger was half the excitement.'

Something more is required to be said here about Ross. Robert ('Robbie') Ross was a Canadian, who had been brought up in England. When he first met Wilde, he was living in London with his mother, a comparatively well-off widow. At this time he was only seventeen years of age. He was shortly to enter King's College, Cambridge, as an undergraduate and he was to leave somewhat abruptly, for reasons undisclosed but not difficult to surmise, after about a year without taking a degree. He then became a journalist and art critic; it seems that he suggested to Wilde the idea of *The Portrait of Mr W. H.*, since we find Wilde writing to him in the month of its original publication in *Blackwood's* (July 1889): 'The story is half yours, and but for you would not have been written.'[2]

Sir William Rothenstein's portrait of Ross, painted a few years later, shows a good-looking young man with dark hair,

1. Frank Harris told Lord Alfred Douglas, when after many years they resumed their acquaintance at Nice in 1925, that Ross had actually boasted to him that he was 'the first boy Oscar ever had', and that the relationship began about 1886. Mr Arthur Ransome, who obtained the biographical details for his study of Wilde from Ross, must be taken to confirm this when he writes that 'in 1886 he [Wilde] began that course of conduct that was to lead to his downfall in 1895': see A. Ransome, *Oscar Wilde* (1912), p. 32.

2. Hart-Davis, p. 247.

The real author was Robert Hichens, who has related the story of its composition and publication in his *Autobiography* (1947).

fine sensitive eyes, and rather sensuous lips. Although not himself 'a creative person', as this artist put it, Robbie Ross had a genius for friendship. 'No man had a wider circle of friends than he,' wrote Rothenstein in his memoirs. 'He had a delightful nature, was an admirable story-teller, and a wit; above all he was able to get the best out of those he admired. Oscar Wilde was never wittier than when at Ross's parties; the same was true of Aubrey Beardsley and Max Beerbohm.' Ross certainly proved himself the most steadfast of all Wilde's friends. Even if he did resume his earlier homosexual relations with Wilde after the latter was released from prison, Ross helped him in many ways during this last unhappy phase; and, as his literary executor, he was to administer his estate for the benefit of his two sons with great care and ability. 'I feel poor Oscar's death a great deal more than I should, and far more than I expected,' Ross told Rothenstein at the time. 'I had grown to feel, rather foolishly a sort of responsibility for Oscar, for everything connected with him except his genius, and he had become for me a sort of adopted prodigal baby. I began to love the very faults which I would never have forgiven in anyone else.'[1]

It is hardly surprising that Constance Wilde, who had no sympathy with smart literary folk, should never have liked this particular friend of her husband's. Before going up to Cambridge, Ross had spent two months as their guest in Tite Street, probably while his mother was abroad; but it was not until several years later – 1891, according to Ross himself, when Wilde was working on *Lady Windermere's Fan* – that they became really close friends. Ross has also put it on record that he wrote down all the witty things his host said when he stayed with him in 1887; he later gave his notes to Wilde, who used them for *The Importance of Being Earnest*, which he wrote in three weeks in the summer of 1894, against time and because he needed the money quickly.[2]

If Wilde had been content to confine his homosexual relations to Robert Ross, and even to Lord Alfred Douglas, it is extremely

1. Sir William Rothenstein, *Men and Memories 1892–1900* (1931), pp. 187 and 362.
2. Margery Ross, *Robert Ross: Friend of Friends* (1952), p. 152.

unlikely that his conduct in this respect would ever have come to the notice of the Director of Public Prosecutions. Unfortunately for him, he made the fatal mistake of extending the range of his homosexual acquaintances to a different social class from his own – to such individuals as a groom, an unemployed clerk, a newspaper boy, also a youth who worked in his publishers' office. In this, of course, Wilde acted with a reckless disregard of his personal safety, since by so doing he exposed himself as a ready victim of the blackmailer's 'loathsome trade'. Most of these youths he met through the introduction of a young man of good education named Alfred Taylor, the son of a wealthy cocoa manufacturer, by whom he had been left a considerable fortune which he was now rapidly running through. Although Wilde probably did not meet Taylor on more than half a dozen occasions, usually in Taylor's exotically furnished rooms in Little College Street, Westminster, Alfred Taylor was to play a significant part in Wilde's undoing and eventually to stand beside him in the dock at the Old Bailey.

The precise mode in which Wilde's peculiar inverted instincts found satisfaction is of interest from the medico-legal standpoint. His conduct with the various youths whom he met, or who were procured for him by the obliging Taylor, usually began with close physical contact and fondling. This would be followed by some form of mutual masturbation or intercrural intercourse. (Amongst the articles of clothing found in Taylor's rooms were several pairs of trousers with slits or vents in place of pockets, a feature plainly designed to facilitate masturbation.) Finally *fellatio* (oral copulation) would be practised with Wilde as the active agent, though this role was occasionally reversed. There seems to have been no question of *pedicatio* (anal penetration). It was suggested by only one of the witnesses who gave evidence at his trials that Wilde had committed sodomy. (This may have been due to a misunderstanding by the witness of the precise meaning of the word.) Nor indeed was Wilde ever charged with this graver offence, which still carries the maximum penalty of life imprisonment. However, such a charge (subsequently dropped) was brought against his confederate Alfred Taylor.

The Background

Wilde was greatly upset by the behaviour of the various young men whom he had entertained and to whom he had given presents of cigarette cases and money. His friend Robert Sherard has recalled that he was with Wilde at the end of the opening day of his last trial, when he was staying at his mother's house in Oakley Street, and that Wilde told him that what was most distressing to him during that painful day was seeing these youths whom the prosecution had now collected to give evidence against him. 'They jeered at me when they saw me,' he told his friend. 'But I never did them any harm. I never tried to be anything but kind to them.'

At that moment, Sherard noted, his eyes were dimmed with tears, and he imagined that his extraordinary love for these boys was nothing but a sisterly or motherly affection. 'It was the most complete case of biological introversion.'[1]

As we shall see, Wilde's experiences at the Old Bailey, and also in prison, failed to convince him that his conduct, however legally wrong, was morally culpable. Even from the witness box he was to attempt to justify his feelings under the guise of so-called Platonic love, or 'the love that dare not speak its name', in a passage in which he was moved to a remarkable flight of eloquence. His only regret in prison was that he had sometimes been guilty of conduct unworthy of an artist. After his release, he was to resume his homosexual practices, with less discrimination than ever in the choice of associates, and, as is now generally known, they continued until the time of his final illness in the autumn of 1900. 'I've been married three times in my life,' he confessed to a French friend, 'once to a woman and twice to men.'

1. Sherard, *Unhappy Friendship*, p. 31.

CHAPTER 2

THE PRELUDE

1

THE cause of Oscar Wilde's first dramatic appearance at the Old Bailey was the friendship he had formed with Lord Alfred Douglas, third son of the eighth Marquess of Queensberry. The father objected to this association on his son's part, and after numerous unsuccessful attempts to break it up, Lord Queensberry finally resorted to a characteristically vulgar and offensive action which was calculated to bring the issue to a head. On the afternoon of the 18 February 1895 he called at Wilde's club in London and left with the porter a card on which he had written some defamatory words. Wilde was handed the card on his next visit to the club, and, having taken legal advice, he embarked on the course which was eventually to land him in prison and his friend in exile.

Wilde and Douglas had then known each other for rather more than three years. At the time of their first meeting Wilde was thirty-eight and Douglas twenty-two. The elder man was well known in London as a witty conversationalist, who had also achieved some success as a poet and writer of fiction, but as yet he had shown little evidence of his skill as a dramatist: he was married to a pretty but not very clever wife, who had borne him two children. The younger man was an undergraduate at Oxford, gifted with decided poetic talents as well as extraordinary good looks. He was known to his friends as 'Bosie' Douglas, 'Bosie' being a contraction for 'Boysie', which he had been called when a child by his fond and indulgent mother. His peculiar good looks and youthful appearance, which lasted well into middle age, proved in many ways a curse rather than a blessing. As Bernard Shaw put it in a letter to Douglas written in 1931, which Douglas showed me in that year, 'that flower-like sort of beauty must have

OSCAR WILDE

(From a contemporary photograph)

LORD ALFRED DOUGLAS

(From a contemporary photograph)

been a horrible handicap to you; it was probably nature's reaction against the ultra-hickory type in your father.'[1]

The two men were introduced by another poet, Lionel Johnson, who bought 'Bosie' to tea at Wilde's house in Tite Street one afternoon early in 1891. They immediately became warm friends. Douglas found in the elder man a most entertaining companion, and it flattered his vanity to be seen in Wilde's company. Wilde, on the other hand, was drawn to Douglas's lively intellect as well as Adonis-like appearance, and he was also influenced by the fact – for like many Irishmen, he had a strong vein of snobbery in his make-up – that his newly-found young friend was a lord. On Wilde's side the friendship rapidly developed into infatuation, and he made no secret of his feelings. 'He was continually asking me to lunch and dine with him,' Douglas subsequently admitted, 'and sending me letters, notes, and telegrams. He flattered me, gave me presents, and made much of me in every way. He gave me copies of all his books, with inscriptions in them. He wrote a sonnet to me, and gave it to me one night in a restaurant.[2] That was after I had known him about six months.' Soon they were hardly ever out of each other's sight. They stayed in each other's houses and occasionally in hotels together and went for trips abroad. Eventually, when Wilde was in Reading gaol, he turned against his friend and, in the suppressed portion of *De Profundis*, accused him of having made him waste his time: however, the fact remains that Wilde wrote his best plays during the period of their association. Gradually Douglas on his side was completely captivated by Wilde's charm, and in the end he was

1. Lord Alfred Bruce Douglas (1870–1945) was educated at Winchester and Magdalen College, Oxford. In spite of the eminence which he subsequently achieved as a poet, his life was almost incessantly dogged by controversy. See his own writings, particularly *Autobiography* (1929) and *Without Apology* (1938) also *Oscar Wilde: A Summing Up* (1940), the biographies of Patrick Braybrooke (1931) and William Freeman (1948), the obituary notice in *The Times*, 21 March 1945, *Lord Alfred Douglas His Poetry and Personality* by Marie Carmichael Stopes (1949), and *Oscar Wilde and the Black Douglas* by the 10th Marquess of Queensberry and Percy Colson (1949).

2. The sonnet was entitled 'The New Remorse', and has been published in the complete edition of Wilde's poems.

without doubt more devoted to Wilde than the elder man had ever been to him. 'He is the most chivalrous friend in the world,' wrote Douglas after they had known each other for about two years; 'he is the only man I know who would have the courage to put his arm on the shoulder of an ex-convict and walk down Piccadilly with him, and combine with that the wit and personality to carry it off so well that nobody would mind.' When Wilde died in 1900, Douglas returned the tribute he had received in the early days of their friendship by writing 'The Dead Poet', a sonnet which has been justly rated amongst the finest in our language.

What impressed Douglas, as it did many others, was the magical quality of Wilde's conversation. 'I have never known anyone to come anywhere near him,' Douglas told me, looking back more than thirty years after Wilde's death. 'He did succeed in weaving spells. One sat and listened to him enthralled. It all appeared to be Wisdom and Power and Beauty and Enchantment. It was indeed enchantment and nothing else.'

> And as of old in music measureless
> I heard his golden voice, and marked him trace
> Under the common thing the hidden grace,
> And conjure wonder out of emptiness,
> Till mean things put on Beauty like a dress
> And all the world was an enchanted place.[1]

Unfortunately there was a less pleasant side to the picture.

1. Lord Alfred Douglas, *Complete Poems* (1928), at p. 82. Cp. the judgement of Robert Ross: 'It will always be difficult for us to convey to those who never knew him, or who, knowing him, disliked him, the extraordinary magnetism which he exerted at least on the needles, if not the silver churns, of life. As in the fable of a gold and silver shield, every one received entirely different impressions according to the method of their approach and the accident of acquaintance. . . . It is impossible to echo even faintly that voice "which conjured wonder out of emptiness". He was indeed a conjurer. To talk with him was to be translated to an enchanted island or to the palaces of the *Fata Morgana*. You could not tell what flowers were at your feet or what fantastic architecture was silhouetted against the purple atmosphere of his conversation.' See further Ross's remarks in Ada Leverson's *Letters to the Sphinx* (1930).

The Prelude

Wilde had begun to indulge in homosexual practices at least five years before he first met Lord Alfred Douglas. Because of the evidence given at his trails by a series of juvenile delinquents with whom Wilde was proved to have been on terms of criminal intimacy, it was generally assumed at the time – and also later – that Douglas was an accomplice in these practices. The foreman of the jury in the last trial actually asked the judge whether a warrant had been issued for Lord Alfred's arrest. In his *Autobiography*, which was published in 1929, Lord Alfred Douglas confessed that for a short time there did occur between them certain 'familiarities' of the kind which not infrequently take place among boys at English public schools; but he went on, 'of the sin which takes its name from one of the cities of the Plain there never was the slightest question. I give this as my solemn word before God, as I hope to be saved.'

Douglas reiterated these remarks in a conversation I had with him shortly after the publication of his *Autobiography*. He admitted that when he first met Wilde he was not any more innocent than other boys of his age.

From the second time he saw me, [Douglas said] when he gave me a copy of *Dorian Gray* which I took with me to Oxford, he made overtures to me. It was not until I had known him for at least six months and he had twice stayed with me in Oxford, that I gave in to him. I did with him and allowed him to do what was done among boys at Winchester and Oxford. . . . Sodomy never took place between us, nor was it attempted or dreamed of. . . . I never liked this part of the business. It was dead against my sexual instincts, which were all for youth and beauty and softness. After a time he tumbled to the fact that I did not like it at all and only consented to it to oblige him, and he very soon cut it out altogether. For at least six months before he went to prison no such thing happened between us, nor was it as much as hinted at after he came out two years later when I met him again.[1]

Wilde always claimed that his love for Douglas was ideal and spiritual. 'It was always a reaching up for the ideal,' Wilde said afterwards, 'and in the end it became utterly ideal.' Nor,

1. See my Foreword to *Oscar Wilde and the Black Douglas* by Lord Queensberry and Percy Colson (1949).

although Douglas's remarkable physique no doubt made a strong impression upon the sensual side of Wilde's nature, was there anything either effete or effeminate about the younger man, either in his appearance or in his manners. As an athlete, Douglas was decidedly above the average. He won several open running events both at Winchester and Magdalen, and he always put up a creditable performance in the hunting field. Apart from the 'familiarities' already referred to, which could hardly in the circumstances have formed the basis of any criminal charge, there was probably little or nothing improper in the relations between the two men.[1] Unfortunately for Douglas, the outside world, including his own father, thought otherwise. This belief gained substance from a number of letters written by Wilde to Douglas in which the writer declared in characteristic terms his admiration for his young friend.

To writers of ordinary day-to-day correspondence, as Sir Edward Clarke put it in his opening speech at the first trial, the language used by Wilde in his communications to Douglas must seem decidedly extravagant in tenor. They certainly were unusual letters for one man to write to another, but though highly coloured, they can scarcely be said to be improper. However, but for an act of carelessness on Douglas's part these communications need never have gone beyond the knowledge of their original sender and recipient.

While still up at Oxford, Douglas gave an old suit of his clothes to an unemployed clerk named Wood, whom he had befriended. In the pockets he had unfortunately overlooked a number of the letters in question, which Wood, in conjunction with

1. On the other hand it would seem beyond dispute that Douglas was fundamentally homosexual at this time and that he indulged in homosexual practices with others, if not with Wilde. The French writer Henri de Régnier is the authority for a curious incident which is stated to have occurred in the Savoy Hotel in London, when Wilde was staying there with Douglas early in 1893. 'A friend of mine who went to see him told me afterwards that there was only one bed in the room, with two pillows, and that while he was there Wilde's wife, who brings him his post every morning, arrived in tears.' *Pages from the Goncourt Journal.* Ed. and tr. by Robert Baldick (1962), p. 384.

two professional blackmailers named Allen and Clibborn, proceeded to use as a means of extorting money from Wilde. Copies of the more seemingly compromising epistles were made by the blackmailers, and one such copy was first sent to the actor-manager Beerbohm Tree, who was then rehearsing Wilde's play *A Woman of No Importance* at the Haymarket Theatre This was the letter beginning 'My own Boy, your sonnet is quite lovely' and subsequently introduced in evidence at the trials. Tree immediately handed the copy to Wilde, remarking as he did so that its sentiments were open to misconstruction. Wilde airily explained that it was really a 'prose poem' and that if put into verse it might be printed in such a respectable anthology as the *Golden Treasury*. A rendering of it in French verse was in fact made shortly afterwards by the French poet Pierre Louÿs, and this version was published in *The Spirit Lamp*, an undergraduate magazine in Oxford then edited by Lord Alfred Douglas.

A little later Wood succeeded in extorting £35 from Wilde in return for a bundle of his letters to Douglas, which he alleged had been stolen from him by Allen and which he had recovered with the aid of a detective. The money was good-humouredly handed over on the pretext of enabling Wood to start a new life in America. But Wood did not remain in America for long. He was soon back in London, and he was to give evidence against his benefactor at the Old Bailey. What is more, on examining the letters more closely after Wood had gone, Wilde discovered that the original of that of which a copy had been sent to Tree was not among them.

In due course Allen turned up at Wilde's house. 'I suppose you have come about my beautiful letter to Lord Alfred Douglas,' Wilde said to him. 'If you had not been so foolish as to send a copy of it to Mr Beerbohm Tree, I would gladly have paid you a very large sum of money for the letter, as I consider it to be a work of art.'

'A very curious construction can be put on that letter,' the blackmailer murmured.

'Art is rarely intelligible to the criminal classes,' rejoined Oscar.

'A man has offered me £60 for it.'

Oscar Wilde

'If you will take my advice you will go to that man and sell my letter to him for £60. I myself have never received so large a sum for any prose work of that length: but I am glad to find that there is someone in England who considers a letter of mine worth £60.'

Allen now looked somewhat taken aback. On recovering his composure he said: 'The man is out of town.'

'He is sure to come back,' answered Wilde, who repeated his advice.

The would-be blackmailer changed his tone and admitted that he was in urgent need of money and had been trying to find Wilde for some time. Wilde said he could not guarantee him his cab expenses, but that he would gladly give him half a sovereign. As Allen pocketed the money, Wilde remarked: 'The letter is a prose poem, will shortly be published in sonnet form in a delightful magazine, and I will send you a copy of it.'

Five minutes later Clibborn, the third blackmailer, rang the bell of the house in Tite Street. By this time Wilde was getting somewhat tired. 'I cannot bother any more about this matter,' he said on going out to him.

To Wilde's surprise the caller produced the original letter from his pocket and said: 'Allen has asked me to give it back to you.'

Wilde did not take it immediately, but asked: 'Why does Allen give me back this letter?'

'Well, he says you were kind to him, and there is no use trying to rent[1] you, as you only laugh at us.'

'I will accept it back,' Wilde now declared, taking the letter, 'and you can thank Allen from me for all the anxiety he has shown about it.'

Then looking at the letter, and seeing that it had become badly soiled, Wilde went on in his customary vein of banter. 'I think it quite unpardonable that better care was not taken of this original manuscript of mine.'

At this Clibborn expressed regret, but pointed out it had been in so many hands.

Wilde thereupon gave him half a sovereign likewise for his

1. A contemporary slang term meaning blackmail.

68

pains, saying as he did so: 'I am afraid you are leading a wonderfully wicked life.'

'There is good and bad in every one of us,' said Clibborn.

'You are a born philosopher,' Wilde told him. And on this note they parted.

Wilde had succeeded in recovering this letter, in which he had written to his friend that 'it is a marvel that those rose-red lips of yours should have been made no less for music of song than for madness of kisses'.

Unfortunately for the writer a copy had fallen into Lord Queensberry's hands. And Queensberry did not see the matter in the same light as Beerbohm Tree had done.

2

John Sholto Douglas, eighth Marquess of Queensberry, was an extremely eccentric Scottish nobleman; indeed, to judge from his recorded actions and utterances, he may be taken to have been mentally unbalanced. His principal preoccupations were sport and atheism, and he knew much more about his horses and dogs than about the human members of his family. He had, however, proved himself a successful steeplechaser and an efficient Master of Hounds, and he had also been an amateur light-weight boxing champion. Apart from his ill-fated quarrel with Wilde, he is chiefly remembered as the author of the rules which govern amateur boxing and which bear his name. But his professions of atheism had already won for him a contemporary notoriety. As a representative peer of Scotland he had refused to take the oath in the House of Lords on the ground that this necessary preliminary was a mere 'Christian tomfoolery'. In his private life he bullied his wife, who subsequently divorced him, and neglected his children, preferring instead the society of his mistresses and his sporting cronies. He was arrogant, vain, conceited, and ill-tempered.[1] His fury at his eldest son, Lord Drumlanrig, who

1. The eighth Marquess of Queensberry (1844–1900) was first married to Sybil, daughter of Alfred Montgomery, by whom he was divorced in 1887.

Oscar Wilde

was Lord Rosebery's private secretary, being created an English peer,[1] led to a ridiculous scene at Homburg, whither the irate Marquess pursued the Prime Minister (as Rosebery then was) with a dog whip. Peace was only preserved as the result of the personal intervention of the Prince of Wales.

It was not long before the eccentric Marquess learned of his third son's being seen about with 'this man Wilde', as he was in the habit of describing Alfred's friend. A few months after the momentous introduction in Tite Street, Queensberry told his son that he must give up knowing Wilde, as he was not a fit man to associate with. Alfred Douglas refused, the Marquess got angry and threatened to cut his allowance. Then the difference was for a while smoothed over. Wilde and Douglas happened to be lunching together one day towards the end of 1892 in the Café Royal and noticed Queensberry glowering at them from an adjoining table. At Wilde's prompting, Douglas got up and went over to his father, who somewhat reluctantly consented to be introduced to Wilde, and the three men sat down and finished their lunch together. In a very short time Queensberry was completely captivated by Wilde's charm of manner and conversation, the lunch was prolonged over liqueurs and cigars, and about three o'clock Douglas left them in an animated discussion of Christianity and atheism. Immediately after this Queensberry wrote to his son saying that he took back everything he had previously said about Wilde, whom he considered charming and extremely

---

1. Francis Archibald (Douglas), Viscount Drumlanrig (1867–1894) was raised to the peerage as Lord Kelhead in 1893. A year later his political career of great promise was suddenly cut short by his death as the result of a shooting accident. Queensberry's fury was caused in part by the fact that since 1880 his own election as a representative peer had not been renewed.

There were four sons and one daughter of this marriage. He married again in 1893, and this marriage, of which there was no issue, was annulled in 1894. On him and the Queensberry family generally, see Lord Alfred Douglas, *Autobiography* (1929), and Francis, tenth Marquess of Queensberry, *The Sporting Queensberrys* (1945), and (with Percy Colson) *Oscar Wilde and the Black Douglas* (1949).

clever. Unfortunately the calm was shoit-lived. Soon Queensberry was writing his son abusive letters threatening once more to cut him off if he did not drop Wilde. This correspondence culminated in a most insulting missive, which was subsequently read out in Court by Sir Edward Clarke at the first trial.

Your intimacy with this man Wilde [wrote Queensberry on 1 April 1894] must either cease or I will disown you and stop all money supplies. I am not going to try and analyse this intimacy, and I make no charge; but to my mind to pose as a thing is as bad as to be it. With my own eyes I saw you both in the most loathsome and disgusting relationship, as expressed by your manner and expression. Never in my experience have I seen such a sight as that in your horrible features. No wonder people are talking as they are. Also I now hear on good authority, but this may be false, that his wife is petitioning to divorce him for sodomy and other crimes. Is this true, or do you not know of it? If I thought the actual thing was true, and it became public property, I should be quite justified in shooting him at sight.

To this amazing effusion Alfred Douglas replied in a celebrated telegram: 'What a funny little man you are.'

Queensberry was now bordering on frenzy, and he threatened to give his impertinent young jackanapes of a son 'the thrashing you deserve', should he send any similar communications in future.

If I catch you again with that man [he continued] I will make a public scandal in a way you little dream of; it is already a suppressed one. I prefer an open one, and at any rate I shall not be blamed for allowing such things to go on.

He then proceeded to visit the various restaurants frequented by Wilde and his son, warning the managers and *maîtres d'hôtel* that he would thrash them both if he discovered them together on the premises. Douglas reacted to these tactics by making a point of going to these restaurants, writing to his father with details of time and place and inviting him to come along and 'see what happened to him' if he started any of his 'ruffianly tricks'.

Oscar Wilde

Wilde was now beginning to feel worried by these unwelcome attentions on Queensberry's part. For one thing they interfered with his professional work and they disturbed the peace of mind which he needed as a writer. On the advice apparently of Robert Ross, he consulted the well-known firm of solicitors, C. O. Humphreys, Son & Kershaw, as to whether the letter about him and his wife was actionable and whether anything could be done to restrain Queensberry's violent and offensive behaviour. He discussed the matter with the senior partner, Mr Charles Octavius Humphreys, a most experienced criminal lawyer, who in fact was to represent Wilde in the subsequent proceedings against Queensberry; but he was eventually dissuaded from taking the matter further by Alfred Douglas's cousin, George Wyndham, M.P., who was prompted to intervene by his natural desire to avert a family scandal.[1] It was agreed between them that Wilde was at least entitled to an apology, and that Humphreys should write to the Marquess and demand one. This was accordingly done, but Queensberry flatly refused to make any amends. 'I certainly shall not tender to Mr Oscar Wilde any apology for letters I have written to my son,' he wrote back to Humphreys.

Had Wilde prosecuted Queensberry for criminal libel at the time of this interview – May 1894 – instead of waiting for nearly twelve months, by which time more damning evidence against himself had become available, it is quite possible that Queensberry would have been convicted and silenced. That Wilde regretted this is apparent from a letter he wrote Douglas almost immediately afterwards. 'Your father is on the rampage again – been to the Café Royal to inquire after us – with threats, etc. I think now it would have been better for me to have had him bound over to keep the peace. But what a scandal! Still, it is intolerable to be dogged by a maniac.'

For a time Wilde managed to escape further bother by going to Worthing, where he took a house and wrote what was to be his best and most successful play, *The Importance of Being Earnest*.

1. George Wyndham (1863–1913), politician and writer, was the elder son of the Hon. Percy Scawen Wyndham and a grandson of the first Lord Leconfield.

But business necessarily brought him back to town from time to time, and it was during one of these visits that there occurred the most extraordinary and dramatic meeting between himself and Queensberry and the last until their final historic encounter in the Courts. One June afternoon, 'the scarlet Marquess', as Wilde called him presented himself at Wilde's house in Chelsea without any previous warning. He was accompanied to quote Wilde again, 'by a gentleman with whom I was not acquainted' – in fact a prize-fighter. The interview took place in the library.

'Sit down,' said the Marquess, as Wilde walked over to the fireplace.

Wilde turned on him. 'I do not allow anyone to talk like that to me in my house or anywhere else.'

Then he continued. 'I suppose you have come to apologize for the statement you made about my wife and myself in letters you wrote to your son. I should have the right any day I chose to prosecute you for writing such a letter.'

'The letter was privileged,' interrupted Queensberry, 'as it was written to my son.'

This time it was Wilde's turn to be angry.

'How dare you say such things to me about your son and me?'

Queensberry went on seemingly unabashed. 'You were both kicked out of the Savoy Hotel at a moment's notice for your disgusting conduct.'

'That is a lie.'

'You have taken furnished rooms for him in Piccadilly.'

'Somebody has been telling you an absurd set of lies about your son and me. I have not done anything of the kind.'

'I hear you were thoroughly well blackmailed for a disgusting letter you wrote to my son.'

Again Wilde protested. 'The letter was a beautiful letter, and I never wrote except for publication.'

Wilde thereupon changed his tone to one of the utmost seriousness. 'Lord Queensberry,' he asked his embarrassing caller, 'do you seriously accuse your son and me of improper conduct?'

Queensberry thought for a moment. 'I do not say you are it,' he said, 'but you look it, and you pose as it, which is just as bad.

If I catch you and my son together in any public restaurant, I will thrash you.'

Although thus confronted with a bully and a bruiser, Wilde did not betray the slightest fear. 'I do not know what the Queensberry rules are,' he told his unwelcome guest, 'but the Oscar Wilde rule is to shoot at sight.'

With this sally Wilde requested Queensberry to leave the house. Queensberry refused, whereupon Wilde threatened to call the police and have him put out.

'It's a disgusting scandal,' foamed the Marquess, as he made for the hallway.

'If it is so,' retorted Wilde, 'you are the author of the scandal and no one else.'

Then, following his visitors into the hall, he pointed out the Marquess to the servant who was waiting there to show them out. 'This is the Marquess of Queensberry, the most infamous brute in London. You are never to allow him to enter my house again.'

It was now a fight to the finish, and no punches were to be pulled, to use a metaphor from the Marquess's favourite sport. Queensberry had already stopped his son's allowance, and he now directed his venom towards the boy's mother, his own divorced wife whom he accused of interfering in the quarrel.

Your daughter [he wrote to her father] is the person who is supporting my son to defy me. ... She evidently wants to make out that I want to make out a case against my son. It is nothing of the kind. I have made out a case against Oscar Wilde and I have to his face accused him of it. If I was quite certain of the thing, I would shoot the fellow at sight, but I can only accuse him of posing. It now lies in the hands of the two whether they will further defy me. Your daughter appears now to be encouraging them, although she can hardly intend this. I don't believe Wilde will now dare defy me. He plainly showed the white feather the other day when I tackled him – damned cur and coward of the Rosebery type. As for this so-called son of mine, he is no son of mine, and I will have nothing to do with him. He may starve as far as I am concerned after his behaviour to me.

At the same time Queensberry wrote to Alfred Douglas, who

had been sending his father postcards, since his letters were now returned to him unopened. Queensberry told him that all future cards would go into the fire unread. He then repeated the threat of a thrashing. 'You reptile,' concluded this paternal epistle. 'You are no son of mine, and I never thought you were.'

Douglas promptly replied that he treated his father's absurd threats with absolute indifference and that he was making a point of being seen with Wilde in as many public restaurants as possible.

If O.W. was to prosecute you in the criminal courts for libel [he continued] you would get seven years' penal servitude for your outrageous libels. Much as I detest you, I am anxious to avoid this for the sake of the family; but if you try to assault me I shall defend myself with a loaded revolver which I always carry, and if I shoot you, or he shoots you, we would be completely justified, as we should be acting in self-defence against a violent and dangerous rough, and I think if you were dead not many people would miss you.

Queensberry was fully determined not to let the matter rest, but for a time his prey eluded him. Having finished *The Importance of Being Earnest*, and the play having gone into rehearsal during the winter, Wilde went abroad on a trip with Douglas. But even here he was pursued by Queensberry's threats and gibes.

At Algiers they fell in with the French writer André Gide. They began to discuss Wilde's work, and the Frenchman asked the dramatist why he failed to put the best of himself into his plays.

'Would you like to know the great drama of my life?' Wilde exclaimed. 'It is that I have put my genius into my life – I have put only my talent into my works.'

According to Gide, whose testimony on this occasion there is no reason to doubt, Wilde went on to speak of returning to London, as a well-known peer was insulting him, challenging him, and taunting him with running away.

'But if you go back what will happen?' asked Gide. 'Do you know the risk you are running?'

'It is best never to know,' answered Wilde. 'My friends are

extraordinary. They beg me to be careful. Careful? But how can I be careful? That would be a backward step. I must go on as far as possible. I cannot go much further. Something is bound to happen . . . something else.'

At this point Wilde broke off the conversation, as if he had a premonition of approaching disaster. On the following day he set out for England.

3

Wilde reached London in time for the first performance of *The Importance of Being Earnest*, which was presented by George Alexander at the St James's Theatre on 14 February 1895. Queensberry planned to create a scene on the opening night and harangue the audience, but he unwisely made known his plan beforehand, so that it reached the ears of the author, who had the theatre surrounded by police. The 'scarlet Marquess' duly arrived with his prize-fighting attendant, and, finding himself unable to obtain admission to the theatre at any of the entrances, prowled about for three hours, and finally left 'chattering', said Wilde, 'like a monstrous ape', having first deposited at the stage-door a 'grotesque bouquet of vegetables' addressed to the object of his enmity. 'This, of course,' as Wilde told Douglas, 'makes his conduct idiotic – robs it of dignity.'

Queensberry accordingly withdrew to consider his next step, and, as the event proved, it was *pour mieux sauter*. Four days later – during the afternoon of 18 February – he called at the Albemarle Club, to which both Wilde and his wife belonged, and left a card with the hall porter. 'Give that to Oscar Wilde,' he said. On the card he had written: 'For Oscar Wilde, posing as a som*domite*,' the latter word being thus misspelled in his fury. The porter looked at the card, but did not understand the meaning of the words. He thereupon put it in an envelope to await Wilde's arrival.

It was not until nearly a fortnight had gone by that Wilde called at the club and was handed the offensive missive by the porter. He immediately went back to the hotel, where he was staying

THE EIGHTH MARQUESS OF QUEENSBERRY

By "Spy"

Letter written on February 28th, 1895, from Oscar Wilde to Robert Ross indicating his intention to prosecute The Marquess of Queensberry for criminal libel

(From the original in the William Andrews Clark Memorial Library, University of California, Los Angeles)

The Prelude

and sent notes to Robert Ross and Alfred Douglas, asking them to come and see him. This is what he wrote to Ross:

Hotel Avondale
Piccadilly
London [28 February 1895]

Dearest Robbie,

Since I saw you something has happened. Bosie's father has left a card at my club with hideous words on it. I don't see anything now but a criminal prosecution. My whole life seems ruined by this man. The tower of ivory is assailed by the foul thing. On the sand is my life spilt.

I don't know what to do. If you could come here at 11.30 please do so tonight. I mar your life by trespassing ever on your love and kindness. I have asked Bosie to come tomorrow.

Yrs,
OSCAR

Ross came to the hotel as requested, and the two men discussed the business into the small hours. Ross advised Wilde once again to see his solicitor and this time to get him to apply for a warrant for the arrest of his tormentor. This is in fact what happened. Next day, which was a Friday, Lord Alfred Douglas arrived, and all three together went to see Humphreys. The solicitor who recalled his previous meeting with Wilde ten months before, was not unnaturally amazed when he heard the details of Queensberry's recent conduct. He asked Wilde point blank on his solemn oath whether there was any truth in the libel. Wilde solemnly assured him that he was absolutely innocent. 'If you are innocent,' said Humphreys, 'you should succeed.' On the strength of this assurance Humphreys agreed to apply for a warrant.

One important question, which arose during the momentous conference in the solicitor's office, was the cost of the contemplated proceedings against the obnoxious Marquess. At this time Wilde was considerably in debt. He therefore told Humphreys that he had no funds immediately available and that he doubted whether he could afford the 'terrible expense' involved in prosecuting Queensberry. At this point, according to Wilde, Lord

Oscar Wilde

Alfred Douglas interposed. Douglas said that his own family 'would be only too delighted to pay the necessary costs', that his father 'had been an incubus to them all', that they 'had often discussed the possibility of getting him put into a lunatic asylum so as to keep him out of the way', and that he was 'a daily source of annoyance and distress' to his divorced wife and to everybody else. Writing from the solitude of his prison cell in Reading eighteen months later, Wilde recalled this incident to his friend's recollection:

The solicitor closed at once, and I was hurried to the Police Court. I had no excuse left for not going. I was forced into it. Of course, your family don't pay the costs, and when I am made bankrupt, it is by your father and *for* the costs – the meagre balance of them – some £700.

This statement requires qualification. It is true that, when a receiving order was eventually made against Wilde and he was adjudicated bankrupt, it was upon the petition of Lord Queensberry, but at the date in question his other disclosed liabilities amounted to more than four times the sum of Queensberry's proved debt, and it was clear that for several years past the debtor had been living to some extent in excess of his income.[1] Also, so far as the immediate proceedings against Queensberry were concerned, Wilde was able to borrow £500 from his friend Ernest Leverson, while Alfred Douglas came to the rescue as well. The young man scraped up all the ready cash he could – about £360 – which he handed over to his friend on the day of his father's arrest.

Another curious but little-known fact which has emerged is that, had Wilde not been in such acute financial embarrassment at the time, he might have gone abroad on the very day that he called at his club, and so might have missed receiving the Marquess's card – at any rate until the lapse of time had either rendered it innocuous or else dictated a different course of action. During most of the preceding fortnight he had been staying at

1. Wilde admitted to the Official Receiver, in the course of his public examination, that as early as July 1893 his liabilities exceeded his assets by £1,450.

the Avondale Hotel, along with Lord Alfred Douglas and a friend of the latter, both of whom Wilde had regarded as his guests. The total bill for the three of them for ten days was £140. As soon as the other two had left the hotel, Wilde had been hoping to go over to France on a fairly long visit, but the hotel proprietor refused to allow his luggage to be moved until the bill had been paid.

Had it not been for the hotel bill, I would have gone to Paris on Thursday morning [Wilde afterwards reminded Douglas]. On that fatal Friday, instead of being in Humphreys's office weakly consenting to my ruin, I would have been happy and free in France, away from you and your father, unconscious of his loathsome card and indifferent to your letters, if I had been able to leave the Avondale Hotel. But the hotel people absolutely refused to let me go. . . . That is what kept me in London.

No doubt the bill was paid out of the cash which had been advanced by Douglas; but, if so, of course, it would have been done after the crucial step of applying for the warrant had been taken, and it was too late to retract.

Since Wilde had previously been in consultation with Mr Humphreys, as we have seen, about Lord Queensbury, it was quite natural for this solicitor to be consulted again on the subject. It is worth noting, however, that Alfred Douglas wished his friend to go to Sir George Lewis. This was the first Sir George Lewis, head of the well-known firm of Lewis & Lewis, and a shrewd lawyer who had a great reputation for settling awkward society cases out of Court.[1] Now Lewis knew a good deal more about the background of Wilde's private life at this time than Humphreys did, and it is quite possible that, if he had been professionally or even privately consulted, he would have taken a different view of Wilde's protestation of innocence and would have told his client to tear up the Marquess's card and do nothing more about it. As it happened, Sir George Lewis was instructed by Queensberry himself.

1. Sir George Henry Lewis (1833–1911) was knighted in 1892, supposedly for his services in connexion with the Parnell Commission. He was created a baronet in 1902.

Oscar Wilde

Lord Queensberry was staying at Carter's Hotel in Albemarle Street, and it was here that he was arrested on Saturday morning, 2 March. 'I have been wanting to find Mr Oscar Wilde for nine or ten days,' he said to the police officer when the warrant was produced. 'This thing has been going on for about two years.' The Marquess was taken to Vine Street police station, where he was formally charged, and thence he was immediately conveyed to the Court in Great Marlborough Street and there brought up before the sitting magistrate.[1]

The initial proceedings at Great Marlborough Street were quite brief. The magistrate was the somewhat irritable seventy-four-year-old Robert Milner Newton, who had presided at that Court for the past thirty years, and before whom Humphreys with his extensive criminal practice had frequently appeared in the past. In opening the case against Queensberry, the solicitor stated that, quite apart from the libel complained of, Wilde had been the object of a most cruel persecution at the hands of the defendant. Humphreys went on to say that his client had consulted him in the matter ten months previously, but that 'in consequence of family affairs Mr Oscar Wilde was very unwilling to take any steps of a criminal nature'. In addition to the libellous words on the card, Humphreys stated that he proposed to refer to other libels which had been published by the defendant before 18 February, and when these had been investigated he would ask the magistrate to commit the defendant for trial. Formal evidence was then given by Sidney Wright, hall porter at the Albemarle Club, as to publication of the libel, and by Inspector Greet, of C Division of Scotland Yard, as to the arrest of the defendant.

1. Queensberry told the officer who arrested him that he thought 'in these cases . . . proceedings were generally taken by summons.' In cases of misdemeanour it was and still is the practice to issue a summons, unless there is reason to believe that the defendant will not appear. It must have been thought that Queensberry might ignore a summons. But in fact he was most anxious to justify what he had written and to prove furthermore that the libel was published for the public benefit. Since the passing of the Act of 1842 (6 & 7 Vict. c. 96), commonly known as Lord Campbell's Act, the establishment of such a plea afforded a complete defence to a charge of criminal libel.

The Prelude

At the conclusion of this evidence, Queensberry's solicitor jumped to his feet.

SIR GEORGE LEWIS: Let me say one word, sir. I venture to say that, when the circumstances of this case are more fully known, Lord Queensberry, acting as he did under feeling of great indignation, and –

MAGISTRATE (*interrupting*): I cannot go into that now.

SIR GEORGE LEWIS: I do not wish this case to be adjourned without it being known that there is nothing against the honour of Lord Queensberry.

MAGISTRATE: You mean that you have a perfect answer to the charge.

On bail being applied for, Humphreys said he would like a surety. 'Lord Queensberry is not going to run away,' answered Lewis. The magistrate, however, agreed with Humphreys, and, in adjourning the case for a week, directed the defendant to find one surety in the sum of £500 and enter into his own recognizances in the sum of £1,000. This was immediately done. One of Queensberry's friends, who was in Court and gave his name and occupation as 'Mr William Tyser, merchant', came forward as the required surety.

During the ensuing week, in which each side began to marshal its forces, a number of important developments took place. First of all, Sir George Lewis declined to act further in the defence and returned his instructions to Queensberry. This may have been due to his previous acquaintance with the prosecutor and the personal regard he had for him. At all events his place was taken by Mr Charles Russell, of Messrs Day & Russell.[1] Russell realized that, as matters then stood, it would be far from easy for Queensberry to justify the libel. It is true there were lots of rumours circulating about the seamy side of Wilde's private life, but at this date

1. Hon. Charles Russell (1863–1928), second son of Lord Russell of Killowen, c.j. His firm, which he founded and of which he was a partner, later became known as Charles Russell & Co. He was created a baronet in 1916.

81

little if anything definite was known against him. So far the main plank of the defence appeared to be copies of letters from Wilde to Alfred Douglas with which, as we have seen, unsuccessful attempts had been made to blackmail Wilde. It would be invidious as well as difficult, since they were addressed to the defendant's son, to show that these letters betrayed an immoral pose on the part of the writer. For the rest, the defence would be thrown back upon Wilde's published writings, where the achievement of proving immoral tendencies in the absence of more definite evidence would indeed be formidable. An able and experienced leading counsel was obviously required for such a case as this, and Charles Russell immediately turned to Mr Edward Carson, Q.C.[1]

According to Edward Marjoribanks's biography of Carson, the first visit paid by Russell to the great Irish counsel's chambers in Dr Johnson's Buildings proved fruitless. As has already been seen, Carson had been at Trinity College, Dublin, with Wilde in the seventies, and he disliked the idea of appearing against a fellow classmate. At all events he refused to accept the brief. Undiscouraged, Russell returned to the charge in a day or two.

Meanwhile, detectives employed on Queensberry's instructions were on the track of evidence of immoral practices with young men carried on by Wilde over a considerable period, evidence calculated to go far beyond the words of the libel which simply alleged 'posing'. Carson still hesitated, and it was not until he had consulted that eminent jurist and former Lord Chancellor, Lord Halsbury, that he finally agreed to take the brief. 'The great thing', Halsbury told him, 'is to arrive at justice, and it is you, I believe, who can best do it.' In fact the dossier against Wilde does not seem to have been completed until some time later, but whatever it was that Carson learned during his second consultation with Russell, it was sufficient in his own mind to justify his appearance at the adjourned hearing before the Great Marl-

---

1. Edward Henry Carson (1854–1935), later Lord Carson. On his life see particularly Edward Marjoribanks, *Life of Lord Carson*, Vol. I (1932), and my *Carson* (1953). Russell is said to have briefed Carson on the advice of his father, Lord Russell of Killowen, who was then Lord Chief Justice of England.

borough Street magistrate on 9 March. He had with him, as junior counsel, Charles Gill, a hard-working as well as hard-headed Ulsterman, who probably possessed the largest practice of any man in those days at the criminal bar.[1] It is said that at this consultation Carson had been strongly inclined to advise his client to plead guilty, but that he changed his mind at the last moment before leaving his chambers for Great Marlborough Street on being informed that Russell had obtained, or was about to obtain, a statement incriminating Wilde from a youth named Charles Parker. Parker, who was to be the first Crown witness called in the subsequent proceedings against Wilde, was then serving as a gunner in the Royal Artillery, and Russell had considerable difficulty in persuading him to come forward, since, of course, the solicitor was not instructed by the Crown and consequently could not confer immunity on a witness whose testimony, being that of an accomplice, might lead to his own prosecution. Russell is believed have been put in touch with Parker by a source in the Savoy Hotel where, as Parker was later to admit, indecencies had taken place between Wilde and himself.

The launching of such a libel prosecution by a successful and popular dramatist against a well-known peer and sporting character was bound to create widespread public interest. It was hardly surprising that the small Court in Great Marlborough Street should have been packed with inquisitive spectators at the adjourned hearing. Incidentally they included, in spite of their previous estrangement, Willie Wilde, who had written to tell his brother that he would be present 'in order to show the world that the family think no evil of you'. When the case was called shortly after 11.30 on the morning of 9 March, there was hardly even standing room, and numbers of prominent people, who had endeavoured to obtain seats beside the magistrate on the Bench, were disappointed. Wilde, who had driven up to the Court in a carriage and pair and was accompanied by the defendant's two sons, Lord Alfred Douglas and Lord Douglas of Hawick, had

---

1. Charles Frederick Gill (1851–1923) was Senior Counsel to the Treasury at the Old Bailey and was also Recorder of Chichester. He was knighted in 1921.

considerable difficulty in obtaining seats; while Humphreys, who again appeared for Wilde, was obliged to apply to the magistrate before accommodation could be found for his clerk. As soon as his name was called, Queensberry entered the dock, but the magistrate ordered a chair to be placed for his convenience outside the rails, and he was later allowed to sit behind his counsel. On looking round, the magistrate then recognized Lord Alfred Douglas and directed him to leave the Court at once. Lord Alfred accordingly withdrew.

Formal evidence not given at the first hearing was now taken, this time the prosecutor himself being in the box. Wilde's examination, however, proceeded slowly, since it was necessary, for the purpose of the depositions, that his testimony should be recorded by the clerk of the Court in long-hand. Wilde could not resist the temptation to show off, a temptation which was later to prove damaging when he was in the box at the Old Bailey. Almost his very first answer called down a mild reproof from the Bench.

MR HUMPHREYS: Are you a dramatist and author?
WITNESS: I believe I am well known in that capacity.
MAGISTRATE: Only answer the questions, please.

Wilde then went on to describe his acquaintance with various members of the Queensberry family, but he had not got very far when his solicitor found himself in a quandary. Humphreys, as he had indicated at the previous hearing, wished to introduce the other libels contained in letters from the defendant to his son, but he was unwilling to read out the full text of these letters on account of the references to Lord Rosebery and other 'exalted personages', as he did not wish their names to transpire. Therefore, when he began to question his witness on the letter dated 1 April 1894, which he had been shown by Lord Alfred Douglas, the magistrate intervened with the suggestion that he should not examine on these letters. 'It would be opening a door to something that ought not to take place in this Court,' Mr Newton added. 'At the trial you can say that you have other libels against Mr Oscar Wilde and mention dates.' In any event he should surely give the defendant notice of his intention to produce these other libels.

At this stage Carson intervened to say he hoped the letters would be put in, his point being that Lord Queensberry was acting in the interest of his son. ('I see your point clearly,' said the magistrate.) 'But', continued Carson, 'unless the documents are produced they cannot be attached to the depositions.' He referred particularly to the letter of 1 April 1894, on which Humphreys was endeavouring to examine Wilde, and he hinted that, when the time came to cross-examine, he 'would go into the question of Lord Queensberry giving advice to his son'. Said Humphreys: 'You don't know that the letter contains only advice to his son.' 'Don't I?' replied Carson. 'I happen to have a copy of it.'

Humphreys now declared that he had intended to produce all the letters for the inspection of the magistrate and the defendant's counsel, but that they should not be read in public. 'It would not be right', he said, 'that the names mentioned should be called in question in matters of this kind.' Carson, however, repeated his objection to examination on these letters without full disclosure of their contents – 'either drop them out altogether or put them in' – and in the face of this opposition Humphreys adopted the magistrate's suggestion and passed on to other matters. The examination concluded with formal evidence of Wilde's receipt of the libellous card and his application through his solicitors for a warrant for Queensberry's arrest.

On Carson's rising to cross-examine, some legal argument took place on the scope of his proposed questions. Carson was, of course, entitled to cross-examine, but not to the truth of the libel, since there was no such issue before the Court. What he proposed to show was why the defendant sent the letters – in other words, that 'Lord Queensberry thought it was well for the morality of his son to put a stop to the relations between the parties'. However, the magistrate ruled that this would amount to quasi-justification and was accordingly not admissible then. Carson thereupon resumed his seat.

The case for the prosecution thus being closed, Wilde's depositions were read over to him by the clerk of the Court. He made one slight correction and was about to affix his signature when he suddenly asked to have a certain portion read a second time. 'If you would just attend,' exclaimed the magistrate testily, 'this would not have happened.' However, the privilege was accorded, and after a whisper from the usher 'initials will do' in reply to whether he should sign in full, the prosecutor without removing his gloves took up a quill pen and appended his initials to the depositions.

The magistrate then turned to the prisoner and asked him whether, having heard the charge, he had anything to say in answer to it.

'I have simply, your worship, to say this,' replied the defendant, who appeared a diminutive figure as he stood up behind his tall counsel. 'I wrote that card simply with the intention of bringing matters to a head, having been unable to meet Mr Wilde otherwise, and to save my son, and I abide by what I wrote.'

'Then', said the magistrate, 'you are committed for trial and the same bail will be allowed you as before.'

4

The next Old Bailey sessions were due to open in less than three weeks from the date of Queensberry's committal, so that neither side had much time to lose before the trial. For the role of leading counsel for the prosecution, Humphreys determined to cast one who was at the top of his profession and would in every way be a match for Carson. Accordingly, within the next few days, the solicitor went along to the Temple and offered the brief to Sir Edward Clarke, Q.C. Then in his early fifties, Clarke was a veritable Titan at the Bar, a former Law Officer of the Crown and a man of the highest personal integrity as well as great forensic ability. His conduct of the defence in two celebrated murder trials – the Penge case and the trial of Mrs Bartlett – had long since established him in the foremost rank of English advocates, while his efforts on behalf of Sir William Gordon-Cumming in the more recent 'Baccarat case', when he examined the Prince of Wales, had shown unexampled courage and fearlessness in his client's

The Prelude

interest when battling against strong Court and society prejudices.[1]

Unlike Sir Frank Lockwood, the Solicitor-General, who had enjoyed some measure of Wilde's friendship and hospitality and was ultimately to appear as his leading prosecutor in the last trial, Clarke had never met Wilde before he was instructed in this case. All he knew about him was what was common knowledge among theatregoers, namely, that he was a brilliant playwright who had two successes running at the same time in the West End. Nevertheless the case was not one which on the face of it appealed to him. Indeed he hesitated before accepting the brief, just as Carson had done with his, though for a different reason. He asked the solicitor if he might first see his prospective client.

Next day Humphreys brought Wilde to Clarke's chambers, and after some conversation a remarkable scene took place between them. 'I can only accept this brief, Mr Wilde,' said Clarke, 'if you can assure me on your honour as an English gentleman that there is not and never has been any foundation for the charges that are made against you.' The fact, apparently overlooked by Clarke in the gravity of the moment, that he was an Irishman did not deter Wilde from standing up and solemnly declaring on his honour that the charges were 'absolutely false and groundless'. It should perhaps be pointed out here that, since his client was technically the prosecutor in this case, Clarke was justified in putting this question to him. Of course, had Wilde been facing a criminal charge himself at this stage, Clarke would obviously not have done so, it being contrary to professional etiquette and the tradition of the Bar for counsel to make his client's declaration of his innocence a condition of defending him.

It was on the strength of this assurance so solemnly and emphatically given, that Clarke consented to appear against Queensberry. As events were to show, the further the case proceeded, the less Clarke relished it. In after years he preferred to forget about it, and it is significant that there is no mention of it in his published memoirs. He did, however, place on record his personal attitude

1. Sir Edward Clarke (1841–1931). On his life, see his memoirs, *The Story of My Life* (1918), and Derek Walker-Smith and Edward Clarke, *Life of Sir Edward Clarke* (1939).

in the case. From the notes discovered among his papers, by his biographers after his death, it is clear that he simply did what he conceived to be his duty towards the client who must have assuredly been one of the most embarrassing he had to represent in the whole course of his career.[1] 'I need hardly say', he wrote, 'I had nothing to do with the institution of that prosecution.' But once briefed, the great leader turned all his attention and energies into the case, along with the two junior counsel instructed with him. These were Willie Mathews, a most experienced criminal practitioner, who had appeared with Clarke in many previous cases,[2] and Travers Humphreys, then a young barrister making his way at the English Criminal Bar.[3]

Meanwhile, in the nearby solicitors' offices of Day & Russell, in Norfolk Street, the defence was busily building up a formidable case against Wilde. For some time past Queensberry had been employing private detectives to collect discreditable evidence of the prosecutor's private life, hitherto with little success. It is a curious fact, which does not seem to be generally known, that the most damning clues were provided by an entirely voluntary agent who received no fee for his services. This was the actor Charles Brookfield, who had conceived a violent hatred of Wilde, although at this time he actually had a part in Wilde's play, *An Ideal Husband*, at the Haymarket Theatre. This appears all the more

1. I am indebted to Sir Edward Clarke's grandson, Mr Edward Clarke, for his kindness in putting this material at my disposal, and I have made full use of it in these pages. It appears that Sir Edward Clarke prepared it with a view to its inclusion in *The Story of My Life* (1918), but on second thoughts decided to omit it from his memoirs, doubtless out of consideration for those readers who, nurtured like himself in Victorian principles of propriety, would have been shocked by the discussion of any case involving charges of indecency.

2. Charles Willie Mathews (1850–1920), later for many years Director of Public Prosecutions. He was knighted in 1907 and created a baronet in 1917.

3. Sir Travers Humphreys, (1867–1956), son of C. O. Humphreys, solicitor, was called to the bar at the Inner Temple in 1889. He was successively Junior and Senior Treasury Counsel at the Old Bailey, and was appointed judge of the King's Bench Division of the High Court in 1928. He was knighted in 1925 and created a Privy Councillor in 1946. See his interesting book of reminiscences, *Criminal Days* (1946), and *A Book of Trials* (1953); also his biography by Douglas G. Browne (1960).

surprising since Brookfield was a man of cultured upbringing who had benefited in various ways from Wilde's theatrical successes. The son of a former royal chaplain and a lady-in-waiting to Queen Victoria – students of Thackeray will remember the dramatic part the elder Brookfields played in that writer's life – Charles Brookfield had begun to read for the Bar on leaving Cambridge, but he soon deserted the Temple for the stage, becoming associated with the Haymarket Theatre at the time the Bancrofts first took over the management of it. He was on the whole a likeable man, in some ways more likeable than Wilde, he had an amusing sense of humour, and he wrote a number of plays, and short stories which, though greatly inferior to Wilde's productions, had attracted a certain amount of passing attention. It seems likely that Brookfield became jealous of Wilde's success. At all events he parodied *Lady Windermere's Fan* in a somewhat spiteful piece entitled *The Poet and the Puppets*. The good-natured tolerance with which Wilde regarded this effort only served to fan the flames of Brookfield's hatred. But it did not prevent him from accepting a part in *An Ideal Husband*. This is how he reconciled his action with his conscience. 'I told him', said Brookfield, 'that as I did not want to learn many of his lines I would take the smallest part, and I took the valet.'

The subject of Oscar Wilde had by this time developed into a positive obsession with Brookfield.[1] Consequently, when the

1. Frank Harris was the first of Wilde's friends to record in detail, in the original edition of his *Oscar Wilde: His Life and his Confessions*, published in New York in 1916, how Brookfield 'constituted himself private prosecutor in this case and raked Piccadilly to find witnesses against Oscar Wilde'. (Vol. I, p. 232.) This passage is omitted from the English edition (1928) of this work. Vincent O'Sullivan, another friend of Wilde's, particularly in his last years, also refers to Brookfield in this connexion in his *Aspects of Wilde* (1936), as also does Stuart Mason in his *Bibliography of Oscar Wilde* (1914). According to Mason (p. 392), after Wilde's conviction Brookfield and some friends entertained Queensberry to dinner in celebration of the event. These details are confirmed by the journalist who introduced Brookfield to Queensberry's solicitor. See John Boon, *Victorians, Edwardians, Georgians*, Vol. I (1928), p. 199ff. Brookfield was later appointed to the post of Censor of plays in the Lord Chamberlain's Office, possibly in recognition of his public-spirited behaviour in Wilde's case, although he had himself written one of the 'riskiest' plays of the period. He died in 1913.

Queensberry storm broke, he went round London getting up opposition wherever he could against the unfortunate dramatist. He induced the commissionaire at the Haymarket to supply the defence with the names and addresses of Wood and the other blackmailers who, as we have seen, had acquired various letters from Wilde to Douglas and had sent a copy of one of them to Beerbohm Tree, the theatre's manager. He also put Inspector Littlechild, one of the detectives employed by Queensberry, in touch with a prostitute whom he knew to possess information about Wilde and his disreputable male associates. This woman, who appeared to be far from prosperous, frankly attributed the falling-off in her business to the unfair competition promoted by Oscar Wilde and his like. Pressed for further details the prostitute told the detective that he only had to visit the rooms of a man named Taylor in a certain house in Chelsea and he would find all the evidence he needed. The detective immediately hastened to No. 3 Chapel Street, the address that had been given him, and pushing past the caretaker, who vainly tried to prevent his entrance, he found a kind of post-box, which contained the names and addresses of numbers of young male homosexuals, mostly in the humbler walks of life, as well as other documents linking them with Wilde. These damning particulars were forwarded to the defendant's solicitors, who now proceeded to amend their client's plea of justification accordingly.

For the time being, Wilde, who had gone off with Lord Alfred Douglas to the south of France to enjoy a short breathing space before the trial, remained ignorant of how the shades of the prison house were beginning to close round him. Nor when the full extent of Brookfield's malevolence was brought home to him some years later by his friend Robert Ross, after he had come out of prison, did he feel the least vindictive. All he said was, 'How absurd of Brookfield!'

According to Marjoribanks's *Life of Lord Carson*, an incident now occurred which caused perhaps the greatest sensation abroad of the whole case and which, in that it involved a name far more illustrious than Wilde's, was destined at a later stage to result in a critical misfortune for the prosecutor of Lord Queensberry. As a further necessary preliminary to his appearance in the dock at the Old Bailey, criminal procedure then required the charge which had been brought against the Marquess to be considered by a Grand Jury, who might return a 'true bill' or not, as they thought warranted by the evidence for the prosecution. If the 'bill' was 'thrown out', of course the prosecution automatically lapsed. Grand jurors were usually well-to-do men with substantial property qualifications. On this occasion a distinguished French journalist, who had lived in England for many years, was empanelled in error. He went down to the Old Bailey in order to excuse himself from attendance on the ground of his French citizenship; but, when he found that Oscar Wilde's prosecution of Lord Queensberry for criminal libel was among the bills before the jury, he decided to remain and say nothing about the mistake which had brought him there. In due course a true bill was returned on the strength of evidence which included, *inter alia*, Queensberry's insulting letters to his son, which Wilde's solicitor had referred to in the Police Court proceedings but had not read, but which mentioned the name of Lord Rosebery, against whom, it will be remembered, the defendant had conceived almost as violent an antipathy as he had expressed against Wilde.

A Grand Jury's deliberations invariably took place in private and its findings were never reported in the newspapers. The French press, however, fully acquainted its readers with what had happened on this occasion, and the information thus imparted was not only spread throughout the Continent but was openly discussed in London bars and clubs. Brookfield and his friends were incited to fresh efforts in the cause of public morality, and all were determined that the fact that the Prime Minister's name had been mentioned in connexion with the case was all the stronger reason that nothing should be hushed up. Hostile feeling about Wilde was increasing, and it seems to have reached as far as the south of France, since it is stated on reliable authority that Wilde and Douglas were refused admission by the manager of one hotel in Monaco.[1]

1. See Robert H. Sherard, *Oscar Wilde: The Story of an Unhappy Friendship* (1902), p. 125.

Oscar Wilde

Writing from prison to Lord Alfred Douglas in the suppressed portion of *De Profundis*, Wilde made the following comments on this interlude:

The warrant once granted, your will, of course, directed everything. At a time when I should have been in London taking wise counsel and calmly considering the hideous trap in which I had allowed myself to be caught – the booby trap, as your father calls it to the present day – you insisted on my taking you to Monte Carlo, of all revolting places on God's earth, that all day and all night as well you might gamble as long as the Casino remained open. As for me – baccarat having no charms for me – I was left alone outside to myself. You refused to discuss even for five minutes the position to which you and your father had brought me . . .

On our return to London those of my friends who really desired my welfare implored me to retire abroad, and not to face an impossible trial. You imparted mean motives to them for giving such advice and cowardice to me for listening to it. You forced me to stay, to brazen it out, if possible, in the box by absurd and silly perjuries. At the end, of course, I was arrested, and your father became the hero of the hour.

The precise circumstances of their visit to Monte Carlo together are obscure, but in any event these circumstances are of relatively minor importance. What happened when the two men returned to London is fairly clear. They arrived about a week before the Old Bailey proceedings were due to begin. A consultation was immediately held in Clarke's chambers, at which Wilde and Douglas were both present in addition to solicitor and counsel; and the opportunity was taken of going through all the particulars of Queensberry's amended plea of justification.[1] In spite of all this new evidence for the defence, the truth of which he persisted in denying, but which must have come as an unpleasant surprise to him, Wilde remained outwardly unmoved. Thanks to the activities of Brookfield and the rest of Queensberry's eager band of assistants, much of this evidence was already common knowledge in London, with the result that during the next few days Wilde was besought by his friends on all sides to leave the country. But to all their entreaties he turned a deaf ear, and in

1. For the text of this document, see Appendix A.

this course he needed no prompting from Douglas. A perverse and foolish sense of obstinacy, amounting indeed to bravado, induced him to stay at all costs to himself and see the thing through. This is amply confirmed by the testimony of a number of independent witnesses.

For instance, two nights before the trial opened he took his wife and Douglas to a box at the St James's Theatre where *The Importance of Being Earnest* was playing to crowded houses. In the interval between the acts he went back-stage to see George Alexander, the theatre's manager, who was also acting a leading part in the play. Alexander reproached him for coming to the theatre at such a time, as people would be sure to consider it 'in bad taste'. Wilde laughingly replied that he might as well accuse every member of the audience of bad taste in coming to see the play. 'I would consider it in bad taste,' he added, 'if they went to see anyone else's play.'

Alexander then proffered this piece of advice: 'Why don't you withdraw from this case and go abroad?'

'Everyone wants me to go abroad,' replied Oscar in the same jesting mood. 'I have just been abroad, and now I have come home again. One can't keep on going abroad, unless one is a missionary, or, what comes to the same thing, a commercial traveller.'

About this time, possibly earlier that same day, Wilde had received similar advice from Frank Harris, formerly editor of *The Fortnightly Review*, to which Wilde had been a contributor.[1] He asked Harris if he would be a witness for him at the trial and

1. Frank Harris (1856–1931), journalist and adventurer. His first editorship was that of the London *Evening News*, which he obtained at the age of twenty-eight. His *Life and Confessions of Oscar Wilde*, though highly coloured and often untrustworthy as regards details, presents on the whole a not unfaithful portrait of its subject. The best account of Harris is by Hugh Kingsmill in his brilliant study *Frank Harris* (1932); see also the 'authorized' biography by the American writers A. I. Tobin and Elmer Gertz (1931), the biography by Vincent Brome (1959), the Introduction to my edition of Harris's play *Mr and Mrs Daventry* (1956), and Harris's own privately printed *My Life and Loves*, which has been published in a drastically expurgated edition in England under the title *Frank Harris: His Life and Adventures* (1947).

testify that in his opinion *The Picture of Dorian Gray*, one of the works which had been singled out for attack by Queensberry in his plea of justification, was a moral story. Harris declined, urging his friend to flee, but on being implored to reconsider his decision he asked Wilde to join him next day at the Café Royal where he had a luncheon engagement with Bernard Shaw. The story of this celebrated encounter has been told by Harris, Shaw, and Douglas (who was also present), and though they differ as to minor details they are agreed on the main outlines.

First of all [argued Harris] we start with the assumption that you are going to lose the case against Queensberry. You don't realize what is going to happen to you. It is not going to be a matter of clever talk about your books. They are going to bring up a string of witnesses that will put art and literature out of the question. Clarke will throw up his brief. ... You should go abroad, and, as ace of trumps, you should take your wife with you. Now for the excuse. I would sit down and write such a letter as you alone can write to *The Times*. You should set forth how you have been insulted by the Marquess of Queensberry and how you went naturally to the Courts for a remedy, but you found out very soon that this was a mistake. No jury would give a verdict against a father, however mistaken he might be. The only thing for you to do, therefore, is to go abroad, and leave the whole ring with its gloves and ropes, its sponges and pails to Lord Queensberry. You are a maker of beautiful things, you should say, and not a fighter, whereas the Marquess of Queensberry takes joy only in fighting. You should refuse to fight with a father under these circumstances. ... But don't stay here clutching at straws like testimonials to *Dorian Gray*. ... I know what is going to happen. ... I know what evidence they have got. You must go.

Shaw, when appealed to, agreed with the force of this argument, and like Harris also he was surprised at the attitude of sulky intransigence which it provoked on the part of the other two. 'Your telling him to run away shows that you are no friend of Oscar's,' said Douglas, getting up from the table. 'It is not friendly of you, Frank,' added Wilde as he followed the younger man out of the restaurant.

There can be no doubt that this line of conduct was reckless in the extreme. Although neither Harris nor Shaw was aware of it at the time, both Wilde and Douglas had already seen Queensberry's amended plea of justification, so that they must have realized that the tactics which the defendant was likely to employ at the trial would take the Court far beyond the relatively innocent realm of the prosecutor's published writings. The only possible explanation has been given by Douglas himself. He was most anxious that the case against his father should proceed, and he naturally resented any arguments in favour of its abandonment. During the meeting in the Café Royal he was, as he subsequently put it in a letter which he wrote to Harris many years later (1925), 'terribly afraid that Oscar would weaken and throw up the sponge.' Hence his desire to get him out of the restaurant as soon as possible, which he did in a manner not noticeably marked by courtesy. 'I did not tell you our case for fear I might not convince you,' he continued in this letter, 'and that you and Shaw might, even after hearing it, argue Wilde out of the state of mind I had got him into.'

What Douglas described as 'our case' was really his private case against his father, and he failed to see at this stage, or at any time subsequently, that the evidence he wished to give would be held inadmissible in any English Court of law. It rested on the mistaken belief that Sir Edward Clarke would begin by launching a violent attack against Queensberry. In later years Douglas liked to assert that he had obtained a promise from Clarke that he would put him into the witness box to prove his father's true character – a claim which, it may be added, has been emphatically denied by Sir Edward Clarke. ('I made no such agreement or promise.') Douglas certainly appears to have expected that he would be allowed to depict Queensberry as outwardly pretending to be a solicitous father trying to save his son, whereas in fact he had behaved like an inhuman brute towards every member of his family. Douglas did not appreciate – indeed he never grasped the point as long as he lived – that such evidence as this had nothing to do with the issue to be decided at the trial, and that, even if he did go into the box, he would never be permitted to give it. 'The question of Lord Queensberry's character was quite irrelevant to the case, and was never mentioned in my instructions or in consultation,' wrote Sir Edward Clarke in answer to a correspondent who had raised the point when *The Autobiography of Lord Alfred Douglas* was published in 1929; 'and if an attempt had been made to give such evidence the judge would of course have peremptorily stopped it.'

The sole issue which the jury would have to decide was a simple one of fact. Did Oscar Wilde pose as a sodomite? If the jury found that he did not, then Queensberry was guilty of libel. On the other hand, if they found that he did, Queensberry was not guilty.

CHAPTER 3

THE FIRST TRIAL

1

THE trial of Lord Queensberry on a charge of criminally libelling Oscar Wilde opened at the Old Bailey on 3 April 1895, before Mr Justice Henn Collins, an excellent criminal judge, later Lord Collins of Kensington.[1] Like Oscar Wilde and Edward Carson, who were in reality the principal protagonists in the case, Henn Collins was also an Irishman and had been educated at the University of Dublin. The trial took place, not in the commodious building which houses the present Central Criminal Court, but in the dingy courtroom, the scene of so many grim tragedies in the past, which was pulled down with the surrounding structure a few years later. The prosecution was represented by Sir Edward Clarke, Q.C., M.P., Mr Willie Mathews and Mr Travers Humphreys, while Mr Edward Carson, Q.C., M.P., along with Mr Charles Gill and Mr Arthur Gill appeared for the defence. Mr Edward Besley, Q.C., and Mr J. L. Monckton held watching briefs for Lord Alfred Douglas and Lord Douglas of Hawick.[2]

As the Court filled up more than an hour before the judge was due to take his seat on the Bench, someone made a joke about 'the

1. Richard Henn Collins (1842–1911) was appointed a judge of the Queen's Bench Division of the High Court in 1891. He became Master of the Rolls in 1901 and went to the House of Lords as a Lord of Appeal in 1907 with the grant of a life peerage.
2. Lord Douglas of Hawick, elder brother of Lord Alfred Douglas, and heir to the Marquessate of Queensberry since Lord Drumlanrig's death, had become acquainted with one of the youths mentioned in the defendant's plea of justification – Ernest Scarfe – whom he had first met on his way out to Australia in 1893. For this reason it was considered desirable for him to be legally represented. He subsequently went bail for Wilde.

97

importance of being early,' which raised a laugh. Soon there was not a seat or corner to be had, while the gangways were crowded with curious bystanders. It was observed, however, that no ladies were present. First of the parties to arrive was Lord Queensberry. He came in alone and stood, hat in hand, in front of the dock, an insignificant and unaristocratic looking figure with his drooping lower lip and red whiskers. He was seen to be wearing a Cambridge blue hunting stock instead of the more conventional collar and tie. He spoke to nobody and nobody spoke to him. He was followed some time later by Wilde, who immediately sat down in front of his counsel and began to talk to them in animated tones. Though smartly dressed in a frock coat and wearing a flower in his buttonhole, he seemed to be in a more serious frame of mind than he had shown at the Police Court, and he asked for a glass of water to be placed in front of him and handed to him when he went into the box. He is also said to have smiled at Carson, who looked coldly past him. Meanwhile, in the seats reserved for the defendant's solicitors, Mr Charles Russell was seen to be in conversation with Inspector Littlechild, the private detective who had been instrumental in procuring the evidence on which the defendant was relying to complete his plea of justification. In another room in the building, carefully guarded from further contamination by the outside world, a wretched band of youths was waiting to substantiate this evidence, laughing together and smoking cigarettes.

The judge was a little late; but when he appeared, no time was wasted on preliminaries. In answer to the usual question put to him by the Clerk of Arraigns, the defendant in a clear voice pleaded not guilty and that the words complained of were true and published for the public benefit. As he did so he cast a glance of undisguised contempt in the direction of the prosecutor. Perhaps it should be added here that, had the charge been one of either treason or felony, instead of misdemeanour, Queensberry could have insisted on his right of being tried by his peers. As things were, of course, he was tried like a commoner. The only right he might have exercised, by virtue of his nobility, was that of remaining covered during the trial, although such a peculiar

Sir EDWARD CLARKE, Q.C., M.P.

By "Spy"

Front and back of the visiting card which the Marquess of
Queensberry left at the Albemarle Club

proceeding was probably regarded as obsolete by this date.[1] By the time the hands of the clock in the courtroom pointed to eleven o'clock, Sir Edward Clarke was well into his opening speech for the prosecution. This stout, short, and bewhiskered figure, albeit extremely dignified, who looked more like an old-fashioned parson than a successful Queen's Counsel, showed himself a master of the advocate's art on this occasion. Although in its studied moderation it did not commend itself to Lord Alfred Douglas, who had been hoping for an all-out attack on his father, the speech was nevertheless a remarkable forensic achievement. 'I never heard anything to equal it in all my life,' Carson said afterwards to a friend in the House of Commons. 'Both matter and manner were superb.' In particular, Clarke's synopsis of *The Picture of Dorian Gray*, which the defence had alleged in the plea of justification to be an immoral and obscene work, was delivered in admirably chosen language.

Clarke began by describing to the jury the circumstances in which Queensberry had published the libel complained of, by calling at Wilde's club and leaving his card with the grossly offensive words written on it, which Clarke read out. 'Of course,' said Clarke, 'it is a matter of serious moment that such a libel as that which Lord Queensberry wrote upon that card should in any way be connected with a gentleman who has borne a high reputation in this country. The words of the libel are not directly an accusation of the gravest of all offences. The suggestion is that there was no guilt of the actual offence, but that in some way or other the person of whom these words were written did appear – nay, desired to appear – and pose to be a person guilty of or inclined to the commission of the gravest of all offences. You will appreciate that the leaving of such a card openly with the porter of a club is a most serious matter and one likely gravely to affect the position of the person as to whom the injurious suggestion was made.'

The question which the jury had to determine was not merely

1. The last peer known to have enjoyed the privilege of remaining covered in Court was the fourth Earl of Abingdon at his trial for criminal libel by Lord Kenyon, C.J., in the Court of King's Bench at Westminster in 1794.

the fact of publication, that is, whether the card had been delivered by the defendant Queensberry, and whether the defendant's conduct could in any way be excused by strong though mistaken feeling. 'By the plea which the defendant has brought before the Court a much graver issue has been raised,' counsel continued. 'The defendant has said that the statement is true and that it is for the public benefit that the statement was made, and he has given particulars in the plea of matters which he has alleged to show that the statement is true in regard to Mr Oscar Wilde.'

As we have seen, Queensberry's lawyers had drawn up a written plea of justification of the libel, and this had been filed with the court, as they were legally obliged to do unless the defendant pleaded guilty. Before 1843 any plea of justification to a charge of criminal libel was inadmissible, and the old maxim 'The greater the truth, the greater the libel' applied. But by the Libel Act of 1843 such a defence was permitted for the first time, provided the defendant could also prove that the libel was published for the public benefit. He was also required to submit a written plea justifying the libellous statement. Although the prosecution was furnished with a copy of this plea, counsel in opening the case did not put it in detail to the jury, because the onus lay with the defendant to prove the truth of the libel. But he necessarily had to refer to it, as Clarke did in this instance.

'There is no allegation in the plea that Mr Oscar Wilde has been guilty of the offence of which I have spoken,' Clarke said, 'but there is a series of accusations in it mentioning the names of persons, and it is said with regard to those persons that Mr Wilde solicited them to commit with him the grave offence, and that he has been guilty with each and all of them of indecent practices. One would gather from the terms of the plea that Mr Wilde has been unsuccessfully soliciting these persons to commit the offence with him, and that, although that offence is not alleged to have been committed, he has been guilty of indecent practices. It is for those who have taken the responsibility of putting into the plea those serious allegations to satisfy you, gentlemen, if they can, by credible witnesses, or evidence which they think worthy of consideration and entitled to belief that these allegations are true. I can understand how it is that these statements have been put in the form in which they are found, for these people, who may be called upon to sustain these charges, are people who will necessarily have to admit in cross-examination that they themselves have been guilty of the gravest of offences.'

Clarke then went on to describe the course of Wilde's friendship with Lord Alfred Douglas and how Wilde had frequently been a welcome guest at Lady Queensberry's house at Salisbury and elsewhere and how Douglas had often stayed with Wilde and his wife. He mentioned the attempt to blackmail Wilde on the basis of his letters to Douglas, and like the good lawyer he was he endeavoured to anticipate the tactics of the defence by reading to the jury the text of the most allegedly compromising example, written by Wilde from a house he had rented in the country and relied upon by Queensberry in support of his case.

My own Boy,
    Your sonnet is quite lovely, and it is a marvel that those red rose-leaf lips of yours should have been made no less for the music of song than for madness of kisses. Your slim gilt soul walks between passion and poetry. I know Hyacinthus, whom Apollo loved so madly, was you in Greek days.
    Why are you alone in London, and when do you go to Salisbury? Do go there to cool your hands in the grey twilight of Gothic things, and come here whenever you like. It is a lovely place – it only lacks you; but go to Salisbury first.
    Always, with undying love,

Yours,

OSCAR

'The words of that letter, gentlemen, may appear extravagant to those in the habit of writing commercial correspondence', Clarke observed amid laughter, 'or those ordinary letters which the necessities of life force upon one every day. But Mr Wilde is a poet, and the letter is considered by him as a prose sonnet, and one of which he is in no way ashamed and is prepared to produce anywhere as the expression of true poetic feeling, and with no relation whatever to the hateful and repulsive suggestions put to it in the plea in this case.'

Wilde's counsel then turned to the conduct of Lord Queensberry preceding his arrest and his ill-mannered attempts to interfere between his son and the prosecutor. ('Whether Lord Queensberry was responsible for his actions is a matter on which you, gentlemen of the jury, may have some doubts before this case has ended.') Finally, Clarke dealt with what he described as two 'extremely curious' allegations at the end of the defendant's plea of justification. The first was that in July 1890 Wilde had published, with his name on the title-page, 'a certain immoral and indecent work with the title of *The Picture of Dorian Gray*, which work was intended to be understood by the readers to describe the relations, intimacies, and passions of certain persons guilty of unnatural practices.' The second allegation was that in December 1894 there appeared a magazine entitled *The Chameleon* 'relating to the practices of persons of unnatural habits'; and that Wilde had joined in procuring the publication of this magazine, with his name on it, as the principal contributor, under the title of 'Phrases and Philosophies for the Use of the Young'. 'Those are two very gross allegations,' observed Clarke, 'and I defy my learned friend Mr Carson to suggest from these contributions anything hostile to the character of Mr Wilde.'

The Chameleon was a new Oxford undergraduate magazine, and Wilde had indeed contributed 'Phrases and Philosophies for the Use of the Young' to the first number, at the request of the editor. Clarke described his contribution as 'epigrammatical statements such as those which many of us have enjoyed when being entertained by such a play as *A Woman of No Importance* – they give brilliancy and effect to dialogue and they even supply wisdom in a witty form.' Unfortunately the same issue of the magazine contained a story called 'The Priest and the Acolyte', which Clarke described as 'a disgrace to literature'. This story had in fact been written by the editor, an undergraduate of Exeter College named J. F. Bloxam. Directly Wilde saw it he wrote to the editor and indignantly insisted that the copies should be withdrawn and the magazine suppressed. 'It is strange indeed, then,' said Clarke, 'to find that publication put upon the particulars as justifying the charge against Mr Wilde.'

'As for the first allegation,' Clarke concluded, 'the volume called *The Picture of Dorian Gray* is one which can be bought at any bookstall in London. It has Mr Wilde's name on the title page and has been published five years. The story of the book is that of a young man of good birth, great wealth, and great personal beauty, whose friend paints a picture of him. Dorian Gray expresses the wish that he could remain as in the picture, while the picture aged with the years. His wish is granted, and he soon knows that upon the picture, and not upon his own face, the scars of trouble and bad conduct are falling. In the end he stabs the picture and falls dead, and the picture is restored to its pristine beauty, while his friends find on the floor the body of a hideous old man.

'I shall be surprised if my learned friend Mr Carson can pitch upon any passage in that book which does more than describe as novelists and dramatists may – nay, must – describe the passions and fashions of life.'

At the conclusion of his opening, Clarke put the Albemarle Club porter in the box, where he repeated the formal evidence of publication of the libel which he had given at the Police Court. He was not cross-examined. Immediately afterwards the prosecutor followed him into the box, and Clarke began the examination-in-chief of his main witness. Wilde answered his counsel's questions with an easy assurance. 'The demeanour of Mr Wilde during his examination-in-chief was excellent,' noted Sir Edward Clarke afterwards. 'He was quiet and clear and definite in his evidence.' However, the statement that his age was thirty-nine caused Carson to cast a sharp glance in the direction of his old classmate and hastily make a note. When the witness was on the subject of his first meeting with Lord Alfred Douglas, the defendant asked for writing materials and from his place in the dock began to scribble furiously, the result ultimately being handed down to Carson by an usher.

During his opening speech, Sir Edward Clarke had unconsciously caused some amusement, first by his comments on the 'prose poem' letter to Douglas, and secondly by a slip of the tongue when in describing the defendant's grotesque appearance at the St James's Theatre with a bouquet of vegetables he inadvertently referred to Lord Queensberry as Lord Rosebery. This unseemly levity was rebuked in indignant tones by Wilde's leading counsel. A third outburst of laughter was caused during his examination-in-chief when his client quoted the defendant's remark when he called at Wilde's house in Tite Street: 'I do not say that you are it, but you look it.' This led the judge to intervene and threaten to have the Court cleared 'if there is the slightest disturbance again'.

The main part of the examination was naturally directed towards the defendant's plea of justification.

'It is suggested that you are responsible for the publication of the magazine *The Chameleon*, on the front page of which some aphorisms of yours appear. Beyond sending that contribution, had you anything to do with the preparation or publication of that magazine?'

'No. Nothing whatever.'

'Until you saw this number of *The Chameleon*, did you know anything about the story "The Priest and the Acolyte"?'

'Nothing at all.'

'Upon seeing that story in print, did you communicate with the editor?'

'The editor came to see me in the Café Royal to speak to me about it'.

'Did you approve of the story of "The Priest and the Acolyte"?'

'I thought it bad and indecent, and I strongly disapproved of it.'

'Was that disapproval expressed to the editor?'

'Yes.'

Slowly and in the most solemn tones, Sir Edward Clarke put his final questions to his client. Wilde answered them with equal solemnity.

'Your attention has been drawn to the statements which are made in the pleadings referring to different persons and impugning your conduct with them?'

'Yes.'

The First Trial

'Is there any truth in any of these accusations?'
'There is no truth whatever in any one of them.'

2

Shortly before the luncheon adjournment, Queensberry's leading counsel rose from his place in the front row of barristers' seats in the Old Bailey courtroom to begin his cross-examination of the prosecutor. As he faced his old college classmate in the witness box, the two figures on whom every eye in court was now fixed presented a striking contrast. There was Wilde, dressed in the height of fashion, a flower in the buttonhole of his frock coat, and exuding an air of easy confidence; opposite him stood Carson, tall, saturnine, and with the most determined expression on his lantern-jawed countenance. The effect of Carson's questions was increased by his rich Irish brogue which, unlike Wilde, he had never lost. This famous cross-examination, which was not completed until the following morning, has long been a favourite theme with students of advocacy in the English courts and it has been justly held up as a brilliant forensic model. At the conclusion of the case it evoked a remarkable tribute from the bench. Carson's performance was particularly impressive because he was suffering from an extremely bad cold at the time.

The opening question immediately revealed the cross-examiner's skill. Carson always attached prime importance to this question. Yet when he went into Court on that April morning, he did not know what it was going to be in this case. Wilde's statement about his age gave Carson his cue.

'You stated that your age was thirty-nine. I think you are over forty. You were born on the 16th of October 1854?' Carson emphasized the point by holding up a copy of the witness's birth certificate.

Wilde appeared momentarily disconcerted, but he quickly recovered his composure. 'I have no wish to pose as being young,' he replied sweetly. 'You have my certificate and that settles the matter.'

105

'But', Carson persisted, 'being born in 1854 makes you more than forty?'

'Ah! Very well,' Wilde agreed with a sigh, as if to congratulate his opponent on a remarkable feat of mathematics.

It was a small point that Carson had scored in this duel of wits, but not without considerable importance. At the very outset Wilde had been detected in a stupid lie, the effect of which was not lost upon the jury, particularly when Carson followed it up by contrasting Wilde's true age with that of Lord Alfred Douglas, with whom Wilde admitted to having stayed at many places, including hotels, both in England and on the Continent. Furthermore, it appeared that Douglas had also contributed to *The Chameleon*, namely two poems. Wilde was asked about these poems, which he admitted that he had seen. 'I thought them exceedingly beautiful poems,' he added. 'One was "In Praise of Shame" and the other "Two Loves".'

'These loves,' Carson asked, with a note of distaste in his voice. 'They were two boys?'

'Yes.'

'One boy calls his love "true love", and the other boy calls his love "shame"?'

'Yes.'

'Did you think they made any improper suggestion?'

'No, none whatever.'

Carson passed on to 'The Priest and the Acolyte', which Wilde admitted that he had read.

'You have no doubt whatever that that was an improper story?'

'From the literary point of view it was highly improper. It is impossible for a man of literature to judge it otherwise; by literature, meaning treatment, selection of subject, and the like. I thought the treatment rotten and the subject rotten.'

'You are of opinion, I believe, that there is no such thing as an immoral book?'

'Yes.'

'May I take it that you think "The Priest and the Acolyte" was not immoral?'

'It was worse. It was badly written.'

106

The First Trial

'Was not the story that of a priest who fell in love with a boy who served him at the altar, and was discovered by the rector in the priest's room, and a scandal arose?'

'I have read it only once, last November, and nothing will induce me to read it again. I don't care for it. It doesn't interest me.'

'Do you think the story blasphemous?'

'I think it violated every artistic canon of beauty.'

'That is not an answer.'

'It is the only one I can give.'

'I want to see the position you pose in.'

'I do not think you should say that.'

'I have said nothing out of the way. I wish to know whether you thought the story blasphemous.'

'The story filled me with disgust. The end was wrong.'

'Answer the question, sir,' Carson rapped out sharply. 'Did you or did you not consider the story blasphemous?'

'I thought it disgusting.'

Professing himself satisfied with this reply, Carson turned to a particular incident in the story. 'You know that when the priest in the story administers poison to the boy, he uses the words of the sacrament of the Church of England?'

'That I entirely forgot.'

'Do you consider that blasphemous?'

'I think it is horrible. "Blasphemous" is not a word of mine.' When Carson put the passage in question to him and asked whether he approved of the words used by the author, Wilde repeated his previous opinion: 'I think them disgusting, perfect twaddle.'

'I think you will admit that anyone who would approve of such a story would pose as guilty of improper practices?'

'I do not think so in the person of another contributor to the magazine. It would show very bad literary taste. Anyhow I strongly objected to the whole story. . . . Of course, I am aware that *The Chameleon* may have circulated among the undergraduates of Oxford. But I do not believe that any book or work of art ever had any effect whatever on morality.'

'Am I right in saying that you do not consider the effect in creating morality or immorality?'

'Certainly, I do not.'

'So far as your works are concerned, you pose as not being concerned about morality or immorality?'

'I do not know whether you use the word "pose" in any particular sense.'

'Is it a favourite word of your own?'

'Is it? I have no pose in this matter. In writing a play or a book, I am concerned entirely with literature – that is, with art. I aim not at doing good or evil, but in trying to make a thing that will have some quality of beauty.'

'Listen, sir,' said Carson, picking up a copy of *The Chameleon*. 'Here is one of the "Phrases and Philosophies" which you contributed to this magazine: "Wickedness is a myth invented by good people to account for the curious attractiveness of others." You think that true?'

'I rarely think that anything I write is true.'

'"Religions die when they are proved to be true." Is that true?'

'Yes. I hold that. It is a suggestion towards a philosophy of the absorption of religions by science, but it is too big a question to go into now.'

'Do you think that was a safe axiom to put forward for the philosophy of the young.'

'Most stimulating.'

'"If one tells the truth, one is sure, sooner or later, to be found out."?'

'That is a pleasing paradox, but I do not set very high store by it as an axiom.'

'Is it good for the young?'

'Anything is good that stimulates thought at whatever age.'

'Whether moral or immoral?'

'There is no such thing as morality or immorality in thought.'

'"Pleasure is the only thing one should live for"?'

'I think that the realization of oneself is the prime aim of life, and to realize oneself through pleasure is finer than to do so

108

through pain. I am, on that point, entirely on the side of the ancients – the Greeks. It is a pagan idea.'

'What would be the effect of "Phrases and Philosophies for the Use of the Young" taken in connexion with such an article as "The Priest and the Acolyte"?'

'Undoubtedly it was the idea that might be formed that made me object so strongly to the story. I saw at once that maxims that were perfectly nonsensical, paradoxical, or anything you like, might be read in conjunction with it.'

It may be noted here that, although he experienced no difficulty in interpreting and elucidating these witty paradoxes, some of which he was at pains to point out were not intended to be taken too seriously, the fact that they had appeared alongside such a scabrous tale as 'The Priest and the Acolyte' was unfortunate for Wilde, since without doubt it inclined the jury in some measure towards the view that at least he had posed in the role which Queensberry attributed to him.

Carson now turned to *The Picture of Dorian Gray*, and it was noticed that the copy he held in his hand had paper covers; it was, in fact, the original version which had appeared in *Lippincott's Monthly Magazine* for July 1890. Carson suggested that owing to certain criticisms which had been made the work was modified a good deal before its publication in book form. This was denied by Wilde, though he admitted that additions had been made. 'In one case', he said, 'it was pointed out to me – not in a newspaper or anything of that sort, but by the only critic of the century whose opinion I set high, Mr Walter Pater – that a certain passage was liable to misconstruction, and I made an addition.'

A characteristic piece of verbal sparring followed, which Carson began by reading a couple of short sentences from the Introduction to *Dorian Gray*.

'"There is no such thing as a moral or an immoral book. Books are well written or badly written." That expresses your view?'

'My view on art, yes.'

'Then I take it, no matter how immoral a book may be, if it is well written, it is, in your opinion, a good book?'

109

'Yes, if it were well written so as to produce a sense of beauty, which is the highest sense of which a human being can be capable. If it were badly written, it would produce a sense of disgust.'

'Then a well-written book putting forward perverted moral views may be a good book?'

'No work of art ever puts forward views. Views belong to people who are not artists.'

'A perverted novel might be a good book?' Carson persisted.

'I don't know what you mean by a "perverted" novel,' Wilde answered crisply.

This gave Carson the opening he sought. 'Then I will suggest *Dorian Gray* is open to the interpretation of being such a novel?'

Wilde brushed aside the suggestion with contempt. 'That could only be to brutes and illiterates,' he said. 'The views of Philistines on art are unaccountable.'

'An illiterate person reading *Dorian Gray* might consider it such a novel?'

'The views of illiterates on art are unaccountable. I am concerned only with my own view of art. I don't care twopence what other people think of it.'

'The majority of persons come under your definition of Philistines and illiterates?'

'I have found wonderful exceptions.'

'Do you think that the majority of people live up to the position you are giving us?'

'I am afraid they are not cultivated enough.'

'Not cultivated enough to draw the distinction between a good book and a bad book?' The note of sarcasm in Carson's voice was unmistakable.

'Certainly not,' Wilde replied blandly.

'The affection and love of the artist of *Dorian Gray* might lead an ordinary individual to believe that it might have a certain tendency?'

'I have no knowledge of the views of ordinary individuals.'

'You did not prevent the ordinary individual from buying your book?'

'I have never discouraged him!'

The First Trial

Counsel now proceeded to read out several lengthy passages from this work, which he put to the witness. He began with the description given by the painter, Basil Hallward, of his first meeting Dorian Gray and the impression the encounter made upon him.

When our eyes met, I felt I was growing pale. A curious instinct of terror came over me. I knew that I had come face to face with someone whose mere personality was so fascinating that, if I allowed it to do so, it would absorb my whole nature, my whole soul, my very art itself. . . . He is all my art to me now. . . . You remember that landscape of mine, for which Agnew offered me such a huge price, but which I would not part with? It is one of the best things I have ever done. And why is it so? Because, while I was painting it, Dorian Gray sat beside me.

'Now I ask you, Mr Wilde, do you consider that that description of the feeling of one man towards a youth just grown-up was a proper or an improper feeling?'

'I think it is the most perfect description of what an artist would feel on meeting a beautiful personality that was in some way necessary to his art and life.'

'You think that is a feeling a young man should have towards another?'

'Yes, as an artist.'

The next passage was of a conversation between the painter and Dorian Gray, in which Basil Hallward declared his admiration for the younger man. When Carson began to read it, Wilde asked for a copy which he could follow, and he was given one of *Lippincott's*. 'I believe it was left out in the purged edition,' Carson remarked, in drawing Wilde's attention to the place.

'I do not call it purged.'

'Yes, I know that. But we will see.'

Carson continued reading:

'It is quite true that I have worshipped you with far more romance of feeling than a man usually gives to a friend. Somehow, I have never loved a woman. I suppose I never had time. . . . Well, from the moment I met you, your personality had the most extraordinary influence over me. I quite admit that I adored you madly, extravagantly, absurdly.

I wanted to have you all to myself. I was only happy when I was with you. When I was away from you, you were still present in my art. It was all wrong and foolish. It is all wrong and foolish still. . . . One day I determined to paint a wonderful portrait of you. It was to have been my masterpiece. It is my masterpiece. But, as I worked at it, every flake and film of colour seemed to me to reveal my secret. I grew afraid that the world would know of my idolatry. . . .'

'Do you mean to say that that passage describes the natural feeling of one man towards another?'

'It would be the influence produced by a beautiful personality.'

'A beautiful person?'

'I said "a beautiful personality". You can describe it as you like. Dorian Gray's was a most remarkable personality.'

'May I take it that you, as an artist, have never known the feeling described here?'

'I have never allowed any personality to dominate my art.'

'Then you have never known the feeling you described?'

'No. It is a work of fiction.'

'So far as you are concerned, you have no experience as to its being a natural feeling?'

'I think it is perfectly natural for any artist to admire intensely and love a young man. It is an incident in the life of almost any artist.'

'But let us go over it phrase by phrase,' said Carson, glancing down at the magazine in his hand. '"I quite admit that I adored you madly." What do you say to that? Have you ever adored a young man madly?'

'No, not madly,' Wilde answered without thinking. 'I prefer love – that is, a higher form . . .'

'Never mind about that,' Carson interrupted. 'Let us keep down to the level we are at now.'

'I have never given adoration to anybody except myself.'

'I suppose you think that a very smart thing?' said Carson, when the laughter which greeted this sally had subsided.

'Not at all,' replied Wilde, who seemed to be almost enjoying this part of Carson's cross-examination.

'Then you have never had that feeling?'

'No. The whole idea was borrowed from Shakespeare, I regret to say – yes, from Shakespeare's sonnets.'

This answer immediately put Carson on to another line of questioning. 'I believe you have written an article to show that Shakespeare's sonnets were suggestive of unnatural vice?'

'On the contrary, I have written an article to show that they are not. I objected to such a perversion being put upon Shakespeare.'[1]

This reply appeared to satisfy Carson, as he returned to his reading of *Dorian Gray*. '"I have adored you extravagantly."' He repeated the sentence in a tone of disgust.

'Do you mean financially?' Wilde queried.

'Oh, yes, financially! Do you think we are talking about finance?'

'I don't know what you are talking about,' said Wilde, attempting once more to be smart at Carson's expense.

'Don't you?' There was a grim look in Carson's face as he spoke to this irritating and self-assured witness. 'Well, I hope I shall make myself very plain before I have done.'

'"I was jealous of every one to whom you spoke."' Carson went on reading. 'Have you ever been jealous of a young man?'

'Never in my life.'

'"I wanted to have you all to myself." Did you ever have that feeling?'

'No. I should consider it an intense nuisance, an intense bore.'

'"I grew afraid that the world would know of my idolatry." Why should he grow afraid that the world should know of it?'

'Because there are people in the world who cannot understand the intense devotion, affection, and admiration that an artist can feel for a wonderful and beautiful personality. These are the conditions under which we live. I regret them.'

'These unfortunate people, that have not the high understanding that you have, might put it down to something wrong?'

Carson's sarcasm left Wilde unmoved. 'Undoubtedly,' he

1. *The Portrait of Mr W. H.*, which originally appeared in *Blackwood's Magazine*, July 1889.

113

agreed with his cross-examiner; 'to any point they chose. I am not concerned with the ignorance of others.'

Carson then mentioned a certain book in the story which Dorian Gray had received.

'Was the book to which you refer a moral book?'

'Not well written, but it gave me an idea.'

'Was not the book you have in mind of a certain tendency?'

'I decline to be cross-examined upon the work of another artist. It is an impertinence and a vulgarity.'

On being further pressed on the point, Wilde admitted that the book he had in mind in the particular passage was a French novel by J. K. Huysmans, entitled *À Rebours*. But when Carson persisted in his attempts to elicit the witness's view as to the morality of this work, Sir Edward Clarke appealed to the judge, who ruled against any further reference to it.[1]

The last passage which Carson read from Wilde's book described the painter's remonstration with Dorian Gray about his 'infamous reputation' and the fact that he had ruined the lives of several other men, including one who had committed suicide and another who had been obliged to leave England 'with a tarnished name'. Carson then asked Wilde whether this passage did not suggest a charge of 'unnatural vice'. Wilde admitted that it described Dorian Gray as a man of very corrupt influence, though there was no statement as to the nature of the influence. 'But as a matter of fact,' he added, 'I do not think that one person influences another, nor do I think there is any bad influence in the world.'

'A man never corrupts a youth?'

'I think not.'

---

1. *À Rebours* was first published in 1884. 'It was a novel without a plot,' wrote Wilde in the passage alluded to by Carson, 'and with only one character, being, indeed, simply a psychological study of a certain young Parisian, who spent his life trying to realize in the nineteenth century all the passions and modes of thought that belonged to every century except his own, and to sum up, as it were, in himself the various modes through which the world-spirit had ever passed, loving for their mere artificiality those renunciations that men have unwisely called virtue, as much as those natural rebellions that wise men call sin.'

'Nothing could corrupt him?'

'If you are talking of separate ages –'

'No, sir,' Carson broke in harshly. 'I am talking common sense.'

Wilde kept his temper, as he replied: 'I do not think one person influences another.'

'You don't think flattering a young man, making love to him, in fact, would be likely to corrupt him?'

'No,' Wilde replied emphatically.

3

Having covered Wilde's published writings, Carson passed on to the allegedly compromising letters Wilde had written to Lord Alfred Douglas, of which one, the so-called 'prose poem' letter, had already been read out by Wilde's counsel. In answer to Carson's questions Wilde explained that this particular letter had been written while Douglas was staying at the Savoy Hotel in London and Wilde was at Babbacombe, near Torquay. The letter was in answer to a poem Douglas had sent him.

'Why should a man of your age address a boy nearly twenty years younger as "My own Boy"?'

'I was fond of him. I have always been fond of him.'

'Do you adore him?'

'No, but I have always liked him.' Wilde then went on to elaborate upon the letter. 'I think it is a beautiful letter. It is a poem. I was not writing an ordinary letter. You might as well cross-examine me as to whether *King Lear* or a sonnet of Shakespeare was proper.'

'Apart from art, Mr Wilde?'

'I cannot answer apart from art.'

'Suppose a man who was not an artist had written this letter, would you say it was a proper letter?'

'A man who was not an artist could not have written that letter.'

'Why?'

'Because nobody but an artist could write it. He certainly could not write the language unless he were a man of letters.'

Oscar Wilde

'I can suggest, for the sake of your reputation, that there is nothing very wonderful in this "red rose-leaf lips of yours"?'

'A great deal depends on the way it is read.'

'"Your slim gilt soul walks between passion and poetry",' Carson continued. 'Is that a beautiful phrase?'

'Not as you read it, Mr Carson. You read it very badly.'

It was now Carson's turn to be nettled. 'I do not profess to be an artist,' he exclaimed, 'and when I hear you give evidence, I am glad I am not.'

These words immediately brought Sir Edward Clarke to his feet. 'I don't think my learned friend should talk like that,' he observed. Then, turning towards his client in the witness box, he added: 'Pray do not criticize my learned friend's reading again.'

This clash caused a buzz of excitement in the courtroom. When it had died down, Carson went on with his cross-examination, indicating the document he was holding in his hand. 'Is not that an exceptional letter?'

'It is unique, I should say.' Wilde's answer produced loud laughter in court, which was still largely on the side of the witness.

'Was that the ordinary way in which you carried on your correspondence?'

'No. But I have often written to Lord Alfred Douglas, though I never wrote to another young man in the same way.'

'Have you often written letters in the same style as this?'

'I don't repeat myself in style.'

Carson held out another sheet of paper. 'Here is another letter which I believe you also wrote to Lord Alfred Douglas. Will you read it?'

Wilde refused this invitation. 'I don't see why I should,' he said.

'Then I will,' retorted Carson.

> Savoy Hotel
> Victoria Embankment
> London

Dearest of all Boys,

Your letter was delightful, red and yellow wine to me; but I am sad and out of sorts. Bosie, you must not make scenes with me. They kill

116

me, they wreck the loveliness of life. I cannot see you, so Greek and gracious, distorted with passion. I cannot listen to your curved lips saying hideous things to me. I would sooner – than have you bitter unjust, hating. . . .

I must see you soon. You are the divine thing I want, the thing of grace and beauty; but I don't know how to do it. Shall I come to Salisbury? My bill here is £49 for a week. I have also got a new sitting-room. . . .

Why are you not here, my dear, my wonderful boy? I fear I must leave – no money, no credit, and a heart of lead.

Your own
OSCAR

'Is that an ordinary letter?' Carson asked, when he had finished reading it.

'Everything I wrote is extraordinary,' Wilde answered with a show of impatience. 'I do not pose as being ordinary, great heavens! Ask me any question you like about it.'

Carson had only one question to ask about this letter, but its effect was deadly. 'Is it the kind of letter a man writes to another?'

Wilde replied as best he could. 'It was a tender expression of my great admiration for Lord Alfred Douglas. It was not, like the other, a prose poem.' He added that he had been in the Savoy for about a month, while he also had his house in Tite Street, and that Douglas had been staying with him at the Savoy immediately before he wrote the letter.

So long as he remained on literary ground, even when questioned about his seemingly equivocal letters to Lord Alfred Douglas, Wilde more than held his own in the duel of wits with his fellow-countryman. But when Carson moved on to the witness's relations with certain other named individuals, which he did later in the afternoon, Wilde began to be less sure of himself, although he maintained his brilliant flow of repartee. The mention of the name of Alfred Wood, followed by the names of other blackmailers, introduced an ominous note into the cross-examination.

Asked first about Wood, Wilde explained that he had originally met him in the Café Royal in response to a telegram from Lord

Alfred Douglas. The same night he took him to supper at the Florence Restaurant in Rupert street, as Douglas had asked him to do what he could for the young man, who was looking for a job as a clerk. 'Otherwise it was rather a bore,' Wilde added. He admitted that he had given him £2 on this occasion, because Lord Alfred Douglas had asked him to be kind to him. Asked about the difference in their social positions, Wilde exclaimed: 'I don't care about different social positions.'

'I suggest that first you had immoral relations with him and then gave him money?'

Wilde denied this charge indignantly. 'It is perfectly untrue.'

'Did you consider that he had come to levy blackmail?' Carson went on.

'I did,' answered Wilde; 'and I determined to face it.'

'And the way you faced it was by giving him £30 to go to America?'

'That is an inaccurate description. I saw that the letters were of no value, and I gave him the money after he had told me the pitiful tale about himself, foolishly perhaps, but out of pure kindness.'

'Did you give him £5 more next day?'

'Yes. He told me that after paying his passage to America he would be left almost penniless. I gave him £5.' Wilde added that the meeting to discuss the letters was arranged by Alfred Taylor in his rooms in Little College Street.

'Did you not think it a curious thing that a man with whom you were on such intimate terms should try to blackmail you?'

'I thought it infamous, but Wood convinced me that such had not been his intention, though it was the intention of other people. Wood assured me that he had recovered all the letters.'

Wilde went on to describe how he noticed that the 'prose poem' letter was missing from the bundle and how Allen, followed by Clibborn, had subsequently called at his house in Tite Street and eventually handed over the letter.

'May I ask why you gave this man [Allen], whom you knew to be a notorious blackmailer, ten shillings?'

'I gave it out of contempt.'

'Then the way you show your contempt is by paying ten shillings?'

'Yes, very often.'

'I suppose he was pleased with your contempt?'

'Yes, he was apparently pleased at my kindness.' Wilde added that he told Allen that the letter was to be published in the form of a sonnet in an Oxford magazine, and that he would send him a copy of it. 'That was to show my indifference.'

'Did you ever have any of your beautiful letters, except the one found out, turned into a sonnet?'

'I require to read a great deal of modern poetry before I can say.'

'Come, sir, answer the question,' Carson barked out. 'Can you tell me if one, except this, was ever turned into a sonnet?'

'Well,' said Wilde, as if searching his memory, 'at the present moment I cannot recollect another.'

'Did you ever ask Lord Alfred Douglas to preserve that letter?'

'No.'

'And therefore you never thought of turning it into a sonnet until it was discovered?'

'I never did turn it into a sonnet,' answered Wilde. 'When the copy was sent to Mr Beerbohm Tree and I saw it, I at once thought it would turn into a sonnet.' (As we have seen, it had been turned into French verse by Pierre Louÿs, and the result published in *The Spirit Lamp*, an Oxford undergraduate magazine edited by Lord Alfred Douglas.)

Carson next proceeded to question the witness about the specific occasions on which Queensberry had alleged in his plea of justification that Wilde had committed sodomy or acts of indecency with certain named individuals. The first such occasion was said to be in February 1892 at the Albemarle Hotel, where Wilde admitted that he had stayed on the date in question.

'At that time were Messrs Elkin Mathews and John Lane, of Vigo Street, your publishers?'

'Yes.'

'Did you become fond of their office boy?'

This question made Wilde extremely indignant. 'I really do

not think that is the proper form for the question to be addressed to me in,' he said, his voice quivering with anger. 'I deny that was the position of Mr Edward Shelley, to whom you are referring. I object to your description.'

Carson allowed this outburst to pass without comment. He merely asked: 'What age was Mr Shelley?'

'I should think about twenty,' said Wilde. He added that he had first met him in the previous October when arranging for the publication of his books. He had later asked him to dinner at the Albemarle Hotel, when he was staying there.

'Was that for the purpose of having an intellectual treat?' asked Carson in tones of undisguised contempt.

'Well, for him, yes,' Wilde answered good-humouredly. 'We dined in my own sitting-room, and there was one other gentleman there.'

At this point Carson caused some surprise by telling the witness that he need not mention this gentleman's name; it would be sufficient if he wrote it down. This Wilde did from his place in the witness box on a sheet of paper, which was then handed to counsel by the court usher. (The name was that of Maurice Schwabe, who was a nephew of Lady Lockwood, wife of the Solicitor-General, Sir Frank Lockwood.)

'On that occasion did you have a room leading into a bedroom?'
'Yes.'
'Did you give him whiskies and sodas?'
'I suppose he had whatever he wanted. I do not remember.'

Questioned as to what happened later, Wilde stoutly denied that any improper conduct had taken place between them. 'He did not stay all night, nor did I embrace him,' he added.

Replying to further questions about his association with Shelley, Wilde said that he had invited him to his house and that he had dined with him and his wife. ('He expressed great admiration for my works.') The witness admitted that he had taken him to the Earl's Court Exhibition, to the Café Royal, and to Kettner's, as well as to the theatre and the Lyric Club. Had he ever given him any money? Yes, on three occasions; the first time £4, the second time £3, and the third time £5. The £3 was for his railway fare to Cromer, where Wilde and his family were staying but Shelley did not come and Wilde wrote to him saying he was not to send back the money.

Wilde also agreed that he had given young Shelley two books. One was a signed copy of the first edition of *The Picture of Dorian Gray*. The other was a novel entitled *The Sinner's Comedy* and inscribed 'From the Author to dear Edward Shelley'. On being handed the work in question, Wilde admitted that the inscription was in his handwriting. But, he added, 'That was purely a piece of nonsense. I was not the author of the book.'[1]

'Did you think this young man of eighteen was a proper or natural companion for you?'

'Certainly.'

Carson's next questions concerned another young lad named Alphonse Conway, whom Wilde admitted that he had met at Worthing and befriended. Carson suggested that he sold newspapers at the kiosk on the pier. 'No, I never heard that up to that time his only occupation was selling newspapers,' Wilde replied, raising another laugh. 'It is the first I have heard of his connexion with literature.'

'What was he?'

'He led a happy, idle life.'

'He was a loafer, in fact?'

'He seemed to me to be just enjoying life.'

'How old was he?'

'He was a youth of about eighteen.'

Asked how he had made his acquaintance, Wilde explained that when he and Lord Alfred Douglas were at Worthing they used to go out in a boat. One day young Conway helped the fisherman to get the craft into the water and Wilde suggested that they should ask Conway to come for a sail. Douglas agreed, and after that Conway and Wilde became great friends. Wilde admitted that he had asked him to lunch, and also that Conway had dined with him at his house and lunched with him at the Marine Hotel.

'Was his conversation literary?'

1. The author of *The Sinner's Comedy* was John Oliver Hobbes (Mrs Craigie), a popular novelist of the day. It was published in 1892.

'On the contrary, quite simple and easily understood. He had been to school where naturally he had not learned much.'

'He was a simple country lad?'

'He was a nice, pleasant creature. His mother kept a lodging-house, and his desire was to go to sea. He told me his father had been an electrical engineer and had died young.'

Pressed further about the nature of his relations with Conway, Wilde emphatically denied that he had met him by appointment one evening and taken him along the road towards Lancing, 'kissing him and indulging in familiarities on the way'. He also denied that he had ever given him any money, but he admitted that he had given him a cigarette case ('Alphonse from his friend Oscar Wilde'), a signed photograph of himself, and a book called *The Wreck of the Grosvenor.*

With a sudden dramatic gesture, Carson produced these gifts, together with a silver-mounted walking-stick, which Wilde had not mentioned, and held them up for the inspection of the jury. The faces of the twelve good men and true in the jury-box plainly showed signs of surprise.

'Were you fond of this boy?' continued Carson.

'Naturally,' Wilde answered, in an attempt to explain away the incident. 'He had been my companion for six weeks.' But worse was to come.

'Did you take the lad to Brighton?'

'Yes.'

'And provided him with a suit of blue serge?'

'Yes'.

'And a straw hat with a band of red and blue?'

'That, I think was his unfortunate selection.'

'But you paid for it?'

'Yes.'

'You dressed this newsboy up to take him to Brighton?'

'No. I did not want him to be ashamed of his shabby clothes.'

'In order that he might look more like an equal?'

'Oh, no! He could not look like that. No, I promised him that before I left Worthing I would take him somewhere, to some place to which he wished to go, as a reward for his being a pleasant

122

companion to myself and my children. He chose Portsmouth, as he was anxious to go to sea, but I told him that was too far. So we went to Brighton. We dined at a restaurant and stayed the night at the Albion Hotel, where I took a sitting-room and two bedrooms.'

'Did the bedrooms communicate by a green baize door?'

'I am not sure.'

Wilde added that they returned to Worthing next day. He had never taken any other boy to the Albion. 'I am quite certain of that.'

At this point Carson broke off his cross-examination, as it was the customary hour for the adjournment of the court at the end of the day.

4

When Carson resumed his cross-examination next morning, Wilde appeared considerably more subdued in the witness box than on the first day of the trial. Nevertheless he seemed confident that he would be able to explain everything satisfactorily, as he kept up a running fire of banter with the defendant's leading counsel.

Carson began by asking Wilde about his friendship with Alfred Taylor, whom Queensberry had alleged in his plea of justification had acted as a procurer of young men for Wilde. The witness stated that he had known Taylor for two and a half years ('I do not call him an intimate friend. He was a friend of mine.'), and that he had arranged the meeting with Wood about the letters to Douglas in his rooms in Little College Street. He had visited these rooms perhaps seven or eight times in all, usually to afternoon tea parties. He said he did not think that Taylor kept a servant.

'Did he use to do his own cooking?'

'I don't know. I don't think he did anything wrong.'

'I have not suggested that he did,' said Carson.

'Well, cooking is an art.'

'Another art?' Carson snorted. Then, after a pause during which Wilde remained silent, he continued: 'Did he always open the door to you?'

'No. Sometimes he did; sometimes his friends did.'

'Did his rooms strike you as being peculiar?'

'No, except that he displayed more taste than usual.'

'There was rather elaborate furniture in the rooms, was there not?'

'The rooms were furnished in good taste.'

'Is it true that he never admitted daylight into them?'

'Really!' Wilde spoke in shocked tones. 'I don't know what you mean.'

Carson proceeded to make himself plain. 'Well, was there always candle or gas light there?' 'No,' said Wilde.

'Did you ever see the curtains drawn back in the sitting-room'?

'When I went to see Taylor, it was generally in the winter about five o'clock – tea-time – but I am under the impression of having seen him earlier in the day when it was daylight.'

'Are you prepared to say that you ever saw the curtains otherwise than drawn across?'

'Yes, I think so,' Wilde replied after a moment's reflection.

'It would not be true, then to say that he always had a double lot of curtains drawn across the windows, and the room, day or night, artificially lighted?'

'I don't think so.'

'Can you declare specifically that any daylight was ever admitted into the room?'

'Well, I can't say as to that.'

'Were the rooms strongly perfumed?'

'Yes, I have known him to burn perfumes. But I would not say the rooms were always perfumed.' Then after another momentary pause to think, Wilde added: 'I am in the habit of burning perfumes in my own rooms.'

The jurymen now began to show by the shocked looks on their faces what they thought of this establishment, so different from their own respectable habitations, while the details which followed, both of the contents of Taylor's rooms and the kind of

124

youth who frequented them, did nothing to improve the un-favourable impression which had been created. For instance, did Wilde know that Taylor kept a lady's costume or fancy dress in his rooms? No, he did not, he assured Carson: nor had he ever seen Taylor with one on. 'He is a man of great taste and intelligence,' added Wilde, 'and I know he was brought up at a good English school.'

'Is he a literary man?'

'I have never seen any created work of his.'

'Did you discuss literature with him?'

'He used to listen. He was a very artistic, pleasant fellow.'

'Was he an artist?'

'Not in the sense of creating anything. He was extremely intellectual and clever, and I liked him very much.'

'Did you get him to arrange dinners at which you could meet young men?'

'No.'

'Now, did you not know that Taylor was notorious for introducing young men to older men?'

'I never heard that in my life.'

'Now, did you know that Taylor was being watched by the police?'

'No, I never heard that.'

'Has he introduced young men to you?'

'Yes.'

'How many young men has he introduced to you?'

'Do you mean of those mentioned in this case?' Wilde queried.

'No,' said Carson; 'young men with whom you afterwards became intimate.'

'About five.'

'They were young men whom you would call by their Christian names?'

'Yes. I always call by their Christian names people whom I like. People I dislike I call something else.'

'Were these young men all about twenty?'

'Yes; twenty or twenty-two. I like the society of young men.'

'What was their occupation?'

125

Oscar Wilde

'I do not know if these particular young men had occupations.'
'Have you given money to them?'
'Yes. I think to all five – money or presents.'
'Did they give *you* anything?' Carson emphasized the word
'you'.
'Me?' said Wilde, in apparent astonishment. 'Me? Oh, no!'
'Among these five did Taylor introduce you to Charles Parker?'
'Yes.'
'Did you become friendly with him?'
'Yes,' Wilde replied, seemingly unaware of the hidden trap in
Carson's question.
'Did you know that Parker was a gentleman's servant out of
employment?'
'No.'
'But if he were, you would still have become friendly with him?'
'Yes. I would become friendly with any human being I liked.'
'How old was he?'
'Really,' said Wilde, now becoming impatient. 'I do not keep
a census.'
'Never mind about a census,' Carson reproved the witness
sharply. 'Tell me how old he was?'
'I should say he was about twenty. He was young, and that was
one of his attractions.'
'Was he a literary character?'
'Oh, no!'
'Was he intellectual?'
'Culture was not his strong point. He was not an artist.'
'Was he an educated man?'
'Education depends on what one's standard is.'
'Where is he now?'
'I haven't the slightest idea. I have lost sight of him.' (At that
moment, Parker was in a side room off the Court, waiting to be
called to give evidence for the defence.)
'How much money did you give Parker?'
'During the time I have known him I should think about £4 or
£5.'
'Why? For what reason?'

'Because he was poor, and I liked him. What better reason could I have?'

'Did you ask what his previous occupation was?'

'I never inquire about people's pasts.'

'Nor their future?' Carson queried.

'Oh, that is problematical.' At this point, Sir Edward Clarke broke in: 'There is no use in arguing about that.'

'Where did you first meet him?' Carson continued.

'At Kettner's,' replied Wilde. 'I was introduced by Mr Taylor.'

'Did you become friendly with Parker's brother as' well?'

'Yes. They were my guests, and as such I became friendly with both of them.'

'On the very first occasion that you saw them?'

'Yes. It was Taylor's birthday, and I asked him to dinner, telling him to bring any of his friends.'

'Did you know that one, Parker, was a gentleman's valet, and the other a groom?' Carson asked sneeringly.

'I did not know it,' Wilde answered with conviction, 'but if I had I should not have cared. I didn't care twopence what they were. I liked them. I have a passion to civilize the community.'

'What enjoyment was it to you to entertain grooms and coachmen?'

'The pleasure to me was being with those who are young, bright, happy, careless, and free. I do not like the sensible and I do not like the old.'

'Taylor accepted your invitation by bringing a valet and a groom to dine with you?'

'That is your account, not mine.'

'Were they persons of that class?' Again there was a sneer in Carson's voice.

'I am surprised at your description of them.' Wilde sounded hurt. 'They did not seem to have the manners of that class. They seemed to me pleasant and nice. They spoke of a father at Datchet as a person of wealth – well, not of wealth, but of some fortune. Charlie Parker told me that he was desirous to go on the stage.'

'Did you call him "Charlie"?'

'Yes.'

'What did you have for dinner?' Carson continued his relentless probing.

'Well, really I have forgotten the menu,' Wilde answered with some petulance.

'Was it a good dinner?'

'Kettner's is not so gorgeous as some restaurants, but it was Kettner at his best.'

'With the best of Kettner's wines?'

'Yes, certainly.'

'All for the valet and the groom?'

'No, for my friends – for Mr Taylor, whose birthday it was.'

'You did the honours to the valet and the groom?'

'I entertained Taylor and his two guests.'

'In a private room, of course?'

'Yes, certainly.'

'Did you give them an intellectual treat?'

'They seemed deeply impressed.'

'During the dinner did you become more intimate with Charles than the other?'

'I liked him better.'

'Did Charles Parker call you "Oscar"?'

'Yes. I like to be called "Oscar" or "Mr Wilde".'

'You had wine?'

'Of course.'

'Was there plenty of champagne?'

'Well, I did not press wine upon them.'

'You did not stint them?'

'What gentleman would stint his guests?' Wilde somewhat incautiously asked the advocate. The opening was too good for Carson to miss. 'What gentleman would stint the valet and the groom?' he retorted in tones of blistering sarcasm.

This remark brought Sir Edward Clarke to his feet, and both he and his client protested vigorously. 'Really, Mr Carson!' Meanwhile there was a hum of excitement among the spectators in court.

Not in the least apologetic for what he had said to the witness, Carson pressed him further. Had he said at the dinner, referring to Charles Parker, 'This is the boy for me'? Certainly not. Had Wilde taken him back to the Savoy Hotel? No, he did not come to the Savoy at all. However, he admitted that other young men had visited him at this hotel.

'Did any of these men who visited you at the Savoy have whiskies and sodas and iced champagne?'

'I can't say what they had.'

'Do you drink champagne yourself?'

'Yes. Iced champagne is a favourite drink of mine – strongly against my doctor's order.'

'Never mind your doctor's orders, sir!' Carson rapped out.

'I never do,' Wilde answered sweetly. A roar of laughter followed this sally.

Replying to further questions about Charles Parker, Wilde stated that he had entertained him and Taylor at Kettner's about a week later and on this occasion the dinner had been arranged by himself. Taylor had also come to tea five or six times in rooms which he had taken in St James's Place. He had given Taylor a cigarette case and £3 or £4, 'as he was hard up and asked me if I could let him have the money'. He did not think that Parker was ever in his bedroom, unless he was putting on his coat to go out or something of that sort.

'Did improprieties take place there?'

'None whatever.'

'When he came to tea, what was he doing all the time?'

'What was he doing? Why, having his tea, smoking cigarettes, and, I hope, enjoying himself!'

'What was there in common between this young man and yourself? What attraction had he for you?'

'I delight in the society of people much younger than myself. I like those who may be called idle and careless. I recognize no social distinctions at all of any kind; and to me youth, the mere fact of youth, is so wonderful that I would sooner talk to a young man for half-an-hour than be – well, cross-examined in Court!'

'Do I understand that even a young boy you might pick up in the street would be a pleasing companion?'

'I would talk to a street arab, with pleasure.'

129

'You would talk to a street arab?' Carson inquired in shocked tones.

'Yes, with pleasure,' Wilde repeated. 'If he would talk to me.'

'And take him into your rooms?'

'Be it so.'

'Did you write him any beautiful letters?'

'I don't think I have ever written any letters to him.'

'Have you any letters of his?'

'Only one.'

Carson now read out the text of the following letter, which was alleged to have been written by Parker to the witness.

> 50 Park Walk
> Chelsea
>
> Dear Oscar,
>
> Am I to have the pleasure of dining with you this evening? If so, kindly reply by messenger or wire to the above address. I trust you can, and we can spend a pleasant evening.
>
> Yours faithfully,
>
> CHARLIE PARKER

Wilde's counsel must have thought that Carson was reading from a copy, as immediately he had finished Sir Edward Clarke intervened: 'I should like to see the handwriting!'

'We will see all about that,' Carson retorted. 'Parker himself will be here, which is better!'

This remark produced a gasp of amazement among the on-lookers in Court, since nobody thought that Parker would dare to go into the witness box and give evidence which in the circumstances would be bound to incriminate him.

'In March or April of last year,' Carson went on, 'did you go one night to visit Parker at 50 Park Walk, about half past twelve at night?'

'No.'

'Is Park Walk about ten minutes from Tite Street?'

'I don't know, I never walk,' said Wilde, as the Court still laughed with him.

'I suppose, when you pay visits, you always take a cab?'

'Always.'

The First Trial

'And, if you visited, you would leave the cab outside?'

'If it were a good cab!'

'When did you see Charles Parker last?'

'I don't think I have seen him since February of last year.'

'Did you ever hear what became of him?'

'I heard that he had gone into the army – enlisted as a private.'

'You saw in the papers of the arrest of Taylor and Parker?'

'Yes, I read that they were arrested.'

'You know that they were charged with felonious practices?'

'I knew nothing of the charges.'

'That when they were arrested they were in the company of several men in women's clothing?'

'I read in the newspapers that two men in women's clothes, music-hall artistes, drove up to the house and were arrested outside.'

'Did you not think it a somewhat serious thing that Mr Taylor, your great friend, and Charles Parker, another great friend, should have been arrested in a police raid?'

'I was very much distressed at the time, and wrote to Mr Taylor, but the magistrates took a different view of the case because they dismissed the charge. It made no difference to my friendship for him.'[1]

'Was this same Taylor lunching with you on Tuesday last?'

'Not lunching. He came to my house to see me.'

Other names rolled from Carson's uncompromising lips – Atkins, Scarfe, Mavor – and the faces of the middle-class jury grew longer and longer. The questions now had a particularity about them which made Wilde's leading counsel distinctly uneasy. What could a man like Wilde have in common with these men? Yet he admitted that he had given them all money or presents, having received nothing in return except the pleasure of their company. And, like Charlie Parker, these other young men had

1. On 12 August 1894 the police raided a club at 46 Fitzroy Street, London, having previously kept watch on the premises. Eighteen persons were taken into custody, including two in female dress. At the subsequent police court proceedings at Great Marlborough Street, two of the accused were bound over, while the remainder, including Taylor and Parker, were discharged.

131

either been introduced to Wilde by Taylor or else Wilde had met them in Taylor's company.

There was Fred Atkins, a bookmaker's tout, who wanted to go on the music-hall stage and asked Wilde to help him. ('I thought him pleasant and young . . . I heard him sing. He was interesting . . . we did not discuss literature. I would not have allowed him to. The art of the music-hall was as far as he got!') Wilde explained that he took him to Paris at the request of 'the gentleman who has been mentioned', who was to meet him there.[1] They stayed at a hotel with communicating bedrooms in the Boulevard des Capucines and Wilde entertained him there on behalf of 'the gentleman I have mentioned'.

'You dined with him?'

'Yes.'

'Gave him an excellent dinner?'

'I never have anything else. I do everything excellently!'

'Did you give him plenty of wine at dinner?'

'As I have said before, anyone who dines at my table is not stinted in wine. If you mean, did I ply him with wine, then I say "No!" It's monstrous, and I won't have it!'

'I have not suggested it,' said Carson.

'But you have suggested it before,' Wilde replied tartly.

'After dinner, did you give him a sovereign to go to the Moulin Rouge?'

'Yes. I went that night, I think, to a French theatre, and when I got back to the hotel, Atkins had gone to bed.' He denied that any impropriety with Atkins had taken place in Paris, adding that 'it would be an infamous lie for anyone to say so'.

Then there was Ernest Scarfe, whom Taylor had originally introduced to Lord Alfred Douglas at a skating rink and Wilde had invited to dine with himself and Taylor at Kettner's. So far as Wilde was aware, he had no occupation, although Wilde said he knew he had been in Australia 'at the gold diggings'.

'Did you know he was a valet and is a valet still?'

'No. I have never met him in Society, though he has been in my society, which is more important!'

1. Maurice Schwabe. See above, p. 120.

The First Trial

'Why did you ask him to dinner?'

'Because I am so good-natured! It is a good action to ask to dinner those beneath one in social station.'

Finally, there was young Sidney Mavor, a youth of rather better social standing, whom Wilde admitted that he had invited to spend a night as his guest at the Albemarle Hotel. 'I asked him to stay with me for companionship, pleasure, amusement,' he explained. 'I like to have people staying with me. I was passing through London, and I wanted his society, as he was a smart, pleasant young fellow.'

'And did you find pleasure in his society that night?' The question was cunningly barbed, but Wilde fended it off neatly. 'Yes, in the evening and at breakfast,' he replied. 'It amused and pleased him that I should ask him to be my guest at a very nice, charming hotel!'

Carson beckoned to the usher and handed him a photograph of Mavor to show the witness. 'Ah!' said Wilde, when he had glanced at it. 'Taken at a period earlier than that at which I knew him!' Carson next held up a cigarette case. 'No, really, I could not!' Wilde declared. 'I have given so many I could not recognize it.'

Once again the Court laughed with this amusing witness – but it was for the last time. A few moments later, Carson reached the climax of his cross-examination with a deadly thrust which at last penetrated Wilde's guard. The question which precipitated the catastrophe concerned a youth named Walter Grainger, whom Wilde admitted that he knew. How old was he? Well, said Wilde, he was about sixteen when he knew him. Wilde went on to explain that Grainger was a servant at a certain house in High Street, Oxford, where Lord Alfred Douglas had rooms. Wilde had stayed there several times, and Grainger had waited at table. 'I never dined with him,' he added. 'If it is one's duty to serve, it is one's duty to serve; and if it is one's pleasure to dine, it is one's pleasure to dine.'

'Did you ever kiss him?'

'Oh, dear no!' said Wilde, in a fatal moment of folly. 'He was a peculiarly plain boy. He was, unfortunately, extremely ugly. I pitied him for it.'

ugly

Quick as lightning Carson pressed home his advantage. 'Was that the reason why you did not kiss him?'

At last, the witness, who had so far shown remarkable self-restraint in the box, lost his temper. 'Oh! Mr Carson: you are pertinently insolent.'

'Did you say that in support of your statement that you never kissed him?' Carson persisted.

'No,' said Wilde, now nearing the verge of tears. 'It is a childish question.'

'Did you put that forward as a reason why you never kissed the boy?' Carson repeated the question.

'Not at all.'

'Why, sir, did you mention that this boy was extremely ugly?'

'For this reason. If I were asked why I did not kiss a door-mat, I should say because I do not like to kiss door-mats. I do not know why I mentioned that he was ugly, except that I was stung by the insolent question you put to me and the way you have insulted me throughout this hearing. Am I to be cross-examined because I do not like it? It is ridiculous to imagine that any such thing could have happened in the circumstances.'

'Then why did you mention his ugliness, I ask you?'

'Perhaps you insulted me by an insulting question.'

'Was that the reason why you should say the boy was ugly?'

At this point, Wilde began several answers almost inarticulately, but was unable to finish any of them. He tried pathetically to collect his thoughts, while Carson rapped out in staccato tones: 'Why? Why? Why did you add that?' At last Wilde managed to get out the words: 'You sting me and insult me and try to unnerve me – and at times one says things flippantly when one ought to speak more seriously. I admit it.'

'Then you said it flippantly?'

'Oh, yes, it was a flippant answer.'

But it was too late now for explanations. The damage had been done; and the foolish slip which caused it could not be covered up.

EDWARD CARSON, Q.C., M.P.

By "Lib"

Mr. JUSTICE HENN COLLINS

By "Quiz"

5

The remainder of Carson's sensational cross-examination was unspectacular. There were a few more questions about Grainger, whom Wilde admitted to having employed as an under-butler when he took a cottage for a month at Goring in the summer of 1893. He denied that Grainger had ever come into his bedroom or that any indecencies had taken place between them. He was also asked about a masseur at the Savoy named Antonio Migge, who used occasionally to massage him in the morning when he stayed in the hotel. But he strenuously denied that he had had boys in his bedroom or that any scandal had occurred there. Nor did he ever bring boys into his bedroom in Paris, he said.

'Only one question more. Would you know the waiter at the hotel in the Boulevard des Capucines in Paris?'

'Yes. I think I would.'

With this Carson gathered up his papers and sat down. Wilde must have breathed a sigh of relief, although he still had some further questions to answer from his own counsel and explanations to offer of his association with the young men whose names had been mentioned.

Sir Edward Clarke began his re-examination by adopting the course, which he had hoped to avoid but to which he felt that Carson's detailed probing had left him with no alternative, of repeating aloud the contents of Queensberry's insulting letters and putting them to his client. The wording of these letters, in which, as we have seen, the writer betrayed the grossest malice towards his family, questioning as he did his son Alfred's legitimacy, created a great stir in Court. The defendant stood up in the dock, every now and then grinding his teeth at Wilde and shaking his head in the most violent manner. The more moving passages in Clarke's monotonous recitation caused the Marquess to bite his lips as if in an effort to restrain his tears.

'Was it from these letters that you first learned that Lord Queensberry objected to your acquaintance with his son, Lord Alfred Douglas?'

'Yes.'

'Is there any foundation for the statement that your wife was petitioning for a divorce?'

'Not the slightest.'

'Your friendship, Mr Wilde, with Lady Queensberry and the other son has continued to the present?'

'Yes.' Wilde added that, having regard to the character of the letters, he had thought it right to disregard entirely the wishes contained in them. 'The letters were brought to my knowledge some time ago by the persons who received them.'

Having finished with this fresh evidence, Clarke now attempted to repair the damage caused by Carson's devastating cross-examination. First, he read a number of passages from *The Picture of Dorian Gray* in order to offset those read by Carson on the previous day. He also read a letter which Wilde had written in defence of the story to W. E. Henley, the editor of the *Scots Observer* and published in that journal at the time of the original publication.

It was necessary, Sir, for the dramatic development of this story, to surround Dorian Gray with an atmosphere of moral corruption. Otherwise the story would have had no meaning and the plot no issue. To keep this atmosphere vague and indeterminate and wonderful was the aim of the artist who wrote the story. I claim, Sir, that he has succeeded. Each man sees his own sin in Dorian Gray. What Dorian Gray's sins are no one knows. He who finds them has brought them.

Clarke next set out to dispel the unfavourable impression created by the mention of Alfred Taylor and his apparently dubious circle of male acquaintances. Wilde explained that he had been introduced to Taylor by 'the gentleman who has been referred to'. This gentleman, who had gone abroad and whom Wilde stated that he had not seen for the past two years, was 'a gentleman of good birth and repute'. (As we have seen, the gentleman in question, Maurice Schwabe, was a nephew by marriage of the Solicitor-General, Sir Frank Lockwood.) Speaking about Taylor, Wilde said that he knew he had lost a lot of money – he had, in fact, been declared bankrupt – but that he still retained a share in some business. 'I knew that he was educated at Marlborough School,' Wilde added.

'Has he any accomplishments?'

'Yes. He played the piano very charmingly.'

'Had you at the time of your introduction to him, or since, had any reason to believe that he was a disreputable and immoral person?'

'None whatever.' Wilde went on to say that he understood that the charge against Taylor and the others in connexion with the Fitzroy Street raid was for assembly at the place for unlawful and felonious purposes. 'He told me that the occasion was a benefit concert, and that he was asked to play the piano. . . . Two men came in women's dress to take part in the concert, and the police immediately broke in and arrested everybody in the place.'

'Was any impression left on your mind that Taylor was at all to blame?' Clarke asked.

'Certainly not,' said Wilde. 'I thought it monstrous!'

Wilde's counsel now turned to the case of Edward Shelley, the youth employed in the office of Wilde's publishers. The witness related how they had been introduced by Mr John Lane, one of the partners in the firm of Elkin Mathews and John Lane, as it then was, which was publishing one of his books.[1] 'I regarded Shelley as a very interesting personality,' said Wilde. 'He was thirsting after information, and had literary tastes. He admired my works, and I acknowledged that by sending him copies.'

'It appears that in the copies which have been produced the flyleaf has been torn out,' said Clarke. 'Did you write in those or in any other books anything that you would object to the whole world seeing?'

'Never in my life!' Wilde declared.

At this point the Court adjourned for luncheon. As they were leaving the building, Clarke explained to his client that his introduction of fresh evidence in the shape of Queensberry's letters gave Carson the right to cross-examine further and that Wilde might therefore have to undergo another ordeal in the witness box. 'Can they examine me about anything and

1. *Salomé.*

137

everything they choose?' Wilde asked his leading counsel. Clarke replied that this was so, and that Carson need not necessarily confine himself to Queensberry's letters, provided the judge had no objection. Wilde went on to inquire whether 'they' could question him about an incident which had not been mentioned at all. 'Certainly,' rejoined the advocate. 'What is it that is in your mind?' 'Well,' said Wilde, 'some time ago I was turned out of the Albemarle Hotel in the middle of the night and a boy was with me. It might be awkward if they found out about that!'

Sir Edward Clarke said nothing. But what his client had just told him worried him considerably. Could there be some foundation for Queensberry's allegations after all? he asked himself. And yet his client had solemnly assured him that they were absolutely false.

When the Court reassembled at two o'clock, Wilde was not in his place in the witness box. As we have seen, his counsel's introduction of fresh evidence in his re-examination had given his opponent the right to cross-examine upon it, and the rumour quickly went round the Old Bailey that Wilde had thrown up the case and was fleeing abroad rather than face Carson again. But the rumour turned out to be false, for about ten minutes later Wilde hurriedly appeared and apologized to the Bench for being late, explaining that the clock in the hotel where he had been lunching was wrong.

Clarke now resumed his re-examination at the point he had left off about Shelley. He read several letters which he had written to Wilde expressing great admiration for Wilde's writings. 'Such beauty of form and arts adds new flavour to life,' Shelley had written after attending the first night of *Lady Windermere's Fan.* 'How miserably poor everything seems beside it, except your books, but your books are a part of yourself.' In another letter, which Clarke seemed to think showed a certain morbid outlook, the writer said he wanted to go away 'and not remember', as he was preparing to lead a Christian life and accepted poverty as part of his religion, 'but I must have health'. Wilde said he gave Shelley £5 to enable him to go away for a change of air.

'Were there ever any relations between you and Edward

Shelley except the relations with a man of letters who admired his poetry and works, and one with whom he had come in contact?'
'Never on any occasion.'

Most of the rest of the re-examination was directed to showing with characteristic skill that in all he had done for the various young men whose names had been mentioned Wilde was activated by the highest motives. Nor had he any reason to suspect them of being immoral or disreputable persons, he said. 'Beyond reading the statements in the papers about the raid in Fitzroy Street,' Wilde added, 'I never saw any intimation that there was anything immoral in the nature of the young men – and in that case they were discharged.'

At the end of this re-examination, the foreman of the jury asked permission of the Bench to put some questions to the witness, and this was granted. Was the editor of *The Chameleon* a personal friend of the witness? No, he was not, said Wilde, who went on to repeat that he had only met him once. 'I first wrote to him to say that I had really nothing to give him at all,' Wilde declared. 'Afterwards I said that I would give him some aphorisms out of my plays. Some of them were unpublished. Some of those quoted yesterday are out of the play at present being performed at the Haymarket [*An Ideal Husband*], and there have been no complaints at the box office of any moral depreciation of the audience!'

'Was *The Chameleon* for private circulation?' continued the foreman.

'Oh, no.'

'We will hand in a copy,' said Sir Edward Clarke. 'Only one hundred copies were printed. They were for the public.'

The foreman of the jury had one more question. Was Mr Wilde aware of the character of the story 'The Priest and the Acolyte'? 'I was not,' said the witness. 'It came upon me as a great shock.'

If the onlookers expected another scintillating series of exchanges between Wilde and Carson, they were disappointed, since Queensberry's counsel intimated that he had no further questions to put by way of cross-examination. Wilde thereupon stepped down from the witness box and left the court.

139

Another surprise immediately followed, when Clarke made it clear that he did not intend to call any more witnesses, at least at that stage of the trial. 'My lord,' he addressed the judge, 'the case for the prosecution is closed for the present.' To this qualification Carson objected, but without success. 'Of course,' Clarke explained, 'I reserve to myself the power to call evidence to rebut anything that may be sprung upon me.'

'Broadly put, the case for the prosecution must close now,' Mr Justice Collins ruled, 'but at my discretion I may admit some other evidence.'

Everyone who followed the case in Court – at least all the lay onlookers – expected Clarke to put Lord Alfred Douglas in the box immediately Wilde had left it. The handsome, fair-haired young man was both ready and eager to give evidence, and great surprise was expressed on all sides when Clarke intimated that his case was closed and sat down. All sorts of reasons have since been advanced, many of them quite fantastic, as to why Wilde's counsel did not call Douglas at this stage. The suggestion, which has been made, that Clarke was in some mysterious and unconscious way subjected to certain social influences which prevented him from pursuing this course, can be dismissed as without foundation. Clarke did not care a jot for social influences – his exertions on his client's behalf in the 'Baccarat case' afford ample proof of that – and all who knew him or have studied his long career with attention must agree that he was, if anything, overscrupulous in his professional conduct. No doubt he consulted with Wilde on this occasion as to the line he actually took, if we may judge from the statement which Wilde himself issued to the press at the conclusion of the trial; and even Alfred Douglas, although he always lamented that he was not given the opportunity of going into the box and showing up his father for the brute that he was, as he subsequently told me, never doubted that Clarke acted otherwise than in what he considered to be the best interests of his client. In any event, for the reasons which have already been noticed, Douglas would not have been permitted to speak as to his father's behaviour towards his wife and family.

In later trials, in which he was called to give evidence, Douglas proved himself a forceful and at times almost terrifying witness, but at this period he was an unknown quantity. How he would have reacted in the face of Carson's fire is a matter of speculation. His testimony, in so far as he would have been allowed to give it, might have diverted some sympathy from Queensberry, but it is difficult to see how it could have secured his father's conviction. Besides this, if Clarke had called Douglas at all, it would almost certainly have been by way of rebuttal. Not being a lawyer, Douglas did not appreciate the rule of evidence which permits fresh facts to be adduced after the close of the defendant's case for the purpose of rebutting evidence given by the defendant upon those issues where the onus of proof lies with him. It was quite possible, in view of Queensberry's letters to his son, which had been read out in Court, that the defendant, when his turn came to go into the box, might be disposed to make the gravest allegations on the subject of his son's relations with Wilde. As a precautionary measure Clarke may have planned to call Douglas in rebuttal of these charges, if and when they were made. However, as events turned out, Queensberry never reached the witness box.

6

Carson's opening speech for the defence, which began shortly after three o'clock, was in his best vein. From the outset the great Irish advocate made it clear that his client adhered to all the charges he had put forward, and he called upon the jury as fathers to say whether Lord Queensberry was not justified in endeavouring by every means in his power to rescue his son from the baneful domination of the prosecutor. 'Gentlemen,' he thundered, 'from beginning to end, Lord Queensberry in dealing with Mr Oscar Wilde has been influenced by one hope alone – that of saving his son.

'Lord Queensberry came to know of Mr Wilde's character [continued Carson], of the scandals in connexion with the Savoy Hotel, that the prosecutor had been going about with young men who were not co-equal with him in position or in age, that he had been associating with men who, it will be proved beyond doubt, are some of the most immoral characters in London. I refer above all to the man Taylor, a most notorious character – as the police will tell the Court – who occupied rooms which were nothing more than a shameful den. Whether Taylor was or was not a procurer in this sense, the fact remains that on Tuesday last, the 2nd of April, he was in company with Mr Wilde at the latter's house in Tite Street and that *he has not been produced by the prosecution*. Taylor has in fact been the right-hand man of Mr Wilde in all the orgies in which artists and valets have taken part; and, if opportunity had only been given of cross-examining him, it might have been possible to get from him at least something as to what was going on near Fitzroy Square on the night of the raid there last year. Taylor is really the pivot of the case, for the simple reason that when the various witnesses for the defence are called and examined – as unfortunately will be necessary – as to the practices of Mr Oscar Wilde, it will be found that it was Taylor who introduced the young men to the prosecutor. Mr Oscar Wilde has undertaken to prove enough to send Lord Queensberry to gaol and to brand him as a criminal, but it is remarkable that the only witness who could have supported Mr Wilde's asseverance of innocence has not been called. Yet Taylor is a friend of Mr Wilde; and nothing, said the prosecutor, has happened to interrupt their friendship.

'It will be painful to be compelled to ask the various witnesses that will be called to describe the manner in which Mr Wilde has acted towards them; but, before the case is ended, you will be obliged to hear a good deal more of the extraordinary den which Taylor kept in Little College Street. Therefore, it is above all things necessary, when we have so much proved by his own admissions, that Mr Wilde should bring any witness he can to bear out his own explanations. We have heard a good deal of the gentleman whose name was written down. On each occasion when it was convenient to introduce somebody, this was the name which Mr Wilde gave, because he was out of the country. But Taylor is still in the country. Why has he not been called?'

The First Trial

When Carson stated that he was proposing to put into the witness box the various young men with whom it was alleged that Wilde had been criminally associated, the atmosphere in the crowded courtroom suddenly became tense, and Wilde's counsel realized that his client now stood in grave personal danger. In particular, there was the blackmailer Wood. 'But who is Wood?' said Carson. 'Why, he too is "Fred", one of Wilde's bosom companions, a friend of Taylor, one of the Little College Street lot! What, then, was the cause of the strained relations between Wilde and Wood? Why did Wilde give Wood £16? When I state that, previous to the possession of those letters, Wood had been carrying on certain practices with Wilde, you will have the key to the whole situation. That is one reason why Wilde would be anxious to get rid of the letters at any cost; and, when Wood came to levy blackmail, then Mr Wilde was very anxious that the man should leave the country. So he paid his passage and, after a farewell luncheon, he shipped him off to New York and, I suppose, hoped that he would never see him again.'

At this point Carson paused dramatically for a moment or two before continuing: 'But, gentlemen, as a matter of fact Wood is here and will be examined before you!'

A gasp of amazement went round the Court at these words, which Carson followed up almost immediately be re-reading Wilde's 'prose poem' letter to the jury.

'I am not here to say anything has ever happened between Lord Alfred Douglas and Mr Oscar Wilde,' he went on. 'God forbid! But everything shows that the young man was in a dangerous position in that he acquiesced in the domination of Mr Wilde, a man of great ability and attainments. Against that letter written by Mr Wilde to Lord Queensberry's son, Lord Queensberry protested; and I wish to know, gentlemen, are you for that protest going to send Lord Queensberry to gaol? Lord Queensberry was determined to bring the matter to an issue, and what other way was open to him than that which he has chosen?'

'Before you condemn Lord Queensberry, I ask you to read Mr Wilde's letter and to say whether the gorge of any father ought not to rise. I ask you to bear in mind that Lord Queensberry's son was so dominated by Mr Wilde that he threatened to shoot his own father. Gentlemen, Lord Queensberry did what he has done most deliberately, and he is not afraid to abide by the issue he has raised in this Court. When you have heard Wood's evidence, the whole story of the payment of those sums of money by Mr Wilde, and the mystery of those letters will be explained; and the suggestion that they were valuable manuscripts, which Mr Wilde desired to obtain, will be dissipated. As a matter of fact Mr Wilde knew that we had all the evidence, and he preferred to discount it as far as possible in advance.'

Carson had been on his feet for about an hour when the Court rose for the day, and Sir Edward Clarke went back to the Temple to consider what should best be done in the light of his opponent's imminent disclosures. That evening he considered the situation very carefully. In view particularly of what his client had told him earlier in the day, during the luncheon adjournment, Carson's speech had already assumed a very serious aspect, and there would be more to come on the following day. Wilde's counsel had appointed a consultation before the sitting of the Court next morning. That night he made up his mind to tell Wilde frankly, when he met him with his solicitor and junior counsel, that in view of the way the case had gone the jury must be expected to acquit Lord Queensberry. In these circumstances he thought it best for his client to withdraw from the prosecution and allow him to make a statement to the Court, consenting to a verdict as regards the charge of 'posing'. By thus admitting the lesser charge, which in fact had not been made out by the defence, Clarke hoped to prevent the intervention of the Public Prosecutor, a development which might lead to Wilde's arrest in open Court if the case were allowed to continue. Mathews, who was one of the two junior counsel, was for fighting the case to a finish, since, as he pointed out, the witnesses whom Carson had indicated his intention of calling were all self-confessed accomplices and themselves criminals whose testimony might well be discredited, and he regarded the case as far from lost. However, Clarke's advice prevailed and his client agreed with it.

The First Trial

When I saw Mr Wilde [Clarke subsequently wrote in his unpublished recollections of the trial], I told him that it was almost impossible in view of all the circumstances to induce a jury to convict of a criminal offence a father who was endeavouring to save his son from what he believed to be an evil companionship. I said that upon full consideration I advised him in his own interest to allow me to make that statement to the Court, and to withdraw from the prosecution; and I said that, if the case went to its end and the jury found that the accusations were justified, the judge would unquestionably order his arrest. He listened quietly and gravely, and then thanked me for my advice and said he was prepared to act upon it. I then told him that there was no necessity for his presence in Court while the announcement was being made. I hoped and expected that he would take the opportunity of escaping from the country, and I believe he would have found no difficulty in doing so.

Meanwhile Carson was again on his feet in Court, continuing his remorseless harangue.

'The wonder is', he told the jury, 'not that the gossip should have reached Lord Queensberry's ears, but that after it was known, this man Wilde should have been tolerated in society in London for the length of time he has. Well, I shall prove that Mr Wilde brought boys into the Savoy Hotel. The masseur of that establishment – a most respectable man – and other servants will be called to prove the character of Mr Wilde's relations with his visitors. Is there any wonder that reports of a scandal at the Savoy should have reached Lord Queensberry, whose son was living a portion of the time at the hotel?

'As to the boy Conway, Conway was not procured by Taylor – he was procured by Wilde himself. Has there ever been confessed in a Court of Justice a more audacious story than that confessed to by Mr Wilde in relation to Conway? He met the boy, he said, on the beach at Worthing. He knew nothing whatsoever about him excepting that he assisted in launching the boats. Conway's real history is that he sold newspapers at Worthing at the kiosk on the pier. . . . If the evidence of Mr Wilde is true – and I sincerely hope it is not – Conway was introduced to Mrs Wilde and her two sons, aged nine and ten. Now, it is clear that Mr Wilde could not take about the boy Conway in the condition he

145

found him in. So what did he do? And it is here that the disgraceful audacity of the man comes in. Mr Wilde procured the boy a suit of clothes to dress him up like a gentleman's son, put some public school colours upon his hat, and generally made him look like a lad fit and proper to associate with Mr Oscar Wilde. The whole thing in its audacity is almost past belief. Why, if the defence had proved the fact, instead of getting it from the mouth of the prosecutor, you would have said it was almost incredible. But why did Mr Wilde dress up Conway? If Mr Wilde were really anxious to assist Conway, the very worst thing he could have done was to take the lad out of his proper sp..ere, to begin by giving him champagne luncheons, taking him to his hotel, and treating him in a manner in which the boy could never in the future expect to live.'

At this moment, Sir Edward Clarke entered the Court with his junior counsel Willie Mathews and was seen to pluck Carson by the gown. A few moments' whispered conversation followed between the two leaders, Carson resumed his seat and Clarke rose to make the announcement which he had carefully prepared, and which he began by saying was made under a feeling of very great responsibility.

SIR EDWARD CLARKE: I think it must have been present to your lordship's mind that those who represent Mr Wilde in this case have before them a very terrible anxiety. They cannot conceal from themselves that the judgement that might be formed on the literature involved in this case, and upon the conduct which has been admitted, might not improbably induce the jury to say that Lord Queensberry in using the word 'posing' was using a word for which there was sufficient justification to entitle the father, who used those words under these circumstances, to the utmost consideration and to be relieved of a criminal charge in respect of his statement. And with this in our clear view, I and my learned friends associated with me in this matter had to look forward to this – that a verdict given in favour of a defendant upon that part of the case might be interpreted outside as a conclusive finding with regard to all parts of the case. And the

The First Trial

position in which we stood was this – that, without expecting a verdict in this case, we should be going through, day after day, an investigation of matters of the most appalling character. Under these circumstances I hope your lordship will think I am taking the right course, which I take after communicating with Mr Oscar Wilde, that is to say that, having regard to what has been referred to by my learned friend Mr Carson in respect of the matters connected with the literature and the letters, I feel we could not resist a verdict of not guilty in this case – *not guilty having reference to the word 'posing'*. Under these circumstances I hope you will think I am not going beyond the bounds of my duty, and that I am doing something to save, to prevent, what would be a most horrible task, however it might close, if I now interpose and say on behalf of Mr Oscar Wilde that I would ask to withdraw from the prosecution. And if you do not think that at this time of the case, and after what has taken place – if you do not think I ought to be allowed to do that on his behalf, I am prepared to submit to a verdict of not guilty, having reference, if to any part of the particulars at all, to that part of the particulars connected with the publication of *The Picture of Dorian Gray* and the publication of *The Chameleon*. I trust that this may make an end of the case.

MR CARSON: I do not know that I have any right whatever to interfere in any way with this application my learned friend has just made. I can only say, as far as Lord Queensberry is concerned, that if there is a verdict of not guilty, a verdict which involves that he has succeeded in his plea of justification, I am quite satisfied. Of course, my learned friend will admit that we must succeed upon the plea in the manner in which he has stated; and that being so, it rests entirely with your lordship as to whether the course suggested by my learned friend is to be taken.

MR JUSTICE COLLINS: Inasmuch as the prosecutor in this case is prepared to acquiesce in a verdict of not guilty against the accused, I do not think it is any part of the function of the judge or of the jury to insist on going through prurient details which can have no bearing on a matter already concluded by the assent of the prosecutor to an adverse verdict. But as to the jury putting any limitation upon the verdict of justification of the charge, which is 'posing as a sodomite' – if that is justified, it is justified; if it is not, it is not. And the verdict of the jury must be 'Guilty' or 'Not Guilty'. There can be no terms and no limitations. The verdict must be 'Guilty' or 'Not Guilty'. I understand him to assent to a verdict of 'Not Guilty', and, of course, the jury will return that.

MR CARSON: Of course, the verdict will be that the plea of justification is proved, and that the words were published for the public benefit.

SIR EDWARD CLARKE: The verdict is 'Not Guilty'.

MR JUSTICE COLLINS: The verdict is 'Not Guilty', but it is arrived at that by that process. I shall have to tell the jury that justification was proved; and that it was true in substance and in fact that the prosecutor had posed as a sodomite. I shall also have to tell them that they will have to find that the statement was published in such a manner as to be for the public benefit. If they find on these two points, the verdict will be 'Not Guilty'.

(*To the jury*) Your verdict will be 'Not Guilty'. But there are are other matters which have to be determined with reference to the specific finding of complete justification, and, as I told you, that involves that the statement is true in fact and substance, and that the publication is for the public benefit. These are the facts on which you will have to find, and if you find them in favour of the defendant, your verdict will be 'Not Guilty'. You will have to say whether complete justification has been proved.

After consulting together for a few moments without leaving the jury box, the jury returned a verdict of 'Not Guilty', finding that the plea of justification had been proved and that the defendant's words were published for the public benefit. A prolonged outburst of cheering amongst the onlookers in Court followed the declaration of this verdict, which the ushers made little attempt to suppress. Soon the news spread to the crowds in the street outside the Old Bailey. Before leaving the Bench, the judge awarded the defendant his costs and also ordered his discharge. Queensberry at once stepped out of the dock and joined his solicitor in the well of the Court. His formal discharge, which immediately followed, was accompanied by renewed applause from the spectators in the public gallery.

When Mr Justice Collins reached the judge's room, he sat down and penned a note to Queensberry's leading counsel. 'I never heard a more powerful speech or a more searching cross-exam,' he wrote. 'I congratulate you on having escaped most of the filth.'

By this time Wilde had left the building by a side door, and so he avoided the ribald scenes which met the eyes of Clarke and Carson when they emerged together shortly afterwards. Prostitutes were dancing on the pavement. 'What a filthy business!' Clarke exclaimed in disgust. 'I shall not feel clean for weeks.'

As soon as he had been released from Court, the victorious defendant sent a characteristic message to his unsuccessful adversary, on whom the tables were now to be savagely turned. 'If the country allows you to leave, all the better for the country!' said Queensberry. 'But, if you take my son with you, I will follow you wherever you go and shoot you!'

CHAPTER 4

THE SECOND TRIAL

1

IT WAS towards noon on the morning of 5 April when Oscar Wilde left the Old Bailey. He was accompanied by Lord Alfred Douglas and Robert Ross, who had remained in Court throughout the trial. Together they drove to a nearby hotel where Wilde wrote the following letter to the *Evening News*:

5 April 1895

To the Editor of the *Evening News*

Sir,

It would have been impossible for me to have proved my case without putting Lord Alfred Douglas in the witness box against his father. Lord Alfred Douglas was extremely anxious to go into the box, but I would not let him do so. Rather than put him into so painful a position, I determined to retire from the case, and to bear on my own shoulders whatever ignominy and shame might result from my prosecuting Lord Queensberry.

Yours, etc.,

OSCAR WILDE[1]

At the same time he sent his wife an urgent note telling her to see no one but her friends and not to let anyone into his bedroom or sitting-room in Tite Street except the servants.

Wilde dispatched these letters and lunched in the hotel with Douglas, while Ross went off to cash a cheque for Wilde for £200. They then went on to call at the offices of Messrs Lewis & Lewis, solicitors, in Ely Place. There they saw Sir George Lewis and asked him if he could suggest anything. 'What is the good of coming to me now?' exclaimed this shrewd old lawyer. 'I am powerless to do anything. If you had had the sense to bring Lord

1. This letter, of which the original is in my Wilde collection, was jotted down by Ross on the back of two hotel envelopes and signed by Wilde after consulting his solicitor. It was then apparently given to a reporter to take to the newspaper offices, so that it could appear in the afternoon editions.

Queensberry's card to me in the first place, I would have torn it up and thrown it in the fire, and told you not to make a fool of yourself.'

But even before this discussion took place Queensberry's solicitor had written to the Director of Public Prosecutions.

> 37 Norfolk Street
> Strand wc
> 5 April 1895

Hon. Hamilton Cuffe
    Director of Prosecutions
            RE OSCAR WILDE

Dear Sir,

In order that there may be no miscarriage of justice, I think it my duty at once to send you a copy of all our witnesses' statements together with a copy of the shorthand notes of the trial.

> Yours faithfully,
> CHARLES RUSSELL

In those days the Director of Public Prosecutions had his office in the Treasury building in Whitehall, and it was here that the decision was taken to apply for a warrant for Wilde's arrest after the Director had examined the papers he had received from Russell in the course of the morning, and after he had had an opportunity of speaking to Russell in person about an hour later. Particulars were also dispatched by hand to the House of Commons, where they were placed before the Home Secretary, Mr Asquith, and the Law Officers, Sir Robert Reid and Sir Frank Lockwood. It was at once agreed that a warrant should be applied for, and the Home Secretary gave instructions that wherever Wilde might be found he should be stopped. A little later, about 3.30 p.m., Detective-Inspector Brockwell of Scotland Yard, accompanied by one of the Treasury lawyers, appeared before Sir John Bridge, the Bow Street magistrate, to apply for the warrant. The magistrate did not immediately grant the application, but adjourned the Court for over an hour and a half. Whether this was to enable Wilde to catch the last train for the Continent, or because he wished to have time to read the documents forwarded by Charles Russell to Mr Hamilton Cuffe, is not clear. It has been said that the magistrate was careful to inquire the time of the boat-train's departure from the clerk of the court, and on receiving this information, to have fixed the time of the application a quarter of an hour later. The fact remains that it was not until past five o'clock, by which time the train had left, that Sir John Bridge actually signed the warrant for Wilde's arrest.

Meanwhile Wilde had gone to the Cadogan Hotel in Sloane Street where Alfred Douglas was staying. Robert Ross, who arrived there soon after lunch, advised him to proceed immediately to Dover and thence try to get over to France. Other friends apparently repeated this advice in the course of the afternoon. Even Wilde's wife, when Ross went to tell her what had happened at the Old Bailey, said between sobs: 'I hope Oscar is going away abroad.' But unfortunately Wilde could not make up his mind what to do, until it was made up for him by the force of events. He remained in a pathetic state of indecision lamenting that 'the train has gone' and that 'it is too late'. Soon after five o'clock Thomas Marlowe, who was then a reporter on the *Star*,[1] called at the hotel and asked to see Wilde. Wilde refused to see him, but sent Ross instead. The journalist then declared that he had just seen a message come through on the tape to the effect that the warrant had already been issued. Ross immediately went into the other room and gave the news to Wilde, who is stated to have gone 'very grey in the face'. Shortly before this, Douglas, who could stand the tension no longer, had gone off to the House of Commons to see his cousin, George Wyndham, and find out whether a prosecution was inevitable. Oscar sat on with his two friends, Robert Ross and Reginald Turner,[2] glumly waiting for

1. Thomas Marlowe (1868–1935) was later editor of the *Daily Mail* and chairman of Associated Newspapers Ltd.

2. Reginald Turner (1869–1938) was one of Wilde's most intimate friends; he helped Ross to nurse him during his final illness in Paris. He was the illegitimate son of the 1st Lord Burnham, proprietor of the *Daily Telegraph*: see Hesketh Pearson, *Oscar Wilde* (1947), p. 266. His letters, written at Wilde's deathbed, have been published by Hart-Davis in the Epilogue to *The Letters of Oscar Wilde* (1962).

the blow to fall and drinking glass after glass of hock and seltzer in an endeavour to steady his nerves.

About half past six there was a knock on the door of Room No. 53. Two men entered. 'Mr Wilde, I believe?' said one of them. 'Yes? Yes?' replied Wilde, who was seated in an armchair by the fireplace, smoking a cigarette. His two companions were seated by a table on which stood some half empty glasses. On the floor lay copies of the evening papers, which had evidently been scanned in haste and thrown aside. 'We are police officers,' said one of the visitors, 'and hold a warrant for your arrest on a charge of committing indecent acts.' The speaker was Inspector Richards of Scotland Yard, and he immediately added: 'I must ask you to accompany me to the police station.'

'Where shall I be taken to?' Wilde then asked.

'You will have to go to Scotland Yard with me and then to Bow Street.'

'Can I have bail?'

'I don't think you can,' replied the detective-inspector. 'But that is a matter for the magistrate to decide.'

'Well,' said Wilde, 'if I must go, I will give you the least possible trouble.'

Before accompanying the detective to Scotland Yard, Wilde asked if he might write a few lines to leave for Lord Alfred Douglas, and permission was granted. In the letter which he now wrote under the eye of the detectives and which he began 'My dear Bosie', he asked his friend to ask his brother Percy, Lord Douglas of Hawick, and also the theatrical managers George Alexander and Lewis Waller, at whose theatres Wilde's plays had been running, to attend to give bail at Bow Street police court. He also asked him to send a telegram to Humphreys, his solicitor, asking him to appear for him in court. 'Also', he added, 'come to see me.'[1]

As he struggled into his overcoat and picked up his gloves and a novel which he had been reading, the effects of the hock and seltzer which he had been imbibing throughout the afternoon

---

1. For the text of this letter, see Hart-Davis, p. 386. The original is in my collection.

were plainly noticeable. He was allowed to take the book with him.[1]

At Scotland Yard the warrant upon which Wilde had been arrested was read over to him. It charged him with committing acts of gross indecency with various male persons. Wilde put out his hand and asked to be allowed to read it. This he was not permitted to do. He then asked: 'What are the mentioned dates?' To this the inspector in charge replied: 'On the 20th March, 1893, and divers other dates.' Prisoner and escort then continued their journey to Bow Street police station, where the prisoner was booked in. In accordance with the current regulations he was searched, a proceeding which revealed £200 in £5 Bank of England notes, also several writs and a letter from Taylor. Taylor's letter showed that he (Taylor) knew he was being watched by Inspector Littlechild and that the detective had searched his room during his absence. The writs had been issued by various firms for money owing in respect of cigarette cases, jewellery, and other goods supplied by them to the prisoner. When these formalities were completed, Wilde was conducted to one of the cells, where he was locked up for the night.

At the time of his arrest, Wilde had asked Robert Ross to go along to his house in Tite Street and collect some clothes and other necessaries which he would require when in custody. In due course Ross arrived at Bow Street, but he was allowed neither to

1. Next morning the newspapers came out with the headlines: ARREST OF OSCAR WILDE. YELLOW BOOK UNDER HIS ARM. This gave rise to the erroneous impression, widely believed at the time and subsequently repeated by R. H. Sherard, Frank Harris, and others of Wilde's biographers, that the work which Wilde had been reading at the time of his arrest was *The Yellow Book*, the famous contemporary periodical. This was published by John Lane, of the Bodley Head, who was also Wilde's publisher. Actually the book in question was *Aphrodite*, a novel by Wilde's friend Pierre Louÿs, and it happened to have a yellow cover. That the contrary impression prevailed at the time is evidenced by the fact that an angry crowd demonstrated outside the offices of the Bodley Head in Vigo Street and broke the windows. 'It killed *The Yellow Book*,' John Lane used to say, 'and it nearly killed me.' Though popularly identified with this publication, in fact Wilde had no connexion whatever with *The Yellow Book*, and he never contributed to its pages. See J. Lewis May, *John Lane And The Nineties* (1936).

see the prisoner nor to leave the Gladstone bag which he had brought with him.[1] A little later Alfred Douglas appeared. He had succeeded in seeing his cousin George Wyndham in the lobby of the House of Commons, only to be told on the authority of the Attorney-General that his friend was to be prosecuted. Returning to the Cadogan Hotel, he found Wilde's letter with the news of his arrest, and so he had hurried off in a cab to Bow Street. He hoped somehow that he might be able to bail him out, and was much distressed when informed by the inspector on duty that on no consideration could his application be entertained. He was also told that, even if bail were subsequently granted by the magistrate, other sureties besides himself would certainly be required. Douglas then went on, at Wilde's previous suggestion, to the Haymarket and St James's Theatres, where Wilde's plays were running, and asked their respective managers, Lewis Waller and George Alexander, if they would be prepared to go bail for the author. Both refused.

That evening the sensational developments of the day were being discussed in hundreds of bars and clubs and homes throughout the country, and pundits of the 'I-told-you-so' type were sanctimoniously holding forth on the dangers of art and literature, at least when pursued by Mr Oscar Wilde. To their discredit the newspapers surpassed themselves in their vulgar gloating. 'And so a most miserable case is ended,' wrote the *Echo*, a London evening paper of the period. 'Lord Queensberry is triumphant, and Mr Oscar Wilde is "damned and done for". He may now change places with Lord Queensberry and go into the dock himself. He appears to have illustrated in his life the beauty and truthfulness of his teachings. He said, in cross-examination, that he considered there was no such thing as morality, and he seems to have harmonized his practice with his theory. The counsel for the

---

1. W. E. Henley, editor of the *National Observer*, wrote to Charles Whibley at this time: 'Yes: Bobbie it was who drove down with the dressing case. I hear that he is ill; and I am very glad to hear it. ... One cheerful feature of the situation is that Bob is scandalized beyond expression by the ingratitude of Oscar's pathics.' See John Connell, *W. E. Henley* (1949), pp. 298–9.

prosecution, the judge, and jury are entitled to public thanks for abruptly terminating the trial, and so preventing the publication of probably revolting revelations.'

But this desire on the part of the *Echo* to spare its readers' feelings was only a sham. Next day it did not hesitate to print what it called a 'detailed report' of the proceedings at Bow Street Police Court where the magistrate heard the first part of the evidence on which he ultimately committed Wilde for trial.

W. E. Henley, who edited the *National Observer*, repaid the kind sympathy which Wilde had shown him when his mother was dying, by publishing a leading article viciously attacking the unsuccessful prosecutor in the Queensberry trial.

There is not a man or woman in the English-speaking world possessed of the treasure of a wholesome mind who is not under a deep debt of gratitude to the Marquess of Queensberry for destroying the High Priest of the Decadents. The obscene imposter, whose prominence has been a social outrage ever since he transferred from Trinity Dublin to Oxford his vices, his follies, and his vanities, has been exposed, and that thoroughly at last. But to the exposure there must be legal and social sequels. There must be another trial at the Old Bailey, or a coroner's inquest – the latter for choice; and the Decadents, of their hideous conceptions of the meaning of Art, of their worse than Eleusinian mysteries, there must be an absolute end.[1]

Meanwhile messages of congratulation were pouring in on Queensberry. On being informed by one of the Sunday newspapers that a further pile of messages was waiting for him, the delighted Marquess said: 'You know, I have not much to do with distinguished people, but I had a very nice letter from Lord Claud Hamilton, and a kind telegram from Mr Charles Danby, the actor, with "Hearty Congratulations", et cetera. Various clubs have telegraphed also. Here is a message: "Every man in the City is with you. Kill the—!."'

1. *National Observer*, 6 April 1895. It is possible that the article was written by Charles Whibley, but in any event Henley must take the responsibility for it.

The Second Trial

2

Before his committal for trial on 19 April, Wilde was twice remanded in custody, since Charles Gill, who appeared for the prosecution, required three hearings before asking for a committal. On each occasion Wilde's defending counsel Travers Humphreys applied for bail, saying that sureties could be offered to any amount and pointing out that the prisoner had made no attempt to get away, although he knew for many hours prior to his arrest that a warrant might be issued. 'You can understand,' urged Travers Humphreys on the third occasion, 'that there are witnesses to be obtained for the defence, and it is very difficult for Mr Wilde to communicate with persons and prepare his defence unless he is to have the facilities of a man at liberty.' But the magistrate persisted in his refusal both in respect of Wilde and also of Alfred Taylor, who had also been arrested. 'In deciding what to do with a case of this kind,' declared Sir John Bridge from the Bench, 'I have to use my discretion according – in the words of a great judge – to the evidence given and the gravity of the accusation. With regard to the gravity of the case, I think there is no worse crime than that with which the prisoners are charged. As to the evidence, all I shall say is that I do not think it slight, and I shall therefore refuse bail.'

In the first part of this declaration the magistrate seems to have allowed his sense of righteous indignation to get the better of him, since he momentarily overlooked the fact that murder, rape and a good many other offences are unquestionably more serious than the misdemeanours with which Wilde and his fellow prisoner were charged. So far as the evidence went, however, the magistrate was on surer ground. The blackmailer Wood, the youth Charles Parker, and the bookmaker's tout Fred Atkins, all deposed to have been introduced to Wilde for immoral purposes, and each swore that misconduct had taken place between himself and Wilde at various times and in various places. Their statements were corroborated generally by two witnesses, a masseur and a

157

chambermaid respectively, who swore that in March 1893 they had seen Wilde in bed with a young man in the Savoy Hotel. The Police Court proceedings, which began on 6 April, continued on 11 April, and concluded on 19 April, were on the whole unspectacular. In reporting them, the daily press displayed the utmost animosity against Wilde, referring to him as 'described as a gentleman', and so forth.[1] At one point the magistrate, who, like the newspapers, seems to have had some difficulty in restraining his feelings, gave a remarkable example of judicial ignorance when he inquired what Kettner's was. It is scarcely credible that Sir John Bridge, who had sat as a magistrate for many years, should not have known of this celebrated restaurant, which was situated barely a mile distant from his own Court. Taylor, whose role as co-defendant was to be particularly unfortunate for Wilde, was brought into the dock when Gill was in the middle of

---

1. With the exception of one daily and one weekly journal, The *Daily Chronicle* and *Reynold's Newspaper*, the whole of the London press was uniformly hostile to Wilde. Lord Alfred Douglas protested publicly against this unfair attitude of the newspapers, to one of which he wrote the following:

I submit that Mr Oscar Wilde has been tried by the newspapers before he has been tried by a jury, that his case has been almost hopelessly prejudiced in the eyes of the public from whom the jury who must try his case will be drawn, and that he is practically delivered over to the fury of a cowardly and brutal mob.

Sir John Bridge, in refusing bail today, stated that he knew of no graver offence than that with which Mr Wilde is charged. Mr Wilde, as a matter of fact, is charged with a 'misdemeanour' punishable by two years' imprisonment with or without hard labour *as a maximum penalty*; therefore, the offence with which he is charged is, in the eye of the law, which Sir John Bridge is supposed to represent, comparatively trifling. I should very much like to know how, in view of that fact, Sir John Bridge can reconcile what he said with his conscience, and with his position as the absolutely impartial exponent of the law, and whether it is not obvious that, in saying what he did, he allowed his personal feelings on a particular point to override his sense of abstract justice, to the prejudice of the man charged before him. If a police magistrate of twenty years' experience shows such flagrant prejudice, what can be expected from the men who will at the Old Bailey form the jury of what the law humorously terms Mr Oscar Wilde's 'peers'? – *Star*, 20 April 1895.

examining one of his witnesses on the first day. He was a dark, clean-shaven man in his early thirties, who appeared well-dressed and greeted his fellow prisoner with a bow.[1]

Perhaps the most sensational moment, although its full implication was not generally realized till the trial, was when Atkins, in describing a visit he had made to Paris with Wilde, stated that on his return from the theatre one night to the hotel where they were staying, he found someone else in bed with Wilde. 'That was Schwabe,' he added in a low, hesitating tone. 'Leave that for the moment,' hurriedly interposed Gill. Reference had been made to a certain Maurice Schwabe during the Queensberry trial, as we have seen, but his name had been written down on a piece of paper and handed up to the judge without actually being mentioned.

While Wilde was making his first appearance before the Bow Street magistrate, Sir Edward Clarke went into his room in the Law Courts and wrote the following letter to the solicitor who had instructed him in the Queensberry case.

Royal Courts of Justice
6 April 1895

Dear Sir,

Having regard to the events of yesterday, I think it right to say that if Mr Oscar Wilde would like me to defend him at his trial my services shall be at his disposal, and in respect of services so offered I, of course, shall not accept any fees. Will you kindly communicate with Mr Oscar Wilde and ascertain his wishes.

Faithfully yours,
EDWARD CLARKE

C. O. Humphreys, Esq.

The solicitor replied the same day that he had seen his client, 'who wishes me to express to you his deepest gratitude for your very kind offer, which he most gladly accepts'. This magnanimous gesture, which also involved the gratuitous services of the two junior counsel who had been with him in the first trial, Willie Mathews and Travers Humphreys, was fully in keeping with

1. Taylor was offered his liberty if he would turn Queen's Evidence and testify against Wilde, but he refused.

Oscar Wilde

Clarke's reputation for personal integrity and his lofty conception of a barrister's duty. 'It was upon these terms', he modestly noted afterwards, 'that I appeared in all subsequent proceedings.' Needless to say, he was thoroughly reviled in certain quarters for his action in defending such a man as Wilde, although he was content to leave his client's interests in the Bow Street proceedings largely in the hands of his able junior, Travers Humphreys.[1]

When Gill had concluded his examination-in-chief of Charles Parker, the first of the Crown witnesses at Bow Street on 6 April, Humphreys announced that he intended to defend, but that the charge had taken his client 'by surprise' and that consequently he was not prepared to cross-examine Parker. The magistrate accordingly allowed the cross-examination of all the Crown witnesses to be postponed. On the resumption of the hearing on 11 April, Clarke – whose offer to defend Wilde without fee had in the meantime been accepted – came into Court and informed the magistrate that he had decided not to cross-examine any of these witnesses, 'as probably no cross-examination could affect the result as far as this Court is concerned, and so far as your action in the matter is concerned'; he also wished to shorten the Police Court proceedings as much as possible. Douglas subsequently blamed Clarke for his failure to cross-examine the Crown witnesses at Bow Street, which he said had resulted in Wilde and

1. Even the reputable *Law Journal* (13 April 1895) censured Clarke for defending Wilde without fee, although it later modified its attitude and sought to justify Clarke's conduct of the defence generally.

'The ludicrous suggestion which has been made in certain quarters that Sir Edward Clarke will suffer politically by his brilliant and strenuous advocacy in the Wilde case might well be passed over in silence were it not that the duty of counsel in defending prisoners is a subject on which many people entertain hazy ideas. It is not necessary to dwell on the supreme ability and courage with which Sir Edward Clarke fought his difficult and losing battle; everyone admits that fact, and indeed it forms the ground for the absurd rumour to which we have referred. We shall merely remark in passing that the English Bar has every right to be, and is to a man, proud of the brilliant intellectual power displayed in this case by one who is amongst the most distinguished of Nisi Prius advocates. ... The most strenuous defence is the right of even the worst criminals, and is in accordance with the best interests of society as a whole.' *Law Journal*, 1 June 1895.

WILLIE MATTHEWS

By "Spy"

TRAVERS HUMPHREYS

(From a contemporary photograph)

The Second Trial

Taylor being committed for trial. He even went so far as to assert in his autobiography that, if he had known as much about the law as he did at the time he wrote, he would have urged Wilde to request Clarke to retire from the case and let someone else – 'even any smart junior' – take over and cross-examine these witnesses. But this only shows how completely ignorant of the English criminal law Lord Alfred Douglas was. The depositions sworn by the Crown witnesses at Bow Street were so strong that committal in the case of both Wilde and Taylor was inevitable, as Clarke rightly realized, and there was nothing to be gained in unnecessarily prolonging the proceedings.

It was widely thought that Alfred Douglas would also be arrested. But the authorities had no evidence against the younger man, a fact revealed in an interesting letter written by George Wyndham, M.P., to his father within forty-eight hours of Wilde's arrest.[1]

Sunday, 7 April 1895

... I ought to tell you that I know on the authority of Arthur Balfour, who has been told the case by the lawyers who had all the papers, that W[ilde] is certain to be condemned, and that the case is in every way a very serious one, involving the systematic ruin of a number of young men.[2] Public feeling is fiercely hostile to him, among all classes.

There is no case against Bosie, but he has associated himself with W[ilde] up to the last moment; and is spoken of as having known the witnesses who will be called. Men like Arthur [Balfour] and Lord Houghton, who have spoken to me, speak in kind terms of him; but are unanimous in saying that he had better go abroad for a year or two. . . .

Bosie took it very well. He thought I was going to ask him to go at once, and began by saying that nothing on earth would make him leave London until the trial was over. You may be sure that nothing will: he is quite insane on the subject. . . . If W[ilde] was released, Bosie would do anything he asked, and no entreaty from you or his mother would weigh with him.

1. The full text of this letter was published many years later by Lord Alfred Douglas in his book *Without Apology* (1938).
2. These young men were nearly all accomplices and no evidence was given at the trials to show that Wilde had 'ruined' any of them.

Oscar Wilde

But W[ilde] is, humanly speaking, sure to be imprisoned. I told Bosie so; and he agreed that it was almost certain.

... Whatever is proved, it is common knowledge in London that there was a sort of secret society around the man Taylor. . . .

Wilde was removed from Bow Street to Holloway Prison, where he remained in custody from the date of his first remand until he was eventually released on bail on the jury's failure to reach a verdict after his first trial nearly a month later. During this period he was deserted by almost all his friends, with the conspicuous exception of Lord Alfred Douglas. In the case of a number of them, however, it must be admitted that their desertion was enforced, since, fearing for their own skins, they crossed in a troupe to the Continent, there to stay until the trials were over and they judged it safe to return. As for Douglas, he visited Wilde at Holloway every day down to the eve of the first trial, when, in response to a request from Sir Edward Clarke, who considered that his continued presence in London was prejudicial to his client, he too withdrew to France.[1]

On 13 April W. E. Henley, editor of the *National Observer*, wrote to another journalist, Charles Whibley, in characteristic language:

Yes: Oscar at bay was on the whole a pleasing sight. The air is alive with rumours, of course: but I believe no new arrests will be made, and that morality will be satisfied if Oscar gets two years: as, of course, he will. Why he didn't stay at Monte Carlo, once he got there, God alone knows. Seeing that . . . he returned to face the music, and play the roman fool to Caesar's Destiny, I can only conjecture that, what between

1. 'I left on the day before his trial at his own most urgent request,' Douglas explained afterwards to Henry Labouchere, 'and at the equally urgent request of his legal advisers, who assured me that my presence in the country could only do him harm, and that, if I were called as a witness, I should infallibly destroy what small chance he had of acquittal. Mr Wilde's own counsel absolutely declined to call me as a witness, fearing the harm I might do him in cross-examination.' From France, after the trial, Douglas also wrote a remarkable letter to W. T. Stead, at that time editor of the *Review of Reviews*, setting out his views on the whole case. For the text of this letter, which Stead declined to publish, see Appendix D.

162

The Second Trial

personal and professional vanity, he was stark mad. Be that as it may,
he is mad no more. Holloway and Bow Street have taken his hair out
of curl in more senses than one. And I am pretty sure that he is having
a damn bad time.[1]

The position in which Wilde now found himself undoubtedly
came as a great shock to him. He could not have believed it
possible. 'With what a crash this fell!' he wrote to his friend Mrs
Ada Leverson whom he called 'The Sphinx', one of the very few
who with her husband stood by him, on his third day in Holloway[2] 'Why did the Sybil[3] say fair things? I thought but to defend
him from his father; I thought of nothing else, and now – ' And
then some days later: 'My counsel seems to wish the case to be
tried at once – I don't – nor does Bosie; – bail or no bail, I think
we had better wait.' About the same time he wrote to another
friend, Robert Sherard: 'I am ill – apathetic. Nothing but Alfred
Douglas's daily visits quicken me into life, but even him I only
see under humiliating and tragic conditions.' Douglas has described these visits in his autobiography, how they sat facing each
other in one of a long row of boxes and separated by a long
corridor about a yard wide, which was patrolled throughout the
interview by a warder. As Wilde was slightly deaf, he had considerable difficulty in hearing what his visitor said owing to the
confused babel of voices from the adjoining boxes, where similar
interviews were taking place. As he looked at Douglas, and
Douglas looked at him, the tears would roll down his cheeks.

1. Connell, op. cit., p. 298.
2. Ada Esther Beddington (1862–1933) married Ernest David Leverson,
the son of a diamond merchant. Leverson had lent Wilde £500 for his legal
expenses in the Queensberry trial. She was a witty contributor to *Punch* and
other journals and was also a successful novelist. In her old age she wrote
some entertaining reminiscences of Wilde in an edition of his letters to her:
see *Letters to the Sphinx from Oscar Wilde* (1930). Sir Osbert Sitwell has
given an interesting account of her in the fifth volume of his autobiography,
Noble Essences (1950).
3. 'The Sybil' was a fortune-teller named Mrs Robinson, whom Wilde
and his wife had previously consulted. Constance Wilde wrote to her at this
time (19 April 1895): 'What is to become of my husband, who has so
betrayed and deceived me and ruined the lives of my darling boys? ...
What a tragedy for him who is so gifted.' See Hart-Davis, p. 389, note.

Although he finally agreed to his friend's departure to Calais, the event greatly depressed him. 'I don't know what to do,' he wrote at this time; 'my life seems to have gone from me. I feel caught in a terrible net. I don't know where to turn. I care less when I think he is thinking of me – I think of nothing else.'

The conduct of the press generally has already been noticed. One paper, in a shocking exhibition of bad taste, not to mention downright cruelty, described with glee an imaginary picture of the prisoner pacing up and down his cell at night like a caged beast. As Frank Harris wrote later, 'his arrest was the signal for an orgy of Philistine rancour such as even London had never known before. The puritan middle class, which had always regarded Wilde with dislike as an artist and an intellectual scoffer, a mere parasite of the aristocracy, now gave free scope to their disgust and contempt, and everyone tried to outdo his neighbour in expressions of loathing and abhorrence.[1] For example, pamphlets attacking him and containing the more salacious portions of the evidence given at Bow Street Police Court were hawked for sale in the streets of the metropolis.

Another calamity, which the major catastrophe brought in its train, was that his income immediately dried up at the source. His plays were taken off and the sales from his books practically ceased. Such of his books as were in print were struck out of the publisher's lists. *An Ideal Husband* was withdrawn from the Haymarket Theatre on the day after his arrest[2]; and, though by a seemingly ignoble compromise, as a result of which his name was

1. A friend and fellow countryman of Wilde's, the late W. B. Yeats, with whom I once discussed the subject, expressed himself in similar terms. He explained the unanimity of the mob by the fact that it had become hypnotized by a word or a notion, and showed the senseless behaviour of an individual under the effect of hypnotic suggestion. 'The rage against Wilde', said Yeats, who was living in London at the time, 'was also complicated by the Britisher's jealousy of art and the artist, which is generally dormant but is called into activity when the artist has got outside his field into publicity of an undesirable kind. This hatred is not due to any action of the artist or eminent man; it is merely the expression of an individual hatred and envy, become collective because circumstances have made it so.'

2. This play was put on a week later by Charles Wyndham at the Criterion Theatre, but was finally withdrawn after a fortnight.

The Second Trial

pasted over on the bills advertising *The Importance of Being Earnest* at the St James's Theatre, the life of this play was prolonged for a few weeks, it too came off.[1] Madame Sarah Bernhardt, the great French tragedienne, had some time ago agreed to produce *Salomé*, with herself in the name part, but on now being asked at Wilde's instance to advance some money on account of royalties, she ignored his request, although it was repeated several times.

A still worse blow fell when his creditors put the bailiffs into his house in Tite Street, and he was sold up. The sale, it may be added, was conducted by the auctioneer in scandalous conditions. Valuable pictures and first editions were knocked down for trifling sums. Other possessions, including some of the author's original manuscripts, were actually pilfered on the spot and were never subsequently recovered.[2]

Since Wilde and Taylor were not committed for trial until 19

1. John Lane, Wilde's publisher, who was in New York on business at the time, wrote home to a colleague: 'The London Theatres on Oscar are very amusing to me, retaining his plays and withdrawing his name! I might just as well have ripped out the title-pages and sold the books!' According to Lane's biographer, Lewis May, the publisher only withdrew Wilde's books from his catalogue under protest and in response to strong pressure exerted by six of the Bodley Head's leading authors: see J. Lewis May, *John Lane And The Nineties* (1936), p. 80. (May does not state the names of the authors, who also demanded and obtained the dismissal of Aubrey Beardsley from the joint editorship of *The Yellow Book*; but it is possible that they included Edmund Gosse and A. C. Benson, and almost certainly William Watson and the Rev. H. C. Beeching. Some years later, on the first publication of *De Profundis*, Beeching, then Canon of Westminster, preached a sermon in the Abbey condemning this work as 'a doctrine of devils'.) It may be added that Lane was extremely worried by the mention in the Queensberry trial of the name of one of his employees at the Bodley Head, Edward Shelley. So far as *The Importance of Being Earnest* is concerned, it is only fair to Sir George Alexander's memory to state the explanation of his action which has been given by his biographer, viz., that to help the author, whose financial condition he knew to be desperate, he hoped thereby to prolong the run of the play: see A. E. W. Mason, *Sir George Alexander and the St James's Theatre* (1935), p. 80.

2. They included *A Florentine Tragedy*, a play in blank verse written in 1893–4.

April, and as the next Old Bailey sessions were due to begin three days later, it would have been useless in point of time for their counsel to have applied for bail to a judge in chambers. However, Willie Mathews, on behalf of Wilde, did apply to Mr Justice Charles, when the sessions opened, to ask for his client's trial to be postponed until the following sessions on the grounds that the defence had not had proper time in which to prepare their case and further that 'in the state of popular feeling existing at the time Mr Wilde would not get a fair and impartial trial'. The application was opposed by Charles Gill for the Crown, and in the circumstances the judge felt that he could not accede to it. As to the defendant's not having a fair trial his lordship thought that 'any suggestion such as that was groundless'.

True bills having already been found by the Grand Jury against Wilde and Taylor, Mr C. O Humphreys, Wilde's solicitor, informed the press that his client intended to plead not guilty and that he would fight the case to the end.

3

Wilde's second appearance at the Old Bailey, his first in the dock, began on 26 April 1895. The presiding judge was Mr Justice Charles[1]; Mr Charles Gill, along with Mr Horace Avory (later the well-known judge),[2] and Mr Arthur Gill appeared for the prosecution; Wilde was represented by the same three counsel as at the previous trial while Mr J. P. Grain[3] appeared for Taylor,

1. Sir Arthur Charles (1839–1921) was appointed a judge of the Queen's Bench Division of the High Court in 1887. He retired in 1897 and was created a Privy Councillor in 1903. He was a distinguished authority on ecclesiastical law.

2. Sir Horace Avory (1851–1935) was appointed a judge of the King's Bench Division of the High Court in 1910 and received a knighthood in the same year. At the time of the Wilde trials he was one of the Junior Treasury Council at the Old Bailey. On his life, see Gordon Lang, *Mr Justice Avory* (1932).

3. John Peter Grain (1839–1916) had a large criminal practice. He was a brother of Corney Grain, the well-known entertainer, and his sister was married to the solicitor, C. O. Humphreys.

The Second Trial

who was jointly indicted with Wilde. The case for the Crown took three days to complete, the greater part of the third day being occupied with the reading of the evidence given at the Queensberry trial, which was put in verbatim.

Wilde and Taylor were charged under a single indictment containing twenty-five counts and alleging: (a) the commission of acts of gross indecency by both men contrary to the Criminal Law Amendment Act, 1885, section 11; and (b) conspiracy to procure the commission of such acts by Wilde. There was a further charge against Taylor of having acted as a procurer for Wilde. The first nine counts in the indictment referred to misconduct with the two Parker brothers; the next three to Frederick Atkins; two more to incidents at the Savoy Hotel; two to the young man Sidney Mavor; three to charges of conspiracy; five to the blackmailer Alfred Wood; and the last to Wilde's conduct in regard to Edward Shelley. In regard to Taylor, the most serious counts in the indictment charged him with attempting to commit the felony of sodomy with both the Parkers. To all these counts the prisoners pleaded not guilty.

This indictment presented an immediate difficulty. Before the year 1885, as the law then stood in England, no accused person could go into the witness box and give evidence on his own behalf. However, the Act of 1885 laid down that any person charged with an offence under that Act could give such evidence if he so wished, although he could not be compelled to do so. In regard to all other offences, both felonies and misdemeanours, including conspiracy, the law remained unchanged.

As soon as the indictment had been read out by the Clerk of Arraigns, Sir Edward Clarke rose to submit that the prisoners could not be called upon to plead to an indictment in this form, since in respect to the conspiracy charges they were not competent witnesses and therefore could not be called. As the counts were at present joined, he argued, the prisoners were liable to be cross-examined on charges to which they were debarred from giving evidence-in-chief should they choose to go into the witness box. Wilde's counsel therefore demurred to the indictment as containing inconsistent counts. The judge, however, ruled against

167

him on the ground that in his opinion the Act of 1885, in spite of making defendants competent witnesses, had not altered the general law with reference to the joinder of counts for misdemeanour. 'I feel the inconvenience of the present state of things,' added Mr Justice Charles, 'but at the same time I do not think that the fact that the prisoners are competent witnesses on some counts and are not competent witnesses on the other counts authorizes me to say that by law these counts cannot be joined in the same indictment.'

As soon as the prisoners had formally pleaded not guilty, Clarke again rose and asked the judge in the exercise of his discretion to put the prosecution to its election as to whether it would proceed with the counts of conspiracy or with the other counts.

'That is impossible,' said Mr Justice Charles. 'If the prisoners are called upon to give evidence at all, they may be cross-examined on the whole case, but they will be entitled to give evidence-in-chief only on the counts of the indictment under the Criminal Law Amendment Act. The fact that the dual indictment is inconvenient does not justify me in requiring the prosecution to abandon one section of it.'

Charles Gill then opened the case for the prosecution in a restrained speech to the jury. 'I must beg you to dismiss from your minds anything you may have heard or read about the prisoners and to abandon all prejudice towards either side, and to approach the case with absolutely open minds carefully and impartially.' Unfortunately the Crown counsel was asking the jury to do the impossible. The majority of the jurymen were no doubt already strongly prejudiced against both prisoners, and the details which Gill now gave them merely served to deepen these prejudices. More than anything else perhaps they were influenced by the description of Taylor's rooms in Little College Street, with their heavily draped windows, candles burning on through the day, and the langorous atmosphere heavy with perfume.

'Here men met together,' said Gill, 'and here Wilde was introduced by Taylor to the youths who will give evidence in this case. Wilde did not hesitate, soon after his first introduction to Taylor, to explain to him to what purpose he wished to put their acquaintance. Taylor was familiar with a number of young men, who were in the habit of giving their bodies, or selling them, to other men for the purpose of sodomy. It appears that there was a number of youths engaged in this abominable traffic, and that one and all of them were known to Taylor, who went about and sought out for them men of means who were willing to pay heavily for the indulgence of their favourite vice. It will be shown that Taylor himself was given to sodomy and that he has himself indulged in these filthy practices with the same youths as he agreed to procure for Wilde. . . . The case of the two Parkers may be given as a sample of the others, on which I prefer to dwell with less minuteness. It will be shown that Taylor corrupted these lads and induced them to meet Wilde by assuring them that he was liberal in his payments.'

Gill went on to describe the charges against Wilde as revealed in the course of the Queensberry trial and the subsequent proceedings at Bow Street Police Court, and he dealt in some detail with Wilde's alleged relations with Charles Parker, Atkins, Mavor and Wood. Coming to the case of Atkins, he said: 'This youth accompanied the prisoner Wilde to Paris, and there can be no doubt whatever that the prisoner endeavoured in the most systematic way to influence the young man's mind towards vicious courses and endeavoured to mould him to his own depraved will.' Counsel then read out a note from Taylor to Mavor, in which the writer asked Mavor to 'come at once and see Oscar at Tite Street'. 'The use of the Christian name of Wilde in so familiar a way', said Gill, 'suggests the nature of the acquaintance which existed between Mavor and Wilde, who was old enough to be the boy's father.' Finally counsel touched on the case of Shelley. 'There is a difference about Wilde's acquaintance with Shelley, the lad whom he met in the shop of his publishers, Messrs Mathews and Lane, where he was employed. It was an acquaintance with a literary side, but it went through the same stages.'

In his place in the dock beside Taylor, Wilde looked haggard and worn, his long hair was dishevelled, and it was plain to the spectators in Court that his confinement had begun to tell upon his physique. He appeared bored, too, by Gill's opening recitation but immediately showed interest when the witnesses were called. The first of these was Charles Parker, a somewhat brash youth who stepped into the witness box with a jaunty air and gave his age as twenty-one.

In reply to Gill's questions, Parker said he had been employed as a valet to a gentleman, but at the beginning of 1893 was out of work. He remembered one day at that time being with his brother William in the bar of the St James's Restaurant. While they were there, Taylor came up and spoke to them. 'He was an entire stranger,' said Parker. 'He passed the compliments of the day, and asked us to have a drink. We got into conversation with him. He spoke about men.'

'In what way?'

'He called attention to the prostitutes who frequented Piccadilly Circus, and remarked: "I can't understand sensible men wasting their money on painted trash like that. Many do, though. But there are a few who know better. Now, you could get money in a certain way easily enough if you cared to." I understood to what Taylor alluded and made a coarse reply.'

'I am obliged to ask you what it was you actually said?'

'I do not like to say.'

'You were less squeamish at the time, I dare say,' Gill remarked to this contemptible witness. 'I ask you for the words?'

After a slight hesitation, Parker replied in a low voice: 'I said that if any old gentleman with money took a fancy to me, I was agreeable. I *was* agreeable. I was terribly hard up.'

'What did Taylor say?'

'He laughed and said that men far cleverer, richer, and better than I preferred things of that kind.' Parker added that they parted after having given Taylor their address.

'Did Taylor mention the prisoner Wilde?'

'Not at that time.'

Asked when he first met Wilde, Parker said that he and his brother met Taylor by invitation next day at his rooms in Little College Street, and Taylor told them he could introduce them to a man 'who was good for plenty of money'. For this purpose

170

they arranged to meet Taylor the following evening at the St James's bar, which they did. Taylor then took them to a restaurant in Rupert Street, which Parker thought was the Solferino, and they were shown upstairs to a private room, where there was a dinner table laid for four. 'After a while,' Parker continued, 'Wilde came in and I was formally introduced. I had never seen him before, but I had heard of him. We dined about eight o'clock. We all four sat down to dinner, Wilde sitting on my left.'

'Who made the fourth?'

'My brother, William Parker. I had promised Taylor that he should accompany me.'

'Was the dinner a good dinner?' went on Gill.

'Yes,' said Parker. 'The table was lighted with red-shaded candles. We had plenty of champagne with our dinner and brandy and coffee afterwards. We all partook of it. Wilde paid for the dinner.'

'Of what nature was the conversation?'

'General, at first. Nothing was then said as to the purposes for which we had come together.'

'And then?'

'Subsequently Wilde said to me "This is the boy for me! Will you go to the Savoy Hotel with me?" I consented, and Wilde drove me in a cab to the hotel. Only he and I went, leaving my brother and Taylor behind. At the Savoy we went first to Wilde's sitting-room on the second floor.'

'More drink was offered you there?'

'Yes, we had liqueurs. Wilde then asked me to go into his bedroom with him.'

'Let us know what occurred there.'

'He committed the act of sodomy upon me.'

'With your consent?'

To this question the witness did not reply, and he was not pressed, since his consent was clearly implied by his behaviour. He went on to state that Wilde had given him £2 on this occasion, telling him to come back to the Savoy in a week. This the witness did, according to his story, one night about eleven o'clock, when they had a champagne supper, and Wilde afterwards committed

171

the same acts as on the first occasion. This time Parker said he got £3.

Asked about his subsequent meetings with Wilde, Parker said that he had met him in Chapel Street when he [Parker] was staying there with Taylor, 'and the same thing occurred as at the Savoy'. Wilde also visited him, he said, when he was living in Park Walk. 'I was asked by Wilde to imagine that I was a woman and that he was my lover. I had to keep up this illusion. I used to sit on his knees and he used to play with my privates as a man might amuse himself with a girl.'

One night, Parker went on, Wilde visited him at Park Walk about half past eleven or twelve. He came in a cab and drove away after staying about a quarter of an hour, having kept the cab waiting outside. In consequence of this incident Parker admitted that his landlady had give him notice and he had left.

'Apart from money, did Wilde give you any presents?'

'Yes, he gave me a silver cigarette case and a gold ring. I don't suppose boys are different to girls in taking presents from them who are fond of them.'

'You pawned the cigarette case and the ring?'

'Yes.'

Asked about other visits, Parker said that Taylor had given him the address of Wilde's rooms in St James's Place, and that he had been there in the morning and to tea in the afternoon. Wilde had a bedroom and a sitting-room opening into each other. Speaking of the misconduct which he alleged had taken place there, Parker said that Wilde invariably began his 'campaign' with indecencies. He used to require him to do what is vulgarly called 'tossing him off', explained Parker quite unabashed, 'and he would often do the same to me.' Parker gave other details equally shocking, and added: 'He suggested two or three times that I would permit him to insert "it" in my mouth, but I never allowed that.'

'Where else have you been with Wilde?'

'To Kettner's Restaurant.'

'What happened there?'

'We dined there. We always had a lot of wine. Wilde would

172

talk of poetry and art during dinner, and of the old Roman days.'

'On one occasion you proceeded from Kettner's to Wilde's house?' Gill prompted the witness's memory.

'Yes,' said Parker. 'We went to Tite Street. It was very late at night. Wilde let himself and me in with a latchkey. I remained the night, sleeping with the prisoner, and he himself let me out in the early morning before anyone was about.'

'Where else have you visited this man?'

'At the Albemarle Hotel. The same thing happened there.'

'Where did your last interview take place?'

'I last saw Mr Wilde in Trafalgar Square about nine months ago. He was in a hansom and saw me. He alighted from the hansom and spoke to me.'

'What did he say?'

'He asked me how I was and said "Well, you are looking as pretty as ever!"' Parker added that he did not ask him to go anywhere with him then.

The remainder of the examination-in-chief of this witness was concerned with the other prisoner. According to Parker, Taylor had told him when Parker and his brother were staying in Little College Street and sleeping with Taylor, that he [Taylor] had gone through a form of marriage with a youth named Mason, that Taylor was in a woman's dress, and that they had a wedding breakfast.

'Who else did you meet at Little College Street?'

'Atkins, Wood, and Scarfe, amongst others.'

'Did you continue your acquaintance with Taylor until a certain incident occurred last August? You were arrested in the course of a police raid on a certain house in Fitzroy Street?'

'Yes.'

'Orgies of the most disgraceful kind used to happen there?'

'Yes.'

This last exchange brought Taylor's counsel, J. P. Grain, to his feet. 'My lord,' he addressed the judge, 'I must protest against the introduction of matter extraneous to the indictment. Surely I have enough to answer!'

The protest had its effect. The Crown counsel did not press the witness for details of what had gone on in the house in Fitzroy Street, but contented himself with explaining that he wished to show that Parker had ceased his acquaintance with Taylor after the incident of the raid. Then, continuing his examination, he asked Parker: 'When did you cease your association with Taylor?'

'In August 1894. I went away into the country and took up another occupation.'

'What was the occupation?' interposed the judge.

'I enlisted,' Parker replied. He then went on to say that, while he was with his regiment, he was seen by Lord Queensberry's solicitor, who took down a statement from him.

'Until you became acquainted with Taylor had you ever been mixed up with men in the commission of indecent acts?'

'No, never.'

This concluded Gill's examination-in-chief of Charles Parker. His cross-examination by Sir Edward Clarke, which followed, was designed to show that not only was this witness a self-confessed accomplice in the offences he described, but he also was a blackmailer and an associate of blackmailers. Clarke began by reminding him that he had admitted at Bow Street that he had received £30, part of moneys extorted from a gentleman with whom he had committed acts of indecency, not to say anything about the case.

'I don't ask the name of the gentleman from whom the money was extorted, but I do ask the names of the two men who got the money and gave you £30?'

'Wood and Allen.'

'You had had indecent behaviour with the gentleman in question?'

'Yes. But only on one occasion – at Camera Square, Chelsea.'

'Where you were living?'

'Yes.'

'Did the gentleman come to your room?'

'Yes.'

'By your invitation?'

'He asked me if he could come.'

'And you took him home with you?'

'Yes.'

'How much did Wood and Allen tell you they got?'

'I can't remember.'

'Try and remember!' Clarke pressed the witness.

There was a pause. Then Parker blurted out: '£300 or £400.'

'Was the £30 the first sum of money you received under circumstances of that kind?'

'Yes.'

'What did you do with the £30?'

'Spent it.'

'And then went into the army?'

'I spent it in about a couple of days.'

'I'll leave that question. You say positively that Mr Wilde committed sodomy with you at the Savoy?'

'Yes.'

'But you have been in the habit of accusing other gentlemen of the same offence?' Clarke again pressed the witness.

'Never,' replied Parker, adding somewhat incautiously, 'unless it has been done!'

'I submit that you blackmail gentlemen?'

'No, sir. I have accepted money, but it has been offered to me to pay for the offence. I have been solicited. I have never suggested this offence to gentlemen.'

At counsel's request the witness wrote down the name and address of his late employer, with whom he said he had been in service as a valet for nine or ten months. He added that he did not leave this place without a character.

'Did you not say that your employer had stated that you had stolen some clothes?'

'Yes.'

'How did you know that he had said so?'

'He wrote and told me so, and asked me to send the things back, which I did. They were not clothes, they were shirts and collars.'

'Well, I call them clothes,' said Clarke. 'Did you have a written character?'

'Yes.'

175

'But was not that written before the robbery of the clothes was discovered?'

'Yes,' Parker answered with obvious reluctance. 'That is so.'

'When Taylor asked you if you ever went with men and got money for it, did you understand what he meant?'

'Yes.'

'You had heard of such things before?'

'Yes.'

'Then it was with the intention of entering upon such practices that you called upon Taylor?'

'No.'

'Then why did you call upon him?'

'Because he asked me to.'

'You meant to go with men and get money?'

'Yes.'

'You understood the practices you were going to enter upon?'

'Yes.'

'When you allowed yourself to be introduced to Mr Wilde, you knew perfectly well the purpose for which the introduction was made?'

'Yes.'

'At the dinner Mr Wilde was the principal conversationalist, I suppose?'

'Yes.'

'And you found him a brilliant and amusing talker?'

'Yes. I told him that I wanted to get some employment on the stage. I knew that Mr Wilde was a dramatist and had much to do with theatres, and I suggested that he might help me. He showed curiosity about my family and affairs, and I told him my father was a horse dealer.'

The rest of Clarke's cross-examination was mainly directed to showing that there was no attempt on Wilde's part to conceal any of the visits Parker paid to him at the Savoy and elsewhere. At the Savoy, for instance, Parker admitted that he gave his name, was shown up to Wilde's suite, and in going away did not attempt to avoid any of the servants.

'Were Mr Wilde's rooms on the ground floor of St James's Place very public ones?'

'Yes. There were menservants about. The sitting-room was a sort of library. There were a good many books about.'

'Do you suggest that in rooms such as you have described and so situated this kind of conduct went on again and again?'

'Yes.'

Finally, Parker admitted that he had heard that Wood had gone to America and that he had in his possession some letters written by Wilde. 'I thought he had taken them away with him.' The witness added that he had also heard – he could not remember from whom – that Wood got the letters out of some clothes which were given to him by Lord Alfred Douglas. 'I never saw the letters,' he said.

Asked by Gill in re-examination if he knew Lord Alfred Douglas, the witness replied that he did and that Taylor had introduced him. 'I know that the letters referred to belonged to Lord Alfred Douglas,' he went on. He added that until he met Taylor he also did not know Atkins, Wood, Allen, or Cliburn.

'When did you first make the acquaintance of Wood?'

'About six months before he went to America.'

4

Charles Parker was followed into the witness box by his brother William, the groom, who, it will be remembered, had made the fourth at the dinner given by Wilde in honour of Taylor's birthday. In corroborating the previous evidence that on this occasion Wilde had paid all his attention to his brother Charles, William Parker was able to add some interesting details to Charles's testimony. He stated that during the meal Wilde often fed his brother off his own fork or out of his own spoon, that his brother accepted a preserved cherry from Wilde's own mouth. ('My brother took it into his, and this trick was repeated three or four times.') Charles then went off to the Savoy with Wilde, while he [William Parker] remained behind with Taylor who remarked:

'Your brother is lucky! Oscar does not care what he pays if he fancies a chap.'

'What did you do after the dinner?' Clarke asked him in cross-examination.

'I went home after having had a drink or two.'

'Hadn't you had enough at the dinner?'

'I know when I have had enough,' replied the witness, who seemed rather put out by the question.

'Did you know when you went with your brother to the dinner that you were to be treated as women, and that you were to have money for it?'

'That was what I understood.'

Four women now gave evidence in succession. Three of them were landladies who had let rooms to Taylor and Charles Parker at various dates; the fourth was a tenant of the house in Park Walk, where Charles Parker had lodged for a time. Mrs Ellen Grant, landlady of the house at 13 Little College Street stated that she had let Taylor four rooms, for which he paid £3 a month. She confirmed that he kept no servant and did his own cooking on a gas stove. The windows of his rooms were covered with strained art muslin and dark curtains and lace curtains, she said. They were furnished sumptuously, and were lighted by different coloured lamps and candles. She swore that the windows were never opened or cleaned, and the daylight was never admitted. ('It could not come in, the curtains being always drawn.') There was no bedstead, she added, but there was a spring mattress on the floor of the bedroom.

'What have you seen in the rooms in the shape of apparel?' Gill asked her.

'I have seen a woman's wig and shoes and stockings. I never saw any dress.'

'Was there any scent there?'

'Yes.'

'Much of it?'

'Mr Taylor used to burn scent.' In answer to another question, this witness said she noticed that her lodger's nightshirt was fastened by a gold brooch pin.

CHARLES GILL

By "Spy"

CHARLES PARKER.

MARGERY BANCROFT.

WILLIAM PARKER.

Sketches of witnesses and Wilde's fellow defendant, Alfred Taylor

ALFRED WOOD.

ALFRED TAYLOR.

MRS. GRANT.

om the contemporary *Reynolds Newspaper*

HORACE AVORY

By "Spy"

The Second Trial

'Were Taylor's visitors, as a class, women or men?'

'Men, young men from sixteen to thirty. ... There were frequent tea parties.'

'Who came to them – men or women?'

'Oh, always gentlemen.' Answering further questions, Mrs Grant said that Taylor used to address his visitors by their Christian names – 'Charlie, dear' and 'Dear boy'. She had heard Taylor talking to someone he called 'Oscar', but she had never seen Wilde there. Once she tried the door, she said, and found it locked. She heard whispering and laughing and her suspicions were aroused, but she 'did not like to take steps in the matter'. Before Taylor left the rooms, in August 1893, a sergeant of police had called and she had shown him the rooms at the officer's request.

In cross-examination this witness confirmed that she had never seen Wilde in the house. She also stated that she understood that the wig and other things were used by her lodger for fancy dress. Re-examined by Gill, she admitted that the house was a very old-fashioned one, and that the ground floor was originally a baker's shop.

Another landlady, Mrs Lucy Rumsby, said she had let a bed-room to Charles Parker at 50 Park Walk, Chelsea, in 1893. When he had been there a fortnight, she gave him notice to quit in consequence of the complaint of another lodger. The lodger in question, Mrs Margery Bancroft, who was next in the witness box, said that late one night she heard a cab drive up and some-one enter the house. Afterwards she heard someone going down-stairs, and, looking out of the window, she saw Wilde enter the cab accompanied by someone who might have been Parker. 'I had my suspicions,' this inquisitive lodger went on, 'and com-plained to the landlady next morning.' Asked how she knew the departing visitor was Wilde, she said he had previously been pointed out to her, when he was standing outside the Royal Academy 'with two ladies'.

The third landlady, Mrs Sophia Gray, stated that Taylor had lodged in her house at 3 Chapel Street, where he occupied two rooms, from August to December 1893. She had seen Parker there and also Mr Oscar Wilde. Mr Wilde was only there on one occasion she could remember, when he stopped but a few minutes. But Parker stayed all night. Other young men called upon Taylor and were alone with him for a long time, she said, but he used to say that they were clerks for whom he hoped to find employment. 'I had no idea of the nature of what was going on,' she added, causing loud laughter in court by this seemingly naïve remark.

Mrs Gray also stated that when Taylor went away he left behind a box of papers which she later handed over to Lord Queensberry's solicitor. She was followed in the witness box by Frederick Kearley, a retired detective-inspector, who said he had examined the documents in question and amongst them he had found the piece of paper on which Charles Parker had written his address at the St James's Restaurant.

Next to go into the witness box was the blackmailer, Alfred Wood, who was examined by Gill's junior counsel, Horace Avory. He said he was formerly a clerk, but was out of work in January 1893, when he first met Taylor and stayed for about three weeks with him in Little College Street.

'Where did you sleep there?'

'In the same room with Taylor. There was only one bed there.'

'When did you first know Wilde?'

'About a month after I made the acquaintance of Taylor.'

'How did you come to know Wilde?'

'I was introduced to him by a gentleman at the Café Royal.'

'Who was the gentleman?'

'Must I give his name?'

'Yes.'

'Lord Alfred Douglas.'

'What took place when you were introduced to Wilde?'

'I was introduced by telegram.'

Here the judge interrupted the witness by remarking: 'You would have led anyone to believe that you were personally introduced!'

After this reproof, the witness went on to relate how, in consequence of the telegram, he went to the Café Royal at nine o'clock one evening. Wilde spoke to him first and asked whether he was Alfred Wood. He then offered the witness a drink which Wood accepted, and later invited him to dinner. Wood said he went with Wilde to the Florence Restaurant in Rupert Street and they dined in a private room.

'What kind of meal was it?' asked Avory.

'Very nice,' replied Wood, 'one of the best to be got.'

'What wine did you have?'

'Champagne.'

During dinner, the witness went on, Wilde would put his hand inside his [Wood's] trousers underneath the table and compel Wood to do the same with him. 'Afterwards I lay on the sofa with him,' Wood said. 'It was a long time, however, before I would allow him to actually do the act of indecency.' This, according to the witness, took place after the dinner, in Tite Street, where Wilde brought him into a bedroom and they first drank hock and seltzer. Wood then swore that Wilde had used his influence to induce him to consent to the act. 'He made me nearly drunk,' he added by way of further explanation.

'Did he give you any money that night?'

'Yes, at the Florence. About £3 I think it was. He said he thought I must need some money to buy things with.'

'Did he give you this money before any suggestion was made about going to Tite Street?'

'Yes.'

Describing further meetings between them, Wood related how on one occasion Wilde called on him in the room in Langham Street where he was living, took him out to tea and bought him half a dozen shirts, some collars and handkerchiefs, and a silver watch and chain, all of which gifts the witness apparently accepted gratefully at the time.

Asked about the letters he found in the old suit of clothes which Lord Alfred Douglas had given him, Wood said he could not remember how many there were, nor did he remember giving them back to Wilde after he had got the £30 to go to America with. 'I might have put them on the table,' he added. He confirmed that he saw Wilde again next day at the Florence, where Wilde had invited him to lunch.

'What sort of lunch was it?'

'Very nice lunch. We had champagne.' While at lunch, he went on, his host said to him: '£30 is very little to go to America with, and I will send you £5.' This he did by messenger, and Wood went off to America two or three days afterwards.

Wood was still in the witness box when the Court rose at the end of the first day of the trial. Next morning he was cross-examined by Sir Edward Clarke, to whom he admitted that he had represented to Wilde in 1893 that he wished to get away from 'a certain class of people' he was connected with, and it was by means of this representation that he obtained the £30 from Wilde.

'What have you been doing since your return from America?'

'Well, I have not done much.'

'Have you done anything?'

'I have had no regular employment.'

'I thought not,' commented Clarke.

'I could not get anything to do,' replied Wood.

'As a matter of fact you have had no respectable work for over three years?'

'Well, no.'

'Charles Parker has told us that you and a man named Allen obtained £300 or £400 from a gentleman and that you gave Parker £30.' Clarke went on to ask. 'Is that true?'

'I didn't get the money,' the witness answered after some hesitation. 'It wasn't paid to me.'

'Well, tell us,' Clarke pressed. 'Did you get £300 from a gentleman?'

'Not me,' said Wood. 'Allen did.' It may be noted here that the witness's answers were not always clearly heard, as he appeared to be chewing something all the time he was giving evidence.

'You were a party to it?'

'I was there, yes.'

'Do you mean by that, that you came into the room whilst the gentleman was there with Parker?'

'I did not. Allen went in first.'

182

'At all events Allen and you got £300 or £400 from the gentleman?'

'Yes.'

'And you gave Parker £30?'

'I did not. Allen might have done.' The witness added that he did not know the exact amount Parker got.

'How much did you get?'

'£175.'

'What for?'

'Well, it was given me by Allen.'

'Then Mr Wilde's giving you £30 to get away from this class of person did not have a very satisfactory result?'

'I was in employment all the time I was in America.'

'How did you live when you came back?'

'On some money left me by my father. I was not twenty-one when I went to America.'

'Was that before you had the £175?'

'No.'

Asked about the Wilde–Douglas letters, the witness said that they came into his possession between January and March 1893, when he was at Oxford. They lay about his rooms for a long time.

'To your knowledge had one of those letters been copied?'

'I don't know,' Wood replied at first. Then he corrected himself and added: 'No. Not to my knowledge was one copied.'

'When you gave the letters back, or left them on the table, or whatever it was you did with them, did you know that there was one which you did not give back?'

'Yes.'

'Where was that one?'

'Allen had it.'

'Did you give it to him?'

'No. He took it out of my pocket.'

'Did it remain in Allen's possession?'

'I don't know. I didn't want to have it back.'

'Since you came back from America have you ever visited Charles Parker?'

'Yes, at Camera Square.'
'Have you stayed there?'
'No.'

Asked by Gill in re-examination whether the people he wanted to get away from when he went to America were people whose names had been mentioned in this case, Wood replied that some of them were, but there were others.

'Whom did you mean by the class of people you had been mixed up with?'

'I meant not only Wilde and Taylor, but several others whose names have not been mentioned here.'

Wood was followed in the witness box by a waiter, Thomas Price, who said he was employed at the private hotel at 10 St James's Place, where Wilde had rooms from October 1893 to April 1894. He recognized Taylor, whom he remembered calling there on one occasion. A number of other young men 'of quite inferior station', including Charles Parker, Atkins, and Scarfe also called to see Wilde there, as well as a man named Barford, whose name was thus introduced into the proceedings for the first time. 'Mr Wilde had a latchkey, but never slept there more than a dozen times,' said the waiter. 'He generally arrived about eleven o'clock in the morning, did some literary work, went out to lunch, and returned in the afternoon.'

5

'What is your business?' Avory for the Crown asked the next witness, twenty-year-old Fred Atkins.

'I have been a billiard marker,' the youth answered. 'I have also been a bookmaker's clerk and a comedian.'

'You are doing nothing now?'
'No.'

'Who introduced you to the prisoners?'

'I was introduced to Taylor by a young fellow named Schwabe in November 1892, and afterwards by Taylor to Mr Wilde.'

'Have you met Lord Alfred Douglas?'

'I have. I dined with him and Mr Wilde at the Florence.'

'What happened at the dinner?'

'Mr Wilde kissed the waiter.'

After this astonishing answer, the witness went on to say that Wilde had invited him to go to Paris with him. 'We were seated at the table, and he put his arm round me and said he liked me. I arranged to meet him two days afterwards at Victoria Station, and went to Paris with him as his private secretary.' He added that they stayed at 29 Boulevard des Capucines, and had two rooms there, a bed-sitting-room and a bedroom, one leading into the other. The day after their arrival in Paris, Atkins said he did some copying for Wilde. 'Afterwards I lunched at the Café Julien with him. We went for a drive in the afternoon. Next day we went to a hairdresser's, and I had my hair cut.'

'Did you tell him to curl it?'

'No. He did it on his own account.'

'Mr Wilde was there?'

'Yes, he was having his hair cut and was talking to the man in French all the time.'

Atkins then described how on their second day in Paris he went to the Moulin Rouge. 'Mr Wilde told me not to go, but I went. I had to pay to go in. I had some money Mr Wilde had given me.'

'What did Mr Wilde tell you?' the judge interposed at this point.

'Mr Wilde told me not to go to see those women, as women were the ruin of young fellows. Mr Wilde spoke several times about the same subject, and always to the same effect.'

Replying to further questions from prosecuting counsel, Atkins said he got back very late to the hotel from the Moulin Rouge. He went into Wilde's bedroom and discovered him in bed with a young man whom he recognized as Schwabe. He then went to bed by himself. Next morning, while he was still in bed, Wilde came into his room and talked about the Moulin Rouge, while Atkins told him he had enjoyed himself. Then, according to Atkins, Wilde said: 'Shall I come into bed with you?' Atkins said he replied that it was time to get up, and Wilde did not get into bed with him. He later returned to London with Wilde, who

185

gave him money and a silver cigarette case. Asked about other meetings with the prisoner, Atkins said he had visited Wilde at Tite Street and once at St James's Place. Wilde had also called on him once at Osnaburgh Street, where he was living; on this occasion a young man named Harry Barford was also present.

'Were you ill at Osnaburgh Street?' Sir Edward Clarke asked him in cross-examination.

'Yes,' said Atkins. 'I had smallpox and was removed to the hospital ship. Before I went I asked Barford to write to Mr Wilde requesting him to come and see me, and he did so. I was removed to the hospital ship the next day.'

'Where did you last see Mr Wilde?'

'At the St James's Theatre when he came forward at the end of a play.'[1]

'When did you first know the gentleman whom you saw in Paris?'

'Early in 1892.'

'Had the gentleman promised to take you to Paris before you met Mr Wilde?'

'Yes.'

'And he could not go at the appointed time?'

'No.'

'So Mr Wilde took you instead?'

'Yes.'

'Are you sure you came back from Paris with Mr Wilde?'

'Yes.'

'Did any impropriety ever take place between you and Mr Wilde?'

'Never.'

The remainder of Clarke's cross-examination of this witness had the object of exposing Atkins as a blackmailer.

'Have you ever lived with a man named Burton?'

'Yes, at Osnaburgh Street, Tachbrook Street, and other places.'

'What was he?'

'A bookmaker. I acted as his clerk when he went to the races.'

1. *The Importance of Being Earnest* opened at the St James's Theatre on 14 February 1895.

Then, as if slightly ashamed of this occupation, Atkins added: 'I have also appeared at music halls.'

'Have you also been engaged in the business of blackmailing?' Clarke asked, eyeing the witness sternly.

'I don't remember.'

'Think!'

'I never got money in that way.'

'Has Burton not obtained money from persons on the ground that they have committed acts of an indecent nature with you?'

'No, sir.'

After Atkins had persisted in this denial, Clarke observed: 'That being your answer, I must particularize. On the 9th of June 1891, did you and Burton obtain a large sum of money from a Birmingham gentleman?'

'Certainly not!'

'What names have you gone by?'

'I have a professional name. I have sometimes called myself Denny.'

Clarke then wrote a name on a piece of paper, which was handed up to the witness.

'Do you know that name?'

'No.'

'Do you know anything about a Birmingham gentleman?'

'No.'

'Where were you living on the 9th June 1891?'

'In Lennox Gardens, Chelsea.'

'On that date did a Birmingham gentleman come with you to the rooms you were living at, and did Burton come in and did you and he get a large sum of money from that gentleman?'

'Certainly not,' said Atkins emphatically. 'Nothing of the kind ever took place.'

'Now I am going to ask you a direct question,' said Clarke, 'and I ask you to be careful in your reply. Were you and Burton ever taken to Rochester Row Police Station?'

'No.'

'Well, was Burton?'

187

'I think not. At least, not that I know of.'

The witness went on to deny that he had taken the gentleman home. Nor had Burton come in and threatened him, nor had he taken the gentleman's watch and chain and given it to Burton.

'And were you taken to the Police Station the following night, and did you there and then give up the watch and chain?'

'No, never.'

'Did not that gentleman give Burton a cheque for £200 made out in the name of St Denis or Denny, which he supposed to be your name?'

'No, I swear the thing never happened.'

As he sat down, Clarke turned to one of his junior counsel sitting in the row behind and whispered something to him. The junior in turn spoke to one of his instructing solicitor's clerks, who immediately left the Court. The significance of this communication will be seen later.

The next witness was a woman, Mrs Mary Applegate, who said she was the housekeeper at the house in Osnaburgh Street where Atkins had lodged until about a month before. She said that Wilde visited the house at least twice in one week to her knowledge, when Atkins was there. He came about five in the afternoon and left at seven. One of the housemaids came to her and complained of the state of the sheets on the bed in which Atkins slept after Wilde's first visit. 'The sheets were stained in a peculiar way,' she added.

Mrs Applegate was followed into the witness box by Sidney Mavor, a youth of some education and better breeding than the others who had so far given evidence. It will be remembered that when he was questioned during the Queensberry trial about his relations with Mavor, Wilde had admitted that this witness had once spent the night with him as his guest at the Albemarle Hotel.

In his evidence-in-chief Mavor said he was in partnership with a friend in business in the city. He first met Taylor at the Gaiety Theatre in 1892, when Taylor had introduced himself and was 'very civil and friendly'. Taylor invited him to Little College

Street and he went there to tea several times; he also admitted to having slept there with Taylor. One day Taylor said to him: 'I know a man in an influential position who could be of great use to you, Mavor. He likes young men when they're modest and nice in appearance. I'll introduce you.' It was arranged that they should dine at Kettner's Restaurant the next evening. Mavor called for Taylor to keep the appointment, and Taylor said: 'I'm glad you've made yourself pretty. Mr Wilde likes nice clean boys!' This was the first time Wilde's name was mentioned, according to Mavor. On arriving at the restaurant they were shown into a private room, where they were joined shortly afterwards by Wilde, Schwabe, and another gentleman, whom Mavor believed to be Lord Alfred Douglas. 'I thought the conversation at dinner peculiar,' Mavor went on, 'but I knew Mr Wilde was a Bohemian, and the talk therefore did not seem strange. I was placed next to Mr Wilde, who used occasionally to pull my ear or chuck me under the chin, but he did nothing that was actually objectionable.'

According to the witness, Wilde said to Taylor at the dinner: 'Our little lad has pleasing manners. We must see more of him.' Mavor added that before they parted Wilde took his address, and soon afterwards he received a silver cigarette case. On opening it he found it inscribed 'Sidney from O. W. October 1892'. 'It was quite a surprise to me!' Mavor said, with an air of innocence.

At this point, in spite of the injunction in *The Importance of Being Earnest* that 'it is a very ungentlemanly thing to read a private cigarette case', the one given by Wilde to Mavor was produced and handed up to the judge on the bench. It was then passed round the jury box, where each juryman apparently examined it with the greatest interest.

Mavor went on to describe the night he spent with Wilde in the Albemarle Hotel and was quite definite that no misconduct occurred between them on that occasion. He confirmed this when Clarke cross-examined him and even went further in his denials. 'No impropriety has ever taken place between me and Mr Wilde,' he said, 'and Mr Wilde has never given me any money. I was always glad of Mr Wilde's friendship.'

This statement followed the evidence which Mavor gave at Bow Street Police Court, when he had made a similar denial, although this denial came as a surprise to the prosecution, since it was directly contrary to what Mavor had previously told the police. According to himself, it was Lord Alfred Douglas who was responsible for this sudden change of front. Douglas happened to meet Mavor in the corridor of the police court while he was waiting to go into the witness box there with the other Crown witnesses. 'Surely you are not going to give evidence against Oscar?' said Douglas. 'Well, what can I do?' answered Mavor, looking round in a frightened manner. 'I daren't refuse to give evidence now. They got a statement out of me.' 'For God's sake,' said Douglas, 'remember you are a gentleman and a public school boy. Don't put yourself on a level with scum like Wood and Parker. When counsel asks you the questions, deny the whole thing, and say you made the statement because you were frightened by the police. They can't do anything to you.' 'All right,' said Mavor, grabbing Douglas's hand. 'I'll do what you say.'[1]

Next to go into the witness box was Edward Shelley, the young man who had been employed in the office of Wilde's publishers. He described the night he had spent with Wilde at the Albemarle Hotel, and how his host had kissed him and invited him to come into his bedroom. 'I felt insulted, degraded, and objected vigorously,' Shelley said. Wilde saw him next day and again kissed him 'and there was a repetition of the previous night's performance'. He went on to say that Wilde had given him inscribed copies of *The Picture of Dorian Gray* and other examples of his works, but he had torn out the pages with the inscriptions after he had heard of the charges suggested by Lord Queensberry. He also explained how he wrote to Wilde, saying that he could not have anything more to do with a man of his morality and he would break off the acquaintance.

'If such a thing as you allege happened, you must have resented the outrage upon you?' Clarke asked him in cross-examination.

'Yes, I did.'

1. Douglas, *Autobiography*, 2nd ed., p. 119.

'Then why did you go and dine with him the very next day?'

'I suppose I was a young fool. I tried to think the best of him.'

Asked why he left the firm of publishers where he worked, Shelley said that his fellow clerks chaffed him about his friendship with Wilde.

'In what way?'

'They implied scandalous things. They called me "Mrs Wilde" and "Miss Oscar".'

'So you left?'

'I resolved to put an end to an intolerable situation.'

'You were in bad odour at home too, I think?'

'Yes, a little.'

'I put it to you that your father requested you to leave his house?'

'Yes. He strongly objected to my friendship with Mr Wilde. But the difference between us was made up again.'

'Were you arrested for an assault upon your father?'

'Yes, I was.'

'Were you quite in your sound mind when you assaulted your father.'

'No, I couldn't have been.'

'Where were you taken?'

'To Fulham Police Station.'

'Did you send to Mr Wilde and ask him to bail you out?'

'Yes.'

'What happened?'

'In an hour my father went to the station and I was liberated. My father withdrew the charge and the case was dismissed.'

As soon as Shelley had left the witness box, Sir Edward Clarke asked for Atkins to be recalled. At the same time counsel handed up a folded document to the judge. It contained a record of the charge sheet at Rochester Row Police Station, and on reading it Mr Justice Charles assumed a grave expression.

'Now,' said Clarke to Atkins, 'I warn you to attend and to be very careful. I am going to ask you a question. Think before you reply!'

'Just be careful now, Atkins,' the judge added.

Oscar Wilde

'On the 10th of June 1891, you were living at Tachbrook Street?'

'Yes.'

'James Burton was living there with you?'

'He was.'

'Were you both taken by two constables, 369A and 500A – you have probably forgotten the officers' numbers – to Rochester Row Police Station and charged with demanding money from a gentleman with menaces?'

The witness looked taken aback. Then he answered in a husky voice: 'I was not charged with that.' Asked what he was charged with, Atkins said it was with hitting a gentleman, whom he had met the same night at the Alhambra music hall and taken home to his room in Tachbrook Street for a game of cards.

'Did the landlady give you and Burton into custody?'

'No, nobody did.'

'Some persons must have done. Who did?'

'All I can say is I did not hear anybody.'

At this point Sir Edward Clarke called Police Constable 396A into Court. The officer took up his position close to the witness box, where Atkins began to wriggle about and eye him uneasily.

'Now I ask you in the presence of this officer, was the statement made at the police station that you and the gentleman had been in bed together?'

'I don't think so.'

'Think before you speak,' Clarke thundered. 'It will be better for you. Did not the landlady actually come into the room and see you and the gentleman naked on or in the bed together?'

'I don't remember that she did.'

'You may as well tell us about it, you know. Was that statement made?'

'Well, yes, it was.' The truth came out at last.

'You had endeavoured to force money out of this gentleman?'

'I asked him for some money.'

'At the police station the gentleman refused to prosecute?'

'Yes.'

'And you and Burton were liberated?'

The Second Trial

'Yes.'

'About two hours ago, Atkins, I asked you these very questions,' said Clarke, 'and you swore upon your oath that you had not been in custody at all, and had never been taken to Rochester Row. How came you to tell me those lies?'

'I did not remember it,' was all Atkins would reply.

The judge turned to the witness. 'Leave the box,' he said sternly, and Atkins slunk out of Court, to face a charge of perjury.

The remaining four witnesses that day were relatively unimportant. There was Elkin Mathews, a former partner in Wilde's firm of publishers, who said that Shelley was asked to leave the firm's employ when it was discovered that Wilde was writing to him. The owner of the Albemarle Hotel said that, owing to the number of young men who called to see Wilde when he was staying in the hotel, he came to the conclusion that it would be better if Wilde did not come to the hotel again, and he accordingly issued a writ for the payment of an outstanding bill. A member of a firm of jewellers in Bond Street gave evidence that he had supplied Wilde with silver cigarette cases and other articles, including the one with the inscription to Mavor, which he had instructions to engrave. Finally, the bookkeeper at the Savoy Hotel stated that Wilde had stayed there in March 1893, and had occupied rooms Nos. 361 and 362, and afterwards Nos. 353 and 346.

The case for the prosecution was continued on the third day. The first witness to be called at the sitting of the Court was Antonio Migge, who described himself as a 'professor of massage' and said that he attended the hotel 'to massage patients,' who included Wilde. On entering Wilde's bedroom one morning, after knocking, he said he saw someone in bed, whom he first took to be a lady, but later recognized as a young man. At the time Wilde was dressing, and according to this witness Wilde told him that he felt so much better and was also very busy, so that he could not stay to have the treatment. The masseur said he never attended Wilde again.

'Was the door of the bedroom locked?' Clarke asked in cross-examination. -

193

'No, the door was not locked.'

'And when you opened the door, Mr Wilde was dressing?'

'Yes.'

'In what part of the room was he?'

'At the washstand.'

The masseur's evidence was confirmed by a chambermaid, Jane Cotter, who said she saw a boy of sixteen, with close cropped hair and a sallow complexion, in Wilde's bed. At this time, Lord Alfred Douglas, she said, occupied the adjoining room. She went on to say that she found it necessary to draw the housekeeper's attention to Wilde's bed sheets, which were 'stained in a peculiar way'. This latter statement was confirmed by the housekeeper, Mrs Annie Perkins, who said she remembered the incident and 'gave instructions accordingly'.

After formal evidence had been given of the arrest of Wilde and Taylor, Gill put in the transcript of Wilde's cross-examination at the Queensberry trial. The reading of this evidence, followed by Sir Edward Clarke's re-examination, occupied the rest of the day. It also concluded the case for the Crown.

Before the Court rose, Wilde's leading counsel renewed the objection which he had taken at the opening of the trial to the inclusion in the indictment of the conspiracy counts, on which the prisoners were debarred from giving evidence. Mr Justice Charles declared that he would take time to consider the matter, and that he would give his decision on the following morning.

The general impression, now that the halfway mark in the trial had been reached, was that Clarke had and would continue to put up an admirable fight for his client. But, as Gill remarked, 'only a miracle can save him'.

6

As soon as the judge had taken his place on the Bench for the fourth day of the trial, Charles Gill rose and addressed a few words to Mr Justice Charles, which relieved the judge of making any further decision in regard to the legal aspect of the indictment, which he had undertaken to reconsider overnight. 'My lord, I have had an opportunity of considering the indictment since the case for the prosecution was closed,' Gill said; 'and, in consultation with my friends Mr Avory and Mr Arthur Gill, I have come to the determination not to ask for a verdict on the counts of the indictment charging conspiracy. Of course, I do that having in my mind that no evidence has been given here at all which was not directly material to the other charges.'

The prosecution's decision to drop the conspiracy charges caused considerable surprise among the spectators in Court. It also brought Sir Edward Clarke to his feet in protest. 'My lord,' he said, 'if those counts had been withdrawn in the first instance, I should have made an application to your lordship for the charges against the two prisoners to be heard separately.' But he agreed, nevertheless, that Crown counsel had a perfect legal right to withdraw the counts at any stage of the case. The judge likewise agreed. 'After the evidence had been given,' he observed, 'it occurred to my own mind that the counts for conspiracy were really unnecessary counts altogether.' The result of Gill's action, in the event of Wilde and his fellow prisoner going into the witness box, was to remove all restrictions on the evidence they might wish to give.[1]

Sir Edward Clarke then opened his defence and addressed the jury at some length. 'I am going to call Mr Wilde as a witness,' he began. 'That decision to call him as a witness has not been arrived at in consequence of the statement just made by Mr Gill – but I certainly felt strengthened in my resolution to call Mr Wilde by the fact of this tardy withdrawal of charges which, if they were not intended to be proceeded with, ought never to have been put in the indictment.'

1. Further on this aspect of the case, which has merely an academic interest now, see articles in the *Law Times*, xcix, 103 (1 June 1895) and *Law Journal*, xxx, 285 (4 May 1895). The arbitrary distinction as to the competency of witnesses in criminal trials was abolished by the Criminal Evidence Act, 1898, which provided that, subject to certain qualifications, every person charged with an offence should be a competent witness for the defence at every stage of the proceedings.

Wilde's counsel went on to discuss what he called the literary part of the case. 'The case has been commented on by a large section of the press in a way that I think is disgraceful,' he said. 'Such conduct is calculated to imperil the administration of justice and is in the highest degree prejudicial to the interests of the prisoners. Mr Gill has asked you to dismiss from your minds anything you may have seen in the newspapers. Mr Gill, in saying that, was quite fair. But I do not think it was quite fair of Mr Gill to have insisted upon reading the cross-examination of Mr Wilde on his writings which you have heard. It is not fair to judge a man by his books. Coleridge said long ago: "Judge no man by his books. A man is better, higher than his books." Hidden meanings have been most unjustly read into the poetical and prose works of my client, and it seems that an endeavour, though a futile one, is being made to convict Mr Wilde because of a prurient construction which has been placed by his enemies upon certain of his works. I allude particularly to *The Picture of Dorian Gray*.'

What he described as 'the strange unfairness in this case', said Clarke, was that an attempt had been made – and repeated by the reading of Wilde's cross-examination at the Queensberry trial – not to judge Wilde by his own books but by books which he did not write, and to judge him by a story ('The Priest and the Acolyte') which he did not write and which he repudiated as horrible and disgusting. 'There was a pretence for such conditions in the former trial, when the question was one as to whether Mr Wilde was "posing" or not, but in the present case there is no such excuse.' Clarke reminded the jury that his client had been most indignant when he saw his name on the title page of a publication which contained such a disgraceful story as 'The Priest and the Acolyte'. Yet he had been cross-examined on it, and it had been sought to attach stigma to him in that connexion. 'Faint and far off as was the justification for the cross-examination with reference to *Dorian Gray*, for that with reference to "The Priest and the Acolyte" there was no justification whatever. As to Mr Carson's cross-examination of Mr Wilde on the French work *À Rebours*, it was grossly unfair and a violent misadministration of every canon of justice. The question of the literature is, therefore, an entirely different question from that which you have now to determine.'

Dealing with the circumstances of the previous trial, Clarke emphasized that it was entirely his client's act in charging Lord Queensberry with criminal libel which had brought the matter before the public and placed Wilde in his present position of peril. 'Men who have been charged with the offences alleged against Mr Wilde shrink from an investigation,' he said, 'and in my submission the fact of Mr Wilde taking the initiative of a public trial is evidence of his innocence. Nor is that all. A few days before the first trial, notice was given of certain charges made against him with names and dates. On the 30th of March Mr Wilde knew the catalogue of accusations which were contained in Lord Queensberry's written plea of justification. Gentlemen of the jury, do you believe that had he been guilty he would have stayed in England and faced those accusations? Men guilty of such offences suffer from a species of insanity. What, then, would you think of a man who, knowing himself to be guilty and that evidence would be forthcoming from half a dozen different places, insisted on bringing his case before the world? Insane would hardly be the word for it, if Mr Wilde really had been guilty and yet faced the investigation.'

Clarke concluded his opening speech to the jury by underlining what he called the remarkable fact that there was only one statement in his client's evidence at the first trial which the prosecution had called an independent witness, who was not an admitted accomplice, to contradict – namely the statement that Wilde had never been to see Charles Parker at Park Walk. 'To my mind that is most significant,' said Clarke, 'and I hope that if any doubt remains in your minds as to whether it is possible for you to convict the defendant upon such evidence as you have heard, the doubt will be at once removed when you hear Mr Wilde deny upon oath that there is any truth whatever in the allegations made on the part of the prosecution.'

Wilde now left the dock and stepped up into the witness box. He answered his counsel's questions quietly and deliberately, and made no attempt to show off as he had done at the previous trial. After he had been taken through the details of his career as an author and dramatist, he said that since the time of his marriage in 1884 he had lived with his wife in Tite Street. 'I have also occupied for a time some rooms in St James's Place, which I took for the purpose of my literary work,' he added, 'it being quite out of the question to secure quiet and mental repose at my own house when my two young sons were at home.'

'Was the evidence you gave at the Queensberry trial absolutely and in all respects true?'

'Entirely true evidence.'

'Is there any truth in any of the allegations of indecent behaviour made against you in the evidence in the present case?'

'There is no truth whatever in any one of the allegations, no truth whatsoever.'

Charles Gill then rose to cross-examine the witness. 'You are acquainted with a publication entitled *The Chameleon*?' he began.

'Very well indeed,' Wilde answered with a wry smile.

'I believe that Lord Alfred Douglas was a frequent contributor?'

'Hardly that, I think. He wrote some verses occasionally, and indeed for other papers.'

'The poems in question were somewhat peculiar, were they not?'

'They certainly were not mere commonplaces, like so much that is labelled poetry.'

'The tone of them met with your critical approval?'

'It was not for me to approve or disapprove. I left that to the reviews.'

'At the last trial you described them as beautiful poems?'

'I said something tantamount to that. The verses were original in theme and construction, and I admired them.'

Here Sir Edward Clarke broke in. 'I do not want to make any difficulty,' he said, 'but I understood from my learned friend that he was willing to confine himself to the specific charges made here.'

'This is cross-examination as to credit,' said Gill, as his opponent turned towards the judge.

The Second Trial

'I do not see how I can interfere,' Mr Justice Charles observed. 'Questions which the learned counsel thinks should go to credit he is entitled to put.'

'Listen, Mr Wilde,' Gill continued. 'I shall not keep you very long in the witness box.' Counsel then picked up a copy of *The Chameleon*, with its distinctive green cover. from which he proceeded to read out the poem entitled 'In Praise of Shame'.

> Last night unto my bed bethought there came
> Our lady of strange dreams, and from an urn
> She poured live fire, so that mine eyes did burn
> At sight of it. Anon the floating flame
> Took many shapes, and one cried: 'I am Shame
> That walks with Love, I am most wise to turn
> Cold lips and limbs to fire; therefore discern
> And see my loveliness, and praise my name.'

> And afterwards, in radiant garments dressed
> With sound of flutes and laughing of glad lips,
> A pomp of all the passions passed along
> All the night through; till the white phantom ships
> Of dawn sailed in. Whereat I said this song,
> 'Of all sweet passions Shame is loveliest.'

'Is that one of the beautiful poems?' Gill asked the witness.

'That is not one of Mr Wilde's,' Clarke commented.

'I am not aware that I said it was,' said Gill.

'I thought you would be glad to say it was not!' Clarke snapped back.

At this point the judge intervened. 'I understand that was a poem by Lord Alfred Douglas.'

'Yes, my lord,' said Gill, adding in tones of heavy sarcasm, 'and one which the witness described as a beautiful poem. The other beautiful poem is the one that follows immediately, and precedes "The Priest and the Acolyte".'

Wilde made as if to speak. 'May I – ', he began. But Gill cut him short with: 'No! Kindly answer my questions.' 'Certainly,' said Wilde.

'If you have any explanation to add to your answer, you may do so,' Mr Justice Charles said, addressing the witness.

199

Oscar Wilde

'I will merely say this, my lord,' Wilde replied. 'It is not for me to explain the work of anybody else. It does not belong to me. But the word "shame" now in that poem is a word used in the sense of "modesty". I mean that I was anxious to point out that "Shame that turns cold lips to fire" – I forget the line exactly – is a quickened sense of modesty.'

'Your view, Mr Wilde,' continued Gill, 'is that the "shame" mentioned here is that shame which is a sense of modesty?'

'That was the explanation given to me by the person who wrote it. The sonnet seemed to me obscure.'

'During 1893 and 1894 you were a great deal in the company of Lord Alfred Douglas?'

'Oh, yes.'

'Did he read that poem to you?'

'Yes.'

'You can perhaps understand that such verses as these would not be acceptable to the reader with an ordinary balanced mind?'

'I am not prepared to say,' Wilde answered. 'It appears to me to be a question of taste, temperament, and individuality. I should say that one man's poetry is another man's poison!'

'I daresay!' commented Gill dryly, when the laughter had subsided. 'The next poem is one described as "Two Loves". It contains these lines:

> Sweet youth,
> Tell me why, sad and sighing, dost thou rove
> These pleasant realms? I pray thee tell me sooth,
> What is thy name?' He said: 'My name is Love',
> Then straight the first did turn himself to me,
> And cried: 'He lieth, for his name is Shame.
> But I am Love, and I was wont to be
> Alone in this fair garden, till he came
> Unasked by night; I am true Love, I fill
> The hearts of boy and girl with mutual flame.'
> Then sighing said the other: 'Have thy will;
> I am the Love that dare not speak its name.'

'Was that poem explained to you?'

'I think that is clear.'

'There is no question as to what it means?'

'Most certainly not.'

'Is it not clear that the love described relates to natural love and unnatural love?'

'No.'

'What is the "Love that dare not speak its name"?' Gill now asked.

'"The love that dare not speak its name" in this century is such a great affection of an elder for a younger man as there was between David and Jonathan, such as Plato made the very basis of his philosophy, and such as you find in the sonnets of Michelangelo and Shakespeare. It is that deep, spiritual affection that is as pure as it is perfect. It dictates and pervades great works of art like those of Shakespeare and Michelangelo, and those two letters of mine, such as they are. It is in this century misunderstood, so much misunderstood that it may be described as the "Love that dare not speak its name", and on account of it I am placed where I am now. It is beautiful, it is fine, it is the noblest form of affection. There is nothing unnatural about it. It is intellectual, and it repeatedly exists between an elder and a younger man, when the elder has intellect, and the younger man has all the joy, hope, and glamour of life before him. That it should be so, the world does not understand. The world mocks at it and sometimes puts one in the pillory for it.'

Wilde's words produced a spontaneous outburst of applause from the public gallery, mingled with some hisses, which moved the judge to say he would have the Court cleared if there were any further manifestation of feeling. There is no doubt, however, that what Wilde said made an unforgettable impression on all those who heard him, not least the jury. The incident also seemed to give Wilde renewed self-confidence in the witness box.

'I wish to call your attention to the style of your correspondence with Lord Alfred Douglas,' Gill went on.

'I am ready,' Wilde replied. 'I am never ashamed of the style of my writings.'

'You are fortunate, or shall I say shameless?' was Gill's neat rejoinder. 'I refer to passages in two letters in particular.'

201

'Kindly quote them.'

'In letter number one you use the expression "Your slim gilt soul" and you refer to Lord Alfred's "red rose lips". The second letter contains the words "You are the divine thing I want" and describes Lord Alfred's letter as being "delightful, red and yellow wine to me". Do you think an ordinarily constituted being would address such expressions to a younger man?'

'I am not, happily I think, an ordinarily constituted being.'

'It is agreeable to be able to agree with you,' said Gill, as he bowed ironically to the witness, who continued his explanation of the controversial correspondence. 'There is nothing, I assure you, in either letter of which I need be ashamed. The first letter is really a prose poem, and the second more of a literary answer to one Lord Alfred Douglas had sent me.'

Gill then turned to the specific charges in the case, beginning with the incidents alleged against Wilde at the Savoy Hotel. 'Are you prepared to contradict the evidence of the hotel servants?' he asked.

'It is entirely untrue,' Wilde declared with some emphasis. 'Can I answer for what hotel servants say years after I have left the hotel? It is childish. I am not responsible for hotel servants. I have stayed at the hotel and been there constantly since.'

'There is no possibility of mistake? There was no woman with you?'

'Certainly not!'

Equally emphatically Wilde denied all the incidents of indecent conduct alleged by Shelley, Charles Parker, Atkins, and Wood, on which prosecuting counsel catechized him. 'These witnesses have, you say, lied throughout?' Gill asked, after he had dealt with each individually.

'Their evidence as to my association with them, as to the dinners taking place and the small presents I gave them is mostly true,' said Wilde. 'But there is not a particle of truth in that part of the evidence which alleged improper behaviour.'

'Why did you take up with these youths?'

'I am a lover of youth!'

'You exalt youth as a sort of god?'

'I like to study the young in everything. There is something fascinating in youthfulness.'

'So you would prefer puppies to dogs and kittens to cats?'

'I think so,' Wilde answered after a slight pause. 'I should enjoy, for instance, the society of a beardless, briefless barrister quite as much as the most accomplished Q.C.' Loud laughter followed this remark.

'I hope the former, whom I represent in large numbers, will appreciate the compliment,' rejoined Gill amid renewed laughter.

'These youths were much inferior to you in station?'

'I never inquired, nor did I care, what station they occupied. I found them, for the most part, bright and entertaining. I found their conversation a change. It acted as a kind of mental tonic.'

'Why did you go to Taylor's rooms?'

'Because I used to meet actors and singers of many kinds there.'

'Did it strike you that this place was at all peculiar?'

'Not at all.'

'Not the sort of street you would usually visit in? You had no other friends there?'

'No. This was merely a bachelor's place.'

'Rather a rough neighbourhood, isn't it?'

'That I don't know. I know it is near the Houses of Parliament.'

'What did you go there for?'

'To amuse myself sometimes; to smoke a cigarette; for music, chatting, and nonsense of that kind, to while an hour away.'

'You never suspected the relations that might exist between Taylor and his young friends?'

'I had no need to suspect anything. Taylor's relations with his friends appeared to me to be quite normal.'

'You have attended to the evidence of the witness Mavor?'

'I have.'

'Is it true or false?'

'It is mainly true, but false inferences have been drawn from it as from most of the evidence.' Then, as if his old self again, Wilde added, to the accompaniment of some mirth, especially from the barristers' seats: 'Truth may be found, I believe, at the bottom of a well. It is, apparently, difficult to find it in a court of law!'

'Nevertheless we endeavour to extract it,' retorted Gill, who had his own brand of dry humour.

'Did the witness Mavor write to you expressing a wish to break off the acquaintance?'

'I received a rather unaccountable and impertinent letter from him, for which he afterwards expressed great regret.'

'Why should he have written to you, if your conduct had been altogether blameless?'

'I do not profess to be able to explain the conduct of most of the witnesses. Mavor may have been told some falsehood about me. His father was greatly incensed at his conduct at the time and, I believe, attributed his son's erratic course to his friendship with me. I do not think Mavor altogether to blame. Pressure was brought to bear on him.'

'What do you say about Alphonse Conway?'

'I met him on the beach at Worthing. He was such a bright, happy boy that it was a pleasure to talk to him. I bought him a walking-stick, a suit of clothes, and a hat with a bright ribbon – but I was not responsible for the ribbon!'

'You made handsome presents to all these young fellows?'

'Pardon me, I differ. I gave two or three of them a cigarette case. Boys of that class smoke a good deal of cigarettes. I have a weakness for presenting my acquaintances with cigarette cases.'

'Rather an expensive habit, if indulged in indiscriminately, isn't it?'

'Less extravagant than giving jewelled garters to ladies!'

This final piece of repartee, which virtually concluded the cross-examination, went down particularly well with counsel, as Gill had the reputation of being a great ladies' man.

Sir Edward Clarke re-examined his client very briefly, confining himself mainly to the letters to Lord Alfred Douglas which Wood had misappropriated. 'Wood gave me three letters back,' Wilde said. 'They were not what I should call matters of great consequence, but no one likes to have his private letters read. They contained some slighting allusions to other people which I should not have liked made public. Then I received an anonymous letter saying that Wood had other letters and intended to try and extort money by means of them. I did not give any money for them at all, but I gave Wood some money to enable him to go to America.'

'Had you anything to do with the publication of the two poems by Lord Alfred Douglas in *The Chameleon*?'

'No, nothing whatever.'

7

Since Clarke called no other witnesses besides his client, Wilde was immediately followed into the witness box by his fellow prisoner, whose testimony occupied the remainder of the morning. Answering his counsel, J. P. Grain, Alfred Taylor said he was thirty-three years old, and the son of a cocoa manufacturer, whose business was now being carried on by a limited liability company, his father having died in 1874. He was educated at Marlborough School, which he left when he was about seventeen to go to a private tutor. His intention had always been to go into the army, which in fact he entered through the militia, serving for a short time in the City of London Regiment. But on coming of age in 1883 he had inherited a fortune of £45,000, and since then he had had no occupation but had lived a life of pleasure. All the allegations of misconduct made against him, he said, were absolutely untrue.

Cross-examined by Gill, Taylor denied that he was expelled from his public school for being caught in a compromising situation with a small boy in the lavatory. He admitted, however, that he used to have a number of young men living in his rooms and sleeping in the same bed. He had never gone through a mock marriage with a youth named Charles Mason, but he admitted to having a woman's dress, 'an Eastern costume', in his rooms, including a woman's wig and stockings.

'At the time you were living in Chapel Street, were you in serious money difficulties?'

'I had just gone through the Bankruptcy Court.'

'Have you not actually made a living since your bankruptcy by procuring lads and young men for rich gentlemen whom you knew to be given to this vice?'

'No.'

'Did you know Mr Wilde well?'

'Yes.'

'Did you tell certain lads that he was fond of boys?'

'No, never.'

'Did you know that he is?'

'I believe he is fond of young people.'

'Why did you introduce Charles Parker to Mr Wilde?'

'I thought Mr Wilde might use his influence to obtain for him some work on the stage.'

'Why did you burn incense in your rooms?'

'Because I liked it.'

Re-examined by his counsel, Taylor explained that the woman's dress which had been found by the police in his rooms was an Oriental dress which he had got in order to go to a fancy dress ball at Covent Garden. 'It came from Constantinople,' he said, 'and I bought it from a lady.'

The remainder of the fourth day of the trial was taken up with counsel's closing speeches to the jury. Sir Edward Clarke began his immediately after the luncheon adjournment and spoke with great power and emotion for nearly two hours. At the outset he attacked the prosecution for their conduct over the conspiracy counts which were later withdrawn. If there was not sufficient evidence to substantiate these charges, why were they included in the indictment in the first place?

'Counsel for the Crown ought to have made up their minds on that point at the outset,' said Clarke. 'A cruel hardship has in consequence been inflicted on Mr Wilde. With whatever anxiety you may seek to separate the evidence in your minds, you will hardly be able to do so. The evidence of literature which has been called against Mr Wilde is not evidence against Taylor, nor is the case of Shelley. At the same time, the character of the young men who frequented Taylor's rooms is no evidence against Mr Wilde. His lordship will tell you that the conversation alleged to have taken place between Taylor and the Parkers at the St James's

Restaurant, when they first met, is no evidence against Mr Wilde. ('It is evidence against Taylor only,' the judge added at this point.) 'In disentangling the evidence, therefore, you will be in a terrible position of responsibility.'

Turning to the question of literature, Clarke castigated Gill for having devoted so much of his cross-examination to interrogating Wilde about two poems of which he was not the author. 'The two poems were written by Lord Alfred Douglas, and with them Mr Wilde had no more to do than I have, or you have, gentlemen. What can be said about the morality of our poets if we are to measure it by the writings, not of themselves, but of others? A poet is no more responsible for what others may have said than an artist is guilty of murder when he paints a picture depicting the murder of Rizzio at the feet of Mary Queen of Scots!

'As to the affection which Mr Wilde has expressed in the letters which have been put in,' Clarke continued, 'he has himself described it as a pure and true affection, absolutely unconnected with, alien to, irreconcilable with the filthy practices which this band of blackmailers you have heard has been narrating. Again, if Mr Wilde were guilty, would he not have recoiled from being put in the witness box? Yet he has gone into the witness box, fearless as to what might be produced against him. Mr Wilde is not an ordinary man. He is a man who has written poetry and prose, brilliant dramas, charming essays; a man who from his youth has been trained in the study of the literature of the world, not of this England of ours alone, but of those empires whose glories are to us only a name. He writes letters in a tone which to others may seem highflown, inflated, exaggerated, absurd. But he is not ashamed or afraid to produce these letters. He goes into the witness box and says that they speak of pure love, and when he says so, is he not to be believed?'

Clarke went on to contrast in the most telling language the instinctive shrinking of the guilty victims of the blackmailers' frightful trade with the open way in which Wilde had himself sought to have the charges against him investigated and the courage which had brought him into the witness box. 'When a man comes forward with such letters as these and says "I do not 'shrink from the judgement of the world upon these productions" you cannot say that such a man is not to be believed. Has the defendant in this case not given the best proof of his innocence? Innocence has courage and faith in the ultimate judgement of mankind.

'Mr Wilde has never made any secret of visiting Taylor's rooms,' Clarke continued. 'He found there society which afforded him variety and change. Nor has Mr Wilde made any secret of giving dinners to some of the witnesses. He thought that they were poorly off and that a good dinner at a restaurant did not often come their way. Only on one occasion did he hire a private room. The dinners were perfectly open and above-board.'

The advocate went over the evidence given by the various witnesses for the prosecution, being careful to distinguish that given by the hysterical Shelley from the others. He ridiculed the testimony of the Savoy Hotel servants, in particular that of the chambermaid and the masseur. 'Migge's story is of the most amazing character,' he said. 'He even admitted that Mr Wilde was expecting him. Yet he says that he opened the door of the room, saw Mr Wilde dressing on one side of the chamber and a boy in the bed on the other side of the room. How was it that no one could be found who ever saw those two boys go into or come out from the hotel?

'As to Parker, Wood, and Atkins, it does not need the experience that these three young men have had in blackmailing to teach them that they must make use of circumstances which actually occurred to suggest others. These wretches who have come forward to admit their own disgrace are shameless creatures incapable of one manly thought or one manly action. They are without exception blackmailers. They live by luring men to their rooms, generally on the pretence that a beautiful girl will be provided for them on their arrival. Once in their clutches, these victims can only get away by paying a large sum of money, unless they are prepared to face and deny the most disgraceful charges. Innocent men consequently pay rather than face the odium attached to the breath even of such scandals. They have, moreover, wives and children, daughters maybe or a sister, whose honour or name they are obliged to consider. Therefore they usually submit to be fleeced, and in this way the wretched Wood and the abject Atkins have been able to go about the West End well fed and well dressed. These youths were introduced to Mr Wilde. They were pleasant-spoken enough, and outwardly decent in their language and conduct. Mr Wilde was taken in by them and permitted himself to enjoy their society. I do not defend Mr Wilde for this. He has unquestionably shown imprudence, but a man of his temperament cannot be judged by the standards of the average individual. Now these youths have come forward to make these charges in a conspiracy to ruin my client. Is it likely that a man of Mr Wilde's cleverness would put himself so completely in the power of these harpies as he would be if he were guilty of only one-tenth of the enormities they have alleged against him?

'I respectfully submit that no jury can find a man guilty on the evidence of these tainted witnesses. Those three witnesses, Charles Parker, Wood, and Atkins, witnesses for the Crown, have admitted their participation in such practices as ought to disentitle their evidence to the slightest credence. You will never forget – for few juries have ever seen such – the scene that happened in the witness box on Saturday. You noticed how Atkins met those questions of mine with steady and solid denial. This young man denied that he had ever been charged at a police station with attempting blackmail. Did the police know who Atkins was, and his shameful history? Was it the public prosecutor alone who was ignorant of Atkins's character? And if he were not, if he knew of these incidents in the shameful record of Burton and Atkins, what was the meaning of the Crown calling Atkins into the witness box for his evidence to be accepted as if it were untainted? Those who conduct criminal prosecutions have a duty towards the defendant as well as to the Crown and the public. It deepens one's horror that Mr Wilde was at the peril of these persons, to think that had the trial been finishing that day the denials made by Atkins might have had their effect upon the jury.'

Clarke then informed the jury that it was through detailed information which he had received in anonymous letters that he had been enabled to convict Atkins of the attempted extortion which he so persistently denied until confronted with the police officers who had taken him into custody. 'It is strange that the public prosecutor, if he knew of this witness's real character, should have permitted Mr Gill to tender his evidence against the accused,' Clarke went on. 'Wood, Parker, and Atkins, too, have shared the profits of blackmailing, and I protest that it should not be accepted, on the uncorroborated evidence of men like them, that before 1892 they were uncorrupted.

'To support the charge, the evidence ought to be convincing – evidence which you believe to be honest, untainted, and in all degrees true. Can you say, gentlemen, with regard to any one piece of the evidence which has attacked the conduct of Mr Wilde, that those epithets can be applied? You are dealing with matters which aie alleged to have taken place a long time ago, and consequently it is impossible that witnesses can be called by Mr Wilde, who can now only meet the allegations with the statement that they are false. I submit that the evidence called by the prosecution is not reliable testimony, that the principal witnesses for the prosecution – whose evidence is wholly uncorroborated – belong to a wretched gang of blackmailers, and that Shelley has admitted that his mind was disordered at the time he wrote the letters that have been produced.'

By this time Wilde's counsel had been speaking for well over an hour in a hushed and silent Court. In a most memorable peroration he brought tears to the eyes of at least one person who heard his final words.

'I know with what extreme difficulty it is that juries are able to efface from their recollection things which bias their judgement, and to address themselves only to that evidence which is sound and true. Before you deal with this case, therefore, I implore you to make the effort, and let your judgement be affected only by those witnesses with regard to whom you can say with a clear conscience that you, as honourable men, are entitled to be guided by true and honest and honourable testimony. Fix your minds firmly on the tests that ought to be applied to evidence before you can condemn a fellow-man on a charge like this. If you guard yourselves from these prejudices which have floated about – they have been dissipated to some extent by the incidents of the last few days, but from them all it is impossible that the atmosphere should be absolutely clear – then I trust that the result of your deliberations will be to gratify those thousands of hopes which are hanging upon your decision, and will clear from this fearful imputation one of our most renowned and accomplished men of letters of today, and, in clearing him, will clear society from a stain.'

A murmur of appreciation went round the Court as Clarke sat down. Most moved of all, who heard this superb example of Victorian advocacy, was the advocate's client. As he wiped a tear from his cheek, Wilde took a piece of paper and wrote a few lines expressing his gratitude to Clarke for the great effort he had put forward on his behalf. The note was handed down to counsel who read it and nodded his thanks to the figure in the dock.

Taylor's counsel, J. P. Grain, who addressed the jury next, had a most difficult task in the face of the evidence he had to meet, but he did his best for his client in the circumstances. An endeavour had been made, he said, to prove that Taylor was in the habit of introducing youths to Wilde whom his client knew to be amenable to Wilde's practices and that he got paid for this degrading work; but the attempt to establish this disgusting association had completely broken down. It was true, he admitted, that Taylor was acquainted with the Parkers, Wood, and Atkins. He had seen them constantly in restaurants and music halls, and they had at first forced themselves upon him and thus got acquainted with a man whom they hoped to blackmail. Counsel went on to point out that the Parkers were the only two witnesses who claimed to have been introduced by Taylor to Wilde, and all the resources of the Crown and the solicitors employed by Lord Queensberry had been unable to produce any corroboration of the charges of misconduct made by those witnesses. If Taylor had been employed by Wilde, where was the proof of any kind of payment? Not a farthing piece, in money or in value, Grain submitted, had passed between the two. As for his client's means of livelihood, he had been living on a small allowance from his late father's firm.

The final speech of the day was made by Charles Gill for the prosecution. 'It has been argued by my learned friend, Sir Edward Clarke,' he began, 'that no man conscious of guilt would have dared to set the criminal law in motion against Lord Queensberry. As to that, I say you cannot tell what was upon the defendant Wilde's mind, or how he was misled by the expectation that the case would take an entirely different course. The fact remains that from the first Lord Queensberry undertook to justify the libel. . . . Sir Edward Clarke has made a courageous and brilliant defence of the prisoner Wilde, and incidentally has made an admission – of which I now take full advantage – that he was in part at least responsible for the course taken on Mr Wilde's behalf at the previous trial, and that in part at least it was due to that circumstance that he – my learned friend – is now appearing on behalf of the accused. So far as the original charge made by Lord Queensberry goes, I have not found it necessary to cross-examine the defendant Wilde, since Mr Wilde's own counsel admitted that the justification was proved and that it was for the public interest that the libel was published.'

Turning to the evidence, including the Wilde–Douglas letters, which seemed to him to 'breathe an unholy passion', the Crown counsel asked what good any of the witnesses could get by giving false evidence. As for corroboration, he pointed out that no direct corroboration of the acts alleged was possible, since it was not in the least likely that they would have been practised before a third party who might afterwards swear to the fact. 'But in respect to many things the evidence is corroborated,' Gill went on. 'A man may conceivably come forward and commit perjury. But these youths are accusing themselves, in accusing another, of shameful and infamous acts, and this they would hardly do it if were not the truth. Mr Wilde has made presents to these youths, and it is noticeable that the gifts were invariably made after he had been alone, at some rooms or other, with one or another of the lads. In these circumstances even a cigarette case is corroboration. . . . All those visits, all those dinners, all those gifts are corroboration. They serve to confirm the truth of the statements made by the youths, who have confessed to the commission of

212

acts for which the things I have quoted were positive and actual payment.'

Dealing with the particular case of Sidney Mavor, Gill argued it was clear that Wilde had in some way continued to disgust this youth. 'Some acts of Mr Wilde, either towards himself or towards others, have offended him,' he said. 'Is not the letter which Mavor addressed to the prisoner, desiring the cessation of their friendship, corroboration?'

At this point the judge interrupted Gill's speech with an observation which was to have a significant result. 'Although the evidence of this witness is clearly of importance,' said Mr Justice Charles, 'yet he has denied that the defendant Wilde has been guilty of impropriety. I do not think, therefore, that the counts in reference to Mavor can stand.' Accordingly, after some further discussion, the judge directed the two counts alleging the commission of acts of indecency with Mavor to be struck out of the indictment.

'At all events,' counsel for the prosecution continued, 'there is nothing to support the suggestion of my learned friend that Shelley, who has shown himself to be an absolutely respectable and trustworthy witness, was in a disordered state of mind; while as to those witnesses who have been described as blackmailers, they can have no conceivable object in bringing these accusations against the accused, unless the charges they have made are true in substance and in fact.'

Gill concluded his speech with these words: 'It is your duty, gentlemen, to express your verdict without fear or favour. You owe a duty to society, however sorry you may feel yourselves at the moral downfall of an eminent man, to protect society from such scandals by removing from its heart a sore which cannot fail in time to corrupt and taint it all.'

8

The judge's summing up of the evidence to the jury, a fine example of judicial impartiality, occupied the whole morning of the fifth and last day of the trial. Mr Justice Charles began by endorsing the admonitory warning which Sir Edward Clarke had given in opening his defence. 'For weeks it has been impossible to open a newspaper without reading some reference to this case, and especially to the prisoner Wilde, and I accordingly entreat you to put away from your minds everything you may have read about the defendants, and to apply your minds fairly to the consideration of the case as it has been presented before you by the witnesses called on the part of the prosecution. I hope that you will not allow any preconceived opinions to weigh with you in trying two persons, both of good education, one of them being a man of high intellectual gifts.'

Mr Justice Charles then proceeded to give the jury his interpretation of the law relating to the corroboration of accomplices; and it is worth noting here that Wilde's junior counsel, Travers Humphreys, who was later to become one of the greatest criminal judges of his day, has expressed the opinion that it was much more favourable to the accused than it would be in similar circumstances today.[1]

By, I will not say the law of England, but by the wholesome practice of our Courts for nearly two hundred years, no defendant can be convicted by a jury on the uncorroborated evidence and testimony of an accomplice in his crime. This is a wise rule of practice. If it were otherwise, to what terrible dangers might not innocent people be exposed by designing or spiteful adversaries? In this case, therefore, had there been no corroboration of the testimony of the young men to whose evidence you have listened, it would have been my duty at once to have told you that you ought to acquit the defendants.

I am sure that you will agree, if you reflect upon it for a moment, that the uncorroborated evidence of an accomplice should not be acted upon, and therefore in this case I have anxiously had to watch the evidence which has been given to see if the witnesses were corroborated in some way or other. I am clearly of opinion that there is corroboration of all the witnesses in the sense that the law requires – not corroboration by eye-witnesses; it would be idle to expect that, and the law does not require it. But there is corroboration as to the acquaintanceship of the defendants with the witnesses, and as to many

1. See Foreword by Sir Travers Humphreys, above, p. 11.

214

particulars of the narrative they gave, which would render it quite impossible for me to withdraw the case for your consideration.

I need not go through the various circumstances now which constitute corroboration and which, therefore, make it my duty to leave the cases of all the witnesses who have been called for your consideration. Not only are some of the witnesses accomplices, but Charles Parker, Wood, and Atkins have been properly described by Sir Edward Clarke, in the eloquent speech which he addressed to you yesterday on behalf of the prisoner Wilde, as persons who levied blackmail; and you will remember what they have admitted themselves. Atkins in the witness box, in your hearing, was out of his own mouth convicted of having told the grossest and most deliberate falsehoods. These witnesses require, therefore, not only corroboration, but also that you should remember their characters.

It is not necessary to follow the judge into the details of his analysis of the evidence. Wherever there might be a doubt in the minds of the jury, the judge invariably urged the jury to give the prisoners the benefit of it. He began by reminding them that Wilde had given evidence under oath, and that it was a point in his favour that he had himself challenged inquiry into the accusations originally made against him by Lord Queensberry. The judge also took care to point out to the jury that they ought not to base any unfavourable opinion on the fact that Wilde was the author of *The Picture of Dorian Gray*. 'If an imaginative writer puts into his novel some consummate villain, and puts into the mouth of that man sentiments revolting to humanity, it must not be supposed that he shares them. . . . While some of our most distinguished and noble-minded writers have passed long lives in producing the most wholesome literature – such as, for instance, Sir Walter Scott and Charles Dickens, who never wrote, so far as I know a single offensive line – it is unfortunately true to say that other great writers, who were perfectly noble-minded men themselves, have somehow or other given to the world, especially in the eighteenth century, works which it is painful for persons of ordinary modesty and decency to read. It would be unfair, therefore, when you are trying a man, to allow yourselves to be unfavourably influenced against him by the circumstances

215

that he has written a book of which you, in so far as you have read any extracts from it, may disapprove.'

On the subject of the two letters to Douglas, of which so much had been made, especially at the Queensberry trial, Mr Justice Charles put the most favourable construction on them he could. 'I question if Mr Carson was right in regarding these letters as of a horrible or indecent character,' he said. 'Mr Wilde himself has said that he is not in any sense ashamed of either of these two letters, and that, although they breathe the language of affection and passion, it is not an impure or unnatural passion. . . . Furthermore, there is this to be said about the first letter of sufficient importance undoubtedly to be worthy of your attention. It was produced by Mr Wilde himself in his examination-in-chief which took place here last session; and so it was said on his behalf by his counsel, "give him credit for not being ashamed of it".'

The judge similarly advised the jury to treat with caution the evidence of the prosecution witnesses, particularly the chambermaid Jane Cotter and the masseur Migge from the Savoy Hotel. 'To my mind it seems strange that, if what the hotel servants alleged is true, there was so little attempt at concealment,' he said. 'However, if the hotel servants were telling the truth, then Wilde's denial that boys had ever been in his bed at the Savoy must be untrue. It is for you to say on which side the balance of credibility lies.

'I do not wish to enlarge upon this most unpleasant part of this most unpleasant case,' the judge went on, 'but it is necessary for me to remind you as discreetly as I can that, according to the evidence of Mary Applegate, the housekeeper at Osnaburgh Street, where Atkins used to lodge, the housemaid objected to making the bed on several occasions after Wilde and Atkins had been in the bedroom together. There were, she affirmed, indications on the sheets that conduct of the grossest kind had been indulged in. I think it my duty to remind you that there may be an innocent explanation of these stains, though the evidence of Jane Cotter certainly affords a kind of corroboration of these charges and of Atkins's own story '

Having gone through all the evidence, the judge concluded by

The Second Trial

saying that he had summed up the case with some minuteness because of its importance to the community at large and its gravity to the accused. 'It is important that, if you think that the practices alleged have been proved, you should fearlessly say so,' he declared; 'but, on the other hand, it is of vast importance that people should not be convicted of acts which they have not committed. The prisoner Wilde has the right to ask you to remember that he is a man of highly intellectual gifts, a person whom people would suppose to be incapable of such acts as are alleged. Taylor, though nothing has been said about his abilities, has been well brought up, and he too belongs to a class of people in whom it is difficult to imagine such an offence. At the same time, you must deal with the evidence fearlessly, remembering the prisoners' position on the one hand and your duty to the public on the other. If you feel you cannot act on the evidence of the witnesses, you should say so; but if you feel constrained to believe that evidence, you must also fearlessly say so.'

Before the jury retired to consider their verdict, Mr Justice Charles put four questions to them which he then wrote down and handed to the foreman.

1. Do you think that Wilde committed indecent acts with Edward Shelley and Alfred Wood and with a person or persons unknown at the Savoy Hotel or with Charles Parker?
2. Did Taylor procure or attempt to procure the commission of these acts or any of them?
3. Did Wilde and Taylor or either of them attempt to get Atkins to commit indecencies?
4. Did Taylor commit indecent acts with Charles Parker or William Parker?

The jury then withdrew, and at the foreman's request the judge ordered that they should be provided with a reasonable amount of food and drink to sustain them during their deliberations. It was just after half past one when they filed out into the jury room. They returned to Court at a quarter past five, having previously sent a message to the judge that they had arrived at a negative finding in regard to the third question above, but that they disagreed about the remainder.

217

Oscar Wilde

'Gentlemen of the jury,' the judge addressed them when they had taken their places in the jury box, 'I have received a communication from you to the effect that, with the exception of the minor question which I put to you in regard to Atkins, you are unable to arrive at an agreement.'

'That is so, my lord,' the foreman replied. 'We cannot agree upon three of the questions you submitted to us.'

'Is there any prospect that if you retire to your room – you have not been inconvenienced, you know, because I ordered what you asked – and continued your deliberations a little longer, you would be able to come to an agreement at least on some of the questions?'

'I put that also to my fellow-jurymen,' answered the foreman. 'We have considered the question for three hours and the only result we have come to is that we cannot agree.'

'Is there anything which you desire to ask me with reference to the case which you think would assist you in further deliberating upon your verdict?'

'It would be useless, my lord. We cannot agree on any of the sub-divisions of questions (1) and (4).'

'I am very unwilling to do anything at any time which should look like compelling a jury to deliver a verdict,' Mr Justice Charles now observed. 'You have been very long in deliberation over this matter, and no doubt you have done your very best to arrive at agreement on the questions. On the other hand, the inconveniences of another trial are very great, and if you thought there was any prospect of agreement after deliberating further, I would ask you to do so.'

'My lord,' said the foreman, 'I fear there is no chance of agreement.'

'That being so, I do not feel justified in detaining you any longer.'

Before they left the box, the jury returned a formal verdict of 'Not Guilty' on the counts relating to Atkins, and also on those concerning Mavor, which had been struck out of the indictment on the judge's directions for lack of evidence, as well as the conspiracy counts, which had been withdrawn by the prosecution.

The Second Trial

This disposed of nine counts in all, out of a total of twenty-five in the indictment which the prisoners had to answer.

Looking back now on this trial, at which the jury disagreed, it must be admitted that, in spite of the judge's honest attempt at impartiality, the scales were unquestionably weighted against Wilde. The evidence against Taylor, though technically not evidence against his fellow prisoner, was in the circumstances bound to influence the jury's minds against Wilde. Taylor had managed to run through a fortune of £45,000, dissipating most of it on various forms of loose living; he was known to be a habitual associate of youths of the lowest class; his rooms had been under police observation for some time; and he had actually been arrested during a police raid on an undesirable house in Fitzroy Street where he had been among those found on the premises. The bracketing of Wilde's name with that of Taylor was a great misfortune for Wilde, both in this trial when he was tried jointly with him, and (as will be seen) in the subsequent trial when, though tried separately, his case was heard immediately after Taylor's. In the former trial the prisoners should also have been tried separately. Had this been so, and had the jurors' minds not been impregnated with prejudicial press comments, there is a chance that on the evidence offered by the prosecution Wilde would have been acquitted on all the counts with which he was charged. That the jury disagreed was, in the circumstances, a considerable tribute to Clarke's advocacy.

As soon as the jury had been discharged, Clarke applied for Wilde to be released on bail pending his re-trial. Mr Justice Charles felt bound to refuse the application, but intimated that he could not object to its renewal before a judge in chambers. Accordingly, next day, 3 May, Willie Mathews made application to Baron Pollock,[1] submitting that in cases of misdemeanour the judge had no option but was bound to grant bail by virtue of a

---

1. Sir Charles Edward Pollock (1823–97) was appointed Baron of the Court of Exchequer in 1873. The consolidation of the Courts effected by the Judicature Acts in 1875 gave him the status of a judge of the High Court, but did not alter his official designation. He was the last surviving holder in England of the ancient judicial title of baron.

219

statute of Charles II. Mathews offered two sureties in the sum of £1,000 each, but Baron Pollock, having consulted with Mr Justice Charles, fixed the total amount at £5,000, directing that Wilde must give his personal security for £2,500 and find two sureties in £1,250 each. In due course this was done, the sureties to come forward being the Marquess of Queensberry's eldest surviving son, Lord Douglas of Hawick,[1] and the Rev. Stewart Headlam, a Church of England clergyman, who, while quite unknown to Wilde, had admired his bearing during the trial and sympathized with him for his treatment by the press and public generally.[2]

Some further delay was occasioned by the need for the police to make the customary inquiries about the sureties, but eventually, on the formal application of Mr Travers Humphreys to the

1. Percy Sholto (Douglas), Lord Douglas of Hawick and Tibbers (1868–1920) succeeded his father as ninth Marquess of Queensberry in 1900. He had a somewhat chequered career, which ended in penury in South Africa.

2. This kind-hearted parson, who was threatened with stoning by a furious mob outside his house in Bloomsbury, published the following statement after Wilde's conviction:

I became bail for Mr Oscar Wilde on public grounds: I felt that the action of a large section of the press, of the theatrical managers at whose houses his plays were running, and of his publisher, was calculated to prejudice his case before his trial had even begun.

I was a surety, not for his character, but for his appearance in Court to stand his trial. I had very little personal knowledge of him at the time; I think I had only met him twice; but my confidence in his honour and manliness has been fully justified by the fact that (if rumour be correct), notwithstanding strong inducements to the contrary, he stayed in England and faced his trial.

Now that the trial is over, and Mr Wilde has been convicted and sentenced, I still feel that I was absolutely right in the course I took, and I hope that, after he has gone through his sentence, Mr Wilde may be able, with the help of his friends, to do good work in his fresh life. – *Church Reformer*, 1 June 1895.

Further details about Stewart Headlam (1847–1924) will be found in the biography by F. G. Bettany (1926). He was an early member of the Fabian Society and a vigorous pioneer of elementary education. Asked by a heckler at a London School Board election meeting whether he was not 'the man that went bail for the notorious convict Wilde', Headlam replied amid cheers: 'Yes, I am the man, and by the laws of England everyone is reckoned innocent until he is proved guilty.'

The Second Trial

Bow Street magistrate on 7 May, Wilde was released in the bail agreed. He had been in custody in Holloway for just over a month 'bored and sick to the death of this place'. 'Oh,' he exclaimed, 'I hope all will come well, and that I can go back to Art and Life.' But, as it happened, he had less than three weeks of freedom ahead of him.

CHAPTER 5

THE THIRD TRIAL

1

FROM Bow Street Police Court, where the formalities for bail were completed, Wilde drove with Lord Douglas of Hawick to the Midland Hotel, St Pancras, where two rooms had been reserved for him. He stayed there for several hours and was about to sit down to dinner with Lord Douglas when the manager burst into their sitting-room. 'You are Oscar Wilde, I believe.' On Wilde's admitting his identity, the manager told him he must leave at once. He now realized that the implacable Queensberry was on his trail again. The Marquess had hired a gang of roughs and instructed them to follow Wilde and see that he did not secure admittance to any hotel in town. They did indeed hunt Wilde from hotel to hotel, and managed to achieve their object even in the surburban localities (as they then were) of Kilburn and Notting Hill, where their unfortunate quarry imagined he would not be known. Towards midnight, however, they lost sight of him. At this time Wilde's mother was living with Willie in Oakley Street, Chelsea, and it was to the door of their house that Wilde at length staggered in a state of complete physical exhaustion. 'Give me shelter, Willie,' he gasped as his astonished brother opened the door. 'Let me lie on the floor, or I shall die in the streets.' With these words he collapsed across the threshold, as Willie Wilde put it, 'like a wounded stag'.

Oscar Wilde remained in Oakley Street for the next few days, feeling ill and miserable. The family atmosphere had the worst possible psychological effect upon him. Both his eccentric mother and his drunken brother kept telling him that he must behave like an Irish gentleman and face the music. 'This house is depressing,' he complained. 'Willie makes such a merit of giving me shelter. He means well, I suppose, but it is all dreadful.' Robert Sherard,

who came over from Paris to see him at this time, found the
wretched man lying on a camp bed in a poorly furnished room,
in which everything was in great disorder. His face was flushed
and swollen and his voice broken. He also showed signs of heavy
drinking.[1] 'Why have you brought me no poison from Paris?' he
kept repeating. Willie Wilde seemed incapable of understanding
his brother. 'Oscar was not a man of bad character,' he naïvely
told Bernard Shaw. 'You could have trusted him with a woman
anywhere.'

The news of Wilde's misadventures was now becoming generally known, and had even passed beyond the channel. On 15 May
Lord Alfred Douglas wrote from his enforced exile in Paris: 'The
proprietor is very nice and most sympathetic; he asked after you
at once and expressed his regret and indignation at the treatment
you had received.'[2] But it was for two ladies to show the greatest
feeling of kindness towards the fallen writer. One of these good
samaritans, Miss Adela Schuster, who had heard of his threatened
bankruptcy, sent him a cheque for £1,000. The other was Ada
Leverson, 'The Sphinx'. She and her husband offered him the
hospitality of their comfortable house in Courtfield Gardens,
where he could rest and be quiet until the beginning of the next
trial.

Meanwhile, in the Treasury offices in Whitehall, preparations
were going ahead for the new prosecution. It had already leaked
out that this would be led, not by Charles Gill, as at the previous
trial, but by Sir Frank Lockwood, the Solicitor-General.[3] Thus
it appeared as if the Crown was now determined to make every

1. W. E. Henley wrote to Charles Whibley at this time: 'As for Hosker
[*sic*], the news is that he lives with his brother, and is all day steeping himself
in liquor and moaning for Boasy [*sic*]. . . . They say he has lost all nerve, all
pose, all everything; and is just now so much the ordinary drunkard that
he hasn't even the energy to kill himself.' Connell, pp. 301–2.
2. For Lord Alfred Douglas's detailed views on this and other aspects
of the Wilde case, see Appendix D.
3. Sir Frank Lockwood (1847–1897) was appointed Solicitor-General by
Lord Rosebery in 1894. Amongst other things he was a clever caricaturist
and contributor to *Punch*. His comparatively early death cut short a fine
career and was a great loss to the English bar. See the excellent biography
by his friend Augustine Birrell (1898).

effort towards securing a conviction. To one member of the Bar at least, such a course did not commend itself. This was Edward Carson, who had defended Queensberry at the first trial, but who had refused to have anything to do with the subsequent proceedings against Wilde.

The great Irish advocate went to Lockwood. 'Cannot you let up on the fellow now?' he said. 'He has suffered a great deal.'

'I would,' replied Lockwood, 'but we cannot: we dare not: it would at once be said, both in England and abroad that owing to the names mentioned in Queensberry's letters we were forced to abandon it.'

The Solicitor-General might have added that the name of his wife's nephew had also cropped up more than once in the two previous trials as having been one of Taylor's notorious circle of acquaintances. The circumstances were extremely unfortunate for Wilde. Indeed, but for their existence, the Crown might conceivably have abandoned the prosecution in the face of the jury's recent disagreement, while at the same time a strong semi-official hint might have been given to Wilde that he should leave the country for a time.

As it was, Wilde was pressed by most of his friends to 'jump' his bail and go abroad. Lord Douglas of Hawick told his co-surety, the Rev. Stewart Headlam, that he would hold himself liable for the whole amount and that he hoped Wilde would bolt. 'It will practically ruin me if I lose all that money at the present moment,' he said, 'but if there is a chance even of a conviction, for God's sake let him go.' Frank Harris is said to have had arrangements in hand for getting him away in a private yacht. Wilde's kind hostess, Ada Leverson added her voice to the others, and even the unfortunate Constance Wilde came round to Courtfield Gardens and pleaded with her husband in tears. But their entreaties were all in vain. Wilde obstinately refused to budge. He would not 'run away' and 'hide' and 'let down' his sureties. 'I could not bear life if I were to flee,' he said. 'I cannot see myself slinking about the Continent, a fugitive from justice.' More than once he remarked to Headlam: 'I have given my word to you and to my mother, and that is enough.' To Lord Alfred Douglas,

who had been the unwitting cause of his misfortunes, he wrote:
'A dishonoured name, a hunted life, are not for me to whom you
have been revealed on that high hill where beautiful things are
transfigured.' And besides that, he considered he had, as he put it,
'a good chance of being acquitted'.

One day, when Wilde was still at his brother's house in Oakley
Street, Frank Harris called in a hansom and persuaded him to
come out to lunch. They avoided his old haunts like the Café
Royal, where he might have been recognized and insulted, going
instead to a quiet restaurant in Great Portland Street. Over
coffee the two men discussed the way the trial had gone. Harris
put forward the view that an English jury with normal healthy
instincts could be expected not to convict a man solely on the
sworn statements of proved blackmailers. The evidence which
Harris felt had weighed most with them was that of the youth
Shelley and the various Savoy Hotel employees, particularly the
chambermaid Cotter, since these witnesses were none of them
connected with the blackmailer's loathsome business.

To Harris's intense surprise Wilde declared that the testimony
of the hotel employees was wrong. 'They are mistaken, Frank,'
he said. 'It was not I they spoke about at the Savoy. *It was Bosie
Douglas. I was never bold enough. I went to see Bosie in the
morning in his room.*'

'Thank God,' explained Harris, 'but why didn't Sir Edward
Clarke bring that out?'

'He wanted to, but I would not let him. I told him he must
not. I must be true to Bosie. I could not let him.'

'But he must,' said Harris. 'At any rate if he does not, I will.
I have three weeks, and in that three weeks I am going to find
the chambermaid. I am going to get a plan of your room and
Bosie's room, and I am going to make her understand that she
was mistaken. She probably remembered you because of your
size. She mistook you for the guilty person.'

'But what good is it, Frank? What good is it?' asked Wilde.
'Even if you convinced the chambermaid and she retracted, there
would still be Shelley, and the judge laid stress on Shelley's
evidence as untainted.'

Oscar Wilde

Harris observed that Shelley appeared in the witness box as an accomplice, and that his testimony consequently required corroboration. There was not a particle of corroboration, he went on. Sir Edward Clarke might have succeeded in having this part of the case withdrawn from the jury like the counts concerning Mavor, had not the issue been complicated by the conspiracy charges. 'You'll see,' he added reassuringly, 'Shelley's evidence too will be ruled out at the next trial.'

'Oh, Frank!' cried Wilde. 'You talk with passion and conviction, as if I were innocent.'

'But you are innocent, aren't you?' asked Harris in amazement.

'No, Frank,' replied the other. 'I thought you knew that all along.'

For some seconds Harris seemed stupefied by this confession. Then he said: 'No, I did not know. I did not believe the accusation. I did not believe it for a moment.'[1]

2

The secret of Wilde's stay with the Leversons was well kept. All the servants, who were asked, gladly agreed to look after him, excepting only the coachman, who was not told but sent away instead on a holiday lest he might talk in the neighbouring public houses. On this occasion Wilde certainly seems to have behaved like a model guest, remaining in his rooms upstairs, actually the nursery, all day, and only coming down for dinner in the evening with the rest of the household.

He remained at No. 2, Courtfield Gardens until 20 May, the date on which he was due to surrender to his bail at the Old Bailey. For the duration of the trial he returned to his brother's house in Oakley Street. Among his visitors during this brief inter-

1. This incident was later described by Harris in his book on Wilde (I, pp. 284–6), but the passages italicized above were for obvious reasons omitted from the account given in the English edition. Mr Hesketh Pearson rejects the story in his biography (p. 308); but, since its substance was confirmed by Wilde himself in the suppressed part of *De Profundis* as well as by R. H. Sherard, I feel it is entitled to belief.

lude of freedom was the brilliant French painter Count Henri de Toulouse-Lautrec, who at a single sitting was able to sketch against a foggy background of Big Ben and the River Thames a most vivid impressionist portrait.[1]

Since no fresh indictments had been preferred, it was unnecessary for the case to go before a grand jury a second time, although several counts had been dropped from the original indictment in addition to those charging Wilde and Taylor with conspiracy on which a verdict of not guilty had been returned by the jury at the previous trial. By special arrangement, the cases of the two defendants were called on the opening day of the sessions. The presiding judge was the seventy-seven year old Sir Alfred Wills, a person of considerable and varied attainments, being a well-known mountaineer, a scholar in classics and mathematics as well as in law, and the editor of a learned work on circumstantial evidence.[2] Sir Frank Lockwood, Q.C., M.P., along with Mr Charles Gill and Mr Horace Avory, appeared for the prosecution. Wilde and Taylor were represented by the same counsel as at the preceding trial.

As soon as the two defendants had taken their places in the dock and their pleas of not guilty had been formally recorded, Sir Edward Clarke applied to the judge that they should be tried separately. He pointed out that, since the conspiracy charges had been withdrawn, there was no single count standing in the indictment on which both prisoners could be convicted together. Although strenuously opposed by the Solicitor-General, his application was granted by the Bench. Lockwood thereupon intimated his intention of taking Taylor's case first. It was now Clarke's turn to protest. He urged that his client's case should have priority since his name stood first on the indictment and the first count was directed against him. 'There are reasons, I am

1. The portrait was used later, in the form of a lithograph reproduction, as part of the programme when *Salomé* was first performed in Paris in 1896, while Wilde was still in prison. On Wilde and Toulouse-Lautrec, see particularly Maurice Joyant, *Henri de Toulouse-Lautrec* (Paris, 1926), pp. 175–8.

2. Sir Alfred Wills (1828–1912) was appointed a judge of the Queen's Bench Division of the High Court in 1884. He was one of the founders of the Alpine Club in 1858 and subsequently became its president.

sure, present to your lordship's mind,' he went on, 'why it would be unjust to Mr Wilde that his case should be tried after, and immediately after, the other defendant.' Lockwood again intervened, and in spite of Clarke's repeated protests, Mr Justice Wills ruled that the prosecution could please itself in the matter. His lordship added that he was sure both the jury and himself would take care that the one trial should have no influence on the other. 'If there should be an acquittal, so much the better for the other prisoner.' He agreed, however, that while Taylor was being tried, Wilde should again be released on bail. Some hours elapsed before the sureties could be found, and Wilde did not leave the building until late in the afternoon.

The point of Clarke's remarks soon became painfully clear. Both Taylor and his defending counsel put up a good showing in the face of severe and, as Grain thought, unfair tactics on the part of the Solicitor-General; but his guilt was plain almost from the beginning. Besides the sworn statements of the Crown witnesses, the inferences to be drawn by the jury from the prisoner's own admission that a series of low-class youths had stayed in his rooms and that they had shared the same bed together were quite inescapable. For instance, Charles Parker swore that Taylor kept him in his rooms for a whole week, during which time they rarely went out, calling him 'Darling' and referring to him as his 'little wife'. According to Parker, when he left, Taylor paid him some money. 'He said I should never want for cash,' Parker declared, 'and that he would introduce me to men prepared to pay for that kind of thing.'

Perhaps the most damaging corroboration of the prosecution's charges was a letter addressed to Taylor from a young man named Charles Mason, with whom, it will be remembered, Taylor at the previous trial had denied going through a mock 'marriage' ceremony.[1] The letter had been discovered by the police in a hat-box which Taylor had left behind in his rooms in Chapel Street. According to Taylor, Mason was 'connected with a newspaper' in the sense of being a shareholder and was 'a very busy man';

1. Wilde wrote to Mason in August 1894: 'I hope marriage has not made you too serious? It has never had that effect on me.' Hart-Davis, p. 364.

The Third Trial

Taylor said he was a very old friend whom he had known since boyhood.

1st November 1891

My dear Alfred,

As soon as you can afford it do let me have some money and I shall be pleased and obliged. I would not ask you if I could get any myself, but you know the business is not so easy. There is a lot of trouble attached to it. I have not met anyone yet. Come home soon, dear, and let us go out sometimes together. Have very little news. Going to a dance on Monday and to a theatre tonight.

With much love,

Yours always,

CHARLIE

'I ask you, Taylor, for an explanation,' said the Solicitor-General after he had read out the letter in the course of his cross-examination, for it requires one, of the use of the words "Come home soon, dear", as between two men.'

'I don't see anything in it,' the witness replied with a nervous laugh.

'Nothing in it?'

'Well, anyhow I am not responsible for the expressions of another.'

'You allowed yourself to be addressed in this strain?'

'It's the way you read it.'

'Then read it yourself, sir,' thundered the Solicitor-General, 'and tell me if that is the kind of language you exchange with the men who were on such intimate terms with you that they slept in your bed?'

'I don't see anything in that,' was all Taylor could answer.

At this point Sir Edward Clarke made as if to rise in his seat, and said something which was inaudible to those in Court. As he did so, the Solicitor-General waved him down. 'You are not engaged in this case!' he reminded him.

Then, turning to the witness, Lockwood continued: 'Do you call it a proper letter, sir?'

'I think it is a perfectly proper letter, seeing the very long friendship which had existed between us,' Taylor replied. 'But, remember, I did not write the letter.'

229

Oscar Wilde

Here Mr Justice Wills intervened. 'In this letter written to you by Mason,' the judge asked, 'how do you explain the passage "I have not met anyone yet"?'

'He had been expecting someone to help him to get work,' the witness lamely explained.

'You are an old public school boy?' the Solicitor-General continued.

'Yes.'

'Was it not repugnant to your public school ideas, this habit of sleeping with men?'

'Not to me,' said Taylor. 'Where there is no harm done, I see nothing repugnant in it.'

Taylor was specifically charged with indecent behaviour with the two Parker brothers and also with procuring them and Wood for Wilde. So far as the indecency charges were concerned, Mr Justice Wills observed in his summing-up that, up to the point where indecency was alleged, the greater part of the Crown evidence had been admitted by the prisoner Taylor. 'It is evidence that shows an association between men of education and position with uneducated menservants,' said the judge, 'and this is certainly remarkable. The two Parkers have declared that improper conduct took place, and in my opinion there is sufficient corroboration to warrant the case going to the jury.' As for the charge of procuration, there was no doubt that the Parkers were introduced to Wilde by Taylor, but the judge warned the jury that unless they were satisfied that the introduction led to the consequences alleged, then it was nothing. 'God forbid,' the judge went on, 'that I should for a moment entertain the thought that for a man to give another a supper – no matter how greatly removed socially they are – is sufficient ground for suspicion; nay, not even though the one gave money to the other.' On the other hand, the judge directed that the counts charging Taylor with procuring Wood for Wilde must fail, as it had been shown that Wood's introduction to Wilde did not take place through Taylor, notwithstanding that Wilde and Wood subsequently met in Taylor's rooms. 'If you have any reasonable doubt as to the prisoner's guilt, he is entitled to the benefit of it,' Mr Justice Wills concluded. 'If, on the other hand, you believe that the charges against the prisoner have been satisfactorily proved, you have but one duty, though it is a sad one, to perform.'

After an absence of three-quarters of an hour, the jury returned to Court and the foreman informed the judge that they could not agree on the counts charging the prisoner with procuring, but that they were agreed on the other counts. Mr Justice Wills observed that in that case he thought it would be sufficient to take the jury's verdict on the counts alleging indecent behaviour with Charles and William Parker, to which course the Solicitor-General assented. The jury thereupon returned the verdict, which had been generally expected, of guilty on both these principal counts. The judge then announced that he would postpone sentence until after the charges against Wilde had been heard.

Some discussion followed as to whether the next trial should begin immediately. Clarke said he was quite ready if the Crown wished to go on, but, of course, with a different jury. Mr Justice Wills agreed that there should be a fresh jury, and on further consideration the Solicitor-General informed the Bench that he thought perhaps, as it was past four o'clock in the afternoon, it would be better to begin the next trial on the following morning.

'Very well,' said the judge, turning to the jury. 'I may repeat what I said yesterday, that I am most anxious to keep these two cases separate, and in these circumstances, gentlemen, having heard the evidence in this case, I think it is most proper, in the interest of securing a fair trial, that you should not try the next case, and that it should be heard by a jury from the next Court who have heard nothing in this case at all.'

Meanwhile, Wilde, who had been waiting in another part of the building with his sureties for most of the day, was at last able to leave, when he learned of the Court's decision not to proceed with his case until the next day.

Among the spectators in Court, who heard the news of Taylor's conviction with intense pleasure was Lord Queensberry. On leaving the Old Bailey, the Marquess drove to the West End of London, where he was staying in a hotel. He stopped first at the bottom of St James's Street, where he got out and went into the post office to send the following telegram to his daughter-in-law, Lady Douglas of Hawick, who was married to his son Percy.

To Lady Douglas: Must congratulate on verdict. Cannot on Percy's appearance. Looked like a dug up corpse. Fear too much madness of kissing. Taylor guilty. Wilde's turn tomorrow.

QUEENSBERRY

Having dispatched this insulting communication – he had already sent a number of similar messages to his daughter-in-law and other members of his family during the preceding weeks – Lord Queensberry continued his journey up St James's Street, and was about to cross Piccadilly in order to reach his hotel in Albemarle Street, when he saw his son Lord Douglas of Hawick on the other side of the road. The two men met at the corner of Bond Street, just opposite Scott's, the hatters. Lord Douglas approached his father, and in a respectful tone asked him to stop writing obscene letters to his wife. The Marquess replied by making a rude noise with his lips, and in a moment the two men were fighting. There was some doubt as to who struck the first blow, but in the subsequent Police Court proceedings the magistrate was satisfied, 'seeing that the Marquess is a boxer', that Queensberry did. A crowd immediately collected, and eventually the antagonists were separated by Police Constable Morrell, who was on duty nearby. The only result of the interference of the arm of the law was that they crossed the street to the pavement outside Stewart's, the confectioners, and there resumed their struggle. By this time another constable had appeared on the scene, and when the two fighters had again been separated they were arrested and taken to Vine Street Police Station. On being charged with disorderly conduct, the pugnacious Marquess said, pointing to Lord Douglas: 'That is my son, who has bailed Oscar Wilde today. He has been following me about, and struck me in Piccadilly.' 'Yes,' added the other, 'that occurred through my father writing letters of a most disgusting character to my wife.'[1]

Next day the two men were bound over at Great Marlborough

1. One of these characteristic messages was subsequently revealed by the Marquess to the London correspondent of the *New York Herald*. In the

232

Street Police Court in their own sureties of £500 to keep the peace for six months. It was a matter of little importance who began the fight, said the magistrate in giving his decision, because both were fighting, both were close to policemen, and neither invoked their assistance.

Meanwhile the town was placarded with Wilde's name as the accused was preparing for the final judicial ordeal. 'Well,' his friend Sherard remarked to him, 'you have got your name before the public at last.'

Wilde laughed. 'Yes,' he said. 'Nobody can pretend now not to have heard of it.'

3

Wilde entered the dock at the Old Bailey to stand trial for the second time on 22 May 1895. There were certain noticeable differences from the previous occasion. The defendant no longer had to meet any charges of conspiracy. The counts relating to Atkins and Mavor had likewise disappeared from the indictment, and with them the testimony of these two youths – Atkins, because he had perjured himself in the witness box, and Mavor, because he had persisted in denying that any indecencies had ever taken place between himself and Wilde. Nevertheless, the accused still had a formidable series of eight counts to meet. Four of these charged him with committing acts of gross indecency with Charles Parker at the Savoy Hotel, St James's Place, and elsewhere; two counts charged him with committing similar offences with unknown persons in the Savoy Hotel; one count related to

---

course of an interview Queensberry held up to the journalist's view a picture, which he had cut out of the *Illustrated London News*, showing a huge iguanodon as it was supposed to have appeared to its prehistoric contemporaries. 'I was struck with a certain resemblance lurking in this picture,' he remarked. 'I have sent a copy of it to my son's wife, endorsing it, as far as I can remember, as a possible ancestor of Oscar Wilde.' He is also stated to have sent a copy to Wilde himself at the Old Bailey. See *Reynold's Newspaper*, 9 June 1895; and Dulau's *Sale Catalogue of Wilde MSS.* (1928), p. 119.

alleged indecency with Wood in Tite Street; and the final count concerned Shelley. In addition, as we have seen, the Solicitor-General led for the prosecution instead of Charles Gill. This meant that the Crown had a decided advantage, since Lockwood as a Law Officer was entitled to the 'last word' in addressing the jury.

When the Solicitor-General had announced that Taylor should be tried first, Sir Edward Clarke had applied to have his client's trial stood over to the next sessions, since he felt that, notwithstanding the presence of a fresh jury, Wilde's position must be adversely affected if he were tried immediately after Taylor. Mr Justice Wills suggested that Clarke should renew his application at the end of Taylor's trial, but when the time came he decided that it would be fruitless to do so, in view of a letter he had received from the judge in the meantime. 'I doubt myself if any earthly purpose can be answered by postponing your case,' the judge had written to Clarke. 'Every man in the kingdom will know, or does know, the outlines of the evidence in this case, and my experience is very much in favour of juries as to mere matters of prejudice in criminal trails. If anything could make the prospect of Wilde's trial tolerable to me or anyone else, it is the fact that you will conduct the defence.'

Since a fresh jury had been empanelled, it was necessary for the prosecution to present its case in detail and to recapitulate much of the evidence given at Taylor's trial and at the two previous trials. However, in view of Mr Justice Charles's remarks in his summing-up as to the probative value of those portions of Wilde's publications which had been quoted by Carson and Gill at the two previous trials, the Solicitor-General wisely made no reference in his opening speech to what had come to be known as the literary part of the case, although the two letters to Lord Alfred Douglas were once more to be used against Wilde with damaging effect.

The first witness called by the prosecution was Edward Shelley, for whose story the Solicitor-General had claimed that there was independent corroboration, although it did not go to the length of describing the actual commission of the offences alleged to have been committed with Shelley. 'Acts like those alleged are not committed in the light of day,' Lockwood told the jury, 'but as far as possible with strictest secrecy and concealment.'

After he had repeated the evidence-in-chief he had given at the previous trial, Shelley was severely cross-examined by Clarke on his letters to Wilde: in these he expressed the most fulsome gratitude to Wilde for past kindnesses, although according to his story Wilde had forced him to commit indecencies with him on two separate occasions. 'I am most anxious to see you,' Shelley wrote in one letter. 'I would have called on you this evening but I am suffering from nervousness, the result of insomnia, and am obliged to remain at home. I have longed to see you all through the week. I have much to tell you. Do not think me forgetful in not coming before, because I shall never forget your kindness to me and am conscious that I can never sufficiently express my thankfulness to you.'

'Now, Mr Shelley,' Clarke asked the witness, 'do you mean to tell the jury that, having in your mind that this man had behaved disgracefully towards you, you wrote this letter?'

'Yes,' Shelley replied, 'because after these two occurrences he treated me very well. He seemed really sorry for what he had done.'

Other letters written by Shelley to Wilde and quoted by Clarke showed the witness to have been constantly complaining about his health. He was 'weak and ill' or 'so nervous and ill' or 'so thin, they think me strange'. He admitted that when he attacked his father and was arrested he was not in his right mind. 'I certainly could not have been sane to assault my father,' he said.

'Was your mental health getting worse and worse?' Clarke asked.

'I made myself ill with studying,' answered Shelley.

'Were you worse than you are today?'

'There is nothing the matter with me now.'

'You are sure of that?' Clarke asked in tones of great disbelief.

'Quite sure.'

The remainder of the day was mostly taken up with Alfred Wood's evidence. He repeated what he had said at the previous trials in his examination-in-chief; and, although cross-examined at length by Clarke, no new facts emerged from his testimony. It was only when he was re-examined by the Solicitor-General – his examination-in-chief had been conducted by Gill – that he said he had seen Wilde and Douglas together in the Savoy Hotel, a fact he had not mentioned before. 'On what terms did Lord Alfred and Mr Wilde appear to be?' the Solicitor-General asked Wood. At this Clarke jumped up and objected to the question. His objection was immediately upheld by the judge, and the re-examination concluded.

Next morning Clarke made a similarly successful objection, for what it was worth, when, in the course of re-examining William Parker, the Solicitor-General asked him what Taylor had said to him at the dinner after his brother and Wilde had gone off together to the Savoy Hotel. This evidence had in fact been given by the witness at the previous trial, when it was admissible, since on that occasion Taylor was being jointly tried with Wilde.[1]

Having, as he felt, successfully disposed of Shelley's evidence, Clarke tried to do the same with the Savoy Hotel servants. Realizing that this was a weak part of its case, the prosecution had brought in two additional witnesses from that establishment, another chambermaid and a waiter. Clarke first dealt with Jane Cotter, the chambermaid who had appeared at the previous trial. On this occasion Clarke noticed that she was wearing spectacles.

'Why do you wear eye-glasses?' Clarke asked her.

'Because my sight is bad,' the witness replied.

'Do you use them when you go about your work?'

'Oh dear, no!'

'Why do you wear them today?'

'Because I thought I might have to recognize somebody.'

'Then you did not wear them when you say you saw the boy in Mr Wilde's room?'

'No.'

'And you had to put them on if you wanted to recognize anybody today?'

'Yes.'

1. See above, p. 177-8.

The Third Trial

Jane Cotter, whose evidence-in-chief had been rendered largely worthless by this courteously brief but devastating cross-examination, was followed into the witness box by her fellow servant, Alice Saunders. The latter stated that her attention had been drawn by the previous witness to the condition of the sheets in Wilde's bedroom at the hotel.

Clarke put one question only. 'When were you first asked to give evidence in this case.'

'Last Friday.'

The next witness was Antonio Migge, the hotel masseur. Again answering Clarke, this witness said that he had no idea whether the door of Wilde's bedroom was locked or not on the morning he called. Clarke then reminded him that at the last trial he had sworn that the door was not locked. Clarke's next question also emphasized the witness's faulty memory.

'Was the boy you say you saw there fair or dark?'

'I cannot remember.'

The waiter, Emile Becker, said he remembered Wilde and Douglas staying in the hotel in March, 1893. After Douglas had left, he had taken champagne and whiskies to Wilde's bedroom, and he remembered seeing several young men there, about five in all. He also said he had served a supper of cold fowl and champagne to Wilde and a dark young man in Wilde's sitting-room. The bill was 16s.

'I suppose you read the accounts of the previous trial?' Clarke asked the waiter in cross-examination.

'Oh, yes.'

'You saw it stated that Parker said he had had chicken and champagne?'

'I think I saw it on Monday.'

'Had you not seen it before?' the judge broke in.

'No,' replied the waiter.

'It was a matter of considerable interest to everybody at the Savoy Hotel?' Clarke continued.

'Yes, it was,' the witness agreed.

'How many rooms had you to look after?'

'Seven sitting-rooms.'

'Plenty of suppers in such a busy place?'
'Not many upstairs.'
'Have you seen Charles Parker?'
'Yes, he was pointed out to me.'
'You did not recognize him?'
'No.'
'When were you asked to give evidence at this trial?'
'Last Friday. I was seen by an inspector from Scotland Yard.'

After the other Crown witnesses had given their testimony and the evidence at the Queensberry trial had been read out a second time, Sir Edward Clarke rose to make a number of submissions to the judge. In the first place, he submitted that, in regard to the counts alleging indecent practices at the Savoy Hotel, there was no case to go to the jury. 'Parker has sworn that he left the hotel on both occasions after midnight,' said Clarke; 'and he cannot, therefore, be identified with the boys whom the hotel servants declared they saw there in the mornings.'

'The condition of the rooms furnishes a certain amount of corroboration of the charges of misconduct,' Mr Justice Wills remarked. 'The very fact that a man in such a position in life as the prisoner is found with a boy in his bedroom seems to me so utterly unusual that very little additional evidence would make the case go to the jury. On the other hand, it has been sworn to by the chambermaid that whatever happened there was reported to the housekeeper, and it is a very strange thing that she should have done nothing about it. I do not know what sort of a person she can have been to take no steps in the matter at once.'

'It might have been', the Solicitor-General intervened to say, 'that the hotel authorities were anxious to avoid the publication of a scandal that would be prejudicial to their establishment.'

'In my submission,' said Wilde's counsel, 'there is no evidence whatever to support the charge that Mr Wilde and a boy were in bed together.'

'The point in respect to the Savoy Hotel incidents is just on the line,' the judge observed. 'The fact that Mr Wilde was said to have rung for the chambermaid to come into the room makes it difficult for me completely to accept this story. The incident deposed to by the masseur Migge is even more slender from the point of view of evidence. It would not be fair to a man charged as Mr Wilde is that a number of nothings should be put to make up a something. I think, however, on the whole the wiser and safer course would be to allow the count in respect to this matter to go to the jury.' The judge added that the question was so completely on the line that he should feel justified in reserving it for the Court of Crown Cases Reserved if counsel so desired.

Clarke went on to submit that there was no corroboration with regard to Shelley, and that his evidence ought likewise to be withdrawn from the jury. 'The letters of Shelley point to the inference that he may have been the victim of delusions,' argued Wilde's counsel, 'and, judging from his conduct in the witness box, he appears to have a peculiar sort of exaltation in and for himself.'

Lockwood, on the other hand, maintained that Shelley's evidence was corroborated as far as it possibly could be. 'What are the relations of these two men of such unequal ages? I shall invite the jury to say that Shelley is a young man who was fascinated by the literary culture of Wilde and brought within Wilde's control and domination – that he was "entrapped", as Shelley put it, and that he was not so much an accomplice as a victim. There is, after all, a certain amount of corroboration – evidence of opportunity.'

'I must confess that Shelley's letters have left on my mind a notion of disturbed intellect,' said the judge. 'It would be a terrible thing for society at large if it were to be considered unnatural for a man to ask a younger man of good character to dine with him.'

'I would remind your lordship of the letter in which Shelley wrote "Let God judge of the past",' the Solicitor-General rejoined, 'and also of the fact that Shelley is not in the position of an accomplice.'

'With regard to Shelley I am very clearly of the opinion that he must be treated, on his own evidence, on the footing of an accomplice, and that his evidence should be corroborated,' Mr Justice Wills now remarked. 'It seems to me there is nothing of *no case here*

A

the kind here. Shelley's own letters to Wilde are rather against the supposition. After a most careful consideration of the point, I adhere to the view, which I had already formed, that there is no corroboration of the nature required by law to warrant conviction, and therefore I feel justified in withdrawing this part of the case from the consideration of the jury.'

This judicial ruling from the Bench, which necessarily involved the acquittal of the prisoner on an important count in the indictment – indeed the only one charging him with an offence against a youth of good education and character – created a great impression, and a buzz of excitement ran round the Court.

Finally, Wilde's counsel referred to the case of Wood, submitting that there was no corroboration of any sort or kind of his evidence that he had been to Tite Street.

'My lord,' said the Solicitor-General, addressing the Bench, 'I must protest against any decision being given on these questions other than by a verdict of the jury. In my opinion the case of the man Wood cannot be withheld from the jury. I submit that there is every element of strong corroboration of Wood's story, having regard especially to the strange and suspicious circumstances under which Mr Wilde and Wood became acquainted. There is also corroboration on the payment by Mr Wilde of the money which enabled Wood to go to America.' The Solicitor-General went on to quote authorities to show that, although Mr Justice Wills had rightly stated the rule of practice, it was not a rule of law, and that it was the duty of a judge to tell the jury that they might, if they so pleased, act on the unconfirmed testimony of an accomplice.

This brought Clarke to his feet. 'It is cruel to suggest', he said, 'that the generous action of a man in giving a lad the means of getting away from bad companions to begin a new life in another country is a corroboration of his own misconduct.' Wilde's counsel then quoted other authorities in answer to Lockwood's, including the admirable words uttered by Mr Justice Charles on the subject of corroboration in the previous trial. 'I rely, therefore,' said Clarke, 'upon this rule of practice

as a wholesome rule of two hundred years' standing, even if it is
not actually a rule of law.'

The judge eventually resolved the matter by saying that he
thought that the counts affecting Wood ought to go to the jury.
'I think that this case is slightly different from that of Shelley,'
he said. 'I have no doubt as to the wholesome rule on which I
acted in the other case, and when it comes to my turn to sum up,
I shall explain why I did not withdraw Wood's case from the jury,
and in what direction I find corroboration. It seems to me, after
hearing the cross-examination of Mr Wilde in the Queensberry
case, that the relations of the two men form a question which the
jury ought to consider.'

4

Sir Edward Clarke opened his defence on the third morning of
the trial. 'I shall call Mr Wilde into the witness box again to
state on his oath for the third time in this Court that there is no
truth whatever in the accusations which are made against him,'
he told the jury, 'and to face for the third time in this Court,
and now with a new assailant, that cross-examination which
may be administered to him in regard to these accusations.' After
relating how the conspiracy charges had been withdrawn in the
previous trial, and how the jury had disagreed upon a verdict as
to the remaining counts, Clarke said he could not imagine any
reason 'of logic or fairness' which could be suggested for the
course which was adopted of trying Taylor first. In Taylor's trial,
moreover, the jury had been unable to agree on the issue referring
to Wilde, and they had been discharged without giving a verdict
as to that issue. 'Practically this is the third time that this issue
has been placed before a jury,' said Clarke. 'There can be no
cause of complaint against me if I feel a little soreness at the
treatment Mr Wilde has received.'

Wilde's counsel then spoke of the Crown evidence and
emphasized that at the previous trial his client had made only one
statement contradicted by an independent witness, namely that

he had never been to Charles Parker's lodgings in Park Walk. 'I ask you to remember that in relation to the question with which you have to deal,' he said. 'It is not enough to discredit the evidence of the accused. The Crown must persuade you to believe the evidence of their witnesses, if their case is to be established. The action of Mr Wilde has not been in the least inconsistent with that of a man who, conscious of innocence, is prepared to face the charges of blackmailers. I ask you to believe that a guilty man could not undergo the terrible ordeal of examination and cross-examination in the witness box on three different occasions. . . . Mr Wilde has heroically fought against the accusations made against him, accusations that have broken down piece by piece.'

As a rule Sir Edward Clarke was most moderate and restrained in his choice of language, but on this occasion he felt impelled to comment severely on the prosecution's conduct of the case against his client. He pointed out that he had himself held the office of Solicitor-General for six years, a longer period than any man had held it during the last hundred years, so that he was unlikely at any place or time to speak lightly of the responsibilities of that office. 'I always look upon the responsibility of a Crown counsel, and especially upon the responsibility of a Law Officer of the Crown, as a public rather than a private interest or responsibility,' he said. 'He is a minister of justice, with a responsibility more like the responsibility of a judge than like that of a counsel retained for a particular combatant in a forensic fray. . . . While, therefore, I say these things without the least unfriendliness of feeling towards the Solicitor-General, I say them in the hope that I may do something to induce my learned friend to remember – what I fear for a moment yesterday he forgot – that he is not here to try to get a verdict by any means he may have, but that he is here to lay before the jury for their judgement the facts on which they will be asked to come to a very serious consideration.'

As the case had been whittled down, Clarke went on, so the efforts of the prosecution had been redoubled. Instead of Gill – 'of the tone of whose conduct of the last case I had never for a moment to complain' – down came a Law Officer of the Crown armed with a strange and invidious privilege, 'which I myself when Solicitor-General never once exercised and will not exercise if ever I fill that distinguished position again', of overriding the usual practice of the Court. 'Whether the defendant calls witnesses or not, the Solicitor-General enjoys the right – though why he should enjoy it I cannot imagine – of the last word with the jury. But for this, I might have relied upon the reading of the defendant's evidence at the last trial. Reckoning with this, the defendant, broken as he is now, as anyone who saw him at the last trial must see he is, by being kept in prison without bail – contrary to practice and, as I believe, contrary to law – will submit himself again to the indignity and pain of going into the witness box. Unfit as he is after the ordeal he has gone through, he will repeat on oath his denial of the charges which have been made against him.'

It was only when Wilde had taken his place in the box and had begun to answer his counsel's questions that the full force of Clarke's remarks became apparent. He looked haggard; his hair, usually so neatly dressed, was in disorder; and his voice sounded hollow and husky. At his counsel's request, he was allowed to remain seated while giving evidence. But, if his customary sparkle and verve seemed largely to have deserted him, he certainly answered Clarke's final question in the examination-in-chief with marked determination.

'Is there any truth in the accusations made against you in this indictment?'

'None whatever!'

When the Solicitor-General began to cross-examine, it was evident that Clarke's remonstrance had exercised some salutary effect, since the tone of his questions was relatively moderate. Lockwood began by asking the witness about his association with Douglas.

'When did your acquaintance with Lord Alfred Douglas begin?'

'In 1892.'

'And when did the Marquess of Queensberry first object?'

'In March 1893.'

'Are you sure?'

Oscar Wilde

'I am very bad about dates,' said Wilde. 'It must have been last year, 1894.'[1]

'Now, Mr Wilde,' the Solicitor-General continued, 'I should like you to tell me where Lord Alfred Douglas is now?'

'He is abroad.'

'Where?'

'In Paris, at the Hotel des Deux Mondes.'

'How long has he been there?'

'About three weeks.'

'Was he in London at the time of the trial of the Marquess of Queensberry?'

'Yes, for about three weeks. He went away to France at my wish before the first trial on these counts came on.'

'Of course,' said Lockwood, 'you have been in communication with him?'

'Certainly,' answered Wilde. 'These charges are founded on sand. Our friendship is founded on a rock. There has been no need to cancel the acquaintance.'

'What did you do when you learned that the Marquess of Queensberry objected to your friendship with his son?'

'I said I was perfectly ready to cease the acquaintance, if it would make peace between him and his father. But he preferred to do otherwise.'

'And the intervention of his father had no effect?'

'No.'

The Solicitor-General then proceeded to read out the now notorious 'prose poem' letter. He also referred to the second letter, which had been written from the Savoy Hotel.

'Are these a sample of the style in which you addressed Lord Alfred Douglas?'

'No! I do not think I should say a sample,' Wilde replied to this question. 'No! The letter written from Torquay was intended to be a kind of prose poem, in answer to a poem Lord Alfred had written to me in verse. It was written under circumstances of great feeling.'

1. Wilde was also mistaken about the date of his first meeting with Douglas. It took place early in 1891: see above, p. 63.

The Third Trial

'Why did you choose the words "My own Boy" as a mode of address?'

'I adopted them because Lord Alfred Douglas is so much younger than myself. The letter was a fantastic, extravagant way of writing to a young man. As I said at the first trial, it does not seem to me to be a question of whether a thing is right or proper, but of literary expression. It was like a little sonnet of Shakespeare.'

'I did not use the word proper or right,' said Lockwood. 'Was it decent?'

'Oh, decent?' Wilde replied. 'Of course. There is nothing indecent in it.'

'Do you think that was a decent way for a man of your age to address a young man of his?'

'It was a beautiful way for an artist to address a young man of culture and charm. Decency does not enter into it.'

'Doesn't it?' said Lockwood sharply. 'Do you understand the meaning of the word, sir?'

'Yes,' Wilde replied, keeping his temper well under control.

'"It is a marvel that those red rose-leaf lips of yours should have been made no less for music of song than for madness of kisses." And do you consider that decent?'

'It was an attempt to write a prose poem in beautiful phraseology.'

'Did you consider it decent phraseology?' Lockwood pressed.

'Oh, yes, yes,' Wilde answered with a touch of impatience.

'Then do you consider that a decent mode of addressing a young man?'

'I can only give you the same answer, that it is a literary mode of writing what is intended to be a prose poem.'

'"Your slim gilt soul walks between passion and poetry ... Hyacinthus, whom Apollo loved so madly, was you in Greek days." You were speaking of love between men?'

'What I meant by the phrase was that he was a poet, and Hyacinthus was a poet.'

'"Always with undying love"?' Lockwood went on quoting.

'It was not a sensual love.'

'Is that again poetic imagery, or an expression of your feelings?'

'That is an expression of my feelings,' said Wilde, rising from his seat in the witness box and bowing with a smile to the Solicitor-General.

Lockwood then read the letter from the Savoy Hotel. When he came to the passage 'My bill here is £49', he broke off. 'That, I suppose is true? That is not poetic?' he asked the witness in his most sarcastic tone of voice.

'Oh, no, no!' Wilde replied good-humouredly. 'That is prose of the most sordid kind!'

After he had finished reading the second letter to Douglas, the Solicitor-General asked: 'He came and stayed with you at the Savoy?'

'Yes, in the month of February 1893.'

'Did he come to you in response to that appeal?'

'He came shortly afterwards, on his way to Germany.'

'How often did he stay with you at the Savoy Hotel?'

'Three times.'

'You were alone, you two?'

'Oh, yes.'

'The approach to your room was through his?'

'Yes.'

'Were you aware of his father objecting to your intimacy?'

'Oh, no! Not at that time.'

'What was the charge Lord Queensberry made against you?'

Wilde hesitated for a few moments before replying: 'Posing as a sodomite.'

'Between Lord Queensberry's committal and his trial, did you and Lord Alfred Douglas go abroad?'

'Yes. We were abroad about a week, and I returned to appear as prosecutor.'

'Before the trial did you see Lord Queensberry's plea of justification?'

'Yes.'

'The plea alleged all the misconduct of which evidence has since been given, besides making charges which have not been heard because they referred to occurrences in Paris?'

'Yes.'

'Did you abandon the prosecution?'

'It was abandoned by the advice of my counsel.'

'With your consent?' queried Lockwood.

'Yes, I admit it was with my consent, but none of those matters had been entered into,' Wilde replied. 'It was entirely about literature, and it was represented to me that I could not get a verdict because of those two letters you have read.'

Questioned about Taylor's rooms in Little College Street and the people he met there, Wilde said he only went there to tea-parties lasting half an hour or so, and after such a lapse of time he could not remember whom he had met there besides Mavor and Schwabe and some of the witnesses. 'You ask me to remember whom I met at a tea-party three years ago. It is childish. How can I?'

'Did you see anything remarkable in the furnishing of Taylor's rooms?'

'No, nothing.'

'The windows were curtained?'

'Yes, but not obscured.'

'Did you know that Taylor's male friends stayed with him and shared his bed?'

'No; I know it now.'

'Does that alter your opinion of Taylor?'

'No, I don't think so. I don't think it is necessary to conclude that there was anything criminal. I don't believe anything criminal took place between Taylor and these boys; and, if they were poor and he shared his bed with them, it may have been charity.'

'Did it shock you that he should have done it?'

'No, I saw no necessity for being shocked.'

This answer did not satisfy the Solicitor-General. 'I must press you,' he persisted. 'Do you approve of his conduct?'

'I don't think I am called upon to express approval or disapproval of any person's conduct,' Wilde replied.

'Would the knowledge that they habitually shared his bed alter your opinion of Taylor?'

'No.'

247

Realizing the dangerous course this line of cross-examination was taking, apart from what he considered to be the inadmissibility of the questions, Clarke now jumped up and objected to the witness being asked his opinion of other people. The judge upheld the objection, but pointed out that it came too late.

Lockwood then turned to the presents Wilde had given the young men he had met at Taylor's. 'Do you remember giving Mavor a cigarette case?'

'Yes, it cost £4.'

'Did you give one to Charles Parker also?'

'Yes, but I am afraid it only cost £1.'

'Silver?' Lockwood queried.

'Well, yes,' said Wilde. 'I have a great fancy for giving cigarette cases.'

'To young men?'

'Yes.'

'How many have you given?'

'I might have given seven or eight in 1892 and 1893.'

'Surely,' the judge broke in, 'a cigarette case conveys no impression to anyone's mind unless he knows what you mean, Sir Frank?'

Ignoring this interruption from the Bench, Lockwood passed on to the next question. 'Was the conversation of these young men literary?'

'No,' said Wilde; 'but the fact that I had written a play which was a success seemed to them very wonderful, and I was gratified by their admiration.'

'By the admiration of these boys, whose very names you don't remember?'

'Yes, I admit that I am enormously fond of praise and admiration and that I like to be made much of by my inferiors – inferiors socially. It pleases me very much.'

'What pleasure could you find in the society of boys much beneath you in social position?'

'I make no social distinctions.'

'What did you do with them?'

'I read to them. I read one of my plays to them.'

The Third Trial

'You, a successful literary man, wished to obtain praise from these boys?' the Solicitor-General asked with an incredulous air.

'Praise from anyone is very delightful,' Wilde replied in one of his best impromptu answers in this cross-examination. 'Praise from literary people is usually tainted with criticism!'

Asked about Taylor's birthday party at which he had been host at Kettner's, Wilde admitted that he had given Taylor *carte blanche* to bring his friends.

'Did you limit the number?'

'Oh dear, no!'

'As many as he liked?'

'Well, I did not ask him to bring a crowd.'

'Then it was a pure coincidence that the table was laid for four and that he brought the two Parkers?'

'No.' said Wilde. 'I think he had ordered the dinner himself. I told him to go to Kettner's, because I have been in the habit for years of dining there.'

'Did you know at the time that the Parkers were a valet and a groom respectively?'

'No, and had I known it I should not have cared.'

'You have no sense at all of social differences?'

'No.'

'You preferred Charles?'

'I make no preferences.'

'You like bright boys?'

'I like bright boys,' Wilde agreed. 'Charles Parker was a bright boy. I liked him.'

'Did you not pause to consider whether it would be the slightest service to lads in their position to be entertained in such style by a man in your position?'

'No. They enjoyed it as schoolboys would enjoy a treat. It was something they did not get every day. I don't suppose they would have cared to be entertained to a chop and a pint of ale – they were used to that.'

'You looked on them as schoolboys?'

'They were amused by the little luxuries of Kettner's, the pink lampshades and so forth.'

'Did you give them wine?'

'Yes. I certainly should not stint a guest.'

'You would let them drink as much as they liked?' the Solicitor-General led the witness on.

'I should not limit their consumption,' Wilde replied. 'But I should consider it extremely vulgar for anyone to take too much wine at table.'

'After dinner what did you do?'

'I bade the Parkers good-bye and they went away with Taylor.'

'Did you not take Charles Parker to the Savoy Hotel?'

'No, certainly not.'

Questioned further about Taylor, Wilde said he thought his rooms were done up with considerable taste, and he also thought it good taste to use perfumes. 'His rooms were cheerful,' he added.

'Not a very cheerful street, Little College Street?'

'Few streets are cheerful. I have known artists who lived quite close there.'

'Did you like the situation?'

'I thought it a particularly nice one – close to Westminster Abbey!'

Asked about Alphonse Conway and when he had last seen him, Wilde said he had seen him outside the Court two days previously. Lockwood was going on to inquire about the 'moral effects' of taking a lad in Conway's position on an outing to Brighton and spending a night with him in a hotel there, when Lord Queensberry suddenly entered the Court. Being unable to find a seat, he remained standing at the back for some time, sucking the brim of his hat and staring at the witness. This unwelcome apparition had a most disconcerting effect upon the man in the witness box, who was seen to take frequent sips of water from a glass by his side.[1]

1. Wilde later wrote to Lord Alfred Douglas from prison, in the 'suppressed' part of *De Profundis*: 'I used to feel bitterly the irony and ignominy of my position when in the course of my three trials, beginning at the Police Court, I used to see your father bustling in and out in the hopes of attracting public attention, as if anyone could fail to note or remember the

The Third Trial

'Did you meet Wood by appointment at the Café Royal?' Lockwood continued.

'Yes,' said Wilde. 'I had been asked to assist him and took him to supper at the Florence. I had already had supper myself.'

'Then why not give him five shillings to go and get his supper?'

'Ah, that would be treating him like a beggar, He was sent to me by Lord Alfred Douglas.'

'Did you know he came from 13 Little College Street?'

'No, I did not know that. He told me he was a clerk out of employment and was anxious to find employment.' Wilde added that he could not get Wood a job, but he gave him money. 'The money was not really from me but was from Lord Alfred Douglas who was at Salisbury.'

'There are such things as postal orders, I believe?'

'Yes.'

'Did you tell him your people were away from home at the time?'

'Yes.'

'Why?'

'Oh, it occurred in the course of conversation.'

Asked about the letters, which Wood had found in the old suit of clothes Douglas had given him, Wilde admitted that he had gone to the meeting in Little College Street prepared to bargain for them if they were worth while buying back, but at the same time he strongly insisted that the money he gave Wood had nothing whatever to do with the delivery of the letters.

The Solicitor-General's concluding questions concerned Wilde's stay in the Savoy Hotel.

'In reference to the Savoy Hotel evidence, is it true that the masseur and the chambermaid saw the boys in your room?'

'Entirely untrue. No one was there.'

---

stableman's gait and dress, the bowed legs, the twitching hands, the hanging lower lip, the bestial and half-witted grin. Even when he was not there, or was out of sight, I used to feel conscious of his presence, and the blank dreary walls of the great courtroom, the very air itself, seemed to me at times to be hung with multitudinous masks of that apelike face.' Hart-Davis, p. 492.

'There was no one there, man or woman?'

'No.'

'You answer also that the chambermaid's statement is untrue?'

'Absolutely.'

'You deny that the bed linen was marked in the way described?'

'I do not examine bed linen when I arise. I am not a housemaid.'

'Were the stains there, sir?'

'If they were, they were not caused by the way the prosecution has most filthily suggested.'

In his brief re-examination of his client, Sir Edward Clarke paid particular attention to the case of Wood and Wilde's account of the transaction over the letters, which Lockwood had clearly shown that he disbelieved.

'Had you any interest in Wood beyond the fact of Lord Alfred Douglas knowing him?'

'None, except that Lord Alfred Douglas asked me to take an interest in the young man and be kind to him.'

'When Wood brought the letters to you, did he attempt to get money for them?'

'No. He at once handed me the letters and said he highly regretted that I should have thought him capable of trying to blackmail me.'

'Is it then positively untrue that you gave Wood £15 for the letters?' Clarke went on.

'I would not have given him fifteen pence for them,' answered Wilde. 'They were of no importance.'

'Was there anything in them you would object to have known?'

'There may be people who would regard some of the words as frivolous, but there was nothing in the letters,' Wilde repeated. 'They were of no importance.'

5

Sir Edward Clarke began his final speech to the jury by paying the Solicitor-General a tribute for the 'absolute fairness' with which he had cross-examined the defendant. 'If earlier in the day I was moved, by what I am glad to think I then described as the momentary forgetfulness of my learned friend yesterday, to expressions which sounded hostile in regard to him, he will let me say at once in the frankest manner that the way in which he has cross-examined absolutely destroys any suggestion which might have lain in my words.'

Wilde's counsel went on to dwell upon the fact, which he had repeatedly underlined throughout, that his client had invited publicity by his action against Lord Queensberry, and that the statements made by him under cross-examination in that action remained with one small exception uncontradicted by independent witnesses. 'I suggest to you, gentlemen, that your duty is simple and clear,' he said, 'and that when you find a man who is assailed by tainted evidence entering the witness box, and for a third time giving a clear, coherent, and lucid account of the transactions such as that which the accused has given today, I venture to say that that man is entitled to be believed against a horde of blackmailers such as you have seen. But there is a larger issue still in this matter. I know not on what grounds the course has been taken in this case which has been taken by the Crown.[1] I will not quarrel with it or discuss it, but it is important to remember that if blackmailers are to be listened to against the defendant in this case, then the profession of blackmailing will become a more deadly mischief than ever before.

'This trial seems to be operating as an act of indemnity for all the blackmailers of London. Wood and Parker, in giving evidence, have established for themselves a sort of statute of limitations. In testifying on behalf of the Crown, they have secured immunity for past rogueries and indecencies. It is on the evidence of Parker and Wood that you are asked to condemn Mr Wilde. And Mr Wilde knew nothing of the characters of these men. They were introduced to him, and it was his love of admiration that caused him to be in their society. The positions should really be changed. It is these men who ought to be the accused, not the accusers. It

1. Clarke was here alluding to the decision that the prosecution in this trial should be led by the Solicitor-General.

is true that Charles Parker and Wood never made any charge against Mr Wilde before the plea of justification in the libel case was put in. But what a powerful piece of evidence that is in favour of Mr Wilde! For if Charles Parker and Wood thought they had material for making a charge against Mr Wilde before that date, do you not think, gentlemen, they would have made it? Do you think that they would have remained year after year without trying to get something from him? But Charles Parker and Wood previously made no charge against Mr Wilde, nor did they attempt to get money from him – and that circumstance is one among other cogent proofs to be found in the case that there is no truth whatever in the accusations against Mr Wilde.'

Clarke then repeated in detail and at some length his already familiar arguments that neither the evidence of Charles Parker nor that of Wood could be relied upon, and that there was no corroboration of it. He likewise submitted that there was nothing to support the counts charging the prisoner with having committed the acts which had been alleged with unknown persons in the Savoy Hotel. As the prosecution had produced two additional witnesses from the Savoy, including a second chambermaid who bore out the testimony previously given by her fellow-servant as to the state of the sheets on Wilde's bed after he had slept in them, Clarke was obliged to deal with this aspect of the case, which he did as briefly and as delicately as he could. There was a perfectly innocent explanation of the stains on the sheets, he suggested. His client had been suffering from attacks of diarrhoea at the time.

'You must not act upon suspicion or prejudice, but upon an examination of the facts, gentlemen,' he concluded in a peroration which moved his listeners to a round of applause when he had finished, 'and on the facts I respectfully urge that Mr Wilde is entitled to claim from you a verdict of acquittal. If upon an examination of the evidence you therefore feel it your duty to say that the charges against the prisoner have not been proved, then I am sure that you will be glad that the brilliant promise which has been clouded by these accusations, and the bright reputation which was so nearly quenched in the torrent of prejudice which a

Mr. JUSTICE CHARLES

By "Spy"

Sir FRANK LOCKWOOD, Q.C., M.P.

By "Spy"

few weeks ago was sweeping through the press, have been saved by your verdict from absolute ruin; and that it leaves him, a distinguished man of letters and a brilliant Irishman, to live among us a life of honour and repute, and to give in the maturity of his genius gifts to our literature of which he has given only the promise in his early youth.'

In his closing speech for the prosecution, which he now began, Sir Frank Lockwood took the utmost advantage of his exclusive right to the last word with the jury. It was certainly an address of great power, and in it the Solicitor-General, as will be seen, showed few signs of the comparatively restrained line he had taken in his cross-examination. After describing Clarke's defence as a brilliant one, the Solicitor-General argued that, so far from being placed at a disadvantage in being cross-examined three times, as Clarke had argued, the prisoner was now better fitted and readier with his answers than before. He denied that the prosecution had behaved with any unfairness towards Wilde, and he went on to say that, in his opinion, the prosecution were quite right in thinking that a Law Officer of the Crown should be instructed to appear for the prosecution. 'With regard to the right of reply on behalf of the Law Officer,' he added, 'and with reference to Sir Edward Clarke's observations that he had never availed himself of that right when he was a Law Officer, I say that my learned friend had no right to lay down a rule which could not affect others who have filled that office.'

'It is upon the evidence only that I ask you to condemn the accused,' Lockwood continued. 'But you will not appreciate the evidence until you know what manner of man it is you are dealing with. Who were his associates? He is a man of culture and literary tastes, and I submit that his associates ought to have been his equals and not these illiterate boys whom you have heard in the witness box.'

The Solicitor-General was still on his feet when the Court rose for the day. Next morning, the fourth and last day of the trial, he went on with his address to the jury with a detailed criticism of the answers which Wilde had given under cross-examination to the various charges and he submitted that these explanations were not worthy of belief. 'You cannot fail to put the interpretation on the conduct of the prisoner that he is a guilty man,' Lockwood urged, 'and you ought to say so by your verdict.

'As to the statement of Sir Edward Clarke that Mr Wilde himself created inquiry into the matter,' continued Lockwood, 'that statement of my learned friend makes it necessary for me to recall to your minds, gentlemen, the relative positions of the parties in the Queensberry case. Sir Edward Clarke has contended that Lord Queensberry's libels referred to events of two years back, and that in the lapse of time witnesses for Mr Wilde have been lost sight of. But I ask you, what witness has been lost sight of? I suggest to you that it was the fact that Mr Wilde had seen nothing of Parker, and that he could rely implicitly on his intimate friend Taylor, that encouraged him to prosecute Lord Queensberry.'

At this point Sir Edward Clarke rose in hot protest. 'I must rise to object to Mr Solicitor-General's rhetorical descriptions of what has never been proved in evidence,' he exclaimed, 'in asserting that an intimate friendship existed between Mr Wilde and Taylor.'

'Gentlemen, it is not rhetoric,' Lockwood replied. 'It is a plain statement of fact. What are the indications of an intimate friendship? They call each other by their Christian names. Is he not a great friend on his own profession? Does he not say to Taylor: "Bring your friends: they are my friends: I will not inquire too closely whether they come from the stables or the kitchen"? No doubt my learned friend desires now to disconnect them. He wishes as a result of this trial that one should be condemned and the other left free to continue his grand literary career.'

'I protest,' said Clarke.

'My friend hopes to preserve Mr Wilde by means of a false glamour of art,' Lockwood went on to taunt his opponent.

'My lord,' said Clarke, appealing to the Bench, 'I must protest against this line of argument. I protest strongly against the line the learned Solicitor-General is taking.'

'Oh, you may protest!' said Lockwood ironically.

'So far no mention has been made of the verdict in the other case,' the judge broke in, hoping to reassure Wilde's counsel. 'All this is as far removed from the evidence as anything ever heard in this Court,' Clarke continued to protest.

'I am alluding, my lord,' Lockwood explained, 'and I maintain I am right in alluding, to my learned friend's last appeal to the jury as to the literary position of his client; and I am dealing, in connexion with that, with his connexion with the man Taylor, and I say that these men must be judged equally.'

'They ought to have been fairly tried in their proper order,' Clarke now complained.

'Oh, my lord,' Lockwood looked up at the judge, 'these interruptions should avail my friend nothing.'

'Mr Solicitor-General is perfectly within his rights,' ruled the judge. 'The only objection is to allusions to the result of the trial of Taylor.'

Lockwood's face now assumed an expression of self-satisfaction as he remarked: 'My learned friend does not seem to have gained a great deal by his superfluity of interruption.'

This remark produced an outburst of laughter which caused the judge to look angrily round the crowded Court and administer a sharp rebuke to those responsible. 'These interruptions are offensive to me beyond anything that can be described,' he said. 'To have to try a case of this kind, to keep the scales even, and do one's duty is hard enough; but to be pestered with the applause or expressions of feeling of senseless people who have no business to be here at all except for the gratification of morbid curiosity is too much. I hope that no further interruption of this kind will be heard throughout the rest of the trial. If there is anything of the kind again, I shall clear the Court.'

Resuming his speech, the Solicitor-General proceeded with characteristic invective to describe the relations between the prisoner and Lord Alfred Douglas in the light of their correspondence, particularly the 'prose poem' letter.

'I contend that such a letter found in the possession of a woman from a man would be open to but one interpretation,' said Lockwood. 'How much worse is the inference to be drawn when such a letter is written from one man to another! It has been attempted to show that this was a prose poem, a sonnet, a lovely thing which I suppose we are too low to appreciate. Gentlemen, let us thank God, if it is so, that we do not appreciate things of this sort save at their proper value, and that is somewhat lower than the beasts. If that letter had been seen by any right-minded man, it would have been looked upon as evidence of guilty passion. And you, men of pride, reason, and honour, are tried to be put off with this story of the prose poem, of the sonnet, of the lovely thing!

'It is a common-sense conclusion that Mr Wilde bargained with Wood and bought the letters. Indeed, Mr Wilde's own admissions, which agree up to a certain point with the evidence of Wood, prove Wood's story to be true. What necessity was there for Mr Wilde to give Wood supper in a private room or to tell him that his family was out of town? If what Mr Wilde has said is true as to his first meeting with Wood, all he had to do was to hand over the money he was deputed to give him, and, if he thought there was aught in this young man that appealed to his own benevolence, to add such sum as provided for such refreshment as Wood might desire. In my submission, Wood has no motive for deceiving you on this occasion. I say that the transaction with regard to the letters is capable of one construction only. Mr Wilde knew they were letters which he must recover; he bought them and tore them to pieces. He kept the one which he had from Allen, because he knew that Mr Beerbohm Tree had a copy of it, so that it was useless to destroy the original. Gentlemen, if you come to the conclusion that Mr Wilde did purchase these letters, it throws a flood of light upon his conduct. It shows that he knew the class of men with whom he had been intimate and with whom he continued to be intimate.'

The Solicitor-General then took the jury through the evidence which had been given by the Parkers. 'The fact of Mr Wilde never having seen William Parker since the dinner at Kettner's corroborates the evidence of the Parkers as to the conversation which took place at dinner,' Lockwood went on. 'Then, as in the case of Wood, Mr Wilde's own evidence contained admission after admission until he came to the point at which admission must cease and confession begin. Further, the evidence of the waiter from the Savoy Hotel corroborates that of Charles Parker. The waiter Becker said that a supper was served to Mr Wilde and a young man in a private room. Parker has described that supper, but Mr Wilde could give no explanation as to who his guest was. He could only say that it was not Charles Parker. Again, the evidence of Mrs Margery Bancroft, who said that she knew Mr Wilde perfectly well by sight, also supplies corroborative evidence. So much impressed was she by what she had seen that she complained to Parker's landlady, and Parker – apparently without complaint or remonstrance – was compelled to leave his lodgings.

'My learned friend has said that these witnesses are blackmailers and has warned you against giving a verdict which would enable this detestable trade to rear its head unblushingly in this city. Gentlemen, I should have as much right to ask you to take care lest by your verdict you should enable another vice as detestable, as abominable, to raise its head with unblushing effrontery in this city. The genesis of the blackmailer is the man who has committed these acts of indecency with him. And the genesis of the man who commits these foul acts is the man who is willing to pay for their commission. Were it not that there are men willing to purchase vice in the most hideous and detestable form, there would be no market for such crime and no opening for these blackmailers to ply their calling.'

Lockwood went on to discuss the relations which, he claimed, had undoubtedly existed between Taylor, Wood, Charles Parker, and the prisoner. He thought it remarkable that Wilde should have made two acquaintances, one after the other, both of whom were recent friends of Taylor and both in a different social position from the prisoner's own. 'With regard to Taylor, who on the occasion of the first trial was charged by Mr Carson with procuration on behalf of Mr Wilde,' the Solicitor-General continued, 'I must point out that Taylor was in Court during the Queensberry trial, and yet he was not put into the witness box. Again, one would have thought that, after the Wood incident, Taylor would have been asked to be careful in the selection of friends he introduced to Mr Wilde. But, no! Taylor had *carte*

259

blanche to bring along any friends he pleased. He brought along Charles Parker, and it is manifest that the prisoner's intimacy with Charles Parker was not a matter of ordinary friendship.' In connexion with Parker's testimony, the Solicitor-General repelled the suggestion that either Lord Queensberry's solicitor or any of the representatives of the Crown had given either fee or reward to any of the youths who had given evidence in this case. All the prosecution had done had been to take precautions to prevent tampering with those witnesses and to ensure their attendance in Court. 'Naturally the witnesses have been removed secretly from place to place,' Lockwood added, 'and I make no apology for the course the Crown has taken in this matter. Charles Parker, whose evidence gave rise to this suggestion, could not possibly have had any sinister motive in telling a story involving his own shame and to some extent his own condemnation, for it has never been shown that Parker, whatever his past conduct may have been, has attempted to extort money from Mr Wilde.'

The Solicitor-General next turned to the other charges alleging misconduct in the Savoy with a person or persons unknown, and he claimed that Sir Edward Clarke had exaggerated – 'unintentionally, of course' – what the judge had said on the previous day with regard to this matter. 'My learned friend made it appear as though the evidence in these cases was exceedingly slender,' said Lockwood, 'but as a matter of fact his lordship has left that part of the case unreservedly for your consideration, gentlemen. Now, I contend that there is ample evidence as to these particular charges. The defendant has given no explanation of the discoveries made by the employees of the hotel. It is no conclusive answer to say that Mr Wilde did everything openly. If crime were always cautious, it would always go unpunished, and it is in moments of carelessness that crime is detected. Why was Lord Alfred Douglas, who slept in the next room, not called to deny the statements of the chambermaid? I maintain that she and the other witnesses from the Savoy Hotel could have no possible object in hatching up a bogus case.'

Finally, Lockwood dealt with the allegation that the prosecution had dragged in matters which were outside the indictment. 'There is no reason why Mr Wilde should not be cross-examined with reference to other offences. You are entitled, gentlemen, in the interests of justice, to put a commonsense interpretation upon the conditions and circumstances under which lads outside the present case were found. The case of the boy Conway, in particular, is very significant. What possible benefit could it be to a boy in his position to be taken from Worthing to Brighton and allowed to stay in a hotel all night?'

As he listened to this damning recitation of his delinquencies, the man in the dock appeared as if stunned. Afterwards he was to recall the effect which such oratory had upon him at the time.

I remember as I was sitting in the dock on the occasion of my last trial, listening to Lockwood's appalling denunciation of me [he wrote in *De Profundis*] – like a thing out of Tacitus, like a passage in Dante, like one of Savonarola's indictments of the Popes at Rome – and being sickened with horror at what I heard. Suddenly it occurred to me: *'How splendid it would be if I was saying all this about myself!'* I saw then at once that what is said of a man is nothing. The point is, who says it. A man's very highest moment is, I have no doubt at all, when he kneels in the dust, and beats his breast, and tells all the sins of his life.

The Solicitor-General had almost done. 'Now, gentlemen, I have been through the whole of this case,' he wound up. 'I have pointed out to you its strength, and I have to ask you to do your duty in regard to it. I have already dealt with that – as I think, unfortunate – appeal which my learned friend has made as to the literary past or the literary future of Mr Oscar Wilde. With that we have in this case nothing whatever to do. He has a right to be acquitted, if you believe him to be an innocent man, be his lot high or low. But if, gentlemen, in your consciences you believe that he is guilty of these charges – well, then you have only one consideration, and that is to follow closely the obligation of the oath which has been laid upon you.'

6

'Whatever may be the guilt or innocence of the accused,' Mr Justice Wills remarked to the jury at the beginning of his summing-up, 'it is clear that Mr Wilde has been obliged, from the result of the Queensberry trial, to confess that his conduct, especially with regard to Lord Alfred Douglas, has been such that Lord Queensberry was justified in applying to him the words of the original libel. It is in my opinion impossible, therefore, for twelve intelligent, impartial, and honest gentlemen to say there was no good ground for an indignant father, a loving and affectionate parent, to charge Mr Wilde with having posed as the Marquess of Queensberry has suggested.'

As befitted an authority on circumstantial evidence, Mr Justice Wills summed up the evidence in this trial in a manner which, while it cannot be said that it was actually unfair to the prisoner, was much less favourable to him than Mr Justice Charles's summing-up in the previous trial, particularly on the subject of the two letters to Lord Alfred Douglas. 'Is the language of those letters calculated to calm and keep down the passions which in a young man need no stimulus?' Mr Justice Wills asked the jury. 'It is strange that it should not occur to a gentleman capable of writing such letters that any young man to whom they were addressed must suffer in the estimation of everybody, if it were known. Lord Queensberry has drawn from these letters the conclusion that most fathers would draw, although he seems to have taken a course of action in his method of interfering which I think no gentleman should have taken, whatever motives he had, in leaving at the defendant's club a card containing a most offensive expression. This was a message which left the defendant no alternative but to prosecute or else be branded publicly as a man who could not deny a foul charge.'

Unlike the previous judge, Mr Justice Wills made no reference to the hostile and vindictive press campaign against Wilde, which had tended to prejudge the issue. However, he deprecated the joining of the charges with those against Taylor at the first trial, which he felt justified the disagreement of the jury on that occasion. 'As to the present trial,' he went on, 'I would have preferred to try the prisoners in a different order; but, on the other hand, I do not think that the defendant has suffered by the course taken by the Solicitor-General, nor do I think that the fact that Taylor's case has been heard first has in any way prejudiced the case of Mr Wilde. Whatever your verdict may be, gentlemen, it cannot leave things precisely as they were before this trial.'

Coming on to the evidence, the judge dealt first with the case of Wood, remarking at the outset that it was impossible for him to do this without also dealing with that of Lord Alfred Douglas. 'Now, Lord Alfred Douglas is not present and is not a party to these proceedings,' he said, 'and it must be remembered in his favour that, if neither side called him, he could not volunteer himself as a witness. Anything, therefore, which I shall have to say to Lord Alfred Douglas's prejudice arises simply out of the facts which have transpired in the course of the evidence you have heard. I am anxious, too, to say nothing, in the case of a young man like this who is just on the threshold of life, which might to a great extent blast his career. I do not desire to comment more than I can help either about Lord Alfred Douglas or the Marquess of Queensberry, but I must say that the whole of this lamentable inquiry has arisen through the defendant's association with Lord Alfred Douglas. It is true that Lord Alfred's family seems to be a house divided against itself. But even if there was nothing but hatred between father and son, what father would not try to save his own son from the associations suggested by the two letters which you have seen from the prisoner to Lord Alfred Douglas? I will avoid saying whether these letters seem to point to actual criminal conduct or not. But they must be considered in relation to the other evidence in the case, and it is for you to say whether their contents lend any colour to Wood's story.'

Describing what he called the 'ill-assorted friendship' between Wood and Douglas, by whom Wood was introduced to Wilde, and from whom he received a suit of clothes, the pockets of which contained the compromising letters, the judge remarked that he found it more understandable that a lad like Wood should be given cast-off clothes than cigarette cases. 'Now, Lord Alfred Douglas, who was on terms of intimacy with Wood, had just previously to that received a letter from the prisoner, of which it is difficult for me to speak with calmness, as addressed from one man to another,' Mr Justice Wills continued. 'It is for you, however, to consider whether or not that letter is an indication of unclean sentiments and unclean appetites on both sides. It is to my mind a letter upon which ordinary people would be very liable to put an uncomfortable construction.' As for the other letters which Wood had got possession of and returned to Wilde, the judge asked why, if they were really harmless, Wilde had not kept them instead of destroying them. From the value which the blackmailers had put upon them, Wilde must have known that they would be useful in answer to any charge which might be brought against him in respect of the two letters which had been produced. 'But I doubt very much', said the judge, 'whether the letters were harmless and trivial.'

In refusing to withdraw the case of Wood from the jury earlier in the trial, it will be remembered that Mr Justice Wills had undertaken to explain the reason for his so doing and in what direction he found corroboration. 'In my opinion,' he now said 'the stress of the case with regard to Wood depends upon the character of the original introduction of Wood to Mr Wilde. Do you believe that Mr Wilde was actuated by charitable motives or by improper motives? On the question of corroboration, you are not expected – because corroboration in cases of such a kind as this is difficult to obtain – to be satisfied with less corroboration than you would be if it were easy to obtain. Unless you feel that Wood's evidence is corroborated, you must not act upon it, because Wood is a blackmailer, a person who belongs to the vilest type of men which great cities produce and which society is pestered with.'

At this point the foreman of the jury rose from his place in the jury box and put a question to the judge. 'In view of the intimacy between Lord Alfred Douglas and Mr Wilde, was a warrant ever issued for the apprehension of Lord Alfred Douglas?'

The Third Trial

'I should think not,' Mr Justice Wills replied. 'We have not heard of it.'

'Was it ever contemplated?' the foreman went on to ask.

'Not to my knowledge,' said the judge. 'A warrant would in any case not be issued without evidence of some fact, of something more than intimacy. I cannot tell, nor need we discuss that, because Lord Alfred Douglas may yet have to answer a charge. He was not called. There may be a thousand considerations of which we may know nothing that might prevent his appearance in the witness box. I think you should deal with the matter upon the evidence before you.'

'But it seems to us', the foreman persisted, 'that if we are to consider these letters as evidence of guilt, and if we adduce any guilt from these letters, it applies as much to Lord Alfred Douglas as to the defendant.'

'Quite so,' remarked the judge somewhat testily, as he disliked being interrupted in his summing-up. 'But how does that relieve the defendant? Our present inquiry is whether guilt is brought home to the man in the dock. We have got the testimony of *his* guilt to deal with now. I believe that to be the recipient of such letters and to continue the intimacy is as fatal to the reputation of the recipient as to the sender, but you have really nothing to do with that at present.

'There is a natural disposition to ask', Mr Justice Wills continued, indicating the prisoner by a motion of the hand, 'why should this man stand in the dock and not Lord Alfred Douglas? But, gentlemen of the jury, the supposition that Lord Alfred Douglas will be spared because he is Lord Alfred Douglas is one of the wildest injustice. The thing is utterly and hopelessly impossible! I must remind you that anything that can be said for or against Lord Alfred Douglas must not be allowed to prejudice the prisoner, and you must remember that no prosecution would be possible on the mere production of Mr Wilde's letters to Lord Alfred Douglas. Lord Alfred Douglas, as you know, went to Paris at the request of the defendant, and there he has stayed, and I know absolutely nothing more about him. I am as ignorant in this respect as you are. It may be that there is no evidence against Lord Alfred

265

Douglas. But even about that I know nothing. It is a thing we cannot discuss, and to entertain any such consideration as I have mentioned would be a prejudice of the worst possible kind.'

Coming to the case of Charles Parker, the judge pointed out that it differed in certain particulars from that of Wood. 'Parker seems to have been introduced to Mr Wilde by Taylor,' said the judge, 'and there can be no doubt that Taylor was a friend of Mr Wilde. On the other hand, the amount of intercourse between Mr Wilde and Taylor proved by the prosecution is not very great. However, the admissions made by Mr Wilde as to the innocent nature of his acquaintance with Parker are certainly remarkable, and it is for you to decide whether the explanations are satisfactory. If you think that the visit to Park Walk has been made out, then it is a very strange thing. It must be remembered that there is nothing to be said against the person who confirmed that part of the case, Mrs Margery Bancroft. If anything could have been found against her, it would have been found by the defence. You must, therefore, recognize that she is not a street walker nor a disreputable woman, and that she has remained for years in her situation.'

At this point the judge had to admit that he was confronted with a difficulty, namely the rule of evidence which prevents a witness from telling what he or she has heard from someone else. Consequently it had not transpired what was the full extent of the complaint made by Mrs Bancroft to the landlady of the house in Park Walk where Charles Parker lodged. 'You will have to draw your own inferences from the witness's evidence, and also to put what construction you think reasonable on Parker's story generally, taken in conjunction with all the surrounding circumstances.

'I must further point out to you that Parker and Wood were introduced to the accused a long time ago,' the judge continued, 'and also that, though they have been very industrious blackmailers during this interval, yet they did not see Mr Wilde again, nor attempt to make any charge against him until now. That in itself appears to me to be a most remarkable fact, and one of overwhelming influence in this case. Again, there is some truth in the aphorism that a man must be judged by the company he

The Third Trial

keeps. Gentlemen, you have seen the Parkers, as you have seen Wood, and the same question must arise in your minds. Are these the kind of young men with whom you yourselves would care to sit down to dine? Are they the sort of persons you would expect to find in the company of men of education?'

What was more, these young men had frequented Taylor's rooms and Taylor had admitted that they had shared his bed. Indeed the jury knew that Taylor had just been convicted of indecencies with both the Parkers, although the judge naturally did not allude to this. 'Now, gentlemen, you must not presume that the mere fact of two men sleeping together is something to be punished,' the judge was careful to add on this aspect of the case. 'Poverty and misery frequently compel this to happen, and drive even men and women to sleep together promiscuously. God forbid that I should say that that in itself is a serious crime! But when we come to a man who is spending £40 or £50 a week (as Taylor was doing), it seems astonishing to me that he should not get at least the whole use of a bed for his money, and it is natural to ask why he did not offer another room to his guest.'

Still on the subject of Charles Parker, the judge mentioned the evidence of the Savoy Hotel waiter who, it will be remembered, had testified to having served a supper of chicken and champagne to Wilde and a guest in a private sitting-room. Although it might conceivably constitute corroboration, the judge told the jury that it was a very long time ago for a waiter to remember. 'The sums too which appeared on the bill are high for such a supper,' the judge added. 'I know nothing about the Savoy, but I must say that in my view "Chicken and salad for two. 16s." is very high! I am afraid I shall never have supper there myself.'

In going on to deal with what the other Savoy Hotel servants had stated in the witness box, the judge expressed regret that medical evidence had not been called. 'It is a loathsome subject,' he said, 'but I make a point of never shrinking from details that are absolutely necessary. The medical evidence would have thrown light on what has been alluded to as marks of grease or vaseline smears. Then, with reference to the condition of the bed, there was the diarrhoea line of defence. That story, I must say, I am not able to appreciate. I have tried many similar cases, but I have never heard that before. It did strike me as being possible; but more than anything else it impressed me with the importance of medical evidence in such a case, which evidence unfortunately we have not had. The worst state of the sheets was not alleged on the date the boy was said to have been seen in the bed by the chambermaid Cotter. There was the same sort of thing, said the woman, but not so bad.

'But, of course, the evidence of the Savoy Hotel servants after a long lapse of time must not be entirely relied upon. If a servant noticed anything wrong and said nothing about it for two years, then I would not consider that as evidence on which I would hang a dog. It is, in my opinion, a strange thing that this should not be made a matter of inquiry until two years afterwards. The evidence of Migge, the masseur, is remarkable, but here again it is not safe to rely on it. The evidence of the woman, Jane Cotter, is no less extraordinary, no matter from what point it is viewed. The thing that strikes me as most remarkable about her story is that, though the housekeeper was acquainted with what had been seen, absolutely no notice was taken of the circumstance. Why, Mrs Perkins, the housekeeper, became an accomplice in the whole affair, and – without saying she is as bad as any of them – I do say it was a very great breach of her sense of right in these matters. She herself has admitted that Cotter, the chambermaid, had made communications to her, and I consider that if the housekeper was informed of the condition of the room and of the boy having been seen in the bed, and if she yet took no steps to prevent such a thing in the future, she was liable to become an accessory before the fact in the event of it being repeated. It is a condition of things one shudders to contemplate in a first-class hotel. If it can be assumed that such practices could be tolerated with a man who was running up a bill of £50 a week, then it will look as if we are coming to a state of society when it will be possible to have a magnificently built place of accommodation on the Thames Embankment!'

Having delivered himself of this homily, Mr Justice Wills once more went through the evidence, this time briefly, and concluded by telling the jury that the question they must answer was whether there was evidence of guilt or of suspicion only. Finally, he thanked the jury for the patience they had displayed throughout the prolonged hearing. It was just 3.30 p.m. by the courtroom clock when the jury retired to consider their verdict. The judge withdrew to his room and the prisoner was taken to a room below the dock. Then began the agonizing period of waiting. One hour passed, then two hours, and still there was no word from the jury room. People were beginning to wonder whether there would be another disagreement, when suddenly an usher was seen bearing a note from the jury room to the judge's room.

'That means an acquittal!' said one of the Treasury counsel. 'You'll dine your man in Paris tomorrow,' Lockwood remarked to Clarke.

But the great advocate who had put up such a brilliant defence of his client was not so sanguine. He shook his head uneasily as they made their way back into the dingy old courtroom.

7

The question which the jury had to ask the judge turned out to be of relatively minor interest. 'My lord,' said the foreman, 'would you read your notes of the evidence of Thomas Price, the waiter, as to the alleged visits of Charles Parker to the prisoner's rooms at 10 St James's Place?'

'There is evidence as to only one of the counts in reference to St James's Place,' replied Mr Justice Wills. The judge then read over his notes of Price's evidence, adding a few words which seemed to imply that this part of the case was not vitally important.

The jury again retired, but were out for only a few minutes. When they filed back to the jury box for the second time, it was clear that they had arrived at a decision.

'Gentlemen,' the Clerk of Arraign addressed them, 'have you agreed upon your verdict?'

'We have,' the foreman replied.

'Do you find the prisoner at the bar guilty or not guilty of an act of gross indecency with Charles Parker at the Savoy Hotel on the night of his first introduction to him?'

'Guilty.'

'Do you find him guilty or not guilty of a similar offence a week later?'

'Guilty.'

'Do you find him guilty or not guilty of a similar offence at St James's Place?'

'Guilty.'

'Do you find him guilty or not guilty of a similar offence about the same period?'

'Guilty.'

'Do you find him guilty or not guilty of an act of gross indecency with Alfred Wood at Tite Street?'

'Guilty.'

'Do you find him guilty or not guilty of an act of gross indecency with a male person unknown in Room 362 of the Savoy Hotel?'

'Guilty.'

'Do you find him guilty or not guilty of a similar offence in Room 346 of the Savoy Hotel?'

'Guilty.'

'Do you find him guilty on all counts in the indictment except that relating to Edward Shelley?'

'Yes. Not guilty on that count.'

'And is that the verdict of you all?'

'It is.'

The prisoner appeared to be dazed by these terrible exchanges, and he only recovered himself when he was joined a minute or two later in the dock by Taylor, whom the judge had directed to be brought up for sentencing along with Wilde. Meanwhile Sir Edward Clarke was on his feet in a last desperate attempt to save his client.

It will be remembered that at the beginning of the previous trial Clarke had demurred to the indictment as containing inconsistent counts; that is, he had objected that the indictment was bad in law because counts alleging conspiracy, on which direct evidence could not be given by the accused, were joined with the others. Although the prosecution had eventually said that it would not ask for a verdict on the conspiracy counts, nevertheless these counts had originally formed part of the indictment, and on this ground Clarke was prepared to argue that the indictment should be quashed and a new trial ordered. In those days there was no Court of Criminal Appeal, to which an appeal would otherwise have lain automatically. But there was a court known as the Court of Crown Cases Reserved, which exercised an appellate jurisdiction in respect of exceptional or difficult points of law in criminal trials which were certified by the Attorney-General as worthy of consideration.

'I have to suggest to your lordship that you will not pass sentence until the next sessions,' said Clarke, addressing the Bench. 'There is a demurrer on record which has to be argued, and I submit that it would be well to postpone passing sentence in order that that argument may be considered.'

'I do not know how far that will affect the case of Mr Taylor,' Taylor's counsel added. 'But I think it would affect him equally. Therefore, if I may re-echo the observation of Sir Edward Clarke, I would make the same application.'

'I oppose the application,' said the Solicitor-General. 'The matter has been argued and decided. It relates to certain counts not included in this indictment, and passing sentence now can in no way affect any arguments that may be raised at any future time.'

'The conspiracy counts are contained in the indictment,' Clarke repeated.

'But there is a verdict of "Not Guilty" on them,' the judge interposed, looking slightly puzzled. 'What is the contention?'

'That the indictment was bad, there being a different mode of trial,' answered Clarke. 'In a case of conspiracy the defendants are not capable of being witnesses, but in the other they are capable of giving evidence and they plead to that indictment alone. The demurrer is just as arguable whatever has taken place since.'

Here Charles Gill, who had led the prosecution at the previous trial, broke in. 'The question was argued before Mr Justice Charles, and he held the indictment to be perfectly good.' To this

271

the Solicitor-General added: 'Sentence can be passed without prejudicing the argument before the Court of Crown Cases Reserved.'

'Of the correctness of the indictment I have myself no doubt,' said Mr Justice Wills, thus dashing Clarke's final forlorn hope. 'In any case, my passing sentence will not interfere with the arguing of the point raised, and I think it my duty to pass sentence at once. It is not a matter about which I entertain any doubt, and to pass sentence now will in no sense prejudice the result of the inquiry. I think it may be well to complete the proceedings here on the other counts.'

The judge then turned to the two prisoners in the dock and continued: 'Oscar Wilde and Alfred Taylor, the crime of which you have been convicted is so bad that one has to put stern restraint upon oneself to prevent oneself from describing, in language which I would rather not use, the sentiments which must rise to the breast of every man of honour who has heard the details of these two terrible trials. That the jury have arrived at a correct verdict in this case, I cannot persuade myself to entertain the shadow of a doubt; and I hope, at all events, that those who sometimes imagine that a judge is half-hearted in the cause of decency and morality, because he takes care no prejudice shall enter into the case, may see that that is consistent at least with the utmost sense of indignation at the horrible charges brought home to both of you.

'It is no use for me to address you. People who can do these things must be dead to all sense of shame, and one cannot hope to produce any effect upon them. It is the worst case I have ever tried. That you, Taylor kept a kind of male brothel it is impossible to doubt. And that you, Wilde, have been the centre of a circle of extensive corruption of the most hideous kind among young men, it is equally impossible to doubt.

'I shall, under such circumstances, be expected to pass the severest sentence that the law allows. In my judgement it is totally inadequate for such a case as this. The sentence of the Court is that each of you be imprisoned and kept to hard labour for two years.'

HOTEL DE LA POSTE

ROUEN

May 26ᵗʰ
1895
Sunday.

Dear Sir Edward.

You will forgive me I am sure
for writing to you now to thank
you from the bottom of my
heart for your noble &
glorious & superb efforts on
my behalf of my friend.
It seems almost an impertinence
for me so miserable as myself
so broken in heart in spirit,
so defamed & ruined to
offer you my poor gratitude.
but believe me I shall never
cease to think of you with
the profoundest gratitude &
admiration. That you
were unable to get a verdict
seems to me, a layman, a piece
of monstrous injustice, & the

47

Letter from Lord Alfred Douglas to Sir Edward Clarke,
May 26th, 1895

[See over

sentence was worse than I
would have thought possible
after the first disagreement.
Forgive this intrusion from
one who is lying in the
lowest hell of misery, &
believe me to be

　　　yours ever gratefully
& sincerely.
　　Alfred Douglas.

See over]

The Third Trial

There were a few murmurs of 'Oh!' and 'Shame!', since the harsh words employed by the judge in passing the maximum sentence had contrasted strongly with the comparatively moderate language of his summing-up. But the protests were quickly drowned in a hum of approval from the majority of the spectators in the gallery. Meanwhile all eyes were focused on the dock. There Taylor heard his sentence with seeming indifference, but the other frock-coated figure swayed slightly, his face suffused with horror, and tried to utter a few words. 'And I?' he began. 'May I say nothing, my lord?' But Mr Justice Wills made no reply beyond a wave of the hand to the warders in attendance, who touched the prisoners on the shoulder and hurried them out of sight to the cells below, there to await the 'Black Maria' to take them to Pentonville Prison.

There is no need to dwell upon the final scene. Among those present in Court who witnessed it were two young men who had known Wilde in his heyday, Seymour Hicks the actor, and Max Beerbohm the writer and caricaturist. On both of them the scene made an unforgettable impression, as indeed they were to tell the present writer many years later. 'I have seen many awful happenings at the Old Bailey,' said Seymour Hicks, 'but to me no death sentence has ever seemed so terrible as the one which Mr Justice Wills delivered when his duty called upon him to destroy and take from the world the man who had given it so much.'[1]

Meanwhile, in the streets outside the Old Bailey the verdict was received with sundry marks of popular approval. A few people literally danced with joy, and some prostitutes were seen to kick up their skirts with glee at the news. ''E'll 'ave 'is 'air cut reglar now!' shouted one of them. This sally provoked a loud chorus of laughter from others on the pavement. Further up the social scale feelings were more decently disguised, except perhaps by Lord Queensberry and his friends.

1. See Sir Seymour Hicks, *Between Ourselves* (1930), p. 86. Sir Seymour told me, in the course of a warm tribute to Wilde for his kindness and help to a young and struggling actor, that he used to drive home with him alone in a hansom cab after the theatre, but that Wilde never by as much as a hint made a single improper advance to him. The side of Wilde's life which was revealed at the trials came, he said, as a complete shock to him.

273

CHAPTER 6

THE AFTERMATH

1

THE punishment which Wilde faced, although by reason of his age and physical condition he was to escape some of its worst features, was still one of terrible severity. Evidence given by a variety of witnesses before a recent Home Office Committee on Prisons had shown that two years' imprisonment with hard labour, involving solitary cell confinement with its attendant laborious and largely useless work in the shape of the tread-wheel, the crank, and oakum picking, which had to be performed on a poor and inadequate diet, were calculated to break a man in body and spirit. Indeed, old offenders greatly preferred penal servitude, which could not be imposed for less than three years, in a convict prison such as Dartmoor or Portland, since the prison labour was largely carried on in the open air and there was always the chance of being released on 'ticket-of-leave' before the expiry of the sentence. With a sentence of imprisonment, on the other hand, the various forms of 'hard labour' were mainly conducted indoors, usually in the prisoner's cell, and there was no provision for remitting any portion of the sentence for good conduct.

The cells in which 'hard labour' prisoners were confined for twenty-three out of the twenty-four hours in the day were badly ventilated, and the sanitary conditions were primitive. The plank bed on which the prisoner was condemned to lie at night was an instrument of torture, which inevitably produced insomnia. Visitors (for twenty minutes each) and the writing and receiving of letters were only allowed once every three months, save in exceptional circumstances. Letters written by prisoners were censored by prison officials for complaints, as well as for 'slang or improper expressions', and on at least one occasion Wilde was to have a passage from one of his letters to Robert Ross excised by the Governor's scissors. According to the current regulations, 'the permission to write and receive letters is given to prisoners for the purpose of enabling them to keep up a connexion with their respectable friends and not that they may be kept informed of public events'. Later on Wilde was to urge strongly that prisoners should be allowed the privilege of both letters and visitors once a month. 'One of the tragedies of prison life is that it turns a man's heart to stone,' he wrote after his release. 'The feelings of natural affection, like all other feelings, require to be fed. They die easily of inanition. A brief letter, four times a year, is not enough to keep alive the gentler and more humane affections by which ultimately the nature is kept sensitive to any fine or beautiful influences that may heal a wrecked or ruined life.'

During the first three months of his imprisonment the prisoner was allowed no books to read, except a Bible, Prayer Book, and hymn-book. Thereafter he was allowed one book a week from the prison library, whose stock consisted chiefly of third-rate theological works which had been selected by the prison chaplain. The first work given to Wilde to read by the chaplain, who had evidently chosen it for its high moral tone, was John Bunyan's *A Pilgrim's Progress*. 'The prison chaplains are entirely useless,' Wilde wrote afterwards. 'They are, as a class, well-meaning, but foolish, indeed silly men. They are no help to any prisoner. Once every six weeks or so the key turns in the lock of one's cell door, and the chaplain enters. One stands, of course, to attention. He asks one whether one has been reading the Bible. One answers "Yes" or "No", as the case may be. He then quotes a few texts, and goes out and locks the door. Sometimes he leaves a tract.' The chaplain at Pentonville appears to have been a typical example of his kind. 'Did you have morning prayers in your house?' he asked Wilde on the occasion of their first meeting. 'I am sorry,' the prisoner replied. 'I fear not.' To which the chaplain rejoined: 'You see where you are now!'

Wilde's first experience of Pentonville Prison was thoroughly disagreeable, and he always remembered it. After he had gone through the reception office, where his particulars were entered

275

in the prison records, he was weighed and he handed over his personal belongings. He was then taken to the baths and told to strip, after which he was made to get into a filthy bath, in which many other prisoners had preceded him. There followed a medical examination, as a result of which he was certified as 'fit for light labour', which meant that he could be put to such tasks as oakum picking and sewing mailbags. He then put on the coarse prison dress with its distinguishing broad arrow marks, and followed a warder to a cell where he was locked in for the night. 'At first it was a fiendish nightmare,' he told Frank Harris; 'more horrible than anything I had ever dreamed of: from the first evening when they made me undress before them and get into some filthy water they called a bath and dry myself with a damp brown rag and put on this livery of shame. The cell was appalling: I could hardly breathe in it, and the food turned my stomach; the smell and sight of it were enough: I did not eat anything for days and days, I could not even swallow the bread; and the rest of the food was uneatable; I lay on the so-called bed and shivered all night long. ... After some days I got so hungry I had to eat a little, nibble at the outside of the bread, and drink some of the liquid; whether it was tea, coffee, or gruel, I could not tell. As soon as I really ate anything it produced violent diarrhoea and I was ill all day and all night. From the beginning I could not sleep, I grew weak and had wild delusions. ... The hunger made you weak; but the inhumanity was the worst of it. What devilish creatures men are! I had never known anything about them. I had never dreamt of such cruelties.'[1]

A rumour that Wilde had become insane during his first few weeks in Pentonville (the prison barber was supposed to have realized his condition) got into the press. As a result the Home Secretary, Mr Asquith, ordered a special medical examination of the prisoner, but this merely revealed that, with the exception of a slightly relaxed throat, he was 'in good health and perfectly sane'. But the truth was that he was far from well, as subsequent events were to show, and Wilde held a low opinion of the doctor who made this diagnosis. As we have seen, Wilde's father had been

1. Harris, II, 331–2.

a distinguished surgeon, and from earliest youth Wilde had always regarded doctors as by far the most humane profession in the country. But his gaol experiences caused him to make a striking exception in the case of prison doctors. At that period, they nearly all had a large private practice and held appointments in other institutions. 'The consequence is that the health of the prisoners is entirely neglected,' wrote Wilde later, 'and the sanitary conditions entirely overlooked.' As for the doctors themselves, they were, 'as far as I came across them, and from what I saw of them in hospital and elsewhere, brutal in manner, coarse in temperament, and utterly indifferent to the health of the prisoners or their comfort.'[1]

The cell in which Wilde found himself at Pentonville, and which was copied by most of the other English prisons at the time, was thirteen feet long, seven feet wide, and nine feet high. This was supposed to be adequate for strictly separate confinement with cell labour. The stone or brick wall surface and ceiling were lime-washed. The door was solidly lined with sheet iron to prevent tampering by ingenious prisoners, and in the middle was a small glass peep-hole, covered by a moveable shutter, to enable the interior of the cell to be observed by patrolling warders. Artificial illumination was provided by flaring gas jets let into the corridor outside. These cast a pale glare through a glazed opening in the cell wall above the door. In daytime, only a relatively small amount of natural light penetrated through the cell window, which consisted of fourteen small opaque panes of glass situated at a height of 6 feet 9 inches above the floor level, shutting out even a glimpse of the sky. Ventilation was provided partly by a ventilator in the window and partly by gratings. But Wilde found that the window ventilator was too small and badly constructed to admit enough fresh air, while the gratings were usually choked up. The result, in his experience, was that for most of the day and night prisoners were breathing the foulest possible air. He was later to describe it in *The Ballad of Reading Gaol.*

> Each narrow cell in which we dwell
> Is a foul and dark latrine,

1. Letter to the *Daily Chronicle*, 24 March 1898.

Oscar Wilde

And the fetid breath of living Death
Chokes up each grated screen,
And all, but Lust, is turned to Dust
In humanity's machine.

The cell was indeed as bare and repellent as it was possible to make it. The only articles of furniture permitted were the plank bed, blanket, hard pillow, and a small table for the prisoner's toilet and feeding utensils. Nothing else was allowed in the way of personal possessions, not even a photograph of the prisoner's wife and children, which might break the monotony of the cell wall or help to keep alive any feeling of family affection. A daily cell inspection was carried out, at which each prisoner had to exhibit the contents of his cell, such as they were, in the prescribed order. These official visitations became a nightmare for Wilde, and in consequence he developed a nervous habit, which his friends noticed when he came out of prison of always arranging objects in front of him symmetrically. 'I had to keep everything in my cell in its exact place,' he said, 'and if I neglected this even in the slightest, I was punished. The punishment was so horrible that I often started up in my sleep to feel if each thing was where the regulations would have it, and not an inch either to right or to the left.' In time, however, he was to learn to do this correctly. One of the warders, who had him in his charge for a time, has described how Wilde, when he had arranged all his tins as they should be, 'would step back and view them with an air of childlike complacency.'[1]

At one time each cell was equipped with a form of latrine, but the closets were later removed because the drainpipes made unauthorized communications between prisoners easier. In place of the old latrine the prisoner was supplied with a small tin chamber pot. This he was allowed to empty three times a day. But he was not allowed to have access to the prison lavatories, except during the one hour when he was at exercise. And after locking-up time, between five o'clock in the afternoon and five the following morning, the prisoner was forbidden to leave his cell under any pretence or for any reason; anyhow the warder on night duty had

1. Sherard, *Life of Oscar Wilde* (1906), p. 389.

278

no key. The prison diet, consisting mostly of weak gruel – so-called 'stirabout' made of coarse Indian meal – suet, water, and greasy cocoa, was a frequent cause of diarrhoea, and the miseries and tortures which sufferers from this endemic prison complaint underwent, especially at night, can be imagined. It was no uncommon thing for warders, when they came on duty in the mornings out of the fresh air, to open and inspect the cells, to be violently sick. Wilde himself witnessed this on a number of occasions, and several warders went out of their way to mention it to him as 'one of the disgusting things which their office entails on them'. At certain times in the day the warders would serve out astringent medicines. But after a comparatively short time, usually about a week, the medicine produced no effect at all. In Wilde's words: 'The wretched prisoner is then left a prey to the most weakening, depressing, and humiliating malady that can be conceived; and if, as often happens, he fails, from physical weakness, to complete the required revolutions on the crank or the mill he is reported for idleness and punished with the greatest severity and brutality.'

Wilde's prison routine was as follows. He got up at 6.0 a.m. and cleaned out his cell. At seven he had breakfast, consisting of cocoa and brown bread. He was then taken out with other prisoners for exercise which lasted an hour. On returning to his cell he picked oakum until midday, when dinner was brought round. This meal consisted of greasy bacon and beans or soup; on one day a week he had cold meat. At 12.30 p.m. oakum picking was resumed and he was expected to continue with this occupation until 6.0 p.m. He then had tea, and at seven the lights were turned out and he went to bed. A newspaper report accurately described his life at this time: 'He is compelled to pick a certain quantity of oakum per day, is not allowed to converse with anyone, and with the exception of an hour's exercise is kept in solitary confinement in his cell.'[1]

> With midnight always in one's heart,
> And twilight in one's cell,
> We turn the crank or tear the rope,

1. *The Morning*, 6 June 1895.

Oscar Wilde

Each in his separate Hell,
And the silence is more awful far
Than the sound of a brazen bell.

And never a human voice comes near
To speak a gentle word:
And the eye that watches through the door
Is pitiless and hard:
And by all forgot, we rot and rot,
With soul and body marred.

The lesson which Wilde set himself to learn in prison was that of humility. From the outset he found it very hard, since he began each day by going down on his knees and washing the floor of his cell. 'For prison life with its endless privations and restrictions makes one rebellious. The most terrible thing about it is not that it breaks one's heart – hearts are made to be broken – but that it turns one's heart to stone. One sometimes feels that it is only with a front of brass and a lip of scorn that one can get through the day at all.' To succeed, he felt that he must overcome this mood of rebellion which 'closes up the channels of the soul and shuts out the airs of heaven'. His achievement he was to epitomize in the composition of the work known as *De Profundis*, which he completed in his prison cell eighteen months later. 'The plank bed, the loathsome food, the hard ropes shredded into oakum until one's fingertips grew dull with pain, the menial offices with which each day begins and finishes, the harsh orders that routine seems to necessitate, the dreadful dress that makes sorrow grotesque to look at, the silence, the solitude, the shame – each and all of these things I had to transform into a spiritual experience.'

2

The first person to give Wilde any feeling of hope in prison was his first visitor from the outside world. This was the Liberal Member of Parliament and lawyer, R. B. Haldane, later Lord Haldane, who had been a member of the Home Office Committee, under the chairmanship of Lord Gladstone, which had recently reviewed in searching terms the whole range of prison administration in England. According to Haldane, he used to meet Wilde in the days of his social success, and although he had not known him well, he was 'haunted by the idea of what this highly sensitive man was probably suffering under ordinary prison treatment'. As a member of the Gladstone Committee Haldane had a warrant which enabled him to go to any prison at any hour and call on the Governor to produce any prisoner he liked. Haldane's visit to Pentonville was probably also prompted by the alarming accounts which had been appearing in the *Daily Chronicle* and other newspapers about Wilde's mental condition.

Before he saw Wilde, the visitor met the prison chaplain in the Governor's room in the prison. This reverend gentleman told Haldane he was glad he had come, since he had 'failed to make any way' with the prisoner, which in view of his remarks to Wilde at their first meeting was hardly surprising. The visitor then saw Wilde alone in a special room. 'At first he refused to speak,' noted Haldane afterwards. 'I put my hand on his prison-dress-clad shoulder and said that I used to know him and that I had come to say something about himself. He had not fully used his great literary gift, and the reason was that he had lived a life of pleasure and had not made any great subject his own. Now misfortune might prove a blessing for his career, for he had got a great subject.' Haldane added that he would try to obtain for him the privileges of books and writing materials, so that in due course he would be 'free to produce'.

Wilde was so overcome by this prospect that he immediately burst into tears. Nevertheless, he promised to make the attempt. For books he asked eagerly, saying that all he had to read was *A Pilgrim's Progress*, and that work, in Haldane's words, 'did not satisfy him'. Among others he asked for Flaubert's works, particularly *Madame Bovary*. To this latter request Haldane replied that the dedication by the author to his advocate, who had successfully defended him on a charge of obscene publication, made such a work as *Madame Bovary* unlikely to be sanctioned.

At this remark, according to Haldane, the prisoner began to laugh and immediately became cheerful. After some discussion they settled on the writings of St Augustine, several books by Cardinal Newman, Pascal's *Pensées*, and Walter Pater's work on the Renaissance. These Haldane succeeded in procuring for him, and they accompanied him to his next prison when he moved, although the Governor of Pentonville objected to several of them as being 'of a controversial character' and consequently not in conformity with the Local Prison Code.[1]

One day, about a year after Wilde's release, Haldane received a small anonymous parcel. When he opened it he found a copy of *The Ballad of Reading Goal* by 'C.3.3.', the pseudonym under which this celebrated poem was originally published. 'It was the redemption of his promise to me,' wrote Haldane afterwards.

Haldane had promised to get in touch with Wilde's wife and family and give them news of the prisoner. He failed to see Mrs Constance Wilde and the two children, as they had gone abroad, but he called at Oakley Street and saw Lady Wilde and Willie, also Willie's second wife, a kind-hearted woman from Dublin, whom Willie had married recently and whom Oscar seems to have known fairly well. This visit prompted Mrs Willie Wilde to write to the Governor of Pentonville, asking him to give 'my unhappy brother-in-law' her 'fondest love' and to say 'how often I think of him and long to see him; also, what perhaps will give him the most pleasure, that his mother is wonderfully well'. This the Governor seems to have done.

Wilde's next visitor brought less pleasant news. He was a clerk from the Marquess of Queensberry's solicitors, who came down to Pentonville to serve the prisoner with a bankruptcy notice. On 21 June 1895 Queensberry had filed a petition in the Bankruptcy Court asking for a receiving order to be made against Wilde. The sum claimed was £677, being the amount of the petitioner's taxed costs in the disastrous action for criminal libel which Wilde had brought against Queensberry. This news came as a cruel blow

1. Haldane later added ten more volumes of Pater and other books. At Haldane's request the collection was later presented to the Wandsworth Prison Library. See Haldane's *Autobiography* (1929), pp. 166–7.

to Wilde and it made him feel very bitter for a long time. At the time of the trial he had received definite assurances from Lord Alfred Douglas that the various members of the Queensberry family who hated its titular head, particularly Douglas's elder brother, Lord Douglas of Hawick, would be responsible for the costs of the libel prosecution into which, as we have seen, Alfred Douglas had vigorously egged Wilde on. This was a subject to which Wilde in his prison correspondence was to revert bitterly again and again. 'I felt most strongly that these costs should have been borne by your family,' he told Douglas. 'You had taken personally on yourself the responsibility of stating that your family would do so. It was that which made the solicitor take up the case the way he did. You were absolutely responsible. Even irrespective of your engagement on your family's behalf, you should have felt that, as you had brought the whole ruin on me, the least that could have been done was to spare me the additional ignominy of bankruptcy for an absolutely contemptible sum of money, less than half of what I spent on you in three brief summer months at Goring.'

In what seems to have been an attempt to stave off the bank-ruptcy proceedings, Wilde's solicitors applied to the Home Office for permission to see their client 'with reference to the translation and publication of some of his works'. The request was made towards the end of June, but it was not until several weeks later that permission was granted. The delay was possibly due to the change in Home Secretaries consequent upon the fall of the Liberal Government of Lord Rosebery, and also perhaps to a misunderstanding of the nature of the publications contemplated. Because Wilde had been convicted of indecent practices, it was assumed by at least one senior Home Office official that the publications might also be indecent. 'Let them see him in the ordinary course as his solicitors to take his instructions in regard to property and business matters,' this official wrote on the relevant file. 'If they publish anything objectionable it will be their look-out, and the Law can intervene.'

When the solicitors received the necessary order and were ready to see their client, they learned that he had been transferred

283

Oscar Wilde

from Pentonville to Wandsworth. What determined the Prison Commissioners on this change, which occurred on 4 July 1895, is not clear. It was possibly due to Haldane, who may have wished to bring Wilde under the influence of the Wandsworth prison chaplain, the Rev. W. D. Morrison, an unusually enlightened clergyman, who could be relied upon to keep a particular eye on him. However, we do know that Wilde was even more unhappy at Wandsworth, where he found the food worse than at Pentonville. ('It even smelt bad. It was not fit for dogs.') 'At Wandsworth I thought I should go mad,' he admitted afterwards. He became more and more mentally depressed and longed to die. 'I was dreadfully unhappy, so utterly miserable that I wanted to kill myself,' he told André Gide after his release. 'But what kept me from doing so was looking at the others, and seeing that they were as unhappy as I was, and feeling sorry for them.'[1] From one fellow-prisoner he received a touching expression of sympathy, which was to land him in trouble. One day at exercise in the prison yard, a prisoner whispered in the hoarse voice men get from long and compulsory silence: 'I am sorry for you. It is harder for the likes of you than it is for the likes of us!' This kindness brought tears to Wilde's eyes. 'No, my friend,' he replied. 'We all suffer alike.' He had not yet learned to speak like other prisoners, without moving their lips. In the result he was punished for talking, and, as he told the Governor that it was he who had begun the conversation, he received double punishment.[2]

The visit of Wilde's solicitors was memorable because it brought the first message which the prisoner received from Lord Alfred Douglas, with whom the solicitors had been in touch in the forlorn hope of receiving some financial help. The firm had sent down one of their clerks to Wandsworth, accompanied by a Commissioner for Oaths in order to take the necessary depositions from their client to file with his Statement of Affairs in connexion with his pending bankruptcy, and the interview took place in the

1. A. Gide, *Oscar Wilde*, tr. Stuart Mason (1905), p. 63.
2. Gide op. cit., 66–8. Gide attributes this incident to Reading, but Wilde states in *De Profundis* that it took place in Wandsworth. The punishment for this breach of regulations was confinement in a dark cell for up to three days on a diet of bread and water.

presence of the customary warder. Suddenly the clerk leaned across the table and, having consulted a piece of paper which he pulled out of his pocket, said in a low voice: 'Prince Fleur de Lys wishes to be remembered to you!' Wilde stared at him. The clerk repeated the message, adding mysteriously: 'The gentleman is abroad at present.' Suddenly the meaning flashed on the prisoner and he laughed bitterly. 'In that laugh was all the scorn of the world,' he later wrote to Douglas, recalling the incident. 'You were, no doubt, quite right to communicate with me under an assumed name. I myself, at that time, had no name at all. In the great prison where I was then incarcerated, I was merely the figure and letter of a little cell in a long gallery, one of a thousand lifeless numbers as of a thousand lifeless lives. But surely there were many real names in real history which would have suited you much better, and by which I would have had no difficulty at all in recognizing you at once? I did not look for you behind the spangles of a tinsel vizard only suitable for an amusing masquerade.'

The first meeting of Wilde's creditors, under the Receiving Order which had been made, took place before the Official Receiver in London on 26 August 1895. According to the Official Receiver the debtor's accounts showed unsecured liabilities of £2,676 and partly secured debts of £915, disclosing a total deficiency of £3,591. Mr Travers Humphreys, who had appeared as Wilde's junior counsel in the three trials and at the preliminary police court proceedings, represented the debtor. He stated that, although every effort had been made, Wilde was not in a position to submit any offer to his creditors. For this reason it had not been considered necessary for the debtor to attend the meeting. In these circumstances it only remained to pass a resolution that he be adjudged bankrupt and to appoint a trustee. This was accordingly done, on the motion of Lord Queensberry, and the Official Receiver was appointed trustee. At the same time, the date of the debtor's public examination was fixed for four weeks later.[1]

Having completed the first three months of his sentence, Wilde was now entitled under the prison regulations to receive and send one letter and also to have a visit from a friend. Feeling that he

1. *The Times*, 27 August 1895.

had to reserve his first letter for the subject of 'family business', Wilde accepted a first letter from his brother-in-law Otho Holland Lloyd, in preference to a letter from Alfred Douglas, who had applied for permission to write to him. What his brother-in-law told him on this occasion was that, if he would only write once to his wife, she would in all probability, for his sake and the sake of the children, take no action for a divorce, as she was being pressed by Sir George Lewis and other family advisers to do. In these circumstances Wilde not unnaturally felt it his duty to send his first letter to her. Surprising as it seemed to some of his friends, he was really very fond of his wife and felt extremely sorry for her, although he was aware that she could not understand him, and on his own admission he had been 'bored to death with married life'.

The text of Wilde's letter to his wife has not survived. But whatever he wrote to her must have touched her deeply. At this time Constance Wilde was staying with friends on the Continent, and she accordingly applied to the Governor of Wandsworth for a visiting order, as she had an opportunity of travelling to England with a friend who had promised to look after her on the journey. The Governor replied that her husband had just received a visit – this was from Robert Sherard – and that he was not due for another visit under the rules for a considerable time, and he advised her to make application to the Prison Commissioners. She did so, and as a result a special visit was authorized. This visit took place on 21 September 1895, in the most painful and humiliating conditions.

'It was indeed awful, more so than I had any conception it could be,' she told Sherard afterwards. 'I could not see him and I could not touch him I scarcely spoke. ... When I go again, I am to get at the Home Secretary through Mr Haldane and try and get a room to see him in and touch him again. He has been mad these last three years, and he says that if he saw Alfred Douglas he would kill him. So he had better keep away and be satisfied with having marred a fine life. Few people can boast of so much.'[1]

1. Sherard, *The Real Oscar Wilde*, p. 173.

The Aftermath

Three days later Wilde underwent a further ordeal, this time in the Bankruptcy Court, to which he was brought in the custody of two policemen for his public examination. A considerable crowd had collected in Carey Street in anticipation of an entertaining spectacle. But, although they caught a glimpse of the prisoner in handcuffs, they were largely disappointed. Pending an application for an adjournment, which was made by counsel on his behalf, Wilde waited with the policemen in an adjoining room. Later he was to pay a warm tribute to these two members of the metropolitan force, 'who, in their homely, rough way strove to comfort me in my journeys to and from the Bankruptcy Court under conditions of terrible mental distress'.

It appeared that several of Wilde's friends had subscribed various sums of money, and with others, which were expected to be forthcoming, there was every reason to believe, said counsel, that there would be sufficient to pay all the creditors twenty shillings in the pound. Since no creditor appeared to oppose the application, the Registrar adjourned the examination for seven weeks. Meanwhile, one of the friends in question, Robert Ross, was waiting in the long dreary corridor outside the courtroom so that, as Wilde put it in a memorable passage in *De Profundis*, 'before the whole crowd, whom an action so sweet and simple hushed into silence, he might gravely raise his hat to me, as handcuffed and with bowed head I passed him by'.

Wilde was now approaching a complete physical and nervous breakdown. He had already lost nearly two stone in weight, and his prison clothes hung loosely on his emaciated frame. One morning, about ten days after his visit to Carey Street, he felt so ill that he could only get up and dress himself with the greatest effort, having previously been accused of malingering by the prison doctor. While he was dressing, he fell and bruised one of his ears badly on the stone floor of his cell. He then went with the other prisoners to the prison chapel for prayers, where he immediately fainted. When he recovered consciousness, he found himself in the hospital, where he was kept for several weeks and seems to have been well treated, given special food, and nursed back to strength. During this period he was examined on the

Oscar Wilde

Home Secretary's instructions by two mental specialists from Broadmoor Criminal Lunatic Asylum. In due course the specialists reported that they could discover no evidence of any mental disease in the prisoner, whom they were first able to observe through a spy-hole in one of the doors leading to the hospital. There they saw Wilde, apparently in excellent spirits, the centre of a group of prisoners, whom he was holding entranced by his talk. In their report the doctors recommended that Wilde should be transferred to a country prison where there would be an opportunity for healthy exercise and employment on garden work, 'with a view of a more wholesome state of his tissues being induced and his mind being thereby roused to more healthy action so far as the subjects of his thoughts are concerned'.

On 12 November 1895 Wilde was considered to have sufficiently recovered to attend his adjourned public examination in Carey Street. Up to the last moment his solicitors hoped that the need for this further trial would be obviated by the subscription of a sufficient sum of money by Wilde's friends to enable his creditors to be paid in full. A certain amount was indeed subscribed, but the balance was not forthcoming. Thus the public examination took place. It was conducted in open court by the Official Receiver.

'Step by step with the Bankruptcy Receiver', Wilde wrote afterwards, 'I had to go over every item in my life. It was horrible.' He had never kept any books or accounts, he told the Official Receiver, but he estimated that his expenditure during the two or three years preceding the receiving order was close on £3,000 a year. Much of this, he admitted, had gone in the entertainment of Lord Alfred Douglas, as he was subsequently to remind that young man in several stinging passages in *De Profundis*. Between the autumn of 1892 and the date of his arrest, he reckoned he had spent over £5,000 on Douglas. In a single week in Paris, for instance, he spent £150, which besides their own expenses included the expenses of Douglas's Italian servant, while in the summer of 1893 he took a house for three months at Goring-on-Thames at a total cost of £1,340. 'Though it may seem strange to you that one in the terrible position in which I am

288

The Aftermath

situated should find a difference between one disgrace and another,' he wrote to Douglas from prison, 'still I frankly admit that the folly of throwing all this money on you, and letting you squander my fortune to your own hurt as well as mine, gives to me and in my eyes a note of common profligacy to my bankruptcy that makes me doubly ashamed of it.'

'You may be interested to know,' he added, 'that your father openly said in the Orleans Club that if it had cost him £20,000 he would have considered the money thoroughly well spent, he had extracted such enjoyment and delight and triumph out of it all. The fact that he was able not merely to put me into prison for two years but to take me out for an afternoon and make me a public bankrupt was an extra refinement of pleasure that he had not expected. It was the crowning point of my humiliation and of his complete and perfect victory.'

3

A few days after Wilde's public examination in Carey Street, the Chairman of the Prison Commissioners, Mr Evelyn Ruggles-Brise informed the Home Secretary that, since the bankruptcy proceedings had now come to an end, Wilde would be transferred to Reading Prison where 'suitable occupation in the way of gardening and bookbinding and library work may be found for him'. Ruggles-Brise, it may be noted here, had been appointed earlier in the year by Asquith, with Haldane's support, and he was perhaps the most enlightened and human prison administrator so far to be in charge of the service.[1] The betterment of Wilde's lot which took place at this time was largely due to Ruggles-Brise, although it was only possible to mitigate the harsher features of the system gradually. The conditions under which the prisoner was removed from Wandsworth to Reading was one of those features.

1. Sir Evelyn Ruggles-Brise (1857–1935) was Chairman of the Prison Commission from 1895 to his retirement in 1921. He founded the Borstal system for juvenile offenders.

289

Oscar Wilde

The transfer was later described by Wilde in *De Profundis* in a passage which has often been quoted and which caught the attention of the critics and the public possibly more than any other when that work was first published in a considerably expurgated edition ten years later. The transfer took place on 20 November 1895.[1]

From two o'clock till half past two on that day I had to stand on the centre platform at Clapham Junction in convict dress and hand-cuffed, for the world to look at. I had been taken out of the hospital ward without a moment's notice being given to me. Of all possible objects I was the most grotesque. When people saw me they laughed. Each train as it came in swelled the audience. Nothing could exceed their amusement. That was, of course, before they knew who I was. As soon as they had been informed they laughed still more. For half an hour I stood there in the grey November rain surrounded by a jeering mob.

No wonder that for a year afterwards Wilde, as he confessed, was to weep every day at the same hour and for the same space of time. According to Sherard, Wilde's initial recognition on the station platform was accompanied by a particularly revolting exhibition of Philistinism and cruelty. A man, who had been staring at the handcuffed figure for some minutes, suddenly exclaimed for the benefit of the other onlookers: 'My God, that's Oscar Wilde!' He then stepped up to him and spat in his face.[2]

Reading Gaol, which has become famous as the place where Wilde was to serve the remainder of his sentence, was one of the smaller county prisons built on the Pentonville model. During Wilde's time its prison population averaged 150, including a number of soldiers who had come from the nearby barracks at Windsor. The Governor, Major Henry Isaacson, was a military despot, under whose harsh rule Wilde was to suffer for the next eight months. He was 'tall and not unlike the headmaster of a public school', according to Robert Ross, who was not un-favourably impressed by him on the occasion of their first meeting.

1. Hart-Davis, pp. 490–1. Wilde mistakenly gave the date in the text as 13 November.
2. Sherard, *Unhappy Friendship*, p. 212.

The Aftermath

But to Frank Harris, a fairly acute observer, to whom the Governor boasted that he was 'knocking the nonsense out of Wilde', Major Isaacson seemed 'almost inhuman'. Wilde himself has put it on record that under him the prison system was carried out with the greatest harshness and stupidity, because, as he subsequently told André Gide, 'he was entirely lacking in imagination'.[1] As for the chaplain, he was kindly enough but ineffective, while the prison doctor, with his greasy white beard, reminded Robert Ross of a bullying director of a sham city company.

At Reading, Wilde was allocated Cell 3 on the third landing of Gallery C, so that his prison number by which he was officially known was C.3.3. It was under this number that *The Ballad of Reading Goal* was originally published.

> The Governor was strong upon
> The Regulations Act:
> The Doctor said that death was but
> A scientific fact:
> And twice a day the Chaplain called
> And left a little tract.

Meanwhile a group of Wilde's friends headed by More Adey had prepared a petition to the Home Secretary asking for Wilde's early release. This document was largely the work of Bernard Shaw, who, although he had never been at all friendly with his fellow-Irishman, felt that he had already been more than sufficiently punished and that confinement for the full term of his sentence under the harsh prison regulations which then prevailed would make him incapable of any further literary work. The difficulty was to find supporters of the petition whose names would carry some weight with the authorities. Bernard Shaw told Willie Wilde at this time, that, while he himself and the Rev. Stewart Headlam, who had gone bail for Wilde after his first trial, were quite ready to sign the petition, 'that would be no use, as we were two notorious cranks and our names would by themselves reduce the petition to absurdity and do Oscar more harm than good.'[2] Willie Wilde replied that he did not think that signatures

1. Gide, p. 65.
2. Harris II (Supplement by G. B. Shaw), p. 5.

would be obtainable, and events speedily proved him right. The only prominent individual whom Adey could persuade to sign the petition was York Powell, Regius Professor of Modern History at Oxford. Several other signatures of influential persons were promised; but, when the time came, they were not forthcoming. Most people who were approached by Adey were afraid to sign. But some refused on moral grounds. Among the latter was Holman Hunt, the Pre-Raphaelite artist and painter of religious pictures, of which the best known is 'The Light of the World'. 'I must repeat my opinion that the law treated him with exceeding leniency,' Hunt wrote to Adey in his letter of refusal, 'and state that further consideration of the facts convinces me that in justice to criminals belonging to other classes of society, I should have to join in the cry for doing away with all personal responsibility, if I took any part in appealing for his liberation before the completion of his term of imprisonment. While such a course might seem benevolent to malefactors, it would scarcely be so to the self-restrained and orderly members of society.' As Wilde's younger son was to put it in his autobiography, it is only fair to suppose that Holman Hunt, when he wrote this letter, had forgotten the quotation which inspired his celebrated painting, now in the Tate Gallery.[1] In these circumstances the project of the petition had to be abandoned.

It is not the purpose of this book, which is primarily concerned with Wilde's trials, to give a detailed account of his prison experiences. But the principal incidents must be briefly mentioned in order to complete the story.

Shortly after his arrival at Reading, his mother became seriously ill with bronchitis. Feeling that her end was near, she asked that Oscar might be allowed to come and see her for the last time. Naturally enough this request was refused. When they brought her the news in bed, she said 'May the prison help him!'

1. 'I expect to pass through this world but once. Any good, therefore, that I can do, or any kindness that I can show to any fellow creature, let me do it now. Let me not defer or neglect it, for I shall not pass this way again.' Cited, with the letter from Hunt dated 30 November 1895, by Vyvyan Holland in his *Son of Oscar Wilde* (1954), p. 204.

and turned her face to the wall. These were her last words.[1]
Like many of the Irish, Wilde was superstitious, and he also
liked to think that he possessed certain psychic qualities. After
he came out of prison, he told Vincent O'Sullivan, the American
writer whom he met in Paris, that on the night of his mother's
death she appeared to him in his cell. She was dressed in outdoor
clothes, and he asked her to take off her hat and cloak and sit
down. But she shook her head sadly and vanished. It was then, he
said, that he knew that she was dead.[2]

As we have seen, Wilde had always been deeply devoted to his
mother, and he was very proud of her achievements in Irish
politics and literature. Even his profligate brother Willie, between
whom and Oscar there was little love lost, had to admit that
'despite all his faults and follies, he was always a good son to her'.
The tribute which Oscar paid to her memory, along with that of
his father, is one of the most striking passages in *De Profundis*.
'Her death was so terrible to me,' he wrote, 'that I, once a lord of
language, have no words in which to express my anguish and my
shame. . . . She and my father had bequeathed to me a name they
had made noble and honoured, not merely in Literature, Art,
Archaeology, and Science, but in the public history of our country in its evolution as a nation. I had disgraced that name etern-
ally. I had made it a low byword among low people. I had dragged
it through the very mire. I had given it to brutes that they might
make it brutal, and to fools that they might turn it into a synonym
for folly. What I suffered then, and still suffer, is not for pen to
write or paper to record.'

It was from his wife ('at that time kind and gentle to me') that
Wilde learned the news of his mother's death. Rather than that he
should hear it from 'indifferent or alien lips', Constance Wilde
travelled from Genoa to Reading to break 'the tidings of so irre-
parable, so irredeemable a loss'. They also discussed the future of
their two children, and Wilde advised her to enlist the help of a
guardian if she could not manage their future upbringing alone.
He begged her not to spoil them, particularly Cyril, the elder, as

1. Harris, II, p. 539. Lady Wilde died in London on 3 February 1896.
2. V. O'Sullivan, *Aspects of Wilde* (1938), p. 63.

Lady Queensberry had done with Lord Alfred Douglas. Later Wilde told Robert Ross how kind his wife had been to him on this occasion. Unfortunately it was to be the last time that Wilde ever saw his wife, although, unknown to him, she is believed to have caught a glimpse of her husband in prison on one other occasion. They became estranged because of the well-meant but ill-judged action by some of Wilde's friends in acquiring a half share of his interest under his marriage settlement from the Official Receiver. Although Wilde himself was opposed to this action, he was blamed for it by his wife and her advisers. Owing to various difficulties, they were never able to meet after his release. Meanwhile she appointed a guardian for the children, and changed their surnames as well as her own married name from Wilde to Holland.

One encouraging piece of news reached the prisoner at this time. On 10 February 1896, his play *Salomé*, which, it will be remembered, the Lord Chamberlain had banned in England, received its first public performance in Paris, where it was produced at Théâtre de l'Oeuvre by the well-known French actor-manager Aurélien Lugne-Poe, who also played the part of Herod. 'Please write to Stuart Merrill in Paris or Robert Sherard to say how gratified I was at the performance of my play and have my thanks conveyed to Lugne-Poe,' Wilde wrote to Ross when he was able to send his next letter from Reading. 'It is something that at a time of disgrace and shame I should still be regarded as an artist. I wish I could feel more pleasure, but I seem dead to all emotions except those of anguish and despair. However, please let Lugne-Poe know that I am sensible of the honour he has done me. He is a poet himself.' Indeed Wilde attributed the change which followed at Reading to this event. 'The production of *Salomé* was the thing that turned the scale in my favour, as far as my treatment in prison by the Government was concerned,' he later told Lord Alfred Douglas, 'and I am deeply grateful to all concerned in it.'[1]

About this time Wilde received a visit from Frank Harris, to

1. Hart-Davis, p. 588. See also A. C. Dennison and Harrison Post. *Some Letters from Oscar Wilde to Lord Alfred Douglas* (1924), p. xxvii.

whom he appears to have complained about his treatment. 'The Governor loves to punish,' he told Harris, 'and he punishes by taking my books from me. It is perfectly awful to let the mind grind itself away between the upper and nether millstones of regret and remorse without respite. With books my life would be livable – any life!'

Harris promised to try to get him more books and also writing materials, of the lack of which Wilde also complained. Wilde repeated these requests in a long petition, which he drafted to the Home Secretary, pointing out that he was only allowed two books a week from the extremely small and poor prison library. Wilde further complained that the abscess which had formed in his ear after his fall at Wandsworth was giving him trouble, and that his eyesight had suffered very much from the enforced living in a whitewashed cell with a flaring gas jet at night.[1]

These representations had some effect, as the Prison Commissioners ordered that the rule as to two books a week should be relaxed in his case, that he should send in a list of requests for books which could be purchased provided that the total cost did not exceed £10, and that he should be provided with foolscap paper, ink, and pen 'for use in his leisure moments, in his cell'. The prison doctor was also directed to watch his general health with care, and call in a second opinion if necessary.

At their meeting Harris had urged Wilde to write something about his prison experiences, or at least to use them for a future literary work. Wilde did not seem particularly enthusiastic about the idea. However, the fact remains that the incident occurred during the summer of 1896 which inspired the composition of his best known poetic work; this at Robert Ross's suggestion, was to be called *The Ballad of Reading Gaol*, and described the last days and execution of a young Guards soldier who was said 'to have cut his wife's throat in a very determined manner, she having excited his jealousy and (so far as the evidence went) greatly annoyed him'.[2]

1. For the text of this petition, dated 2 July 1896, see Hart-Davis, pp. 401–5.
2. *Reading Mercury*, 10 July 1896.

Oscar Wilde

> The man had killed the thing he loved,
> And so he had to die.

Harris always claimed that it was as a result of the report which he made to Ruggles-Brise after seeing Wilde that a change of Governors took place at Reading. However that may be, in July 1896 Isaacson was transferred to another post in the service and his place was taken by Major J. O. Nelson, a very different type from his predecessor. While Isaacson, according to Wilde, was unable to enjoy his breakfast unless someone was punished before he ate it, Nelson on the other hand was 'the most Christ-like man' he had ever met. 'The present Governor of Reading is a man of gentle and humane character, greatly liked and respected by all the prisoners,' wrote Wilde at the time of his release. 'Though he cannot alter the rules of the prison system, he has altered the spirit in which they used to be carried out by his predecessor. He is very popular with the prisoners and the warders. Indeed he has quite altered the whole tone of prison life.'[1]

It was under Major Nelson's kindly dispensation that Wilde served out the remaining ten months of his sentence, and that he was able to make use of his privilege of writing materials by composing the work which, as we shall see, was first given to the world in considerably abbreviated form under the title of *De Profundis*. At the same time he had one further most painful experience. This was the handing over of his children by an order of the High Court to the joint guardianship of his wife and her cousin Adrian Hope, while he was to be restrained from attempting to remove them from their mother's custody or otherwise 'interfering' with them. For their father this was an appalling blow. 'My two children are taken from me by legal procedure,' he wrote shortly afterwards in *De Profundis*. 'That is and always will remain to me a source of infinite distress, of infinite pain, of grief without end or limit. That the law should decide and take upon itself to decide that I am one unfit to be with my own children is something quite horrible to me. The disgrace of prison is as nothing compared with it. I envy the other men who tread the yard along with me. I am sure that their children

1. Letter to *Daily Chronicle*, 27 May 1897.

wait for them, look for their coming, will be sweet to them.' Eventually, after a lengthy correspondence between Constance Wilde's solicitors and the solicitors employed by Ross and Adey on Wilde's behalf, Wilde's wife agreed to make him an allowance of £150 a year, provided that the contingent interest in his marriage settlement which Ross and Adey had bought in for him from the Official Receiver was surrendered and furthermore that Wilde did nothing which would entitle his wife to a divorce or judicial separation and was not guilty of any moral misconduct and did not 'notoriously consort with evil or disreputable persons'. This agreement was embodied in a Deed of Arrangement, which was signed by Wilde in the presence of the respective solicitors a few days before his release.

On this occasion Constance Wilde is stated to have accompanied her solicitor to Reading and to have waited in the corridor outside the 'solicitor's room', a pathetic, tearful figure dressed in black. In response to her request to have 'one glimpse of my husband', the warder on duty in the corridor stepped back silently so as to enable her to look through the glass peep-hole in the door. In the warder's words: 'Mrs Wilde cast one long lingering glance inside and saw the convict-poet, who, in deep mental distress himself, was totally unconscious that any eyes save those of the stern lawyer and myself witnessed his degradation.' At that precise moment Wilde was in the act of putting his signature to the deed. She drew back, 'apparently labouring under deep emotion', and a few minutes later left the prison with her solicitor, still unseen by Wilde. She never saw him again. To the warder it remained the saddest story he knew of the prisoner.[1]

4

'I don't defend my conduct. I explain it.' Thus wrote Wilde on the eve of his release from Reading Gaol to his friend and literary executor, Robert Ross. The explanation is to be found in a curious document, a mixture of apology, self-abasement, and

1. *Evening News*, 2 March 1905.

violent recrimination, which Wilde composed during his last three months in prison. This document took the form of a long letter to Lord Alfred Douglas, and it was originally entrusted to Ross for the purpose of having copies made of it before its dispatch to Douglas. In 1905 Ross published parts of it – actually less than half – under the title *De Profundis*, to which a few other excerpts were added in a new edition which appeared four years later, but without any indication that it was really a letter to Douglas. In 1913, Lord Alfred Douglas brought an action for libel against Mr Arthur Ransome, who had written a study of Wilde in which he described *De Profundis* as having been written to 'a man to whom Wilde felt that he owed some at least of the public circumstances of his disgrace'. In his plea of justification, the defendant put in substantial portions which had been 'suppressed' by Ross in the published versions. These passages, which were read out in Court, were far from complimentary to Douglas.[1] In this manner the public, including Douglas himself (so he said), learned for the first time the true nature of the work known as *De Profundis*. Meanwhile, Ross – who swore he had sent Douglas a copy and that Douglas had received it during Wilde's lifetime – presented the original manuscript to the British Museum, on condition that it should remain sealed up for fifty years. In accordance with this condition, the MS was opened to the public for the first time on 1 January 1960.[2]

1. This libel action, which was tried before Mr Justice Darling in the King's Bench Division in April 1913, resulted in a verdict for Mr Ransome: for details see my *Cases that Changed the Law* (1951).
2. Before handing over the original to the British Museum, Ross had fifteen copies hurriedly printed in the United States, of which two were deposited for copyright purposes in the Library of Congress, Washington, D.C.; only one was offered for sale, at what Ross considered to be the prohibitive price of $1,000, and was bought by an unknown purchaser at that figure. A page of the original was photographed at the same time lest the authenticity of the work should be doubted: it was reproduced by Mason in his bibliography of Wilde. Those passages from the 'suppressed' portions, which were read out in Court during the case of *Douglas v. Ransome*, were published by Frank Harris, op. cit. II, 552–75. The complete text, taken from the original MS, will be found in Hart-Davis, pp. 423–511. For further details, see my article in the *Sunday Times*, 3 January 1960.

The Aftermath

It may well be asked what caused Wilde to turn so bitterly against his friend in prison, particularly as Wilde had written to him in terms of deep affection whilst he was in Holloway on remand awaiting his first trial; after all, it was only at Wilde's earnest entreaty that Douglas, who was certainly ready to stand by him, had reluctantly consented to leave the country. From his chosen place of exile in France, Douglas had continued to write to the English press on Wilde's behalf, and he had even addressed a petition to Queen Victoria pleading for the exercise of royal clemency, 'Most gracious lady,' he wrote, 'your heart is kind and tender, and even in these latter days the arm of the Queen is strong. Will you not save this man, who even if he be guilty has already been punished more, a thousand times more cruelly than he deserves, seeing that in addition to the ruin of his life, the destruction of his art and the loss of every worldly possession, he has been condemned to a sentence which the highest authorities have declared to be equivalent to a sentence of "death or madness", and which has been unanimously condemned as inhuman by the Prison Commission which has just recently laid its report before Your Majesty's Court?'[1]

While he was in prison Wilde had plenty of time to reflect upon the consequences of his unfortunate friendship with Douglas, which, as Mr Justice Wills had remarked in his summing up at the last trial, had led to 'the whole of this lamentable inquiry'. We have already noticed the unfavourable impression which Douglas had made by his first message to Wilde from 'Prince Fleur de Lys' and Wilde's reaction to it. But what really produced the most bitter feelings in Wilde was Douglas's intention (which Wilde first heard of from Sherard and which was later confirmed by the Governor of Wandsworth when Douglas wrote to him) to include the Holloway letters in an article which he had written for the French literary monthly the *Mercure de France* – 'the letters', as Wilde subsequently reproached Douglas, 'that should have

---

1. The Queen never saw this petition, dated 25 June 1895: it was intercepted by her private secretary and forwarded to the Home Secretary, who rejected it immediately.

been to you of all things sacred and secret beyond anything in the whole world!'

No doubt Douglas had acted from the best of intentions. He honestly believed that, if it were published, the article would have the effect 'of completely rehabilitating Oscar, at any rate in France'. It is much more likely that the appearance of these letters in print, even in a French translation, would have done Wilde even more harm than the two compromising letters which had been quoted in the trials. Wilde himself seems to have realized this. But, as events turned out, he had alarmed himself unnecessarily. Sherard was already in touch with the editor of the *Mercure de France*, and although the article was already in type, the editor wrote to Douglas asking him to omit the letters. This Douglas refused to do, and in consequence the whole article was withdrawn.[1]

Wilde was not allowed to send his letter to Douglas, surely one of the longest ever written – it runs to over 30,000 words – but he was permitted to take it with him when he left Reading on his release. He was also allowed to write before his release to Ross, telling him the underlying reasons for its composition and giving directions for its copying, as he wished several copies to be made.

Well, if you are to be my literary executor, you must be in possession of the only document that really gives any explanation of my extraordinary behaviour with regard to Queensberry and Alfred Douglas. When you have read the letter, you will see the psychological explanation of a course of conduct that from the outside seems a combination of absolute idiocy with vulgar bravado. Some day the truth will have to be known – not necessarily in my lifetime or in Douglas's. But I am not prepared to sit in the grotesque pillory they put me into for all time; for the simple reason that I inherited from my father and mother a name of high distinction in literature and art, and I cannot for eternity allow that name to be the shield and catspaw of the Queensberry's. I don't defend my conduct, I explain it.

1. Sherard, *Unhappy Friendship*, pp. 204–5. Douglas has given his version of the affair in his *Autobiography* (1929), Chapter XXI. He refused to hand over the letters to Ross, who undertook to seal them up until Wilde came out of prison, and subsequently destroyed them. However, it has been possible to reconstruct the text from the French translation which was later retranslated into English: see Hart-Davis, pp. 393–4 and 396–8.

The Aftermath

As for the mode of copying the document, Wilde felt that 'the only thing is to be thoroughly modern and have it typewritten'. He suggested that a girl from the agency, where he had had his last play typed, might be sent to More Adey's flat in London to do the work under Ross's supervision. ('Women are the most reliable, they have no memory for the important.') 'I assure you', he wrote to Ross, 'that the typewriting machine, when played with expression, is no more annoying than the piano when played by a sister or near relation. Indeed many among those most devoted to domesticity prefer it.' He playfully suggested that the typist 'might be fed through a lattice in the door, like the Cardinals when they elect a Pope, till she comes out on the balcony and can say to the world "*Habet mundus Epistolam*"; for indeed it is an Encyclical letter, and as the Bulls of the Holy Father are named from their opening words, it may be spoken of as the *Epistola in Carcere et Vinculis*'.

It was Ross who gave the work its title *De Profundis*, when he published the first truncated version eight years later, having for obvious reasons been obliged to suppress more than half of the original text. From the point of view of the trials, the interest of *De Profundis*, particularly as regards the suppressed portions, lies in the author's allusions to the central catastrophe and the events which caused it.

Here, for example, is his account of the fatal 'prose poem' letter, which formed such an important link in the chain of events encompassing his ruin and which, it will be remembered, had been written as the result of a poem sent by Douglas to him.

... You send me a very nice poem of the undergraduate school of verse for my approval. I reply by a letter of fantastic literary conceits: I compare you to Hylas, or Hyacinth, Jonquil, or Narcissus, or some one whom the great god of Poetry favoured, and honoured with his love. The letter is like a passage from one of Shakespeare's sonnets transposed to a minor key. ...

It was, let me say frankly, the sort of letter I would, in a happy, if wilful moment, have written to any graceful young man of either University who had sent me a poem of his own making, certain that he would have sufficient wit or culture to interpret rightly its fantastic phrases. Look at the history of that letter! It passes from you into the hands of a loathsome companion, from him to a gang of blackmailers, copies of it are sent about London to my friends, and to the manager of the theatre where my work is being performed, every construction but the right one is put upon it. Society is thrilled with the absurd rumours that I have had to pay a huge sum of money for having written an infamous letter to you; this forms the basis of your father's worst attack.

I produce the original letter myself in Court to show what it really is; it is denounced by your father's Counsel as a revolting and insidious attempt to corrupt innocence; ultimately it forms part of a criminal charge: the Crown takes it up: the Judge sums up on it with little learning and much morality: I go to prison for it at last. That is the result of writing you a charming letter.

Of course, Wilde did not go to prison, as he suggests here, simply because he had written an extravagant letter. There was another side of the picture, which he himself admitted. It was repeatedly made clear at various stages during the trials that Wilde could not be convicted on the sole evidence of this letter he had written Douglas. But there is no doubt that its cumulative effect, when considered with the rest of the evidence against him was damning in the eyes of the jury, although he himself had actually produced the letter. It was a dead weight he had to carry throughout the Old Bailey drama, and it may well have eventually turned the scales against him.

In what is perhaps the most interesting passage in the suppressed portion of *De Profundis* from the point of view of the trials, Wilde makes the remarkable statement that, but for the sake of his friend whose reputation he was shielding, he might have said much more than he did when he went into the witness box.

The sins of another were being placed to my account. Had I so chosen, I could on either trial have saved myself at his expense, not from shame indeed, but from imprisonment.[1] Had I cared to show that the Crown witnesses – the three most important – had been carefully coached by your father and his solicitors, not in reticences merely, but

1. Wilde made a similar admission after his release to his future biographer, R. H. Sherard: 'It would have meant betraying a friend.' See Sherard, *Life of Oscar Wilde* (1906), p. 368.

in assertions, in the absolute transference, deliberate, plotted, and rehearsed, of the actions and doings of someone else on to me, I could have had each one of them dismissed from the box by the judge, more summarily than even wretched perjured Atkins was. I could have walked out of Court with my tongue in my cheek, and my hands in my pockets, a free man. The strongest pressure was put upon me to do so, I was earnestly advised, begged, entreated to do so by people whose sole interest was my welfare, and the welfare of my house. But I refused. I did not choose to do so. I have never regretted my decision for a single moment, even in the most bitter periods of my imprisonment. Such a course of action would have been beneath me. Sins of the flesh are nothing. They are maladies for physicians to cure, if they should be cured. Sins of the soul alone are shameful. To have secured my acquittal by such means would have been a lifelong torture to me. But do you really think you were worthy of the love I was showing you then, or that for a single moment I thought you were?

The full effect of this passage appears in the light of the conversation which Wilde had had with Frank Harris, when he was out on bail before the last trial, and which has been described in these pages.[1] But it does not follow that, if Wilde had incriminated his friend by relating the true facts of the Savoy Hotel visit from the witness box, he would have succeeded in exculpating himself at the same time. As Bernard Shaw pointed out in his preface to the English edition of Frank Harris's controversial book on Wilde, this may merely mean that the police 'constructed' their story confusedly, not that the charges were untrue or the verdict wrong.[2] Nevertheless, there is just the possibility, which cannot be entirely overlooked, that if Wilde at either trial had told the whole story of Lord Alfred Douglas at the Savoy, he would with the aid of Clarke's powerful advocacy, have been acquitted.

In *De Profundis*, Wilde showed how fully he realized that, but for his precipitate action with Queensberry, he would probably not have been writing, as he was, from Reading Gaol.

1. See above, p. 225. The Crown witnesses referred to were most probably the masseur Migge, the chambermaid Cotter, and the housekeeper Perkins, who were all employed at the Savoy Hotel when Wilde stayed there with Douglas in March 1893.
2. Frank Harris, *Oscar Wilde* (1938), p. xxvii.

Oscar Wilde

Remember how and why I am here at this very moment. Do you think I am here on account of my relations with the witnesses on my trial? My relations, real or supposed, with people of that kind were matters of no interest to either the Government or Society. They knew nothing of them and cared less. I am here for having tried to put your father into prison. My attempt failed, of course. My own Counsel threw up their briefs. Your father completely turned the tables on me, and had *me* in prison, has me there still. That is why there is contempt felt for me. That is why people despise me. That is why I have to serve out every day, every hour, every minute of my dreadful imprisonment. That is why my petitions have been refused.[1]

Of the folly of his conduct Wilde had no illusions. 'I became the spendthrift of my genius,' he wrote, 'and to waste an eternal youth gave me a curious joy. Tired of being on the heights, I deliberately went to the depths in search of a new sensation. What the paradox was to be in the sphere of thought, perversity became to me in the sphere of passion.' Yet, however he may have censured himself in his prison cell for his indulgence in 'perverse pleasures', he returned to these pleasures very soon after his release. He resumed, too, his relations with Lord Alfred Douglas; and he forgot everything he had formerly written about his friend in the bitterness of his heart. 'I feel that my only hope of again doing beautiful work in art is being with you,' he told him a few months after he left Reading. 'Everyone is furious with me for going back to you, but they don't understand us. I feel that it is only with you that I can do anything at all. Do remake my ruined life for me, and then our friendship and love will have a different meaning to the world.'

Not even during his imprisonment did the fact that he had been on intimate terms with the kind of individual, who had testified against him at the Old Bailey, fill Wilde with any conscious sense

1. Wilde also reminded Douglas that he [Douglas] had laughed when, in the early days of their association, Wilde told him how Taylor ('that unfortunate young man who ultimately stood beside me in the dock') had warned Wilde more than once that Douglas would prove 'far more fatal' in bringing Wilde to 'utter destruction' than any of the 'common lads' whom he was foolish enough to know.

of shame. What disturbed him was the false role which he was consequently forced to play in the ensuing tragedy.

People thought it dreadful of me to have entertained at dinner the evil things of life, and to have found pleasure in their company. But they, from the point of view through which I, as an artist in life, approach them, were delightfully suggestive and stimulating. It was like feasting with panthers; the danger was half the excitement. I used to feel as a snake-charmer must feel when he lures the cobra to stir from the painted cloth or reed basket that holds it and makes it spread its hood at his bidding and sway to and fro in the air as a plant sways restfully in a stream. They were to me the brightest of gilded snakes. Their poison was part of their perfection. I did not know that when they were to strike at me it was to be at another's piping and at another's pay. I don't feel at all ashamed at having known them, they were intensely interesting; what I do feel ashamed of is the horrible Philistine atmosphere into which you brought me. My business as an artist was with Ariel, you set me to wrestle with Caliban. Instead of making beautiful coloured musical things such as *Salomé* and the *Florentine Tragedy* and *La Sainte Courtisane*, I forced myself to send long lawyer's letters to your father and was constrained to appeal to the very things against which I had always protested. Clibborn and Atkins were wonderful in their infamous war against life. To entertain them was an astounding adventure; Dumas père, Cellini, Goya, Edgar Allan Poe, or Baudelaire would have done just the same. What is loathsome to me is the memory of interminable visits paid by me to the solicitor Humphreys, in your company, when in the ghastly glare of a bleak room you and I would sit with serious faces telling serious lies to a bald man till I really groaned and yawned with *ennui*. *There* is where I found myself after two years' friendship with you, right in the centre of Philistia, away from everything that was beautiful or brilliant or wonderful or daring. I had come forward on your behalf as the champion of respectability in conduct, of puritanism in life, and of morality in art.

The truth is that Oscar Wilde was amoral rather than immoral; and, in looking back upon the scandal of the trials in which he was involved, the English public has an uneasy conscience about him. For a good deal of the mud thrown at the time has stuck. It is still thought in some quarters that Wilde was a debaucher of youth. In passing sentence upon him Mr Justice Wills described

305

Wilde as having been 'the centre of a circle of extensive corruption of the most hideous kind among young men'. Strictly speaking, this statement is not true; Wilde was never proved to have corrupted any youthful innocence. In respect of the charges relating to the only two young men of decent background with whom he was accused of immoral practices – Mavor and Shelley – he was acquitted. On the other hand, that he was guilty of the crimes of which he was accused is now beyond dispute. But for the sake of English justice it is regrettable that Wilde's guilt was not brought home to him, and to the world at large, beyond all reasonable doubt – in other words, with that measure of certainty in proof which the English law demands in criminal trials.

It is given to few to be the central figure in three Old Bailey trials before three different judges at three consecutive sessions. Such was the lot of Oscar Wilde. He realized the consequences which they entailed for him, and that, even when his offence had been purged, he would still have to reckon with the enmity of society.

All trials are trials for one's life, just as all sentences are sentences of death [he wrote in the conclusion of *De Profundis*], and three times have I been tried. The first time I left the box to be arrested, the second time to be led back to the house of detention, the third time to pass into a prison for two years. Society, as we have constituted it, will have no place for me, has none to offer; but Nature, whose sweet rains fall on just and unjust alike, will have clefts in the rocks where I may hide, and secret valleys in whose silence I may weep undisturbed. She will hang the night with stars so that I may walk abroad in the darkness without stumbling, and send the wind over my footprints so that none may track me to my hurt: she will cleanse me in great waters, and with bitter herbs make me whole.

5

Although he petitioned the Home Secretary to be released a little before the due date, so as to avoid unwelcome attentions by the press, this was not permitted, and Wilde was obliged to serve out the whole of his two-year sentence to the day. He was actually released from Pentonville early in the morning of 19 May 1897, having been brought up from Reading the previous evening, since the regulations in those days required that a prisoner should be released from the same prison to which he had been originally admitted. Fortunately everything went off well. His friend More Adey and Stewart Headlam, the kindly clergymen who had gone bail for him, arrived at Pentonville in a brougham with the blinds drawn shortly after 6.0 a.m. and they were able to drive away unobserved to Headlam's house in Bloomsbury, where Wilde was able to change and have breakfast. 'He was given the first cup of coffee after two years,' his host noted. 'How grateful he was!'

After breakfast, the Leversons and other friends called, and Wilde stayed talking so long that he missed the day boat train to Newhaven, on which it had been arranged for him to travel with Adey, so as to join Robert Ross and Reggie Turner who had gone on ahead to Dieppe. Some delay was also caused by Wilde sending a letter by hand to one of the Jesuit priests at the Roman Catholic Church in Farm Street requesting to be allowed to go into retreat with them for six months, and waiting for the disappointing reply that he could not be accepted on the impulse of the moment but must first consider the matter for a least a year.

Leaving Headlam's house by cab the same afternoon, Wilde and Adey drove off to catch the night boat from Newhaven. They stopped for a few minutes at Hatchard's bookshop in Piccadilly, where Wilde had once been a favoured customer. Here someone recognized him and they left hurriedly. Taking care to avoid Victoria Station for fear of further recognition, they drove on to West Croydon, where they boarded the train for Newhaven. In the early hours of the following morning they reached Dieppe, where Ross and Turner were waiting on the quayside to welcome the exile. As he came down the gangway with an odd elephantine gait which Ross had never remarked in anyone else, Wilde was seen to be holding a large sealed envelope. 'This, my dear Robbie, is the great manuscript about which you know,' Wilde exclaimed, as he handed over the text of *De Profundis* to be dealt with according to his instructions.

Dieppe was too crowded with English visitors for Wilde to

stay in for long. After looking round the neighbourhood, he eventually settled under the name 'Sebastian Melmoth' at the nearby seaside village of Berneval, where he was able to complete the first draft of *The Ballad of Reading Gaol* in the course of the summer. Early in September, while the manuscript was being typed, Wilde came to a fateful and unfortunate decision. He had begun to feel very lonely at Berneval, and was out of patience with his wife who for one reason or another had put off seeing him. Meanwhile he was in touch with Alfred Douglas, whom he had forgiven and whom he now planned to meet secretly at Rouen. By a coincidence – for there is no evidence that Constance knew anything of his intention – she wrote to him that she would see him now that she had got the children 'out of the way'. But it was too late. Also, Wilde was so irritated by what he considered his wife's extraordinary want of tact that he disregarded the advice given him by Ross and other friends and refused to go to her, saying that he was 'utterly lonely, treated like a pariah and worn out with her perpetual procrastination' and was therefore going to live with the only person ready to give him companionship.

After a tearful but happy reunion between Oscar and Bosie at Rouen, where they walked about hand in hand all day, they arranged that Wilde should return to Berneval, pack his bags and rejoin Douglas, going off to Naples together, where they planned to take a villa. They did in fact share a villa for about two months at Posilipo, outside Naples, where Wilde was able to revise *The Ballad* and Douglas also wrote some poetry. But the experiment of living together was soon brought to an abrupt conclusion by Lady Queensberry threatening to cut off her son's allowance if he continued to live with Wilde; at the same time Wilde's solicitors intimated that his small income would be stopped for the same reason. This caused Wilde to turn against his friend for the second time, accusing him of having offered to provide him with a home, for which Wilde found he was expected to put up the money, and then deserting him when he saw that Wilde could no longer do so. 'It is, of course, the most bitter experience of a bitter life,' Wilde told Ross.

Although they were to meet from time to time in Paris during the next three years, the old spell was finally broken and they never resumed their former intimacy. At the end, Douglas arrived too late, in reponse to a telegram from Ross summoning him to Wilde's deathbed in Paris, to see his old friend alive. But he was in time to take the part of chief mourner at his grave and to pay for the funeral expenses.

The Ballad of Reading Gaol, for which Wilde had some difficulty in finding a publisher, appeared in February 1898 under the imprint of Leonard Smithers, an original and eccentric Yorkshireman, who started his career as a solicitor in Sheffield and had later migrated to London, where he set up as a publisher in the Royal Arcade, off Bond Street, combining the publication of finely produced books by poets and artists with a surreptitious business in retailing pornography.[1] About 7,000 copies of *The Ballad* were sold during Wilde's lifetime, the later editions bearing Wilde's name on the title page in addition to his prison number 'C.C.3.', under which it first came out. A French prose translation by Henri Davray was published side-by-side with the original text by *Mercure de France* in Paris. Smithers also brought out editions of *The Importance of Being Earnest* and *An Ideal Husband*, for the publication of which Wilde had had no time to arrange before his arrest and trials. But apart from *The Ballad*, two letters on prison conditions to the *Daily Chronicle*, and a brief scenario, which he sold to several people including Frank Harris who based his play *Mr and Mrs Daventry* on it, Wilde wrote nothing after he came out of Reading Gaol. 'Something is killed in me,' he told Ross. 'I feel no desire to write – I am unconscious of power. Of course my first year in prison destroyed me body and soul. It could not be otherwise.'

Constance Wilde lived just long enough to see the publication of *The Ballad*, of which her husband sent her a copy of the first edition and which, she told him through a mutual friend, she

1. Further details about Leonard Charles Smithers (1862–1909) will be found in Wilde's letters edited by Hart-Davis; Vincent O'Sullivan, *Aspects of Wilde* (1936); *Letters from Aubrey Beardsley to Leonard Smithers*, edited by R. A. Walker (1937); and the autobiography of Smithers's son, *The Early Life and Vicissitudes of Jack Smithers* (1939).

found 'exquisite'. Shortly afterwards she entered a nursing home in Genoa, where she died a few days later from the effects of an operation to correct a spinal injury. Wilde was overwhelmed by the unexpected news. 'It is awful,' he told a friend who came to comfort him. 'I don't know what to do. If we had only met once and kissed each other. It is too late. How awful life is.' She was buried in the Protestant cemetery in Genoa, where Wilde went to visit her grave about a year later. 'It was very tragic seeing her name carved on a tomb,' Wilde noted at the time, 'her surname – my name not mentioned of course – just "Constance Mary, daughter of Horatio Lloyd, q.c." and a verse from *Revelations*. I bought some flowers. I was deeply affected, with a sense, also, of the uselessness of all regrets. Nothing could have been otherwise, and Life is a very terrible thing.'[1]

Except for short visits to the south of France, where he stayed with Frank Harris, and to Switzerland and Italy, where he was the guest and travelling companion of a young man of independent means named Harold Mellor (described by Wilde as having been sent away from Harrow at the age of fourteen 'for being loved by the captain of the cricket eleven'), Wilde spent his remaining days after parting company with Douglas in or near Paris. But wherever he was he appears to have been dominated by an overpowering homosexual passion, of which his sojourn at Reading had not effected the slightest cure. 'After he came out of prison he had literally no other interest in life at all,' Douglas has said, perhaps a little unkindly in the circumstances. 'All he thought about and dreamed about was the gratification of his vice and getting money by any means, and at whatever cost of honour and decency and honesty, to gratify it.'

On one occasion only during this last phase of his life does Wilde appear to have deviated from what had become his habitual course of sexual conduct. This was when he was living at Berneval in the summer of 1897. One day he went into Dieppe where he met the poet Ernest Dowson in a café. According to

1. Constance Wilde died on 7 April 1898, aged forty. A copy of her death certificate from the British consular records in Genoa is reproduced in Sherard's *Life* p. 375.

The Aftermath

W. B. Yeats, who claimed to have had the story from Dowson himself, Dowson kindly offered to conduct Wilde to a local brothel for the purpose of acquiring 'a more wholesome taste'. They managed to scrape up enough cash between them to defray the cost of the expedition, and thereupon set off together for the brothel, to which apparently Dowson was no stranger. Meanwhile the news of the incident quickly became known in the neighbourhood and a small crowd began to collect round the entrance to the brothel where Dowson was waiting. Presently Wilde emerged from the building, evidently disappointed by his experiences within. 'The first these ten years,' he said to Dowson in a low voice, 'and it will be the last. It was like cold mutton!' And then, raising his voice so that the crowd could hear, he added: 'But tell it in England, for it will entirely restore my character!'[1]

Lord Alfred Douglas assured me as 'an absolute fact' that it was Robert Ross who 'dragged' Wilde back to homosexual practices when they were staying together at Berneval. 'Oscar told me this himself one night after dinner in Paris when he had had a great many drinks. I did not mention it in my *Autobiography* because I thought everyone would think I was inventing it to get even with Ross.[2] Also the idea was so revolting that I preferred not to say anything about it.' As for Wilde's last years in Paris, Douglas went on, 'the manner of his life there was notorious and

1. W. B. Yeats, *Autobiographies* (1926), p. 404.
2. Douglas considered that he had been robbed of the verdict to which he was entitled when he was prosecuted by Ross at the Old Bailey in November 1914 on a charge of criminal libel – he had described Ross as a sodomite and habitual associate of male prostitutes – and the jury disagreed. The case was then dropped. In the light of the evidence given at this trial it must be admitted that Ross, who at this time occupied the post of Assessor of Picture Valuations to the Inland Revenue, was extremely fortunate in not being prosecuted himself on similar charges to Wilde. Shortly afterwards he was the recipient of a substantial sum of money and a public testimonial which was drawn up by Edmund Gosse and included the name of the Prime Minister, Mr Asquith. In intimating that he desired to apply the money to some charitable object, Ross showed a certain unconscious sense of humour, since the bequest was accepted by the University of London for the purpose of founding *a scholarship for boys* to be known as 'The Robert Ross Scholarship'.

he was quite open about it. He was hand in glove with all the little boys on the Boulevard. He never attempted to conceal it. Oscar believed, as many other eminent people do, that he had a perfect right to indulge his own tastes. He would not thank you for trying to make people believe it was otherwise. In fact, nothing irritated him more than to meet – as he occasionally did – admirers who refused to believe that he was addicted to the vices for which he was condemned. This used to infuriate him.'[1]

During his last years, Wilde discussed the subject with his friend Frank Harris, whose passions were strongly heterosexual (Ross used to call him a 'mulierast'), and Harris subsequently reproduced, in one of the most controversial chapters of his book on Wilde, what he alleged to have been Wilde's conversation with him on this occasion.[2] Whether the words which Harris puts into Wilde's mouth were actually uttered by him is not of great consequence. What is beyond doubt is that they do reflect Wilde's views on this topic, to which he clung with an obstinate persistence.

'What you call vice, Frank, is not vice,' said Wilde, according to Harris. 'It is as good to me as it was to Caesar, Alexander, Michelangelo, and Shakespeare. It was first of all made sin by monasticism, and it has been made a crime in recent times by the Goths – the Germans and English – who have done little or nothing since to refine or exalt the ideals of humanity. A brutal race; they over-eat and over-drink and condemn the lusts of the flesh, while revelling in all the vilest sins of the spirit. If they would read the twenty-third chapter of St Matthew and apply it to themselves, they would learn more than by condemning a pleasure they don't understand. Why, even Bentham refused to put what you call a "vice" in his penal code, and you yourself admitted that it should not be punished as a crime, for it carries no temptation with it. It may be a malady, but, if so, it appears

1. When he said this, Douglas had become a convert to the Roman Catholic faith and forsworn his own former homosexual practices. Otherwise this statement might be regarded as a case of the pot calling the kettle black.
2. Chapter xxiv.

only to attack the highest natures. It is disgraceful to punish it. The wit of man can find no argument which justifies its punishment.'

Harris's rejoinder that homosexual practices had been 'condemned by a hundred generations of the most civilized races of mankind' apparently left Wilde unimpressed. 'Mere prejudice of the unlettered, Frank,' was his alleged reply. At all events, Wilde seems to have stuck to his point. 'Of course everything can be argued,' Harris makes him say in conclusion, 'but I hold to my conviction – the best minds even now don't condemn us, and the world is becoming more tolerant.' He made a simliar admission to the criminologist, George Ives, 'I have no doubt we shall win,' he told him at this time, 'but the road is long, and red with monstrous martyrdoms. Nothing but the repeal of the Criminal Law Amendment Act would do any good. That is the essential. It is not so much public opinion as public officials that need educating.'

After trying various small hotels and pensions in Paris and its environs, Wilde finally settled in the Hotel d'Alsace in the Rue des Beaux Arts on the left bank. Although it was a small place of the 'bed and breakfast' variety, the Hotel d'Alsace was perfectly clean and respectable, and the proprietor, M. Jean Dupoirier, whom Ross rightly described as a most charitable and humane man, let him run up a large bill, of which nearly £100 was outstanding at the time of Wilde's death. Dupoirier also paid for necessities and even little luxuries ordered by the doctors during Wilde's last illness and never as much as mentioned to Ross what he was owed until after the funeral, while all the other creditors came flocking round as soon as they heard that the case was hopeless. Nor was there any truth in the press report that Wilde died in a sort of neglected or sordid way. Throughout his illness, which began with an abscess following an operation on the ear which had been injured by his fall in prison, he wanted for nothing. He had a special nurse, food was sent in from a nearby restaurant, he was attended by the British Embassy doctor, and a brain specialist was called in when meningitis declared itself. As long as the doctors allowed it, he had as much champagne as he could drink, a feature of his sickroom diet which no doubt provoked the celebrated quip to Ross 'I am dying beyond my means!' When earlier Ross had remonstrated with him, telling him to pull himself together and lay off the bottle, Wilde merely laughed and said that he could never outlive the century, as the English people 'would not stand it' and that he was already responsible for the failure of the Paris Exhibition, as English people on seeing him there had gone away. He was received into the Catholic Church during his last hours, and died on 30 November 1900.[1]

Because Wilde had registered in the hotel under an assumed name, which was contrary to French law, his body was nearly taken to the Morgue, a 'ghastly contingency' which it required all Ross's tact with the local municipal authorities to prevent, particularly as the latter could not understand the absence of relatives and other legal representatives. Wilde's remains were first interred in Bagneaux cemetery, in a temporary grave on which rested a pathetic tribute from Dupoirier of a wreath of artificial flowers inscribed '*À mon locataire*'. Some years later, in 1909, the remains were exhumed and transferred to their present resting place in Père Lachaise cemetery beneath Jacob Epstein's noble monument, on which Ross caused the following lines to be carved from *The Ballad of Reading Gaol*.

> And alien tears will fill for him
> Pity's long broken urn,
> For his mourners will be outcast men
> And outcasts always mourn.

'Though everyone who knew him well enough to appreciate his wonderful power and the sumptuous endowment of his intellect will regret his death,' wrote Ross at the time to a mutual friend, Miss Adela Schuster, 'apart from personal affection, the terrible commonplace "It was for the best" is really true in his case. Two things were absolutely necessary for him, contact with comely things, as Pater says, and social position. Comely things meant

1. For the details of Wilde's final illness and death, see Hart-Davis, p. 845ff.

314

for him a certain standard of living, and this since his release he was unable to have except for a few weeks at a time or perhaps months. Social position, he realized after five months, he could not have. . . . He chose, therefore, a Bohemian existence entirely out of note with his genius and temperament. There was no use arguing or exhorting him. The temporary deprivation of his annuity produced no result. You cannot ask a man who started on the top rung of the ladder to suddenly start again from the lowest rung of all. Among his many fine qualities he showed in his later years was that he never blamed anyone but himself for his own disasters. He never bore any ill will to anybody and in a characteristic way was really surprised that anyone should bear any resentment against him. For example, he really did not understand how cruel he was to his wife, but I never expect anyone to believe that.

'I was not surprised by the silence of the press. Journalists could hardly say very much, and it was better to be silent than point a moral. Later on I think everyone will recognize his achievements, his plays and essays will endure. Of course, you may think with others that his personality and conversation were far more wonderful than anything he wrote, or that his written works give only a pale reflexion of his power. Perhaps that is so, and of course it will be impossible to reproduce what is gone for ever. . . .'[1]

Wilde's posthumous rehabilitation began, not in England, as he himself thought it would, but on the Continent, particularly in Germany, where *Salomé* was set to music as an opera by Richard Strauss. Indeed the royalties from the German editions of his books enabled Ross, within six years of his death, to pay off all his creditors twenty shillings in the pound plus four per cent interest, and have his bankruptcy annulled. Meanwhile, Ross's edition of *De Profundis* had appeared, first in Germany and then in England, to be followed three years later by the first collected edition of Wilde's works, which fully justified Ross's courage in

---

1. Margery Ross, *Robert Ross*, pp. 62–9. The original MS. of this letter, dated 23 December 1900, giving intimate details of Wilde's last days, is in my collection.

bringing them out, although his action was attacked by a few fanatics such as Canon H. C. Beeching, who, as we have seen, preached a sermon in Westminster Abbey denouncing *De Profundis* as 'a doctrine of devils'. The publication of *De Profundis* and its reception marked the turning-point in the public attitude towards Wilde, when the critics on the whole showed themselves ready to estimate the writer, whether favourably or unfavourably, without emphasizing their prejudice against his later career. 'Society', wrote J. A. Spender in his review, 'has vindicated itself towards this sinner, and can afford to be Christian to his memory.'[1]

'Its reception seems to me remarkable, unprophesiable five or six years ago,' Laurence Housman wrote to Ross on the first appearance of *De Profundis* in 1905. 'Perhaps before we die a tablet will be put up in Tite Street on the house where he used to live. . . .'[2] Housman, though not Ross, was to live to see these words come true almost exactly half a century later, when a plaque was erected by the London County Council and unveiled by Sir Compton Mackenzie on the centenary of Wilde's birth, 16 October 1954. Housman, who had already recaptured something of the brilliance of Wilde's table talk in his *L'Écho de Paris*, was able to send an appropriate message for the occasion: 'His unhappy fate has done the world a signal service in defeating the blind obscurantists; he has made people think. Far more people of intelligence think differently today because of him. And when he wrote his *Ballad of Reading Gaol*, he not only gave the world a beautiful poem, but a much needed lesson in good will, pity, pardon and understanding for the down-and-out.'

1. *Westminster Gazette*, 23 February 1905.
2. Margery Ross, *Robert Ross*, p. 100.

LEADING DATES

Leading Dates

Oct. 1893–March 1894	Wilde occupied rooms at 10 and 11 St James's Place. Alleged offences with Sidney Mavor and Charles Parker.
1 April 1894	Queensberry threatened to disown his son, Lord Alfred Douglas, unless he ceased his association with Wilde.
May	Wilde consulted the solicitor, Mr C. O. Humphreys, but on consideration decided to take no action against Queensberry.
June	Queensberry called on Wilde at his house in Tite Street with a prize-fighter and, after an insulting interview, was expelled.
December	Publication of *The Chameleon* containing 'Phrases and Philosophies for the Use of the Young' by Wilde.
14 February 1895	First performance of *The Importance of Being Earnest* at the St James's Theatre. Queensberry unsuccessfully attempted to gain admission to the theatre with the object of creating a scene.
18 February	Queensberry left libellous card for Wilde at Albemarle Club.
28 February	Wilde received Queensberry's card from hall-porter of Albemarle Club.
1 March	After consultation with his solicitor, Wilde obtained a warrant for Queensberry's arrest.
2 March	Queensberry arrested and charged at Great Marlborough Street Police Court with criminal libel.
9 March	Queensberry committed for trial.
18 March	Grand Jury returned a true bill against Queensberry.
30 March	Queensberry filed amended plea of justification.
3 April	Trial of *Reg.* v. *Queensberry* opened at Old Bailey before Henn Collins, J.
5 April	Withdrawal of prosecution and acquittal of Queensberry. Arrest of Wilde. Taken to Holloway Prison.
6 April	Wilde and Taylor charged jointly at Bow Street Police Court with offences under Criminal Law Amendment Act, 1885, sec. 11. Bail refused by magistrate, Sir John Bridge.
19 April	Wilde and Taylor committed for trial.
23 April	Grand Jury returned true bills against Wilde and Taylor.

Leading Dates

26 April	Trial of *Reg.* v. *Wilde and Taylor* opened at Old Bailey before Charles, J.
1 May	Disagreement of jury on principal counts of indictment.
7 May	Wilde released on bail in £5,000, pending re-trial.
21 May	Wilde and Taylor arraigned at Old Bailey before Wills, J., who ordered prisoners to be tried separately.
22 May	Taylor found guilty on all remaining counts except that charging him with procuring Wood for Wilde.
25 May	Wilde found guilty on all remaining counts except that relating to Edward Shelley. Wilde and Taylor sentenced to two years' imprisonment with hard labour.
26 August	Wilde adjudicated bankrupt.
12 November	Public examination of Wilde in bankruptcy.
21 November	Wilde transferred from Wandsworth to Reading Gaol.
March 1897	Wilde completed *De Profundis* in the form of a long letter to Lord Alfred Douglas. He entrusted the MS. to Robert Ross, who retained it in his possession.
19 May	Wilde released from prison.
14 February 1898	Publication of *The Ballad of Reading Gaol*.
7 April	Death of Mrs Constance Wilde.
30 November 1900	Wilde died in the Hôtel d'Alsace, rue des Beaux Arts, Paris. Robert Ross constituted Wilde's literary executor.
23 February 1905	*De Profundis* first published in English in a drastically expurgated edition, with a preface by Robert Ross.
28 May 1906	Wilde estate declared solvent through payment of final dividend giving creditors in bankruptcy 20s. in £ together with 4 per cent interest.
November 1909	MS. of *De Profundis* presented by Robert Ross to the British Museum on condition that it should remain sealed up until 1960.
April 1913	Portions of the suppressed part of *De Profundis* read out in Court during trial of *Douglas* v. *Ransome* before Darling, J., in King's Bench Division.
August–September	Fifteen copies of the suppressed part of *De Profundis* privately printed in New York on Robert Ross's instructions in order to protect U.S. copyright.

Leading Dates

20 March 1945	Death of Lord Alfred Douglas.
16 October 1954	Plaque erected by London County Council on outside wall of Wilde's house, 16 (now 33) Tite Street, Chelsea, and unveiled by Sir Compton Mackenzie.
1 January 1960	MS. of *De Profundis* opened to the public in the British Museum in accordance with terms of Robert Ross's bequest.

APPENDICES

Mr. JUSTICE WILLS

By "Spy"

APPENDIX A.

PLEA OF JUSTIFICATION FILED BY THE DEFENDANT IN *REGINA (WILDE)* v. *QUEENSBERRY*.[1]

Central Criminal Court. To wit: At the Sessions of Oyer and Terminer and General Gaol Delivery holden for the Central Criminal Court District at Justice Hall Old Bailey in the Suburbs of the City of London on the twenty-fifth day of March in the year of our Lord One thousand eight hundred and ninety-five comes into Court the said John Sholto Douglas Marquess of Queensberry in his own proper person and having heard the said Indictment read says he is not guilty of the premises in the said Indictment above specified and charged upon him and of this the said John Sholto Douglas Marquess of Queensberry puts himself upon the Country.

Second Plea.

And for a further plea in this behalf to the Second Count of the said Indictment the said John Sholto Douglas Marquess of Queensberry says that our Lady the Queen ought not further to prosecute the said Second Count of the said Indictment against him because he says that the said alleged libel according to the natural meaning of the words thereof is true in substance and in fact in that the said Oscar Fingal O'Flahertie Wills Wilde between the month of February in the year of our Lord One thousand eight hundred and ninety-two and the month of May in the same year at the Albemarle Hotel in the County of London did solicit and incite one Edward Shelley to commit sodomy and other acts of gross indecency with him the said Oscar Fingal O'Flahertie Wills Wilde and that the said Oscar Fingal O'Flahertie Wills Wilde did then indecently assault and commit acts of gross indecency and immorality with the said Edward Shelley.

And that the said Oscar Fingal O'Flahertie Wills Wilde in the month of October in the year of our Lord One thousand eight hundred and ninety-two at the said Albemarle Hotel did solicit and incite one Sidney Mavor to commit sodomy and other acts of gross indecency and immorality and did then and there commit the said

---

[1] From the original preserved in the records of the Central Criminal Court, London.

other acts of gross indecency and immorality with the said Sidney Mavor.

And that the said Oscar Fingal O'Flahertie Wills Wilde on the twentieth day of November in the year of our Lord One thousand eight hundred and ninety-two at a house situate at 29 Boulevard des Capucines in Paris in the Republic of France did solicit and incite one Frederick Atkins to commit sodomy and other acts of gross indecency and immorality with him the said Oscar Fingal O'Flahertie Wills Wilde and did then and there commit the said other acts of gross indecency and immorality with the said Frederick Atkins.

And that the said Oscar Fingal O'Flahertie Wills Wilde on the twenty-second day of November in the year of our Lord One thousand eight hundred and ninety-two at the said house in Paris did solicit and incite one Maurice Salis Schwabe to commit sodomy and other acts of gross indecency and immorality with the said Maurice Salis Schwabe.

And that the said Oscar Fingal O'Flahertie Wills Wilde at the said house situate in Paris between the twenty-fifth day of January in the year of our Lord One thousand eight hundred and ninety-three and the fifth day of February in the said year did solicit and incite certain boys to the Defendant unknown to commit sodomy and other acts of gross indecency and immorality with him the said Oscar Fingal O'Flahertie Wills Wilde and did then and there commit the said other acts of gross indecency and immorality with the said boys.

And that the said Oscar Fingal O'Flahertie Wills Wilde in the month of January in the year of our Lord One thousand eight hundred and ninety-three at the house situate at and being No. 16 Tite Street in the County of London did solicit and incite one Alfred Wood to commit sodomy and other acts of gross indecency and immorality with him the said Oscar Fingal O'Flahertie Wills Wilde and did then and there commit the said other acts of gross indecency and immorality with the said Alfred Woods.

And that the said Oscar Fingal O'Flahertie Wills Wilde about the seventh day of March in the year of our Lord One thousand eight hundred and ninety-three at the Savoy Hotel in the County of London did solicit and incite a certain boy to the Defendant unknown to commit sodomy and other acts of gross indecency and immorality with him the said Oscar Fingal O'Flahertie Wills Wilde and did then and there commit the said other acts of gross indecency and immorality with the said boy unknown.

And that the said Oscar Fingal O'Flahertie Wills Wilde on or about the twentieth day of March in the year of our Lord One thousand eight hundred and ninety-three at the said Savoy Hotel did solicit and incite another boy to the Defendant unknown to commit sodomy and other acts of gross indecency with the said Oscar Fingal O'Flahertie Wills Wilde and did there commit the said other acts of gross indecency with the said last mentioned boy.

And that the said Oscar Fingal O'Flahertie Wills Wilde in the said month of March in the year of our Lord One thousand eight hundred and ninety-three at the said Savoy Hotel and again in or about the month of April in the year of our Lord One thousand eight hundred and ninety-three at a house situate and being No. 7 Camera Square and again in or about the month of April in the year of our Lord One thousand eight hundred and ninety-three at a house situate at and being No. 50 Park Walk and again between the month of October in the year of our Lord One thousand eight hundred and ninety-three and the month of April in the year of our Lord One thousand eight hundred and ninety-four at a house situate and being No. 10 St. James Place all in the County of London did on each of the said occasions incite one Charles Parker to commit sodomy and other acts of gross indecency and immorality with him the said Oscar Fingal O'Flahertie Wills Wilde and did then and there commit the said other acts of gross indecency and immorality with the said Charles Parker.

And that the said Oscar Fingal O'Flahertie Wills Wilde between the month of October in the year of our Lord One thousand eight hundred and ninety-three and the month of April in the year of our Lord One thousand eight hundred and ninety-four at the said house No. 10 St. James Place did solicit and incite one Ernest Scarfe to commit sodomy and other acts of gross indecency and immorality with him the said Oscar Fingal O'Flahertie Wills Wilde and did then and there commit the said other acts of gross indecency and immorality with the said Ernest Scarfe.

And that the said Oscar Fingal O'Flahertie Wills Wilde in the said month of March in the year of our Lord One thousand eight hundred and ninety-three at the said Savoy Hotel did take indecent liberties with one Herbert Tankard.

And that the said Oscar Fingal O'Flahertie Wills Wilde on several occasions in the month of June in the year of our Lord One thousand eight hundred and ninety-three in the City of Oxford and also upon several occasions in the months of June July and August in the year of our Lord One thousand eight hundred and ninety-three at a house called "The Cottage" at Goring in the

325

County of Oxford did solicit and incite one Walter Grainger to commit sodomy and other acts of gross indecency and immorality with him the said Oscar Fingal O'Flahertie Wills Wilde and did then and there commit the said other acts of gross indecency and immorality with the said Walter Grainger.

And that the said Oscar Fingal O'Flahertie Wills Wilde upon several occasions in the months of August and September in the year of our Lord One thousand eight hundred and ninety-four at Worthing in the County of Sussex and on or about the twenty-seventh day of September in the said year at the Albion Hotel Brighton in the same County did solicit and incite one Alfonso Harold Conway to commit sodomy and other acts of gross indecency and immorality with him the said Oscar Fingal O'Flahertie Wills Wilde.

And that the said Oscar Fingal O'Flahertie Wills Wilde did in fact at the said times and places commit the said other acts of gross indecency with the said Alfonso Harold Conway.

And that the said Oscar Fingal O'Flahertie Wills Wilde in the month of July in the year of our Lord One thousand eight hundred and ninety did write and publish and cause and procure to be printed and published with his name upon the title page thereof a certain immoral and obscene work in the form of a narrative entitled "The Picture of Dorian Gray" which said work was designed and intended by the said Oscar Fingal O'Flahertie Wills Wilde and was understood by the readers thereof to describe the relations intimacies and passions of certain persons of sodomitical and unnatural habits tastes and practices.

And that in the month of December in the year of our Lord One thousand eight hundred and ninety-four was published a certain other immoral and obscene work in the form of a magazine entitled "The Chameleon" which said work contained divers obscene matters and things relating to the practices and passions of persons of sodomitical and unnatural habits and tastes and that the said Oscar Fingal O'Flahertie Wills Wilde published his name on the contents sheet of the said magazine as its first and principal contributor and published in the said magazine certain immoral maxims as an introduction to the same under the title of "Phrases and Philosophies for the Use of the Young."

And the said John Sholto Douglas Marquess of Queensberry further says that at the time of the publishing of the said alleged libel in the second count charged and stated it was for the public benefit that the matter contained therein should be published because before and at the time of the publishing of the said alleged libel the said Oscar Fingal O'Flahertie Wills Wilde was a man of letters and a dramatist of prominence and notoriety and a person who exercised considerable influence over young men, that the said Oscar Fingal O'Flahertie Wills Wilde claimed to be a fit and proper person to give advice and instruction to the young and had published the said maxims hereinbefore mentioned in the said magazine entitled "The Chameleon" for circulation amongst students of the University of Oxford, and that the said works entitled "The Chameleon" and "The Picture of Dorian Gray" were calculated to subvert morality and to encourage unnatural vice, and that the said Oscar Fingal O'Flahertie Wills Wilde had corrupted and debauched the morals of the said Charles Parker, Alfonso Harold Conway, Walter Grainger, Sidney Mavor, Frederick Atkins, Ernest Scarfe and Edward Shelley as aforesaid, and that the said Oscar Fingal O'Flahertie Wills Wilde had committed the offences aforementioned and the said sodomitical practices for a long time with impunity and without detection wherefore it was for the public benefit and interest that the matter contained in the said alleged libel should be published and that the true character and habits of the said Oscar Fingal O'Flahertie Wills Wilde should be known that the said Oscar Fingal O'Flahertie Wills Wilde might be prevented from further committing such offences and further debauching the liege subjects of our said Lady the Queen and that such liege subjects being forewarned might avoid the corrupting influence of the said Oscar Fingal O'Flahertie Wills Wilde.

And this the said John Sholto Douglas Marquess of Queensberry is ready to verify wherefor he prays Judgment and that by the Court he may be discharged and dismissed from the said premises in the said indictment above specified.

(Signed) CHARLES F. GILL.

Dated and filed this thirtieth day of March, 1895, by Charles Russell, solicitor to the said Marquess of Queensberry.

APPENDIX B

LORD ALFRED DOUGLAS AND SIR EDWARD CLARKE

In later life Lord Alfred Douglas severely impugned Sir Edward Clarke's conduct of all three cases in which he appeared for Wilde. However, it is worthy of record that at the time of the trials themselves Douglas professed himself more than satisfied with Clarke's forensic endeavours on his client's behalf.

It will be remembered that Douglas was present throughout the proceedings taken by Wilde at the Old Bailey against his father, but he was subsequently prevailed upon by Wilde's solicitors to leave the country on the eve of the next trial. In France, where he stayed first at Calais and later at Rouen, he received the newspaper reports of the proceedings. He again offered to give evidence for Wilde and he telegraphed in this sense to Clarke, only to receive a well-merited rebuke from the solicitors, who informed him that his telegram was most improper and adjured him not to attempt any further interference "which can only have the effect of rendering Sir Edward's task still harder than it is already."

After the conclusion of the last trial Douglas sent Clarke a further communication, this time in the form of a letter, in which he expressed his warm appreciation of what Clarke had done. In view of the blame which Douglas subsequently attached to Clarke, this letter is of considerable interest.[1]

> "Hotel De La Poste,
> Rouen.
> Sunday, 26th May, 1895.
>
> Dear Sir Edward,
>   You will forgive me I am sure for writing to you now to thank you from the bottom of my heart for your noble generous and superb efforts on behalf of my friend.
>   It seems almost an impertinence from one so miserable as myself, so broken in heart [and] in spirit, so defamed and ruined to offer you my poor gratitude, but believe me I shall

---

[1] I am indebted to Sir Edward Clarke's grandson, Mr. Edward Clarke, for enabling me to reproduce the text of his letter and the two others quoted in this appendix.

never cease to think of you but with the profoundest gratitude and admiration. That you were unable to get a verdict seems to me, a layman, a piece of monstrous injustice, and the sentence was worse than I would have thought possible after the first disagreement.

Forgive this intrusion from one who is lying in the lowest hell of misery, and believe me to be

Yours ever gratefully and sincerely,

ALFRED DOUGLAS."

In his book, *Oscar Wilde and Myself,* which was published in 1914, Lord Alfred Douglas continued to write favourably of Clarke, pointing out that far from throwing up the sponge after the collapse of the Queensberry prosecution, he had defended Wilde in the two subsequent trials without fee.[2]

During the following years Douglas came to adopt and to lose no opportunity in expounding a very different view. In a long letter which he wrote to Frank Harris in 1925, and which was designed to form part of a new preface to Harris's life of Wilde, Douglas attributed the collapse of the Queensberry prosecution to Clarke's having abandoned his declared intention to conduct the case on certain pre-arranged lines.[3]

According to Douglas, during the consultation which took place in Clarke's chambers when Queensberry's amended plea of justification was discussed, he told Clarke that if he (Clarke) did not put him in the box they might as well throw up the case at once.

"Make your mind at rest, Lord Alfred," said Clarke, according to Douglas's version, "I agree with everything you say. My idea of the way to conduct this case is to launch out at the outset with a deadly attack on Lord Queensberry for his conduct to his family, of which we have ample proof in his letters to you and to your grandfather, Mr. Alfred Montgomery, supplemented by your own evidence."

---

[2] *Op. cit.,* pp. 107-109.

[3] See Frank Harris and Lord Alfred Douglas, *New Preface to "The Life and Confessions of Oscar Wilde,"* (1925). Harris and Douglas disagreed before the publication of the new edition of Harris's book with the result that Douglas published the Preface separately with his comments.

The reason for their disagreement is noteworthy. "About the Preface," wrote Harris to Douglas on 30th July, 1925, "months ago I sent it to London to be printed. My printers kept it some time and then returned it to me with the statement that every printer in London thought your attack on Sir Edward Clarke too libellous to print. I couldn't believe it, and tried my luck everywhere, then I sent it to a most distinguished lawyer . . . he implores me not to attack Clarke, says the reply would be crushing, even if he didn't prosecute us for libel. If Clarke did, he adds, you haven't the ghost of a chance of a verdict in your favour." A. J. Tobin and Elmer Gertz, *Frank Harris* (Chicago, 1931), at pp. 290-291.

Appendix B

"Yes," said Douglas, "but will you promise faithfully to put me in the box?"

"I promise you I will. You shall go into the box immediately after my opening speech."

Douglas repeated and amplified this assertion in his *Autobiography*, first published in 1929.[4] By this time Douglas had become convinced that, if he had testified on Wilde's behalf, he would have won the case for him; and he now blamed Clarke for his failure to call him. The real reason why Clarke did not put Douglas in the box has already been given in the Introduction to this book.[5] It is confirmed by Clarke's own words.

On the appearance of Douglas's autobiography the late R. H. Sherard wrote the following letter to Clarke:—

"Calvi, Corsica,
9th September, 1929.

The Right Hon. Sir Edward Clarke, P.C., K.C.,
Peterhouse, Staines.

Dear Sir,

May I first of all apologize for venturing to trouble you? It is only my recollection of the extreme courtesy with which you met a request of mine nearly twenty years ago that encourages me to write to you.

I am obliged in self-defence to answer certain aspersions made upon me in his Autobiography by Lord Alfred Douglas. In this book, which I trust you have not read, there is a very foolish comment on the way in which you conducted Oscar Wilde's case against Lord Queensberry for criminal libel at the Old Bailey in April, 1895. Douglas declared that you had agreed to put him in the witness-box immediately after your opening speech on the prosecutor's behalf. He was to give evidence to show the character of his father, the Marquis, and a full account of Lord Queensberry's alleged brutalities to his family, &c. He adds that you promised to do so, and that you did not keep this promise. He says that if he had been called and had been allowed to destroy his father's character, Wilde would have certainly won his case.

May I be allowed to point out to my readers the utter absurdity of this statement, and shall I not be right in saying that the judge would not have allowed such evidence to be

---

[4] *Op. cit.*, p. 90, *et seq.*
[5] See above, p. 46.

330

given as being entirely irrelevant to the point at issue?
Douglas's statements might be treated with contempt were
it not for the support that is being given to them by a certain
Frank Harris, who joins in this attack on your conduct of
the case, in his widely circulated book.
I have the honour to remain, with profound respect,
Your obliged, obedient servant,
ROBERT H. SHERARD."

To this letter Sir Edward Clarke replied as follows:—

"Peterhouse, Staines,
16th September, 1929.
Dear Sir,
I have not seen the Autobiography of Lord Alfred
Douglas, and certainly shall not trouble to read it. But I am
glad of the opportunity of contradicting the statements about
me which you quote.
It is, you say, alleged that I agreed with Oscar Wilde that
he should 'give evidence to show the character of his (Lord
Alfred's) father, the Marquess, and a full account of Lord
Queensberry's alleged brutalities to his family, &c.' That I
'promised to do this and did not keep the promise.' It is
added that 'if he (Lord Alfred) had been called and had been
allowed to destroy his father's character Wilde would certainly have won his case.' There is not a fragment of truth
in any of these statements. I made no such agreement or
promise. The question of Lord Queensberry's character was
quite irrelevant to the case, and was never mentioned in my
instructions or in consultation, and if an attempt had been
made to give such evidence the judge would of course have
peremptorily stopped it. You are at liberty to make any use
you please of this letter.
Yours faithfully,
EDWARD CLARKE."

A further charge brought against Clarke by Douglas in his book
is that the great counsel "put the lid on" his performance at the
Queensberry trial by failing to cross-examine the Crown witnesses
at Bow Street Police Court, with the result that Wilde and Taylor
were committed for trial. Douglas goes on to state that if he had
known as much about the law then as he did at the time of
writing, he would have urged Wilde to say that if Clarke would

not cross-examine the witnesses at the Police Court he must request him to retire from the case and let someone else ("even any smart junior") do it instead. Here again we fortunately have Sir Edward Clarke's personal explanation, and his words speak for themselves,

It will be remembered that Wilde was first brought up at Bow Street on Saturday, 6th April, 1895, the day following his arrest. Evidence for the prosecution was given by the two brothers Parker, Mrs. Ellen Grant, Alfred Wood, Sidney Mavor, Antonio Migge, and Jane Cotter. When Charles Gill for the Crown had concluded his examination-in-chief of the first of these witnesses, Charles Parker, Mr. Travers Humphreys, who appeared for Wilde, announced that he intended to defend but that the charge had taken his client by surprise and that consequently he was not prepared to cross-examine Parker. The magistrate accordingly allowed the cross-examination of all the Crown witnesses to be postponed.

On the resumption of the hearing on the 11th April, Sir Edward Clarke, whose offer to defend Wilde without fee had in the meantime been accepted by Wilde's solicitors, came into Court and made the following statement as soon as the magistrate had taken his seat on the bench.

> "I appear in this case with my friend Mr. Travers Humphreys for the defence of Mr. Oscar Wilde. I have had the opportunity of reading the depositions which were taken last Saturday, and I am much obliged for the permission to postpone the cross-examination of those witnesses. But upon consideration I have decided not to ask for those witnesses to be recalled for cross-examination, as probably no cross-examination could affect the result as far as this Court is concerned, and so far as your action in the matter is concerned. And of course it is desirable on all grounds that the investigation shall be taken in as short a time as possible in this Court. And, saying that with regard to the witnesses who have been called, I shall probably take the same course with regard to other witnesses, with a view to shorten the proceedings before you."

Needless to say, the magistrate agreed that the course proposed by Clarke was highly desirable. Indeed Clarke could not with advantage have taken any other.

All Douglas's criticisms of Clarke and his representation of his client in the various trials are, therefore, without foundation. It is to be regretted that Douglas should have persisted in them until the end of his life and should have recurred to them in his last two books, *Without Apology*[5] (1938) and *Oscar Wilde: A Summing Up*[6] (1940). He repeated them to me in a long conversation which I had with him in 1931, when he declared that in his opinion Sir Edward Clarke had broken his promise to him and "entirely let down his client." He told me that at the time of the trials he and Wilde were both such simpletons in legal matters that it never occurred to either of them that Clarke was not performing prodigies of skill and courage in his conduct of the case. "I have even recollections," he added, "of writing Sir Edward a long and pathetic letter of thanks for what he had done, after poor Oscar's conviction. It does not bear thinking of."

But, although he no longer remembered Sir Edward Clarke "with the profoundest gratitude and admiration" which he had expressed after the trials in 1895, Lord Alfred Douglas did make one admission about him to me which it is well to remember : "I don't for a moment suggest that he acted otherwise than in what he considered to be the best interests of his client."

[5] *Op. cit.*, pp. 209-212.
[6] *Op. cit.*, pp. 124-125.

APPENDIX C.

BANKRUPTCY PROCEEDINGS.

IN RE WILDE.

The petition in Wilde's bankruptcy was presented by Lord Queensberry on 21st June, and a receiving order was made on 25th July, 1895. Adjudication and public examination of the debtor followed in due course. The Official Receiver was appointed trustee.[1]

Meeting of Creditors.

The first meeting of creditors under a receiving order made against Oscar Fingal O'Flahertie Wills Wilde, described as late of 16 Tite Street, Chelsea, and now of Her Majesty's Prison, Wandsworth, took place on 26th August, 1895, before the Official Receiver, Mr. A. H. Wildy. The petitioning creditor was the Marquess of Queensberry, who claimed £677 in respect of law costs in connexion with legal proceedings instituted by the debtor.

The OFFICIAL RECEIVER—The accounts show unsecured liabilities of £2676 and partly secured debts of £915, a deficiency of £3591 being disclosed. The assets, of which the value is not stated, comprise royalties on literary works and plays. The debtor states that his income has averaged not less than £2000 per annum derived from royalties. He is at present interested in four dramatic works, namely "Lady Windermere's Fan," "A Woman of No Importance," "An Ideal Husband," and "The Importance of Being Earnest." He is also interested in the novel *The Picture of Dorian Gray* and a book of poems entitled *The Sphinx*. The debtor

---

[1] These particulars have been obtained from the Official Court of Bankruptcy files and also from the reports of bankruptcy proceedings published in *The Times*. There are numerous references to the bankruptcy in *De Profundis* as well as in Wilde's extensive prison and post-prison correspondence with his literary executor Robert Ross, partly published in *After Reading* and *After Berneval* (1921) and in the *Dulau Sale Catalogue of Wilde Letters* (1928).

Bankruptcy Proceedings

that my expenditure during the two or three years preceding the
date of the receiving order was at the rate of about £2900 a year.
In July, 1893, my liabilities exceeded my assets by about £1450. I
remember being examined at the instance of the Official Receiver on
29th July last, and the information which I then gave in relation
to my plays and royalties due thereon is substantially correct. It
was usual for me to receive payment in advance for royalties, with
the result that certain theatrical managers appear in my account as
creditors, their security consisting of acting rights in respect of my
plays. It was about the time of my conviction that I first became
aware that I did not possess sufficient property to enable me to
pay all my debts in full. I adhere to the statements which I have
already made as to the causes of my insolvency.

On the occasion of my marriage in May, 1884, a settlement was
executed comprising property belonging to my wife, and an
income derived therefrom has amounted to about £800 per year. I
have a life interest in the property comprised in the deed subject
to my surviving my wife. She is about 35 years of age. The
trustees of the settlement have made me an advance of £1000 at
5 per cent. interest. I have also an interest in a small property
under my father's will. It is situate in Ireland, and produced
between £100 and £150 a year. The household furniture and
effects at my residence in Tite Street were sold in April last by the
Sheriff under an execution. I have never previously been bankrupt,
nor effected an arrangement with my creditors.

Mr. GRAIN did not ask the debtor any questions.

In the absence of opposition by any creditor, the examination
was concluded.

On 7th May, 1897, a first interim dividend of 1s. 5d. in the £
was declared, and this was followed on 23rd July, 1897, by a supple-
mental dividend of 2¾d. The Official Receiver ceased to act as
trustee on 13th December, 1897, and other trustees were appointed.
No further dividends were declared during Wilde's lifetime, since
he never applied to the Court for his discharge, and he died a
bankrupt.

Meanwhile Robert Ross had been appointed the debtor's literary
executor. Early in 1900, whilst Wilde was still alive, Queensberry
died and Lord Alfred Douglas came in for a share of his father's
fortune amounting to about £25,000. Ross therefore asked him to
pay off Wilde's debts and thereby acquire the copyrights in his

writings, which Ross undertook to administer on his behalf until he was repaid. To his subsequent lasting regret Douglas declined to do this.[2] The estate, which Douglas might thus have rescued from bankruptcy, did not become solvent until 1906, when all the creditors were paid 20s. in the £ together with 4 per cent. interest on the amount of their debts. It is interesting to note that in this final settlement Douglas received with interest approximately a quarter of the amount of his father's debt, the legal costs of the libel prosecution which of course ranked as an asset in the Queensberry estate.[3]

The remaining dividends were declared as follows: 13s. 4d. (3rd July, 1903), 4s. 0¼d. (23rd July, 1904), 1s. with 4 per cent. interest (28th May, 1906)—thus amounting in all to a payment to Wilde's creditors of 20s. in the £ with interest.

---

[2] See Hesketh Pearson, *Modern Men and Mummers* (1921), at p. 168.
[3] See *The Library of William Andrews Clark, jun., Wilde and Wildeana,* Vol. II. (1922) at p. 70.

further states that he had 10 per cent. cf the gross weekly receipts from the play "The Importance of Being Earnest" up to £1000, and 15 per cent. on anything over that amount. As to "A Woman of No Importance" and "An Ideal Husband" the terms were as follows: if the receipts were over £600 and under £800 per week he was to receive 5 per cent.; over £800 and under £1000 7½ per cent., and on anything over £1000 10 per cent. Those royalties were all paid weekly, and, to the best of the debtor's belief there was nothing outstanding in respect of them at the date of his arrest. He attributes his insolvency to the failure of the legal proceedings instituted by him against the Marquess of Queensberry, and to his arrest and conviction in the recent trial of *Regina* v. *Wilde*.

[Mr. TRAVERS HUMPHREYS, who attended on behalf of the debtor, stated that, although every effort had been made, the debtor was not at present in a position to submit an offer to the creditors.]

The OFFICIAL RECEIVER—[Having dealt with the proofs, including in addition to that of the Marquess of Queensberry one showing £233 in respect of tobacco, wines and jewelry supplied to the debtor, he said] : The debtor in consequence of the present position is not in attendance, it not being considered necessary to obtain an order to bring him up. The summary and observations recently issued sufficiently indicate the position in the matter, and it appears that the debtor has been insolvent for some time past. There being no proposal before the meeting, the only course will be to pass a resolution that the debtor be adjudged bankrupt and to elect a trustee.

The resolution for bankruptcy having been agreed to, a proposal for the appointment of a trustee was made, but negatived by the vote of the Marquess of Queensberry, who was desirous that the matter should remain in the hands of the Official Receiver.

The public examination of the debtor was fixed for 24th September next at 11 o'clock.

Public Examination.

BEFORE MR. REGISTRAR GIFFARD.

24th September, 1895.

Mr. C. A. POPE attended as Assistant Official Receiver, and Mr. J. P. GRAIN for the debtor.

The DEBTOR was brought up in the custody of two warders from Wandsworth Prison, but was not brought into Court.

Mr. J. P. GRAIN—I am instructed to apply for an adjournment. The debtor's accounts show liabilities of about £3500 and substantially, so far as could be ascertained at the present time, there are no assets, although there are certain of the royalties on his plays which may at some future date prove to be of value. Several of the debtor's friends, however, have already subscribed sums amounting to between £1000 and £1500, and I have every reason to believe that when many other of his friends return from their vacation they will also render such financial assistance as will be sufficient to pay all the creditors 20s. in the pound, with the exception of a liability of £1557 due to the trustees of his marriage settlement. It is intended that some arrangement shall be made whereby that claim will be satisfied by the execution of a deed transferring to the trustees of the marriage settlement all the debtor's interest in his plays and literary works. By this means all the creditors will be paid in full, and an application will then be made to rescind the receiving order. Under these circumstances I ask that the sitting may be adjourned for so long a time as the Court may think fit.

The ASSISTANT OFFICIAL RECEIVER—I shall not oppose the application if there is any prospect of the creditors being paid in full.

Mr. REGISTRAR GIFFARD, on no creditor appearing to oppose, adjourned the examination to 12th November at 11.30 o'clock.

Public Examination—continued.

BEFORE MR. REGISTRAR LINKLATER.

12th November, 1895.

Mr. A. H. WILDY appeared as Official Receiver, and Mr. J. P. GRAIN represented the debtor.

The DEBTOR, examined by Mr. WILDY—I am 40 years of age. For about ten or eleven years previously to March last I resided at 16 Tite Street, Chelsea. I kept no books of accounts. I estimate without any one even dreaming of any scandal. Between persons of the same sex suspicion of impropriety or the thought of indecency has been so effectually banished that the mere suggestion of the possibility will seem to most an incredible absurdity. Between individuals of opposite sexes no such free unfettered communion of life is possible. That, however, is the goal towards which we ought to progress; and it would be a fatal blunder at the very moment when we are endeavouring to rid friendship between man and woman of the blighting shadow of possible wrong-doing, were we to acquiesce in the re-establishment of that upas shade over the relations between man and man and man and woman.

The Sacrosanct Male. At the same time it is impossible to deny that the trial and the sentence bring into very clear relief the ridiculous disparity there is between the punishment meted out to those who corrupt girls and those who corrupt boys. If Oscar Wilde, instead of indulging in dirty tricks of indecent familiarity with boys and men, had ruined the lives of half a dozen innocent simpletons of girls, or had broken up the home of his friend by corrupting his friend's wife, no one could have laid a finger upon him. The male is sacrosanct: the female is fair game. To have burdened society with a dozen bastards, to have destroyed a happy home by his lawless lust—of these things the criminal law takes no account. But let him act indecently to a young rascal who is very well able to take care of himself, and who can by no possibility bring a child into the world as the result of his corruption, then judges can hardly contain themselves from indignation when inflicting the maximum sentence the law allows. Another contrast, almost as remarkable as that which sends Oscar Wilde to hard labour and places Sir Charles Dilke in the House of Commons, is that between the universal execration heaped upon Oscar Wilde and the tacit universal acquiescence of the very same public in the same kind of vice in our public schools. If all persons guilty of Oscar Wilde's offences were to be clapped into gaol, there would be a very surprising exodus from Eton and Harrow, Rugby and Winchester, to Pentonville and Holloway. It is to be hoped that our headmasters will pluck up a little courage from the result of the Wilde trial, and endeavour to rid our Protestant schools of a foul and unnatural vice which is not found in Catholic establishments, at all events in this country. But meanwhile public school boys are allowed to indulge with impunity in practices which, when they leave school, would consign them to hard labour."

When he read these comments Lord Alfred Douglas wrote the following letter to the editor. It is clear from its contents that this document was composed, so to speak, at fever heat :—

"Hotel De La Poste,

Rouen, 28th June, 1895.

Sir,

I have just read your comments on the Oscar Wilde case in the *Review of Reviews*. I believe you to be a man with a conscience and one who, if he thought a terrible wrong had been done, would not sit with his hands folded and do nothing. Now, sir, you admit that the common cant about 'unnatural' offences is not worth anything, you have sufficient philosophy to understand and sufficient boldness to say that to call a thing unnatural is not only not necessarily to condemn it but is even to a certain extent to commend it. Everything that diverges from the normal may to a certain extent be called unnatural, genius and beauty among them. But while you admit broadly all this, you uphold the horrible and barbarous law which condemns a man who is guilty of these so called 'offences' to a sentence which you calmly describe as 'probably capital,' and you give surely the flimsiest and feeblest reason· for this. Your argument apparently is that if these laws did not exist a taint or suspicion might be thrown on friendships between people of the same sex which at present does not exist. Now, sir, you are probably aware that such laws as ours do not exist in France, and that these 'offences' are there ignored by the law just as fornication is ignored in England, and yet you will hardly venture to say that this taint or suspicion exists in connexion with friendships between people of the same sex in France. Why then do you anticipate that a similar absence of laws in England would produce the result you dread? My opinion is that no such taint would attach to friendships between those of the same sex unless the suspicion was justified by facts. Thus in England there are no laws against 'Lesbianism' or intercourse of an erotic character between women, and yet there are several women in London whose friendship with other women does carry a taint and a suspicion, simply because these women are obviously 'sapphic' in their loves. On the other hand a

APPENDIX D.

LORD ALFRED DOUGLAS AND THE AFTERMATH OF THE WILDE TRIALS.

While in France, where he had been obliged to retire on the eve of Wilde's prosecution, Lord Alfred Douglas received a copy of *The Review of Reviews* for June, 1895. In this issue the editor, Mr. W. T. Stead, had commented in characteristic style on the trials and their tragic outcome. Stead's remarks in turn provoked Douglas to address a letter to the editor which set out his own views on the case, and which must rank as one of the most amazing literary outbursts on any subject. This letter, which for obvious reasons Stead dared not publish, has remained concealed from the light of day until the present.

W. T. Stead, destined eventually to lose his life in the "Titanic" disaster, was one of the most courageous and out-spoken Radical journalists of the period, as well as a tireless antagonist of social abuses with a strong Nonconformist conscience. Strangely enough, it was Stead more than anyone else who was responsible for the passing of the Criminal Law Amendment Act in 1885, although not for the specific section of it under which Wilde was charged. This statute was entitled "An Act to make further provision for the Protection of Women and Girls, the suppression of brothels and other purposes," and it was the culminating point in the campaign against prostitution and white slavery in England which Stead had been carrying on for some time in the pages of the *Pall Mall Gazette.* When the Bill was being debated in the committee stage in the House of Commons, Henry Labouchere, the well-known Radical M.P. and editor of *Truth,* moved an amendment designed to cover indecent practices between males or "outrages on decency" whether committed in public or *in private,* although this was never within the original scope and purpose of the Bill. After some discussion, and the increase of the maximum punishment of one year's imprisonment with hard labour, as proposed by Labouchere, to two years, the amendment was carried and subsequently incorporated as Section 11 of the Act.[1]

---

[1] See Hansard, *Parliamentary Debates* (3rd Series) CCC., at p. 1398. The Act (48 & 49 Vict. c. 69) came into force on 1st January, 1886. See also remarks by Sir Travers Humphreys above, pp. 5-7.

Appendix D

Unfortunately for himself, Stead's zeal in the social purity campaign outran his discretion. While the Criminal Law Amendment Bill was still before Parliament, he published a series of articles under the title of "The Maiden Tribute of Modern Babylon" in the *Pall Mall Gazette,* which it is no exaggeration to say produced a world-wide sensation. Anxious to show how relatively simple a matter it was for anyone with £20 in his pocket to acquire a young girl for the purposes of prostitution or white slavery, Stead himself entered into an arrangement of this kind with a mother of a young girl, and although the girl was immediately handed over to the tender care of the Salvation Army and the police were informed, Stead was charged with abducting the girl, and on his conviction which followed he was sent to prison for three months.[2]

Stead continued his social work after his release, and having severed his connexion with the *Pall Mall Gazette* he proceeded to found a new journal which he called *The Review of Reviews.* It was in the editorial notes of this periodical, entitled "The Progress of the World," that in due course he came to comment on the Wilde case.

"The Conviction of Oscar Wilde."

". . . The trial of Oscar Wilde and Taylor at the Old Bailey, resulting in their conviction and the infliction of what will probably be a capital sentence—for two years' hard labour in solitary confinement always breaks up the constitution even of tough and stalwart men—has forced upon the attention of the public the existence of a vice of which the most of us happily know nothing. The heinousness of the crime of Oscar Wilde and his associates does not lie, as is usually supposed, in its being unnatural. It would be unnatural for seventy-nine out of eighty persons. It is natural for the abnormal person who is in a minority of one. If the promptings of our animal nature are to be the only guide, the punishment of Oscar Wilde would savour of persecution, and he might fairly claim our sympathy as the champion of individualism against the tyranny of an intolerant majority. But we are not merely animal. We are human beings living together in society, whose aim is to render social intercourse as free and as happy as possible. At present, fortunately, people of the same sex can travel together, and live together in close intimacy,

---

[2] Frederic Whyte, *Life of W. T. Stead,* vol. 1 (1925), p. 185.

published in his version over Douglas's name. The appearance of the article in this form produced considerable excitement on both sides of the channel, and Douglas was under such concentrated attack from various quarters that he was eventually persuaded to say that the French version did not accurately reflect his views.[4] But in later years he admitted that the translation was entirely faithful.[5] In any event the survival of the original English text, from which the following extracts are taken, places the matter beyond doubt.

At the beginning of the article Douglas stated that in France he was regarded as "the young friend of Oscar Wilde, or to be more explicit, the child that Oscar Wilde loved," and as such he was pitied by some and detested by others. "It is curious to reflect that had I the good fortune to live in Athens in the time of Pericles," he went on, "the very conduct which at present has led to my disgrace would then have resulted in my glory. To-day I am proud that I have been loved by a great poet who, perhaps, esteemed me because he recognized that besides a beautiful body I possessed a beautiful soul." For the reversal of public opinion, and the "ignorant persecution of the excellent persons who are in very truth the salt of the earth," he blamed the church. But he admitted that the church, while severe on sodomy, had countenanced the passionate love which existed between friends of the same sex provided it was chaste. "On this question, she adopts the Platonic view. The ordinary man, the man in the street, however, detests and despises such passionate affection whether they be pure or otherwise and, however laudable they may be, his indignation is directed against the affection itself and not against that which, after all, is only an accident of the affection." Hence, as he put it, "there has always been and always will be a thousand Queensberrys for one Oscar Wilde."

When he came to write about the trial, Douglas's remarks were scarcely less restrained and unwise than they had been on the subject of his relations with Wilde. Indeed, had they been uttered in England they might well have involved him in a prosecution for criminal libel.

---

[4] The article, which appeared in the *Revue Blanche* for 1st June, 1896, was entitled *"Une introduction à mes poemes avec quelque considérations sur l'affaire Wilde."* Its authenticity was denied by Douglas in his book *Oscar Wilde and Myself* (1914), Ch. xiv. R. H. Sherard, who was living in Paris at the time of the projected appearance of the article, tried unsuccessfully to have it stopped: see *The Real Oscar Wilde* (1915), at p. 390.

[5] cp. Leon Lemonnier, *La Vie d'Oscar Wilde* (1931), at p. 203: "Au cours entretien particulier, Lord Alfred m'a avoué qu'il était l'auteur de l'article et que son traducteur, Felix Fenéon, ne l'avait nullement trahi."

"Everyone is familiar with the origin of the Oscar Wilde case. It is sufficient for me to say—but is it not clear to everyone—that the pretentions of my Lord Queensberry to have acted in the interests of virtue to save his son was pure hypocrisy. If in the mind of anyone there may linger the possibility of the thought that Lord Queensberry could be capable of a sentiment of moral indignation, I would refer them to his life and tell them that if his deeds of bestiality have not been made known to the rabble to make him an object of disgust he owes it to the superhuman generosity of his wife— my mother—whom he besought that she should keep his conduct secret. What right, I ask, had such a man to pose as the patron of virtue? . . .

To return to the trial. I am confident thàt the Government did not wish to let the prosecution of Oscar Wilde take its regular course. My readers will recall that the first criminal trial resulted in disagreement of the jury and the question is consequently pertinent—why did the Crown take the very irregular course of having a second trial—why was the prosecution conducted with this extraordinary animosity; briefly why did the Crown manifest so eager a desire to obtain a verdict of guilty? The reason is very simple. The Government was intimidated; the second trial was the result of a political intrigue. I would wish to ask Mr. Asquith, the then Home Secretary and an old friend of Oscar Wilde, if he was not threatened by Lord Rosebery that if a second trial was not instituted and a verdict of guilty obtained against Mr. Wilde, the Liberal party would be removed from power. The fact is that the Liberal party then contained a large number of men whom I have referred to as the salt of the earth. The maniacs of virtue threatened a series of legal actions which would have created an unprecedented scandal in Europe—a scandal in political circles. If Oscar Wilde was found guilty the matter would be hushed up. This was the cause of the second trial, and the verdict of guilty. It was a degrading *coup-d'état*—the sacrifice of a great poet to save a degraded band of politicians.

The conviction of Oscar Wilde was one of the last acts of this disgraceful and discredited Liberal party who is now in an exceptional minority in the House of Commons.

There is nothing more to say. Oscar Wilde is in jail and will remain there till the expiration of his sentence. A national crime has been committed, a crime from which no great friendship may exist between two ordinary women and nobody would think of imputing to them 'improper' motives, I hope you follow my argument and observe the analogy.

Perhaps you are not aware that 'Lesbianism' exists to any extent in London, but I can assure you that it does, and though of course I cannot mention names, I could point out to you half a dozen women in society or among actresses who would be considered as 'dangerous' to young girls as Oscar Wilde will I suppose henceforth be considered to boys. Why on earth in the name of liberty and common sense a man cannot be allowed to love a boy, rather than a woman when his nature and his instinct tell him to do so, and when he has before him the example of such a number of noble and gifted men who have had similar tastes (such as Shakespeare, Marlowe, Michael Angelo, Frederick the Great, and a host of others), is another question and one to which I should like to hear a satisfactory answer. Certain it is that persecution will no more kill this instinct in a man who has it, than it killed the faith of the Christian martyrs. I am not pleading for prostitution, but I think if a man who affects female prostitutes is unmolested it is disgraceful that a man who prefers male prostitutes should be thus barbarously punished. The only difference is that the man who brings bastards into the world, who seduces girls or commits adultery does an immense amount of harm, as you have yourself pointed out, whereas the pæderast does absolutely no harm to anyone.

While on the point, sir, may I ask you if it ever occurred to you to consider the relative deserts of Mr. Oscar Wilde and the man who ruined him, my father, Lord Queensberry? Mr. Oscar Wilde seduced no one, he did no one any harm, he was a kind, generous and astoundingly gifted man, utterly incapable of meanness or cruelty. Lord Queensberry was divorced from my mother after, for twelve years, she had silently endured the most horrible suffering at his hands.

He broke her heart, ruined her health and took away all joy from her life, and after his divorce till the present day he has not ceased to persecute her with every fiendish ingenuity of cruelty and meanness that a man could devise. Hardly a week passes without her receiving some letter from him containing some horrible insult, he has been to beat on the door of her house when she was nearly dying upstairs, and he has taken away from her every penny of money that as an honourable man he should have given her, and left her only that which he is forced to give by the Scotch law which is so hard on a woman who divorces her husband. In the meanwhile he flaunts about with prostitutes and kept women and spends on them the money which he should give to his children, for he has cut off all money supplies from my brother, myself and my sister.

Last year he induced a girl of seventeen to marry him in a registry office against the wish of her people.

On the following day he deserted her, and has since been divorced for a second time. Not content with practising fornication and adultery, he has written pamphlets and given lectures advocating what he calls a 'sort of polygamy' which is neither more nor less than free love. This is the man who has been made into a hero by the English people and the *press,* who is cheered in the streets by the mob, and who has crowned his career by dishonouring and driving out of England his son who now writes to you.

I am, sir, your obedient servant,

ALFRED DOUGLAS."

Containing as it did such a spirited defence of homosexual conduct, it was scarcely surprising that W. T. Stead should decline to publish this letter in his review. Douglas wrote another letter in similar terms to Henry Labouchere, the editor of *Truth,* and Labouchere likewise declined to publish it. Unfortunately for Douglas, this second letter was to be produced with damaging effect to the writer's character in the libel action brought by Douglas against Mr. Arthur Ransome, his publisher, and The Times Book Club eighteen years later.[3]

In 1896 Douglas succeeded in getting his views on the subject into print in a French journal. It came about in this way. Unable to find a publisher for his poems in England, Douglas managed to arrange for their publication by the *Mercure de France,* the well-known Paris monthly magazine. Another journal of rather more advanced opinions, called the *Revue Blanche,* had already published several of these poems, and when the editor of the latter learned that they were shortly all to appear, he asked Douglas to write an article by way of introducing them to the French public and at the same time setting forth his comments on the Wilde case. Douglas's knowledge of the French language was not sufficient to enable him to write the article in French, so it was arranged that he should write it in English and it should be translated by the editor and

---

[3] See above, p. 95, and note.

APPENDIX E

THE PREVALENCE OF MALE HOMOSEXUALITY IN ENGLAND.

Although this was the most conspicuous prosecution of its kind which had taken place under the Criminal Law Amendment Act of 1885, it must not be supposed from the evidence in *Regina* v. *Wilde and Taylor* that homosexual acts were any novelty in England at the time of the conviction of the two defendants in this case. For, as Marcus Aurelius has said, "who can change the desires of men?" Male homosexuality has certainly been prevalent in this country since the time of the Norman Conquest.[1] At least four English kings have been inverts, as also have been a number of distinguished soldiers, clergy, poets, peers of the realm, Members of Parliament and others prominent in one rank or another of English society. Further, the prevalence of homosexual conduct is attested by the fact that sodomy was regarded from early times as an ecclesiastical offence, although it did not become a felony and thus subject to ordinary criminal jurisdiction until the reign of Henry VIII.

The spread of sodomitical habits in France about the eleventh century has been attributed to the Normans, and there is little doubt that the arrival of the Normans in England had a similar effect. We are told on good authority that the gilded youth of Normandy and of Norman England began to wear long garments like women, and let their hair grow long and they copied the walk and behaviour of women and wore long pointed shoes like women. The younger son of William the Conqueror, who succeeded his father in 1087 and is usually called William Rufus, was unquestionably homosexual. Indeed his conduct was so scandalous that, after his accidental death while hunting in the New Forest in 1100, his corpse was denied Christian burial by the Church. "Into the details of the private life of Rufus it is well not to grope too narrowly," wrote the historian Bishop Freeman in the eighties of

[1] On this subject generally see Havelock Ellis, *Studies in the Psychology of Sex,* vol. II, part 2, *Sexual Inversion* (New York, 1936); Eugen Dühren (Ivan Bloch), *Das Geschlechtsleben in England,* vol. III (Berlin, 1903); Marc-André Raffalovich *Uranisme et Unisexualité* (Paris and Lyon, 1896), and works therein cited.

the last century; "in him England might see on her own soil habits of the ancient Greek and the modern Turk."[2] William II's two nephews and most of their companions who perished in the wreck of the White Ship in 1102, were likewise inclined : indeed, the contemporary historian Henry of Huntingdon regarded the loss of this vessel as divine judgment for the crime of sodomy. About the same time too we find Archbishop Anselm of Canterbury writing to one of his clergy that "this sin has been so public that hardly anyone has blushed for it, and many, therefore, have plunged into it without realizing its gravity."

Two centuries later another homosexual, or more probably bisexual monarch, sat on the English throne in the person of Edward II. His love of low company and his association with various favourites, notably Piers Gaveston, are now matters of fairly common knowledge. Edward was murdered at the instigation of his wife and her lover in Berkeley Castle, and it seems probable that the peculiarly revolting manner in which he met his death was dictated by popular knowledge of his habits.[3]

Although the church took cognizance of the crime of sodomy, it does not appear to have been dealt with at all severely. There seems to have been a prevailing opinion that, if the church relinquished convicted offenders to the secular arm, they would be burned like sorcerers and witches. It is practically certain that they were not burned and that on the contrary they enjoyed comparative immunity until the passing of the Statute of 1533, which made the offence a felony and punishable capitally. It was only a few years previously that Henry VIII had decided upon the suppression of the monasteries, and it is probable that the act was occasioned by the unsatisfactory state of affairs revealed by some of the inhabitants of these institutions. The Act (25 Henry VIII, c. 6) was repealed in 1547 by Edward VI, along with other legislation passed in his father's time, but it was re-enacted in the following year, again repealed in 1553 and finally re-enacted in 1562 (5 Elizabeth, c. 17), when Parliament ordained that it was to be perpetual. It remained a capital offence until the beginning of the nineteenth century, when the death penalty was abolished for this as for many other offences at the instigation of Sir Robert Peel, then Home Secretary.

---

[2] Edward A. Freeman, *The Reign of William Rufus*, I, 159 (1882). For further details see *op. cit.* II, 499-502.

[3] According to the contemporary chronicler, Higden, Edward II "was sleyne with a hoote broche putte thro the secret place posteriale" (*cum vero ignito inter celanda confossus ignominiose peremptus est*): Rolls Series, *Polychronicon Ranulphi Higden*, VIII, 324 (1882).

element of morbid intrigue, sensuality, cruelty and hypocrisy is wanting. . . ."

In English politics the Liberals had been succeeded by a Conservative administration headed by Lord Salisbury, with Mr. Arthur Balfour as Leader of the House of Commons. Douglas pointed out in the final paragraphs of his article that Balfour was a man of culture and a philosopher who had been a friend of Wilde's and was an admirer of his genius. This was the person who might help. Accordingly, Douglas appealed to the leading writers in France, in particular to Henri Bauër, Paul Adam, and Octave Mirbeau, whom he mentioned by name, to write personally to the Conservative leader and urge him to release the prisoner. The new Government had shown solicitude for Dr. Jameson and his band of filibusters in the Transvaal. Certainly a poet and an artist had an equal claim to their protection. And now, asked Douglas in conclusion, who would play the part of Nicodemus to Mr. Balfour?

Opinion in France at this time as expressed in the literary journals was unanimous in condemning the sentiments expressed in this article. Writers such as Henri Bauër, who had been prominent for their sympathy towards Wilde in the hour of his tragedy, stigmatized Douglas's intervention as clumsy and sensational. The repercussions were not slow in making themselves felt on the editor's head; and it is significant that, in the following issue of the *Revue Blanche,* Douglas was at pains to point out in the course of an explanatory statement that *"l'amour de mon ami pour moi était platonique, c'est-a-dire pur."* But there is no doubt that the article did Douglas a great deal of harm, and it made his stay in France much more difficult and embarrassing for him than it otherwise might have been.[6]

However he may have continued to feel about Lord Rosebery and the late Liberal administration, it must always be remembered in justice to his reputation that Lord Alfred Douglas lived to modify very considerably his views on the controversial subject of homosexuality. Nevertheless, for many years after the publication of the notorious *Revue Blanche* article these views remained unchanged.

---

6 In the previous year, when he was staying in Le Havre, his action in hiring a small yacht with two boys as deck hands produced a violent attack by a local newspaper which accused him of corrupting the youth of the town. "Pour moi," he replied in a letter to the *Journal de Havre,* dated 1st August, 1895, "c'est déjà trop évident que le monde a le droit de m'insulter et de m'injurier parce que je suis l'ami d' Oscar Wilde. Voilà mon crime, non pas que j'étais son ami, mais que je serai jusqu'à la mort (et même après si Dieu le veut)."

Appendix D

On being reunited with Wilde after the latter's release from prison—the first reunion took place in the same hotel in Rouen in which the letter reproduced above had been dashed off so feverishly—we find Douglas writing in similar if somewhat more guarded terms to his mother. "Don't think that I have changed about him or that I have changed my views about morals," he told Lady Queensberry at the end of 1897. "I still love and admire him, and I think he has been infamously treated by ignorant and cruel brutes. I look upon him as a martyr to progress. I associate myself with him in everything. I long to hear of his success and rehabilitation in the post which is his by right at the very summit of English literature, nor do I intend to cease corresponding with him or not to see him from time to time in Paris and elsewhere. I give up nothing and admit no point against him or myself separately or jointly."[7]

Douglas continued in this frame of mind for some time after Wilde's death. The change was gradual : its completion coincided with his reception into the Roman Catholic Church in 1911. Henceforward he openly expressed his abhorrence of homosexuality, particularly in his *Autobiography* (1929) and in his later and final study of Wilde, which was published in 1940.[8] Looking back to the period of his youthful folly, he wrote : "At that time I not only loved and admired Wilde as a friend and a man of genius, but I entirely sympathized with his vices, which I did not regard as vices at all. I was a complete and frank pagan and scorned the Christian ethic." For this reason Douglas considered that his original attitude was in a measure justified. The truth was that the subject of homosexuality was regarded with exaggerated horror at the time of Wilde's conviction, an attitude which Douglas felt squared very imperfectly with the private lives of many of those, such as his own father, who were most conspicuous in condemning it.

"The fact that I now loathe and detest what I then thought innocuous, if not actually a fine thing in itself," he went on to say in his last book not long before he died, "cannot prevent me from seeing that, according to my then lights, the attitude I took up was courageous and admirable. I was fifty years in advance of my time. I was persecuted, almost as badly as Wilde was himself, for that attitude which never varied right up to the time of Wilde's death. I was in perfect good faith; my only fault was that I declined to conform to what I considered to be the hypocritical pretence that homosexuality was an offence in a class by itself and worse than murder."

[7] Lord Alfred Douglas, *Without Apology* (1938), at p. 304.
[8] *Oscar Wilde: A Summing Up.*

otherwise directed, as novelists and others who embroider history are never tired of telling us; but there were strong grounds for supposing that William III, who became king after the revolution of 1688, was homosexual, although probably not in so pronounced a degree as James I. Sir John Vanbrugh was not afraid to introduce the subject into his play, *The Relapse,* which received its first public performance in 1696. The King's habits seem to have been widely shared at Court, particularly by the King's Minister, Lord Portland, who shocked the French by his behaviour when he went to Paris as Ambassador in 1698. "Nothing is more ordinary in England than this unnatural vice, as I was told by an Englishman himself," wrote Elizabeth, Duchess of Orleans, at this time, "and all those who followed Lord Portland to Paris led a terrible life with the debauchees of Paris. Lord Westmoreland and Lord Raby and three or four others did not hesitate to make public what their inclinations were. . . . You ask why people persist in tasting such forbidden pleasures, but since the days of Adam it has always been so, that forbidden fruits taste better than those that are allowed."[7]

In spite of the severe penalties to which those practising it were liable, homosexuality continued to flourish in England in the eighteenth century. The Old Bailey and Middlesex Sessions papers abound with trials for sodomy at this time, and many death sentences are recorded, although the law seems to have been very fairly, if severely, applied. Readers of Smollett's *Roderick Random,* which first appeared in 1748, may remember how Lord Strutwell observed that homosexuality "gains ground apace and in all probability will become in a short time a more fashionable device than simple fornication." Male brothels were certainly not unknown in London in 1726. There is a remarkable trial of one Margaret Clap "for keeping a sodomitical house off Holborn," where between forty and fifty men were found one Sunday evening "making love to one another, as they called it." Mistress Clap was duly convicted and sentenced to two years' imprisonment as well as to stand in the pillory.[8]

Among the more notorious trials of this century may be mentioned that of the Rev. Robert Thistlewayte, of Wadham College, Oxford, and that of Samuel Foote, the actor and dramatist—the former, in 1739, for an assault upon one of his pupils in college, and the latter, in 1776, for an assault upon a servant whom he had

[7] G. S. Stevenson, *The Letters of Madame,* I, 256-257 (1924), "The King (William III)," wrote the Duchess of Orleans in 1701, "is said to have been in love with Albemarle as with a woman, and they say he used to kiss his hands before all the Court ": *op. cit.,* I, 217.

[8] *Select Trials at the Sessions-House of the Old Bailey,* III, 37 (1742).

discharged from his employ. There were other cases which never came to Court, such as that of the Reverend John Fenwick, Vicar of Bryall, in Northumberland, who conveniently removed himself to Naples in 1797, and William Beckford, wealthy squire of Font-hill and author of *Vathek*, who was obliged to spend many years in exile and seclusion for his part in a suppressed scandal in 1784. King George III is said to have wished Beckford to be hanged, also the fifteen-year-old Lord Courtenay, with whom in the course of a country-house visit Beckford is supposed to have been discovered in bed. Certain it is that the patent of peerage which had been prepared for Beckford was cancelled, and the suspect immediately betook himself abroad, there to remain for the next ten years.

One gains the impression that, relative to the population at the time, male inversion flourished in London in considerably greater measure than it does to-day. Nothwithstanding the frequent infliction of the death penalty, homosexual practices continued in a marked degree until the offence ceased to be punishable capitally in 1828; nor, as we have seen, were these practices confined to the more humble members of the community. The poet Byron, to quote another example, experienced very strong emotions towards his male friends, but it is probably true to say that he was bisexual. That not even members of the Royal Family were free from suspicion at this time appears from the prosecution of the publisher Joseph Phillips for a libel arising out of an account which he published of the suicide of the Duke of Cumberland's valet Sellis in St. James's Palace in 1810.

The most prominent case in the early part of the nineteenth century was that of the Hon. Percy Jocelyn, Bishop of Clogher. The bishop, who was a younger son of the first Earl of Roden, was detected with a private soldier in the back room of the White Lion Tavern, off the Haymarket, in a situation which led to his instant apprehension on the night of 19th July, 1822.[9] The case caused a tremendous sensation at the time, particularly when it became known that the bishop, who had been released on bail by the magistrate, had fled the country.[1] Particular animosity was popularly felt towards him as the soldier who was arrested remained to stand his trial and was condemned.

---

[9] For details, see *Annual Register,* 1822, Appendix, pp. 425-432.

[1] *The Greville Memoirs* (ed. Lytton Strachey and Roger Fulford), vol. I (1938), at pp. 125-126. The bishop later returned to live for many years in Scotland with the assumed name of Thomas Wilson. He died in Edinburgh in 1843, and was buried incognito: *The Times,* 2nd January, 1844.

Male Homosexuality in England

In the sixteenth century several eminent homosexual men stand out, particularly in the field of drama and scholarship. Nicholas Udall, author of *Ralph Roister Doister,* a work generally regarded as the first comedy in the English language, was an invert and even a pervert. As headmaster of Eton, he was noted for his love of inflicting corporal punishment on the boys, which no doubt implied a sadistic sexual impulse. In 1541, the year in which *Ralph Roister Doister* was first publicly performed, Udall was charged with unnatural crime and confessed his guilt before the Privy Council. He was dismissed from his headmastership and imprisoned, but his reputation does not appear to have been greatly injured, for he subsequently enjoyed a number of lucrative ecclesiastical livings and Queen Mary appointed him headmaster of Westminster School in 1553. Elizabethan writers were, of course, accustomed to use extravagant language in paying compliments to members of their own sex, but, as the late Edmund Gosse has said in his biography of one of them, Richard Barnfield, their verses are sometimes "dedicated to a sentiment of friendship so exaggerated as to remove them beyond wholesome sympathy."[4]

Among the dramatists of the period must be included Christopher Marlowe, one of the most brilliant writers of the age, whose works as well as whose conduct betrayed his feelings. In his most powerful drama, *Edward II,* he deals with the relations between the King and his favourites. In 1593 Marlowe was accused, amongst other things, of having openly stated that "all thei that love not tobacco and boyes are fooles."[5] A warrant was issued by the Privy Council for his arrest, and it was only his sudden death immediately afterwards which prevented his execution. He was involved in a tavern brawl in Bedford and was fatally stabbed, according to a contemporary, "by a bawdy serving man, a rival of his in his lewd love."

Shakespeare has also been discussed in this connexion. A view was expressed rather more than a century ago by the historian and critic Henry Hallam that it would have been better for Shakespeare's reputation if the sonnets had never been written. This view is still held in certain quarters. All that can be said, however, is that Shakespeare addressed a long series of sonnets to a youthful male friend, whose identity is still in dispute, and that, although written in tender language, the imputation of any shameful relationship or feeling is scarcely justified. Shakespeare is so preoccupied with women in his other writings, particularly in the

---

4 See article on Barnfield in *Dictionary of National Biography,* I, 1182.
5 See Havelock Ellis, *Christopher Marlowe* (1887), at p. 429.

twenty-six sonnets to the so-called "Dark Lady," as well as in such dramas of heterosexual passion as *Troilus and Cressida, Measure for Measure,* and *Anthony and Cleopatra,* that there can be little if any doubt that he was free from traits of abnormality.

Shakespeare's eminent contemporary, Francis Bacon, does not escape judgment so easily. Both the contemporary writers Aubrey and Sir Symonds D'Ewes assert that he was a pederast, while the latter produced evidence which there is no reason to doubt of Bacon's homosexual practices with his own servants. These charges are supported by a letter from Bacon's mother reproving him for his alleged behaviour. It may be added that Bacon's writings show no evidence of any interest in or attraction to women, whilst the essay on beauty deals exclusively with masculine beauty.

Rex fuit Elizabeth, nunc est regina Jacobus. King James I's proclivities in this direction are too notorious to need comment. That sovereign had numerous favourites and there can be little doubt that Robert Carr, whom the King advanced from being a page to the earldom of Somerset, was pardoned for his part in the murder of Sir Thomas Overbury for fear that he might make public the details of his criminal association with the monarch.

The first trial of anyone of social prominence, and the first to be included in the published collection of State Trials, did not take place until almost a century after the passing of the first penal statute in the reign of Henry VIII. In 1631 the thirty-eight-year-old Earl of Castlehaven was arraigned before his peers on charges of having committed sodomy with two of his servants, as well as for a rape on his own wife. It is a curious case, since the Earl was convicted solely on the testimony of his wife and servants, while the motives of the Countess, who seems to have been carrying on an intrigue with another member of the household, are not above suspicion. Further, the fact that Castlehaven had recently changed his religion from Protestant to Catholic did not help him at the trial. He was convicted and was duly sentenced to death and beheaded on Tower Hill. The two servants, Lawrence Fitzpatrick and Giles Broadway, were subsequently charged with the same serious offence, and being commoners were hanged at Tyburn.[6]

As might be expected, the Restoration brought a considerable wave of homosexuality in its train. It was the opinion of the diarist Pepys, for example, that the Court had never been so bad as it was during the reign of Charles II for "the most abominable vices that ever were in the world." Charles's own interests were

---

[6] *State Trials,* III, 402-426.

copies of this volume for the printer to be prosecuted. This was in 1898. In the result Havelock Ellis was obliged to bring out the remaining volumes of his great work in the United States, and it is only in recent years that they have been reprinted in this country. Besides W. T. Stead's remarks in the *Review of Reviews*,[5] one of the few frank expressions of opinion on the subject of sexual inversion in England, published by the press at the time of Wilde's conviction, was contained in a letter to *Reynold's Newspaper* over the initials "C. S. M." These initials concealed the identity of Christopher Sclater Millard, who was later to compile several bibliographies of Wilde's writings under the pseudonym "Stuart Mason."[6] Unfortunately for him, this writer was also to be convicted of offences under the Criminal Law Amendment Act as Wilde had been.

"Sir,

Mr. Oscar Wilde has been sentenced to two years' imprisonment with hard labour. What for? For being immoral? No. A man may commit adultery with another man's wife or fornication with a painted harlot who plys her filthy trade in the public streets unmolested with impunity. It is because this man has dared to choose another form of satisfying his natural passions the law steps in. Yet he has not injured the State or anybody else against their will.

Why does not the Crown prosecute every boy at a public or private school or half the men in the Universities?

In the latter places "poederism" is as common as fornication, and everybody knows it.

May I say a word about the conduct of the press in this case? *The Daily Chronicle* and yourselves are the only papers which have ever given the poor wretch in prison a fair hearing. Other papers, which a few weeks ago devoted columns to reviews of his splendid plays or books, now scorn him as poison. Because a fellow-creature has fallen, why should they cast stones at him? Are the writers of such articles themselves immaculate in their passions?

---

[5] See above, p. 358.
[6] His *Bibliography of Oscar Wilde* (1914) contains much interesting information. For further details of C. S. Millard (1872-1927), see A. J. A. Symons, *The Quest for Corvo* (1934), pp. 1-3, and Osbert Burdett, *Memory and Imagination* (1935), pp. 104-108.

Appendix E

Prosecuting a man on such a charge as this does not tend to diminish this form of immorality; it rather increases it tenfold.

Yours, &c.,

C. S. M.

29th May, 1895."

Considerable research has now been carried out on the subject by psychologists and psychopathologists of such eminent international reputation as Krafft-Ebing and Bloch. According to their findings, the tendency of modern penologists is to treat the offender in the light of psychology and psychiatry. Homosexual offences are no longer regarded with the same degree of horror as they were in Wilde's time, and one satisfactory feature of this development is that opportunities of blackmail in connexion with this offence have proportionately decreased. If it is no longer customary to describe homosexuality as "vice," homosexual conduct, at least when punished by the law, still carries a certain social stigma with it. But public opinion continues to moderate as more scientific knowledge is brought to bear on the subject and popular education is extended.

"We now look upon homosexuality as a pathological condition," said Lord Dawson of Penn, in a debate in the House of Lords (7th July, 1937). "I am not at all sure that in the future it may not be regarded as an insufficiency disease, and although it is true that the law must take cognizance of it and punish it in order to act as a preventive to potential offenders, the more reasonable view is gradually being adopted that it at any rate has one foot in the realm of disease and it not wholly in the realm of crime." However, there are still many who will agree with the words of the late Lord Atkin, who referred to his judicial experiences in the same debate: "It is not correct to say that these cases . . . are the result of something in the nature of disease . . . they are the result of wicked impulses which, like other wicked impulses, are capable of being controlled . . . they can be checked by advice and by resolution."

A tragic sidelight on this case was reflected a few weeks later, when the Foreign Minister and Leader of the House of Commons, the Marquess of Londonderry (better known by his courtesy title of Viscount Castlereagh), had a dramatic interview with King George IV at Carlton House, in which he made it clear that he was under a delusion that he was about to be prosecuted for this type of offence. "I am a fugitive from justice," the Minister told the King. "I am accused of the same crime as the Bishop of Clogher." There is no evidence to show that Castlereagh had any homosexual inclinations, although he has been credited with them. It is possible, however, that he was being blackmailed by a gang of ruffians who threatened to denounce him as a pederast, and that his mind gave way under the strain. He committed suicide three days later.[2]

Although not so numerous perhaps as in the preceding century, there were plenty enough cases of this description in the later Georgian and Victorian period. Richard Heber, the famous book collector and one of the founders of the Athenæum Club, who represented Oxford University in the House of Commons, was obliged to resign his seat in 1826 as the result of a libel action brought by a Mr. Hartshorn against the editor of a newspaper, in which pointed allusions were made to a supposed intimacy between Heber and Hartshorn's son. As a result, Heber was obliged altogether to withdraw from society, and was still ostracized at the time of his death, a few years later.

In 1833 another M.P. was similarly involved, William John Bankes, who sat for the County of Dorset and was well known to the literary world for his travels in the East. He was accused of having committed an act of indecency with a soldier in a public lavatory outside Westminster Abbey. At his trial, many well-known persons, including the Duke of Wellington, Samuel Rogers, and Dr. Butler, the Master of Harrow, testified as to his good character, with the result that he was acquitted. Some years later, however, in 1841, he was brought before a magistrate for indecently exposing himself in Green Park, and was set at liberty on bail. This time he forfeited his recognizance and withdrew to the Continent, where he died in Venice in 1855.

Similar cases occurred later in the century, and during the earlier part of Wilde's life, before his own prosecution, there were a number of cases involving more or less socially prominent individuals of which he must have had some knowledge.

---

[2] See J. Richardson, *Recollections of the Last Half Century*, vol. I (1855), at p. 283, *et seq.*, and *Private Letters of Princess Lieven to Prince Metternich* (1939), at p. 189.

Appendix E

In 1883 two officials in Dublin Castle, named Cornwall and French, were publicly involved in an extensive homosexual circle. The latter included a Conservative M.P. named De Cobain. In 1889 details of a male brothel patronized by members of society, including the peerage, came to light in the so-called Cleveland Street scandal. This was largely the result of an editorial article in a journal called *The North London Press,* dated 16th November, 1889, in which it was alleged that the house at 19 Cleveland Street, off Tottenham Court Road in London, was frequented by certain aristocrats for homosexual purposes. Names were given, but unfortunately for the editor, he failed to justify the circumstances in regard to one of them, the Earl of Euston, son of the Duke of Grafton. As a result, although the article was in part justified, the editor was sentenced to twelve months' imprisonment by Hawkins, J., at the Old Bailey for criminal libel.[3] It may be added that another member of the nobility whose name had been mentioned in these proceedings, and who was an officer in the Prince of Wales's household, Lord Arthur Somerset, was allowed to leave the country.

Lord Queensberry's action and the resultant trials involving Oscar Wilde served in a measure to focus public attention on the subject, but it was still regarded with feelings akin to horror, and no one except the reporters in the baser journals were expected to write about it. When it was necessary for historians to refer to it in the course of their work, similar feelings were expected to prevail.

In 1866, W. E. H. Lecky, writing in his *History of European Morals,* described what he called "the lowest abyss of unnatural love" as the "deepest and strongest taint of Greek civilization," adding that "my task in describing this aspect of Greek life has been an eminently unpleasant one." John Addington Symonds, who was a contemporary of Lecky, wrote two scientific monographs on the subject, *A Problem in Greek Ethics* (1873) and *A Problem in Modern Ethics* (1891), but, fearing prosecution, he limited the editions to a few privately printed copies. Symonds pressed Oscar Browning to devote some research to the subject, but Browning deemed it prudent to decline the invitation.[4] On the other hand, Havelock Ellis, with whom Symonds had collaborated in the original first volume of the celebrated *Studies in the Psychology of Sex,* which dealt with inversion, published a sufficient number of

---

[3] *Reg.* v. *Parke,* reported in *The Times,* 16th-17th January, 1890. See also Frank Harris's comments on this curious case in his autobiography (ed. Grant Richards), at pp. 240-241.

[4] H. E. Wortham, *Oscar Browning,* 261.

Index

Index

INDEX

A CATALOG OF SELECTED
DOVER BOOKS
IN ALL FIELDS OF INTEREST

A CATALOG OF SELECTED DOVER
BOOKS IN ALL FIELDS OF INTEREST

CONCERNING THE SPIRITUAL IN ART, Wassily Kandinsky. Pioneering work by father of abstract art. Thoughts on color theory, nature of art. Analysis of earlier masters. 12 illustrations. 80pp. of text. 5⅜ x 8½. 23411-8 Pa. $3.95

ANIMALS: 1,419 Copyright-Free Illustrations of Mammals, Birds, Fish, Insects, etc., Jim Harter (ed.). Clear wood engravings present, in extremely lifelike poses, over 1,000 species of animals. One of the most extensive pictorial sourcebooks of its kind. Captions. Index. 284pp. 9 x 12. 23766-4 Pa. $12.95

CELTIC ART: The Methods of Construction, George Bain. Simple geometric techniques for making Celtic interlacements, spirals, Kells-type initials, animals, humans, etc. Over 500 illustrations. 160pp. 9 x 12. (USO) 22923-8 Pa. $9.95

AN ATLAS OF ANATOMY FOR ARTISTS, Fritz Schider. Most thorough reference work on art anatomy in the world. Hundreds of illustrations, including selections from works by Vesalius, Leonardo, Goya, Ingres, Michelangelo, others. 593 illustrations. 192pp. 7⅛ x 10¼. 20241-0 Pa. $9.95

CELTIC HAND STROKE-BY-STROKE (Irish Half-Uncial from "The Book of Kells"): An Arthur Baker Calligraphy Manual, Arthur Baker. Complete guide to creating each letter of the alphabet in distinctive Celtic manner. Covers hand position, strokes, pens, inks, paper, more. Illustrated. 48pp. 8¼ x 11. 24336-2 Pa. $3.95

EASY ORIGAMI, John Montroll. Charming collection of 32 projects (hat, cup, pelican, piano, swan, many more) specially designed for the novice origami hobbyist. Clearly illustrated easy-to-follow instructions insure that even beginning papercrafters will achieve successful results. 48pp. 8¼ x 11. 27298-2 Pa. $3.50

THE COMPLETE BOOK OF BIRDHOUSE CONSTRUCTION FOR WOODWORKERS, Scott D. Campbell. Detailed instructions, illustrations, tables. Also data on bird habitat and instinct patterns. Bibliography. 3 tables. 63 illustrations in 15 figures. 48pp. 5¼ x 8½. 24407-5 Pa. $2.50

BLOOMINGDALE'S ILLUSTRATED 1886 CATALOG: Fashions, Dry Goods and Housewares, Bloomingdale Brothers. Famed merchants' extremely rare catalog depicting about 1,700 products: clothing, housewares, firearms, dry goods, jewelry, more. Invaluable for dating, identifying vintage items. Also, copyright-free graphics for artists, designers. Co-published with Henry Ford Museum & Greenfield Village. 160pp. 8¼ x 11. 25780-0 Pa. $10.95

HISTORIC COSTUME IN PICTURES, Braun & Schneider. Over 1,450 costumed figures in clearly detailed engravings–from dawn of civilization to end of 19th century. Captions. Many folk costumes. 256pp. 8⅜ x 11¾. 23150-X Pa. $12.95

CATALOG OF DOVER BOOKS

STICKLEY CRAFTSMAN FURNITURE CATALOGS, Gustav Stickley and L. & J. G. Stickley. Beautiful, functional furniture in two authentic catalogs from 1910. 594 illustrations, including 277 photos, show settles, rockers, armchairs, reclining chairs, bookcases, desks, tables. 183pp. 6½ x 9¼. 23838-5 Pa. $9.95

AMERICAN LOCOMOTIVES IN HISTORIC PHOTOGRAPHS: 1858 to 1949, Ron Ziel (ed.). A rare collection of 126 meticulously detailed official photographs, called "builder portraits," of American locomotives that majestically chronicle the rise of steam locomotive power in America. Introduction. Detailed captions. xi + 129pp. 9 x 12. 27393-8 Pa. $12.95

AMERICA'S LIGHTHOUSES: An Illustrated History, Francis Ross Holland, Jr. Delightfully written, profusely illustrated fact-filled survey of over 200 American lighthouses since 1716. History, anecdotes, technological advances, more. 240pp. 8 x 10¾. 25576-X Pa. $12.95

TOWARDS A NEW ARCHITECTURE, Le Corbusier. Pioneering manifesto by founder of "International School." Technical and aesthetic theories, views of industry, economics, relation of form to function, "mass-production split" and much more. Profusely illustrated. 320pp. 6⅛ x 9¼. (USO) 25023-7 Pa. $9.95

HOW THE OTHER HALF LIVES, Jacob Riis. Famous journalistic record, exposing poverty and degradation of New York slums around 1900, by major social reformer. 100 striking and influential photographs. 233pp. 10 x 7⅞. 22012-5 Pa. $10.95

FRUIT KEY AND TWIG KEY TO TREES AND SHRUBS, William M. Harlow. One of the handiest and most widely used identification aids. Fruit key covers 120 deciduous and evergreen species; twig key 160 deciduous species. Easily used. Over 300 photographs. 126pp. 5⅜ x 8½. 20511-8 Pa. $3.95

COMMON BIRD SONGS, Dr. Donald J. Borror. Songs of 60 most common U.S. birds: robins, sparrows, cardinals, bluejays, finches, more—arranged in order of increasing complexity. Up to 9 variations of songs of each species. Cassette and manual 99911-4 $8.95

ORCHIDS AS HOUSE PLANTS, Rebecca Tyson Northen. Grow cattleyas and many other kinds of orchids—in a window, in a case, or under artificial light. 63 illustrations. 148pp. 5⅜ x 8½. 23261-1 Pa. $4.95

MONSTER MAZES, Dave Phillips. Masterful mazes at four levels of difficulty. Avoid deadly perils and evil creatures to find magical treasures. Solutions for all 32 exciting illustrated puzzles. 48pp. 8¼ x 11. 26005-4 Pa. $2.95

MOZART'S DON GIOVANNI (DOVER OPERA LIBRETTO SERIES), Wolfgang Amadeus Mozart. Introduced and translated by Ellen H. Bleiler. Standard Italian libretto, with complete English translation. Convenient and thoroughly portable—an ideal companion for reading along with a recording or the performance itself. Introduction. List of characters. Plot summary. 121pp. 5¼ x 8½. 24944-1 Pa. $2.95

TECHNICAL MANUAL AND DICTIONARY OF CLASSICAL BALLET, Gail Grant. Defines, explains, comments on steps, movements, poses and concepts. 15-page pictorial section. Basic book for student, viewer. 127pp. 5⅜ x 8½. 21843-0 Pa. $4.95

BRASS INSTRUMENTS: Their History and Development, Anthony Baines. Authoritative, updated survey of the evolution of trumpets, trombones, bugles, cornets, French horns, tubas and other brass wind instruments. Over 140 illustrations and 48 music examples. Corrected and updated by author. New preface. Bibliography. 320pp. 5⅜ x 8½. 27574-4 Pa. $9.95

HOLLYWOOD GLAMOR PORTRAITS, John Kobal (ed.). 145 photos from 1926-49. Harlow, Gable, Bogart, Bacall; 94 stars in all. Full background on photographers, technical aspects. 160pp. 8⅜ x 11¼. 23352-9 Pa. $12.95

MAX AND MORITZ, Wilhelm Busch. Great humor classic in both German and English. Also 10 other works: "Cat and Mouse," "Plisch and Plumm," etc. 216pp. 5⅜ x 8½. 20181-3 Pa. $6.95

THE RAVEN AND OTHER FAVORITE POEMS, Edgar Allan Poe. Over 40 of the author's most memorable poems: "The Bells," "Ulalume," "Israfel," "To Helen," "The Conqueror Worm," "Eldorado," "Annabel Lee," many more. Alphabetic lists of titles and first lines. 64pp. 5³⁄₁₆ x 8¼. 26685-0 Pa. $1.00

PERSONAL MEMOIRS OF U. S. GRANT, Ulysses Simpson Grant. Intelligent, deeply moving firsthand account of Civil War campaigns, considered by many the finest military memoirs ever written. Includes letters, historic photographs, maps and more. 528pp. 6⅛ x 9¼. 28587-1 Pa. $11.95

AMULETS AND SUPERSTITIONS, E. A. Wallis Budge. Comprehensive discourse on origin, powers of amulets in many ancient cultures: Arab, Persian Babylonian, Assyrian, Egyptian, Gnostic, Hebrew, Phoenician, Syriac, etc. Covers cross, swastika, crucifix, seals, rings, stones, etc. 584pp. 5⅜ x 8½. 23573-4 Pa. $12.95

RUSSIAN STORIES/PYCCKNE PACCKA3bl: A Dual-Language Book, edited by Gleb Struve. Twelve tales by such masters as Chekhov, Tolstoy, Dostoevsky, Pushkin, others. Excellent word-for-word English translations on facing pages, plus teaching and study aids, Russian/English vocabulary, biographical/critical introductions, more. 416pp. 5⅜ x 8½. 26244-8 Pa. $8.95

PHILADELPHIA THEN AND NOW: 60 Sites Photographed in the Past and Present, Kenneth Finkel and Susan Oyama. Rare photographs of City Hall, Logan Square, Independence Hall, Betsy Ross House, other landmarks juxtaposed with contemporary views. Captures changing face of historic city. Introduction. Captions. 128pp. 8¼ x 11. 25790-8 Pa. $9.95

AIA ARCHITECTURAL GUIDE TO NASSAU AND SUFFOLK COUNTIES, LONG ISLAND, The American Institute of Architects, Long Island Chapter, and the Society for the Preservation of Long Island Antiquities. Comprehensive, well-researched and generously illustrated volume brings to life over three centuries of Long Island's great architectural heritage. More than 240 photographs with authoritative, extensively detailed captions. 176pp. 8¼ x 11. 26946-9 Pa. $14.95

NORTH AMERICAN INDIAN LIFE: Customs and Traditions of 23 Tribes, Elsie Clews Parsons (ed.). 27 fictionalized essays by noted anthropologists examine religion, customs, government, additional facets of life among the Winnebago, Crow, Zuni, Eskimo, other tribes. 480pp. 6⅛ x 9¼. 27377-6 Pa. $10.95

FRANK LLOYD WRIGHT'S HOLLYHOCK HOUSE, Donald Hoffmann. Lavishly illustrated, carefully documented study of one of Wright's most controversial residential designs. Over 120 photographs, floor plans, elevations, etc. Detailed perceptive text by noted Wright scholar. Index. 128pp. 9¼ x 10¾. 27133-1 Pa. $11.95

THE MALE AND FEMALE FIGURE IN MOTION: 60 Classic Photographic Sequences, Eadweard Muybridge. 60 true-action photographs of men and women walking, running, climbing, bending, turning, etc., reproduced from rare 19th-century masterpiece. vi + 121pp. 9 x 12. 24745-7 Pa. $10.95

1001 QUESTIONS ANSWERED ABOUT THE SEASHORE, N. J. Berrill and Jacquelyn Berrill. Queries answered about dolphins, sea snails, sponges, starfish, fishes, shore birds, many others. Covers appearance, breeding, growth, feeding, much more. 305pp. 5¼ x 8¼. 23366-9 Pa. $8.95

GUIDE TO OWL WATCHING IN NORTH AMERICA, Donald S. Heintzelman. Superb guide offers complete data and descriptions of 19 species: barn owl, screech owl, snowy owl, many more. Expert coverage of owl-watching equipment, conservation, migrations and invasions, etc. Guide to observing sites. 84 illustrations. xiii + 193pp. 5⅜ x 8½. 27344-X Pa. $8.95

MEDICINAL AND OTHER USES OF NORTH AMERICAN PLANTS: A Historical Survey with Special Reference to the Eastern Indian Tribes, Charlotte Erichsen-Brown. Chronological historical citations document 500 years of usage of plants, trees, shrubs native to eastern Canada, northeastern U.S. Also complete identifying information. 343 illustrations. 544pp. 6½ x 9¼. 25951-X Pa. $12.95

STORYBOOK MAZES, Dave Phillips. 23 stories and mazes on two-page spreads: Wizard of Oz, Treasure Island, Robin Hood, etc. Solutions. 64pp. 8¼ x 11. 23628-5 Pa. $2.95

NEGRO FOLK MUSIC, U.S.A., Harold Courlander. Noted folklorist's scholarly yet readable analysis of rich and varied musical tradition. Includes authentic versions of over 40 folk songs. Valuable bibliography and discography. xi + 324pp. 5⅜ x 8½. 27350-4 Pa. $9.95

MOVIE-STAR PORTRAITS OF THE FORTIES, John Kobal (ed.). 163 glamor, studio photos of 106 stars of the 1940s: Rita Hayworth, Ava Gardner, Marlon Brando, Clark Gable, many more. 176pp. 8⅜ x 11¼. 23546-7 Pa. $12.95

BENCHLEY LOST AND FOUND, Robert Benchley. Finest humor from early 30s, about pet peeves, child psychologists, post office and others. Mostly unavailable elsewhere. 73 illustrations by Peter Arno and others. 183pp. 5⅜ x 8½. 22410-4 Pa. $6.95

YEKL and THE IMPORTED BRIDEGROOM AND OTHER STORIES OF YIDDISH NEW YORK, Abraham Cahan. Film Hester Street based on Yekl (1896). Novel, other stories among first about Jewish immigrants on N.Y.'s East Side. 240pp. 5⅜ x 8½. 22427-9 Pa. $6.95

SELECTED POEMS, Walt Whitman. Generous sampling from *Leaves of Grass.* Twenty-four poems include "I Hear America Singing," "Song of the Open Road," "I Sing the Body Electric," "When Lilacs Last in the Dooryard Bloom'd," "O Captain! My Captain!"—all reprinted from an authoritative edition. Lists of titles and first lines. 128pp. 5³⁄₁₆ x 8¼. 26878-0 Pa. $1.00

THE BEST TALES OF HOFFMANN, E. T. A. Hoffmann. 10 of Hoffmann's most important stories: "Nutcracker and the King of Mice," "The Golden Flowerpot," etc. 458pp. 5⅜ x 8½. 21793-0 Pa. $9.95

FROM FETISH TO GOD IN ANCIENT EGYPT, E. A. Wallis Budge. Rich detailed survey of Egyptian conception of "God" and gods, magic, cult of animals, Osiris, more. Also, superb English translations of hymns and legends. 240 illustrations. 545pp. 5⅜ x 8½. 25803-3 Pa. $13.95

FRENCH STORIES/CONTES FRANÇAIS: A Dual-Language Book, Wallace Fowlie. Ten stories by French masters, Voltaire to Camus: "Micromegas" by Voltaire; "The Atheist's Mass" by Balzac; "Minuet" by de Maupassant; "The Guest" by Camus, six more. Excellent English translations on facing pages. Also French-English vocabulary list, exercises, more. 352pp. 5⅜ x 8½. 26443-2 Pa. $8.95

CHICAGO AT THE TURN OF THE CENTURY IN PHOTOGRAPHS: 122 Historic Views from the Collections of the Chicago Historical Society, Larry A. Viskochil. Rare large-format prints offer detailed views of City Hall, State Street, the Loop, Hull House, Union Station, many other landmarks, circa 1904-1913. Introduction. Captions. Maps. 144pp. 9⅜ x 12¼. 24656-6 Pa. $12.95

OLD BROOKLYN IN EARLY PHOTOGRAPHS, 1865-1929, William Lee Younger. Luna Park, Gravesend race track, construction of Grand Army Plaza, moving of Hotel Brighton, etc. 157 previously unpublished photographs. 165pp. 8⅞ x 11¾. 23587-4 Pa. $13.95

THE MYTHS OF THE NORTH AMERICAN INDIANS, Lewis Spence. Rich anthology of the myths and legends of the Algonquins, Iroquois, Pawnees and Sioux, prefaced by an extensive historical and ethnological commentary. 36 illustrations. 480pp. 5⅜ x 8½. 25967-6 Pa. $8.95

AN ENCYCLOPEDIA OF BATTLES: Accounts of Over 1,560 Battles from 1479 B.C. to the Present, David Eggenberger. Essential details of every major battle in recorded history from the first battle of Megiddo in 1479 B.C. to Grenada in 1984. List of Battle Maps. New Appendix covering the years 1967-1984. Index. 99 illustrations. 544pp. 6½ x 9¼. 24913-1 Pa. $14.95

SAILING ALONE AROUND THE WORLD, Captain Joshua Slocum. First man to sail around the world, alone, in small boat. One of great feats of seamanship told in delightful manner. 67 illustrations. 294pp. 5⅜ x 8½. 20326-3 Pa. $5.95

ANARCHISM AND OTHER ESSAYS, Emma Goldman. Powerful, penetrating, prophetic essays on direct action, role of minorities, prison reform, puritan hypocrisy, violence, etc. 271pp. 5⅜ x 8½. 22484-8 Pa. $6.95

MYTHS OF THE HINDUS AND BUDDHISTS, Ananda K. Coomaraswamy and Sister Nivedita. Great stories of the epics; deeds of Krishna, Shiva, taken from puranas, Vedas, folk tales; etc. 32 illustrations. 400pp. 5⅜ x 8½. 21759-0 Pa. $10.95

BEYOND PSYCHOLOGY, Otto Rank. Fear of death, desire of immortality, nature of sexuality, social organization, creativity, according to Rankian system. 291pp. 5⅜ x 8½. 20485-5 Pa. $8.95

A THEOLOGICO-POLITICAL TREATISE, Benedict Spinoza. Also contains unfinished Political Treatise. Great classic on religious liberty, theory of government on common consent. R. Elwes translation. Total of 421pp. 5⅜ x 8½. 20249-6 Pa. $9.95

CATALOG OF DOVER BOOKS

MY BONDAGE AND MY FREEDOM, Frederick Douglass. Born a slave, Douglass became outspoken force in antislavery movement. The best of Douglass' autobiographies. Graphic description of slave life. 464pp. 5⅜ x 8½. 22457-0 Pa. $8.95

FOLLOWING THE EQUATOR: A Journey Around the World, Mark Twain. Fascinating humorous account of 1897 voyage to Hawaii, Australia, India, New Zealand, etc. Ironic, bemused reports on peoples, customs, climate, flora and fauna, politics, much more. 197 illustrations. 720pp. 5⅜ x 8½.   26113-1 Pa. $15.95

THE PEOPLE CALLED SHAKERS, Edward D. Andrews. Definitive study of Shakers: origins, beliefs, practices, dances, social organization, furniture and crafts, etc. 33 illustrations. 351pp. 5⅜ x 8½.   21081-2 Pa. $8.95

THE MYTHS OF GREECE AND ROME, H. A. Guerber. A classic of mythology, generously illustrated, long prized for its simple, graphic, accurate retelling of the principal myths of Greece and Rome, and for its commentary on their origins and significance. With 64 illustrations by Michelangelo, Raphael, Titian, Rubens, Canova, Bernini and others. 480pp. 5⅜ x 8½.   27584-1 Pa. $9.95

PSYCHOLOGY OF MUSIC, Carl E. Seashore. Classic work discusses music as a medium from psychological viewpoint. Clear treatment of physical acoustics, auditory apparatus, sound perception, development of musical skills, nature of musical feeling, host of other topics. 88 figures. 408pp. 5⅜ x 8½.   21851-1 Pa. $10.95

THE PHILOSOPHY OF HISTORY, Georg W. Hegel. Great classic of Western thought develops concept that history is not chance but rational process, the evolution of freedom. 457pp. 5⅜ x 8½.   20112-0 Pa. $9.95

THE BOOK OF TEA, Kakuzo Okakura. Minor classic of the Orient: entertaining, charming explanation, interpretation of traditional Japanese culture in terms of tea ceremony. 94pp. 5⅜ x 8½.   20070-1 Pa. $3.95

LIFE IN ANCIENT EGYPT, Adolf Erman. Fullest, most thorough, detailed older account with much not in more recent books, domestic life, religion, magic, medicine, commerce, much more. Many illustrations reproduce tomb paintings, carvings, hieroglyphs, etc. 597pp. 5⅜ x 8½.   22632-8 Pa. $11.95

SUNDIALS, Their Theory and Construction, Albert Waugh. Far and away the best, most thorough coverage of ideas, mathematics concerned, types, construction, adjusting anywhere. Simple, nontechnical treatment allows even children to build several of these dials. Over 100 illustrations. 230pp. 5⅜ x 8½.   22947-5 Pa. $7.95

DYNAMICS OF FLUIDS IN POROUS MEDIA, Jacob Bear. For advanced students of ground water hydrology, soil mechanics and physics, drainage and irrigation engineering, and more. 335 illustrations. Exercises, with answers. 784pp. 6⅛ x 9¼.   65675-6 Pa. $19.95

SONGS OF EXPERIENCE: Facsimile Reproduction with 26 Plates in Full Color, William Blake. 26 full-color plates from a rare 1826 edition. Includes "TheTyger," "London," "Holy Thursday," and other poems. Printed text of poems. 48pp. 5¼ x 7.   24636-1 Pa. $4.95

OLD-TIME VIGNETTES IN FULL COLOR, Carol Belanger Grafton (ed.). Over 390 charming, often sentimental illustrations, selected from archives of Victorian graphics—pretty women posing, children playing, food, flowers, kittens and puppies, smiling cherubs, birds and butterflies, much more. All copyright-free. 48pp. 9¼ x 12¼.   27269-9 Pa. $7.95

PERSPECTIVE FOR ARTISTS, Rex Vicat Cole. Depth, perspective of sky and sea, shadows, much more, not usually covered. 391 diagrams, 81 reproductions of drawings and paintings. 279pp. 5⅜ x 8½. 22487-2 Pa. $7.95

DRAWING THE LIVING FIGURE, Joseph Sheppard. Innovative approach to artistic anatomy focuses on specifics of surface anatomy, rather than muscles and bones. Over 170 drawings of live models in front, back and side views, and in widely varying poses. Accompanying diagrams. 177 illustrations. Introduction. Index. 144pp. 8⅜ x11¼. 26723-7 Pa. $8.95

GOTHIC AND OLD ENGLISH ALPHABETS: 100 Complete Fonts, Dan X. Solo. Add power, elegance to posters, signs, other graphics with 100 stunning copyright-free alphabets: Blackstone, Dolbey, Germania, 97 more–including many lower-case, numerals, punctuation marks. 104pp. 8⅛ x 11. 24695-7 Pa. $8.95

HOW TO DO BEADWORK, Mary White. Fundamental book on craft from simple projects to five-bead chains and woven works. 106 illustrations. 142pp. 5⅜ x 8. 20697-1 Pa. $4.95

THE BOOK OF WOOD CARVING, Charles Marshall Sayers. Finest book for beginners discusses fundamentals and offers 34 designs. "Absolutely first rate . . . well thought out and well executed."–E. J. Tangerman. 118pp. 7¾ x 10⅝. 23654-4 Pa. $6.95

ILLUSTRATED CATALOG OF CIVIL WAR MILITARY GOODS: Union Army Weapons, Insignia, Uniform Accessories, and Other Equipment, Schuyler, Hartley, and Graham. Rare, profusely illustrated 1846 catalog includes Union Army uniform and dress regulations, arms and ammunition, coats, insignia, flags, swords, rifles, etc. 226 illustrations. 160pp. 9 x 12. 24939-5 Pa. $10.95

WOMEN'S FASHIONS OF THE EARLY 1900s: An Unabridged Republication of "New York Fashions, 1909," National Cloak & Suit Co. Rare catalog of mail-order fashions documents women's and children's clothing styles shortly after the turn of the century. Captions offer full descriptions, prices. Invaluable resource for fashion, costume historians. Approximately 725 illustrations. 128pp. 8⅜ x 11¼. 27276-1 Pa. $11.95

THE 1912 AND 1915 GUSTAV STICKLEY FURNITURE CATALOGS, Gustav Stickley. With over 200 detailed illustrations and descriptions, these two catalogs are essential reading and reference materials and identification guides for Stickley furniture. Captions cite materials, dimensions and prices. 112pp. 6½ x 9¼. 26676-1 Pa. $9.95

EARLY AMERICAN LOCOMOTIVES, John H. White, Jr. Finest locomotive engravings from early 19th century: historical (1804–74), main-line (after 1870), special, foreign, etc. 147 plates. 142pp. 11⅜ x 8¼. 22772-3 Pa. $10.95

THE TALL SHIPS OF TODAY IN PHOTOGRAPHS, Frank O. Braynard. Lavishly illustrated tribute to nearly 100 majestic contemporary sailing vessels: Amerigo Vespucci, Clearwater, Constitution, Eagle, Mayflower, Sea Cloud, Victory, many more. Authoritative captions provide statistics, background on each ship. 190 black-and-white photographs and illustrations. Introduction. 128pp. 8⅞ x 11¾. 27163-3 Pa. $13.95

EARLY NINETEENTH-CENTURY CRAFTS AND TRADES, Peter Stockham (ed.). Extremely rare 1807 volume describes to youngsters the crafts and trades of the day: brickmaker, weaver, dressmaker, bookbinder, ropemaker, saddler, many more. Quaint prose, charming illustrations for each craft. 20 black-and-white line illustrations. 192pp. 4⅝ x 6. 27293-1 Pa. $4.95

VICTORIAN FASHIONS AND COSTUMES FROM HARPER'S BAZAR, 1867–1898, Stella Blum (ed.). Day costumes, evening wear, sports clothes, shoes, hats, other accessories in over 1,000 detailed engravings. 320pp. 9⅜ x 12¼. 22990-4 Pa. $14.95

GUSTAV STICKLEY, THE CRAFTSMAN, Mary Ann Smith. Superb study surveys broad scope of Stickley's achievement, especially in architecture. Design philosophy, rise and fall of the Craftsman empire, descriptions and floor plans for many Craftsman houses, more. 86 black-and-white halftones. 31 line illustrations. Introduction 208pp. 6½ x 9¼. 27210-9 Pa. $9.95

THE LONG ISLAND RAIL ROAD IN EARLY PHOTOGRAPHS, Ron Ziel. Over 220 rare photos, informative text document origin (1844) and development of rail service on Long Island. Vintage views of early trains, locomotives, stations, passengers, crews, much more. Captions. 8⅞ x 11¾. 26301-0 Pa. $13.95

THE BOOK OF OLD SHIPS: From Egyptian Galleys to Clipper Ships, Henry B. Culver. Superb, authoritative history of sailing vessels, with 80 magnificent line illustrations. Galley, bark, caravel, longship, whaler, many more. Detailed, informative text on each vessel by noted naval historian. Introduction. 256pp. 5⅜ x 8½. 27332-6 Pa. $7.95

TEN BOOKS ON ARCHITECTURE, Vitruvius. The most important book ever written on architecture. Early Roman aesthetics, technology, classical orders, site selection, all other aspects. Morgan translation. 331pp. 5⅜ x 8½. 20645-9 Pa. $8.95

THE HUMAN FIGURE IN MOTION, Eadweard Muybridge. More than 4,500 stopped-action photos, in action series, showing undraped men, women, children jumping, lying down, throwing, sitting, wrestling, carrying, etc. 390pp. 7⅞ x 10⅝. 20204-6 Clothbd. $25.95

TREES OF THE EASTERN AND CENTRAL UNITED STATES AND CANADA, William M. Harlow. Best one-volume guide to 140 trees. Full descriptions, woodlore, range, etc. Over 600 illustrations. Handy size. 288pp. 4½ x 6⅜. 20395-6 Pa. $6.95

SONGS OF WESTERN BIRDS, Dr. Donald J. Borror. Complete song and call repertoire of 60 western species, including flycatchers, juncoes, cactus wrens, many more—includes fully illustrated booklet. Cassette and manual 99913-0 $8.95

GROWING AND USING HERBS AND SPICES, Milo Miloradovich. Versatile handbook provides all the information needed for cultivation and use of all the herbs and spices available in North America. 4 illustrations. Index. Glossary. 236pp. 5⅜ x 8½. 25058-X Pa. $6.95

BIG BOOK OF MAZES AND LABYRINTHS, Walter Shepherd. 50 mazes and labyrinths in all—classical, solid, ripple, and more—in one great volume. Perfect inexpensive puzzler for clever youngsters. Full solutions. 112pp. 8⅛ x 11. 22951-3 Pa. $4.95

CATALOG OF DOVER BOOKS

PIANO TUNING, J. Cree Fischer. Clearest, best book for beginner, amateur. Simple repairs, raising dropped notes, tuning by easy method of flattened fifths. No previous skills needed. 4 illustrations. 201pp. 5⅜ x 8½.   23267-0 Pa. $6.95

A SOURCE BOOK IN THEATRICAL HISTORY, A. M. Nagler. Contemporary observers on acting, directing, make-up, costuming, stage props, machinery, scene design, from Ancient Greece to Chekhov. 611pp. 5⅜ x 8½.   20515-0 Pa. $12.95

THE COMPLETE NONSENSE OF EDWARD LEAR, Edward Lear. All nonsense limericks, zany alphabets, Owl and Pussycat, songs, nonsense botany, etc., illustrated by Lear. Total of 320pp. 5⅜ x 8½. (USO)   20167-8 Pa. $6.95

VICTORIAN PARLOUR POETRY: An Annotated Anthology, Michael R. Turner. 117 gems by Longfellow, Tennyson, Browning, many lesser-known poets. "The Village Blacksmith," "Curfew Must Not Ring Tonight," "Only a Baby Small," dozens more, often difficult to find elsewhere. Index of poets, titles, first lines. xxiii + 325pp. 5⅜ x 8¼.   27044-0 Pa. $8.95

DUBLINERS, James Joyce. Fifteen stories offer vivid, tightly focused observations of the lives of Dublin's poorer classes. At least one, "The Dead," is considered a masterpiece. Reprinted complete and unabridged from standard edition. 160pp. 5⁵⁄₁₆ x 8¼.
26870-5 Pa. $1.00

THE HAUNTED MONASTERY and THE CHINESE MAZE MURDERS, Robert van Gulik. Two full novels by van Gulik, set in 7th-century China, continue adventures of Judge Dee and his companions. An evil Taoist monastery, seemingly supernatural events; overgrown topiary maze hides strange crimes. 27 illustrations. 328pp. 5⅜ x 8½.   23502-5 Pa. $8.95

THE BOOK OF THE SACRED MAGIC OF ABRAMELIN THE MAGE, translated by S. MacGregor Mathers. Medieval manuscript of ceremonial magic. Basic document in Aleister Crowley, Golden Dawn groups. 268pp. 5⅜ x 8½.
23211-5 Pa. $8.95

NEW RUSSIAN-ENGLISH AND ENGLISH-RUSSIAN DICTIONARY, M. A. O'Brien. This is a remarkably handy Russian dictionary, containing a surprising amount of information, including over 70,000 entries. 366pp. 4½ x 6⅛.
20208-9 Pa. $9.95

HISTORIC HOMES OF THE AMERICAN PRESIDENTS, Second, Revised Edition, Irvin Haas. A traveler's guide to American Presidential homes, most open to the public, depicting and describing homes occupied by every American President from George Washington to George Bush. With visiting hours, admission charges, travel routes. 175 photographs. Index. 160pp. 8¼ x 11.   26751-2 Pa. $11.95

NEW YORK IN THE FORTIES, Andreas Feininger. 162 brilliant photographs by the well-known photographer, formerly with *Life* magazine. Commuters, shoppers, Times Square at night, much else from city at its peak. Captions by John von Hartz. 181pp. 9¼ x 10¾.   23585-8 Pa. $12.95

INDIAN SIGN LANGUAGE, William Tomkins. Over 525 signs developed by Sioux and other tribes. Written instructions and diagrams. Also 290 pictographs. 111pp. 6⅛ x 9¼.   22029-X Pa. $3.95

CATALOG OF DOVER BOOKS

ANATOMY: A Complete Guide for Artists, Joseph Sheppard. A master of figure drawing shows artists how to render human anatomy convincingly. Over 460 illustrations. 224pp. 8⅜ x 11¼. 27279-6 Pa. $10.95

MEDIEVAL CALLIGRAPHY: Its History and Technique, Marc Drogin. Spirited history, comprehensive instruction manual covers 13 styles (ca. 4th century thru 15th). Excellent photographs; directions for duplicating medieval techniques with modern tools. 224pp. 8⅜ x 11¼. 26142-5 Pa. $12.95

DRIED FLOWERS: How to Prepare Them, Sarah Whitlock and Martha Rankin. Complete instructions on how to use silica gel, meal and borax, perlite aggregate, sand and borax, glycerine and water to create attractive permanent flower arrangements. 12 illustrations. 32pp. 5⅜ x 8½. 21802-3 Pa. $1.00

EASY-TO-MAKE BIRD FEEDERS FOR WOODWORKERS, Scott D. Campbell. Detailed, simple-to-use guide for designing, constructing, caring for and using feeders. Text, illustrations for 12 classic and contemporary designs. 96pp. 5⅜ x 8½. 25847-5 Pa. $2.95

SCOTTISH WONDER TALES FROM MYTH AND LEGEND, Donald A. Mackenzie. 16 lively tales tell of giants rumbling down mountainsides, of a magic wand that turns stone pillars into warriors, of gods and goddesses, evil hags, powerful forces and more. 240pp. 5⅜ x 8½. 29677-6 Pa. $6.95

THE HISTORY OF UNDERCLOTHES, C. Willett Cunnington and Phyllis Cunnington. Fascinating, well-documented survey covering six centuries of English undergarments, enhanced with over 100 illustrations: 12th-century laced-up bodice, footed long drawers (1795), 19th-century bustles, 19th-century corsets for men, Victorian "bust improvers," much more. 272pp. 5⅝ x 8¼. 27124-2 Pa. $9.95

ARTS AND CRAFTS FURNITURE: The Complete Brooks Catalog of 1912, Brooks Manufacturing Co. Photos and detailed descriptions of more than 150 now very collectible furniture designs from the Arts and Crafts movement depict davenports, settees, buffets, desks, tables, chairs, bedsteads, dressers and more, all built of solid, quarter-sawed oak. Invaluable for students and enthusiasts of antiques, Americana and the decorative arts. 80pp. 6½ x 9¼. 27471-3 Pa. $8.95

HOW WE INVENTED THE AIRPLANE: An Illustrated History, Orville Wright. Fascinating firsthand account covers early experiments, construction of planes and motors, first flights, much more. Introduction and commentary by Fred C. Kelly. 76 photographs. 96pp. 8¼ x 11. 25662-6 Pa. $8.95

THE ARTS OF THE SAILOR: Knotting, Splicing and Ropework, Hervey Garrett Smith. Indispensable shipboard reference covers tools, basic knots and useful hitches; handsewing and canvas work, more. Over 100 illustrations. Delightful reading for sea lovers. 256pp. 5⅜ x 8½. 26440-8 Pa. $7.95

FRANK LLOYD WRIGHT'S FALLINGWATER: The House and Its History, Second, Revised Edition, Donald Hoffmann. A total revision–both in text and illustrations–of the standard document on Fallingwater, the boldest, most personal architectural statement of Wright's mature years, updated with valuable new material from the recently opened Frank Lloyd Wright Archives. "Fascinating"–*The New York Times*. 116 illustrations. 128pp. 9¼ x 10¾. 27430-6 Pa. $11.95

CATALOG OF DOVER BOOKS

PHOTOGRAPHIC SKETCHBOOK OF THE CIVIL WAR, Alexander Gardner. 100 photos taken on field during the Civil War. Famous shots of Manassas Harper's Ferry, Lincoln, Richmond, slave pens, etc. 244pp. 10⅝ x 8¼.   22731-6 Pa. $9.95

FIVE ACRES AND INDEPENDENCE, Maurice G. Kains. Great back-to-the-land classic explains basics of self-sufficient farming. The one book to get. 95 illustrations. 397pp. 5⅜ x 8½.   20974-1 Pa. $7.95

SONGS OF EASTERN BIRDS, Dr. Donald J. Borror. Songs and calls of 60 species most common to eastern U.S.: warblers, woodpeckers, flycatchers, thrushes, larks, many more in high-quality recording.   Cassette and manual 99912-2 $9.95

A MODERN HERBAL, Margaret Grieve. Much the fullest, most exact, most useful compilation of herbal material. Gigantic alphabetical encyclopedia, from aconite to zedoary, gives botanical information, medical properties, folklore, economic uses, much else. Indispensable to serious reader. 161 illustrations. 888pp. 6½ x 9¼. 2-vol. set. (USO)   Vol. I: 22798-7 Pa. $9.95
Vol. II: 22799-5 Pa. $9.95

HIDDEN TREASURE MAZE BOOK, Dave Phillips. Solve 34 challenging mazes accompanied by heroic tales of adventure. Evil dragons, people-eating plants, blood-thirsty giants, many more dangerous adversaries lurk at every twist and turn. 34 mazes, stories, solutions. 48pp. 8¼ x 11.   24566-7 Pa. $2.95

LETTERS OF W. A. MOZART, Wolfgang A. Mozart. Remarkable letters show bawdy wit, humor, imagination, musical insights, contemporary musical world; includes some letters from Leopold Mozart. 276pp. 5⅜ x 8½.   22859-2 Pa. $7.95

BASIC PRINCIPLES OF CLASSICAL BALLET, Agrippina Vaganova. Great Russian theoretician, teacher explains methods for teaching classical ballet. 118 illustrations. 175pp. 5⅜ x 8½.   22036-2 Pa. $5.95

THE JUMPING FROG, Mark Twain. Revenge edition. The original story of The Celebrated Jumping Frog of Calaveras County, a hapless French translation, and Twain's hilarious "retranslation" from the French. 12 illustrations. 66pp. 5⅜ x 8½.   22686-7 Pa. $3.95

BEST REMEMBERED POEMS, Martin Gardner (ed.). The 126 poems in this superb collection of 19th- and 20th-century British and American verse range from Shelley's "To a Skylark" to the impassioned "Renascence" of Edna St. Vincent Millay and to Edward Lear's whimsical "The Owl and the Pussycat." 224pp. 5⅜ x 8½.   27165-X Pa. $4.95

COMPLETE SONNETS, William Shakespeare. Over 150 exquisite poems deal with love, friendship, the tyranny of time, beauty's evanescence, death and other themes in language of remarkable power, precision and beauty. Glossary of archaic terms. 80pp. 5³⁄₁₆ x 8¼.   26686-9 Pa. $1.00

BODIES IN A BOOKSHOP, R. T. Campbell. Challenging mystery of blackmail and murder with ingenious plot and superbly drawn characters. In the best tradition of British suspense fiction. 192pp. 5⅜ x 8½.   24720-1 Pa. $6.95

THE WIT AND HUMOR OF OSCAR WILDE, Alvin Redman (ed.). More than 1,000 ripostes, paradoxes, wisecracks: Work is the curse of the drinking classes; I can resist everything except temptation; etc. 258pp. 5⅜ x 8½. 20602-5 Pa. $5.95

SHAKESPEARE LEXICON AND QUOTATION DICTIONARY, Alexander Schmidt. Full definitions, locations, shades of meaning in every word in plays and poems. More than 50,000 exact quotations. 1,485pp. 6½ x 9¼. 2-vol. set.
Vol. 1: 22726-X Pa. $16.95
Vol. 2: 22727-8 Pa. $16.95

SELECTED POEMS, Emily Dickinson. Over 100 best-known, best-loved poems by one of America's foremost poets, reprinted from authoritative early editions. No comparable edition at this price. Index of first lines. 64pp. 5$\frac{3}{16}$ x 8¼.
26466-1 Pa. $1.00

CELEBRATED CASES OF JUDGE DEE (DEE GOONG AN), translated by Robert van Gulik. Authentic 18th-century Chinese detective novel; Dee and associates solve three interlocked cases. Led to van Gulik's own stories with same characters. Extensive introduction. 9 illustrations. 237pp. 5⅜ x 8½. 23337-5 Pa. $6.95

THE MALLEUS MALEFICARUM OF KRAMER AND SPRENGER, translated by Montague Summers. Full text of most important witchhunter's "bible," used by both Catholics and Protestants. 278pp. 6⅝ x 10. 22802-9 Pa. $12.95

SPANISH STORIES/CUENTOS ESPAÑOLES: A Dual-Language Book, Angel Flores (ed.). Unique format offers 13 great stories in Spanish by Cervantes, Borges, others. Faithful English translations on facing pages. 352pp. 5⅜ x 8½.
25399-6 Pa. $8.95

THE CHICAGO WORLD'S FAIR OF 1893: A Photographic Record, Stanley Appelbaum (ed.). 128 rare photos show 200 buildings, Beaux-Arts architecture, Midway, original Ferris Wheel, Edison's kinetoscope, more. Architectural emphasis; full text. 116pp. 8¼ x 11. 23990-X Pa. $9.95

OLD QUEENS, N.Y., IN EARLY PHOTOGRAPHS, Vincent F. Seyfried and William Asadorian. Over 160 rare photographs of Maspeth, Jamaica, Jackson Heights, and other areas. Vintage views of DeWitt Clinton mansion, 1939 World's Fair and more. Captions. 192pp. 8⅞ x 11. 26358-4 Pa. $12.95

CAPTURED BY THE INDIANS: 15 Firsthand Accounts, 1750-1870, Frederick Drimmer. Astounding true historical accounts of grisly torture, bloody conflicts, relentless pursuits, miraculous escapes and more, by people who lived to tell the tale. 384pp. 5⅜ x 8½. 24901-8 Pa. $8.95

THE WORLD'S GREAT SPEECHES, Lewis Copeland and Lawrence W. Lamm (eds.). Vast collection of 278 speeches of Greeks to 1970. Powerful and effective models; unique look at history. 842pp. 5⅜ x 8½. 20468-5 Pa. $14.95

THE BOOK OF THE SWORD, Sir Richard F. Burton. Great Victorian scholar/adventurer's eloquent, erudite history of the "queen of weapons"–from prehistory to early Roman Empire. Evolution and development of early swords, variations (sabre, broadsword, cutlass, scimitar, etc.), much more. 336pp. 6⅛ x 9¼.
25434-8 Pa. $9.95

AUTOBIOGRAPHY: The Story of My Experiments with Truth, Mohandas K. Gandhi. Boyhood, legal studies, purification, the growth of the Satyagraha (nonviolent protest) movement. Critical, inspiring work of the man responsible for the freedom of India. 480pp. 5⅜ x 8½. (USO) 24593-4 Pa. $8.95

CELTIC MYTHS AND LEGENDS, T. W. Rolleston. Masterful retelling of Irish and Welsh stories and tales. Cuchulain, King Arthur, Deirdre, the Grail, many more. First paperback edition. 58 full-page illustrations. 512pp. 5⅜ x 8½. 26507-2 Pa. $9.95

THE PRINCIPLES OF PSYCHOLOGY, William James. Famous long course complete, unabridged. Stream of thought, time perception, memory, experimental methods; great work decades ahead of its time. 94 figures. 1,391pp. 5⅜ x 8½. 2-vol. set.
Vol. I: 20381-6 Pa. $12.95
Vol. II: 20382-4 Pa. $12.95

THE WORLD AS WILL AND REPRESENTATION, Arthur Schopenhauer. Definitive English translation of Schopenhauer's life work, correcting more than 1,000 errors, omissions in earlier translations. Translated by E. F. J. Payne. Total of 1,269pp. 5⅜ x 8½. 2-vol. set. Vol. 1: 21761-2 Pa. $11.95
Vol. 2: 21762-0 Pa. $12.95

MAGIC AND MYSTERY IN TIBET, Madame Alexandra David-Neel. Experiences among lamas, magicians, sages, sorcerers, Bonpa wizards. A true psychic discovery. 32 illustrations. 321pp. 5⅜ x 8½. (USO) 22682-4 Pa. $8.95

THE EGYPTIAN BOOK OF THE DEAD, E. A. Wallis Budge. Complete reproduction of Ani's papyrus, finest ever found. Full hieroglyphic text, interlinear transliteration, word-for-word translation, smooth translation. 533pp. 6½ x 9¼.
21866-X Pa. $10.95

MATHEMATICS FOR THE NONMATHEMATICIAN, Morris Kline. Detailed, college-level treatment of mathematics in cultural and historical context, with numerous exercises. Recommended Reading Lists. Tables. Numerous figures. 641pp. 5⅜ x 8½.
24823-2 Pa. $11.95

THEORY OF WING SECTIONS: Including a Summary of Airfoil Data, Ira H. Abbott and A. E. von Doenhoff. Concise compilation of subsonic aerodynamic characteristics of NACA wing sections, plus description of theory. 350pp. of tables. 693pp. 5⅜ x 8½. 60586-8 Pa. $14.95

THE RIME OF THE ANCIENT MARINER, Gustave Doré, S. T. Coleridge. Doré's finest work; 34 plates capture moods, subtleties of poem. Flawless full-size reproductions printed on facing pages with authoritative text of poem. "Beautiful. Simply beautiful."–*Publisher's Weekly.* 77pp. 9¼ x 12. 22305-1 Pa. $6.95

NORTH AMERICAN INDIAN DESIGNS FOR ARTISTS AND CRAFTSPEOPLE, Eva Wilson. Over 360 authentic copyright-free designs adapted from Navajo blankets, Hopi pottery, Sioux buffalo hides, more. Geometrics, symbolic figures, plant and animal motifs, etc. 128pp. 8⅜ x 11. (EUK) 25341-4 Pa. $8.95

SCULPTURE: Principles and Practice, Louis Slobodkin. Step-by-step approach to clay, plaster, metals, stone; classical and modern. 253 drawings, photos. 255pp. 8⅛ x 11.
22960-2 Pa. $11.95

CATALOG OF DOVER BOOKS

THE INFLUENCE OF SEA POWER UPON HISTORY, 1660–1783, A. T. Mahan. Influential classic of naval history and tactics still used as text in war colleges. First paperback edition. 4 maps. 24 battle plans. 640pp. 5⅜ x 8½. 25509-3 Pa. $12.95

THE STORY OF THE TITANIC AS TOLD BY ITS SURVIVORS, Jack Winocour (ed.). What it was really like. Panic, despair, shocking inefficiency, and a little heroism. More thrilling than any fictional account. 26 illustrations. 320pp. 5⅜ x 8½. 20610-6 Pa. $8.95

FAIRY AND FOLK TALES OF THE IRISH PEASANTRY, William Butler Yeats (ed.). Treasury of 64 tales from the twilight world of Celtic myth and legend: "The Soul Cages," "The Kildare Pooka," "King O'Toole and his Goose," many more. Introduction and Notes by W. B. Yeats. 352pp. 5⅜ x 8½. 26941-8 Pa. $8.95

BUDDHIST MAHAYANA TEXTS, E. B. Cowell and Others (eds.). Superb, accurate translations of basic documents in Mahayana Buddhism, highly important in history of religions. The Buddha-karita of Asvaghosha, Larger Sukhavativyuha, more. 448pp. 5⅜ x 8½. 25552-2 Pa. $12.95

ONE TWO THREE . . . INFINITY: Facts and Speculations of Science, George Gamow. Great physicist's fascinating, readable overview of contemporary science: number theory, relativity, fourth dimension, entropy, genes, atomic structure, much more. 128 illustrations. Index. 352pp. 5⅜ x 8½. 25664-2 Pa. $8.95

ENGINEERING IN HISTORY, Richard Shelton Kirby, et al. Broad, nontechnical survey of history's major technological advances: birth of Greek science, industrial revolution, electricity and applied science, 20th-century automation, much more. 181 illustrations. ". . . excellent . . ."–*Isis*. Bibliography. vii + 530pp. 5⅜ x 8¼. 26412-2 Pa. $14.95

DALÍ ON MODERN ART: The Cuckolds of Antiquated Modern Art, Salvador Dalí. Influential painter skewers modern art and its practitioners. Outrageous evaluations of Picasso, Cézanne, Turner, more. 15 renderings of paintings discussed. 44 calligraphic decorations by Dalí. 96pp. 5⅜ x 8½. (USO) 29220-7 Pa. $4.95

ANTIQUE PLAYING CARDS: A Pictorial History, Henry René D'Allemagne. Over 900 elaborate, decorative images from rare playing cards (14th–20th centuries): Bacchus, death, dancing dogs, hunting scenes, royal coats of arms, players cheating, much more. 96pp. 9¼ x 12¼. 29265-7 Pa. $11.95

MAKING FURNITURE MASTERPIECES: 30 Projects with Measured Drawings, Franklin H. Gottshall. Step-by-step instructions, illustrations for constructing handsome, useful pieces, among them a Sheraton desk, Chippendale chair, Spanish desk, Queen Anne table and a William and Mary dressing mirror. 224pp. 8⅛ x 11¼. 29338-6 Pa. $13.95

THE FOSSIL BOOK: A Record of Prehistoric Life, Patricia V. Rich et al. Profusely illustrated definitive guide covers everything from single-celled organisms and dinosaurs to birds and mammals and the interplay between climate and man. Over 1,500 illustrations. 760pp. 7½ x 10⅛. 29371-8 Pa. $29.95

Prices subject to change without notice.

Available at your book dealer or write for free catalog to Dept. GI, Dover Publications, Inc., 31 East 2nd St., Mineola, N.Y. 11501. Dover publishes more than 500 books each year on science, elementary and advanced mathematics, biology, music, art, literary history, social sciences and other areas.